CIVIC POWER

What will it take to restore American democracy and rescue it from this moment of crisis? *Civic Power* argues that the current threat to U.S. democracy is rooted not just in the outcome of the 2016 election, but in deeper, systemic forms of inequality that concentrate economic and political power in the hands of the few at the expense of the many. Drawing on historical and social science research and case studies of contemporary democratic innovations across the country, *Civic Power* calls for a broader approach to democracy reform focused on meaningfully redistributing power to citizens. It advocates for booth reviving grassroots civil society and novel approaches to governance, policymaking, civic technology, and institutional design – aimed at dismantling structural disparities to build a more inclusive, empowered, bottom-up democracy where communities and people have greater voice, power, and agency.

K. Sabeel Rahman is the President of Demos, a think-and-do tank committed to building a more inclusive and equitable democracy and economy. He is also Associate Professor of Law at Brooklyn Law School, where he teaches constitutional law and administrative law. He is a leading scholar of democracy, law, and inequality, and is the author of *Democracy against Domination* (2017), which won the American Political Science Association's Dahl Award.

Hollie Russon Gilman is Lecturer at Columbia University and holds research fellowships at New America and Georgetown's Beeck Center. Her work focuses on the intersection of civic engagement, technology, and governance. She is the author of *Democracy Reinvented: Participatory Budgeting and Civic Innovation in America* (2016). She served in the Obama Administration in the White House Office of Science and Technology Policy.

Civic Power

REBUILDING AMERICAN DEMOCRACY IN AN
ERA OF CRISIS

K. SABEEL RAHMAN
Brooklyn Law School

HOLLIE RUSSON GILMAN
Columbia University, New York

CAMBRIDGE
UNIVERSITY PRESS

University Printing House, Cambridge CB2 8BS, United Kingdom

One Liberty Plaza, 20th Floor, New York, NY 10006, USA

477 Williamstown Road, Port Melbourne, VIC 3207, Australia

314–321, 3rd Floor, Plot 3, Splendor Forum, Jasola District Centre, New Delhi – 110025, India

79 Anson Road, #06–04/06, Singapore 079906

Cambridge University Press is part of the University of Cambridge.

It furthers the University's mission by disseminating knowledge in the pursuit of education, learning, and research at the highest international levels of excellence.

www.cambridge.org
Information on this title: www.cambridge.org/9781108422116
DOI: 10.1017/9781108380744

© K. Sabeel Rahman and Hollie Russon Gilman 2019

This publication is in copyright. Subject to statutory exception and to the provisions of relevant collective licensing agreements, no reproduction of any part may take place without the written permission of Cambridge University Press.

First published 2019

Printed and bound in Great Britain by Clays Ltd, Elcograf S.p.A.

A catalogue record for this publication is available from the British Library.

ISBN 978-1-108-42211-6 Hardback
ISBN 978-1-108-43184-2 Paperback

Cambridge University Press has no responsibility for the persistence or accuracy of URLs for external or third-party internet websites referred to in this publication and does not guarantee that any content on such websites is, or will remain, accurate or appropriate.

Contents

Preface   *page* vii

1   Democracy in Crisis   1
Inequality, Exclusion, and the Chronic Crisis of Democracy   3
The Failure of Conventional Democracy Reform   13
Reclaiming Democracy's Radicalism   22
Civic Power   27
A Road Map for Reconstructing Our Democracy   37
Of, For, and By the People   43

PART I   CIVIC POWER THROUGH ORGANIZING   45

**2   Democracy and Inequality as a Function of the Balance
of Power**   47
Organizations, Political Power, and Organizing   49
The Democratizing Force of Progressive Organizational Power   53
Inequality as a Problem of Organizational Power   60
Organizing Exclusionary Populism   68
Conclusion   79

3   Organizing for Power   81
The Promise and Peril of "Thin" Organizing   82
Toward Inclusive, Empowered Civic Capacity   90
Conclusion   107

PART II   CIVIC POWER THROUGH GOVERNANCE   111

4   From Governance to Power – Rethinking Democracy Reform   113
Administrative Procedure and the Limits of Good Governance   116
The Limits of "Innovating Government"   120

v

vi   *Contents*

The Rise – and Limits – of the "Civic Tech" Movement   124
Governance Reform as Power Shifting: An Alternative Tradition 134
From Citizen as Consumer to Citizen as Agent   140

5   **Bureaucratizing Participation**   142
     Bureaucratizing Engagement: The Case of the CFPB   143
     Cultivating Internal Support for Participatory Governance 150
     Democratizing Government from Within   163

6   **Power-Oriented Policy Design**   169
     Participatory Policymaking: The Case of Participatory Budgeting 172
     Downstream Participation: Monitoring and Enforcement   183
     Institutionalized Representation   194
     Conclusion: Power, Participation, and Policy Design   200

     PART III CONCLUSION   203

7   **Democracy's Future**   205
     Democratic Resistance and Reconstruction   205
     Recommendations: Building Civic Power   212

Bibliography   224
Index   261

Preface

In the fall of 2013, we had the good fortune of working with a group of remarkable scholars and organizers concerned about the state of American democracy. The Gettysburg Project, as we came to call it (in reference to Abraham Lincoln's defense of democracy in his Gettysburg Address), brought together leading organizers, democracy reformers, foundations, and academics to think deeply about how the crisis of American democracy could be addressed in the long term. Since then, we have continued working with an ever-growing network of inspiring and incredible leaders, across community organizations, policymakers, and foundations. A few years later, we convened a similar cross sector gathering of leaders at Open Society Foundations to discuss the possibilities for building more inclusive democracy in the United States of America, spurred by debates over the United Nations Sustainable Development Goals. Most recently, in the spring of 2017, we gathered a group of organizers, movement leaders, thinkers, and policymakers at New America, a think tank based in Washington, DC, to revisit this question of democratic renewal in the aftermath of the 2016 election.

These conversations connected us to a wide world of amazing leaders in democracy reform. They also underscored the importance of building communities of practice where such conversations can be conducted at a deep level – and where silos between research and practice, between organizing and policymaking, can be broken down to build genuine relationships and dialogue. While committed to the same core values, these different groups had rarely engaged with one another in a deep and generative way. Academics studying democracy often do not do so in dialogue with on-the-ground movement organizers. Advocacy groups, while adept at challenging governments, are not often engaged in collaborative and honest dialogues with policymakers about how to design different institutions and governance regimes. This project emerged out of a desire to build on the lessons learned from those discussions and to spur further dialogue.

The 2016 election intensified this motivation. For many Americans, the election of Donald Trump seemed implausible, a refutation of a sense of democratic progress toward ever-greater inclusion. Yet while we shared acute concerns about the future of American democracy, we were also deeply aware that many of today's concerns, though novel in some ways, are rooted in familiar and long-running challenges: inequality, racial and gender subordination, globalization, and the like. Indeed, while the election has spurred a powerful partisan battle over control of policy in Washington, there is a notable gap between this partisan fight and efforts at more structural reforms to address threats to democracy that have often arisen from – and been fueled by – policy decisions made by both major parties. At the same time, the urgency of these threats to democracy seemed at odds with some other democracy reform conversations based in the civic technology movement and emerging from Silicon Valley. The techno-utopian vision of a democracy optimized by apps and online tools appeared woefully limited in the face of such deep and chronic concerns as well as the critique of the distorting capacities of such technology that other scholars and activists have voiced since the election.

Our discussion in this book openly centers on the United States; this is not a book about the global crisis of liberal democracy. But that national focus enables us to highlight what we think are very real areas of innovation and creativity as well as potentially transformative work to enhance the power of communities from the bottom up and thereby radically transform our institutions of governance to be more inclusive, responsive, and democratic.

We could not have produced this volume without the support, guidance, and thoughtfulness of many wonderful colleagues, mentors, and collaborators. Thanks are owed particularly to Xavier de Souza Briggs, Anna Burger, Archon Fung, Marshall Ganz, Hahrie Han, and the participants in the Gettysburg Project convenings from 2013 to 2016. The Harvard Kennedy School's Roy and Lila Ash Center for Democratic Governance and Innovation helped incubate the earliest stages of this book as part of its support for the Gettysburg Project (and for each of us!) in those early years. Thanks are also due to the many academics, researchers, and practitioners whose work has inspired us and who have offered us generous feedback and support, including Susan Crawford, Michael Dawson, Claudine Gay, Jacob Hacker, Sarah Holloway, Merit Janow, David Karpf, Taeku Lee, Matt Leighninger, Zach Markovits, Tina Nabatchi, Beth Simone Noveck, Tiago C. Peixoto, Paul Pierson, Andrew Rasiej, Donata Secondo, Sonal Shah, Micah Sifry, Dennis Thompson,

Preface

Edward T. Walker, Ari Wallach, Brian Wampler, Vanessa Williamson, and Nicole Wong. We are grateful to the many practitioner collaborators who shared their work and their insights with us and granted us permission to highlight them in the book as case studies, including Whitney Kimball Coe, Dee Davis, and the Center for Rural Strategies; Jess Kutch, Michelle Miller, and Coworker.org; Lydia Bean and Faith in Texas; Regina Schwartz and the Mayor's Public Engagement Unit in New York City; Nigel Jacob and the Mayor's Office of New Urban Mechanics in Boston; Josh Lerner and the Participatory Budgeting Project; and Nikki Bas, Lauren Jacobs, and the Partnership for Working Families. We also thank the participants from the April 2017 convening at New America.

The development of this book has been supported by a number of colleagues and collaborators. We are grateful to the Political Reform Program team at New America, including especially Rachel Black, Lee Drutman, Heather Hurlburt, Chayenne Polimedio, Mark Schmitt, Anne-Marie Slaughter, Elena Souris, and others. We are also grateful for the support of the Beeck Center at Georgetown University, the School of International and Public Affairs at Columbia University, and the faculty and administration of Brooklyn Law School. As the manuscript was being finalized, we were also lucky to engage with our new colleagues at Demos, whose enthusiasm and support have been enormously helpful as well. We thank the Democracy Fund, the Ford Foundation, Knight Foundation, and Open Society Foundations for supporting various convenings and research that helped develop the ideas in this book.

Jannon Stein has been a phenomenal colleague and editor throughout the manuscript. Sabrina Detlef provided excellent copy-editing support. John Berger and Cambridge University Press were excellent publishers, and their enthusiasm and flexibility made this book possible. Thank you as well to our excellent research assistants for their hard work and dedication, including: Aliya Bhatia, Ian Eppler, Harleen Gambhir, Emma Goold, Audrey Litvak, Lawrence McDonald, Pablo Andres Mandiola, Carolyn Morway, Michael Myones, Rebecca Rosen, Gemma Torras Vives, and Jonathan Yang.

Finally, Hollie would like to thank Daniel Benaim for being the best life partner and father to the newest family member, Charlotte Mia Benaim. She's our hope for the future and a reminder of why this work matters to us. She also thanks her parents Gail Russon and Stephen Gilman for their boundless love and spirit of generosity and kindness. Sabeel would like to thank Noorain Khan for her boundless enthusiasm and support in this and all things, and his family Kazi A. Rahman, Shegufta Rahman, Wasima Rahman, Marc Garrett, and Sadia Rahman for all their love and support.

Portions of this manuscript draw on research that each of us previously published, particularly on our previous articles and papers: K. Sabeel Rahman, "Policymaking as Power-Building," *Southern California Interdisciplinary Law Journal* 27 (2018): 315–77; K. Sabeel Rahman, "(Re)Constructing Democracy in Crisis," *UCLA Law Review* 65 (2018): 1552–72; K. Sabeel Rahman, "From Civic Tech to Civic Capacity: The Case of Citizen Audits," *Political Science and Politics* 50 (2017): 751–57; Hollie Russon Gilman and Jessica Gover, *The Architecture of Innovation: Institutionalizing Innovation in Federal Policymaking* (Washington, DC: Beeck Center at Georgetown University, 2016); Hollie Russon Gilman, "Government as Government, Not Business," *Stanford Social Innovation Review*, October 5, 2017, https://ssir.org/articles/entry/government_as_go vernment_not_business; and Hollie Russon Gilman and K. Sabeel Rahman, *Building Civic Capacity in an Era of Democratic Crisis* (Washington, DC: New America, September 2017). We thank the respective editors and journals for their support for these earlier works and their permission to reproduce and repurpose them in this larger project.

1

Democracy in Crisis

On a frigid January evening in 2008, Barack Obama, then merely a junior senator from Illinois, shocked the political establishment by winning the Iowa Caucus. At the boisterous celebration rally, Obama delivered what would become one of the signature speeches of his political career, defining many of the central themes of his campaign and his presidency. "[T]he time has come," Obama declared, "to tell the lobbyists who think their money and their influence speak louder than our voices that they don't own this government – we do. And we are here to take it back!"[1] If there was a central message in Obama's 2008 campaign for the White House, it was this faith in a revival of American democracy – the belief "that in the face of impossible odds, people who love this country can change it."[2]

Obama would go on to win the presidency, but within the next eight years, the aspirational hope of the early Obama era faded away, supplanted by something much darker. While the Obama administration achieved several significant policy changes, his term was also marked by the fallout from the Great Recession as well as increasingly vociferous opposition from conservatives in Congress. At its close, Donald Trump, a real estate mogul, shocked the country by winning the next presidential election, after rising to political prominence as the leader of the "birther" movement that questioned the very legitimacy of the nation's first African American President.

In some ways, the Trump candidacy channeled a sharper frustration with the corrupt and rigged political and economic system than even that evoked by Obama in 2008. But Trump garnered his "populist" grassroots base by fusing this antiestablishment ire with virulent appeals to racism, misogyny, and

---

[1] "Barack Obama's Caucus Speech," *New York Times*, January 3, 2008, www.nytimes.com/2008/01/03/us/politics/03obama-transcript.html.
[2] Ibid.

2   *Civic Power*

xenophobia. As president, Trump has provoked widespread concerns about
the threat he and his politics pose to democratic institutions.[3] His public
rhetoric has helped foster and encourage the resurgence of openly white
supremacist and anti-feminist movements in American politics. The lack of
transparency around his and his family's business interests – as well as proliferating conflicts of interest and opportunities for self-dealing connected to
them – raise concerns about kleptocracy and corruption. His attacks on the
free press, independent judges, independent law enforcement, and his calls
for criminalization of his political opponents all raise the specter of democratic decline in the United States.

Yet fears about rising exclusionary populism, lack of accountability, and
erosion of existing democratic checks and balances all speak to deeper, more
chronic problems of American democracy. Although Trump poses some
unique threats to American democracy, in many ways Trump is as much
symptom as he a cause of the weakness of American democratic structures. In
a polity where trust in and responsiveness of political institutions is already
low, where racial and gender disparities lurk just beneath the surface, and
where many constituencies struggle to make themselves heard even in settings
of "politics as usual," conventional political structures – even those of the pre-
Trump era – already fall short of democratic aspirations and ideals. The
Trump era has exacerbated chronic failures into a more virulent and urgent
form of democratic crisis. Thus, the democratic threats posed by the rise of far-
right populism raise a subsidiary danger: that efforts to reform American
democracy will focus too narrowly on restoring an imagined pre-Trump era
of civility and the accompanying "norms" of ordinary political behavior in
a status quo ante.[4] Even if such reform were possible, it would be unwise.
Trumpism is reflective of the deeper and more chronic crisis of American
democracy.

It is this deeper level of crisis that is the focus of this book. The threats to the
ideal of democracy are widespread and arise from day-to-day failures of
democratic governance: in how constituencies struggle to organize and exercise a share of political power; in the perpetual fracturing of communities
along racial, gender, and class lines; and in how institutions of ordinary, daily
governance – from cities to regulatory bodies – fail to operate inclusively and
responsively. Rebuilding democracy – or rather building it anew so that it will

---

[3] Jack Goldsmith, "Will Donald Trump Destroy the Presidency?" *Atlantic*, October 2017, www
     .theatlantic.com/magazine/archive/2017/10/will-donald-trump-destroy-the-presidency/537921/.
[4] Jedediah Purdy, "Normcore," *Dissent*, Summer 2018, www.dissentmagazine.org/article/norm
     core-trump-resistance-books-crisis-of-democracy.

Democracy in Crisis 3

include many for the first time – requires addressing these deeper structural challenges. Yet conventional democracy reform discourses themselves pose obstacles to this process. As we argue in this book, often ideas of "good governance" reforms and the allure of "civic technology" platforms capture attention and resources, but such efforts frequently fall short in addressing deeper problems of inequality, exclusion, and disparate political power. What we need is a clear-eyed sense of these chronic crises of democracy – and an approach to democracy reform that is sufficiently transformative and bold to tackle these crises. This book represents an attempt to map out what such an alternative, transformative approach to democracy reform – that places power and inequality at its center – might look like. As we will argue below, building a truly inclusive democracy will require deep investments in building bottom-up, membership-driven civil society organizations, and radically more participatory and democratic policymaking institutions that these organizations can engage and influence.

But before we can explore these forward-looking directions, the rest of this chapter explores in more depth three key background arguments that serve as the foundation for this book: first, that the crisis of democracy is a structural and chronic one, based in deep patterns of inequality and exclusion that cut beyond the current debates over the Trump administration; second, that many conventional approaches to democracy reform fail to address these deep disparities in power and inequality; and third, that a democratic rebuilding agenda that does take these inequities seriously will have to look closely at both the building of grassroots civil society and social movement power on the one hand, and transformations to the day-to-day operation of policymaking institutions and processes on the other.

INEQUALITY, EXCLUSION, AND THE CHRONIC CRISIS OF DEMOCRACY

In the years since Trump's electoral victory in 2016, there has been an explosion of scholarly concern for the dangers of "democratic backsliding," much of which is devoted to unpacking the political, institutional, and sociological factors that tend to accompany or provoke the collapse of democratic regimes into authoritarianism.[5] These accounts tend to share some common areas of focus, highlighting the threats posed by autocratic leaders, who by disposition

---

[5] See for example, Steven Levitsky and Daniel Ziblatt, *How Democracies Die* (New York: Crown, 2018), 5–6; and Aziz Huq and Tom Ginsburg, "How to Lose a Constitutional Democracy," *UCLA Law Review* 65 (2018): 78–169.

are hostile to democratic institutions and civil liberties,[6] warning that such autocrats can gain political power through conventional and legitimate means, particularly by building coalitions with existing parties and gatekeepers causing a gradual subversion of existing checks and balances and a consolidation of power.[7] Some of these scholars warn that democratic backsliding can also arise in a less direct form, through increasingly polarized and scorched-earth forms of political conflict between rival parties for power.[8]

Given this fear of backsliding, much of this literature has tended to highlight the importance of defending existing institutional checks and balances, as well as restoring informal "norms" that govern political behavior – norms such as the "mutual toleration"[9] of political opponents and "forbearance,"[10] which require political actors, once in power, to hold themselves back from deploying the full range of their coercive powers to snuff out their rivals. In the American context, a variety of other norms have also been central to maintaining democracy, including norms against conflicts of interest for elected officials, and norms promoting internal deliberation (such as the expectation that the president will consult with legal and other internal experts before advancing policy proposals). It is these norms that prevent the executive branch from overreaching in normal circumstances.[11] And it is these norms that have been most blatantly violated by the current administration, contributing to concerns about presidential overreach and arbitrariness.[12]

Yet a narrow focus on norms as the primary site for the threat of autocracy risks glossing over a much-needed investigation into deeper, more chronic

---

[6] Levitsky and Ziblatt describe the views and dispositions of authoritarian leaders as revolving around a shared rejection of democratic institutions, of legitimate opposition, and of civil liberties (*How Democracies Die*, 65–68).

[7] Levitsky and Ziblatt describe how autocrats, once in power, erode opposition through attacks on media and use of patronage relationships (*How Democracies Die*, 78–96); and Huq and Ginsburg, "How to Lose a Constitutional Democracy."

[8] Jack M. Balkin, "Constitutional Hardball and Constitutional Crises," *Quinnipiac Law Review* 26 (2008): 579–98; see also Levitsky and Ziblatt, *How Democracies Die*, 217.

[9] Levitsky and Ziblatt, *How Democracies Die*, 102.

[10] Ibid., 106.

[11] Daphna Renan maps out different norms that structure the exercise of executive power in "Presidential Norms and Article II," *Harvard Law Review* 131 (2018): 2187–2282.

[12] Goldsmith, "Will Donald Trump Destroy the Presidency?":

> Trump has been less constrained by norms, the nonlegal principles of appropriate behavior that presidents and other officials tacitly accept and that typically structure their actions. Norms, not laws, create the expectation that a president will take regular intelligence briefings, pay public respect to our allies, and not fire the FBI director for declining to pledge his loyalty. There is no canonical list of presidential norms. They are rarely noticed until they are violated.

Democracy in Crisis 5

problems of contemporary American democracy. The election of 2016 did not so much produce a democratic crisis as reveal one. The reality is that American democracy had already been deeply broken for years prior to that campaign cycle. The deeper, more troubling, crisis of American democracy stems first from the growing problem of economic inequality and its magnifying of disparities of political power, and second from systemic patterns of social exclusion that have limited political agency along racial and gendered lines.

Inequality and the Problem of Power

One major long-term threat to democracy stems from economic inequality and the ways it can enable durable and often hidden forms of political inequality. Much of the scholarship on the democratic threat posed by concentrated wealth has explored the terrain of campaign finance reform and focused concerns on the ability of wealthy donors to influence elected officials to favor their interests.[13] But economic inequality skews democratic politics beyond the campaign finance context. Indeed, this disparity in political influence extends even beyond the electoral arena to the day-to-day practice of politics and governance. Through a variety of mechanisms, wealthier constituencies and business interests are able to steer policymaking to favor their interests over others. In the process, they also undermine the ability of other constituencies to advocate for themselves on fair and equal terms. An extensive social science literature has in recent years documented more pervasive disparities in how public policy skews toward the preferences of wealthier and more elite constituencies.[14]

Democracy in practice is less about "the mass public" as it is about the contest between organized interests – but in practice some interests have been vastly more effective at exercising influence than others. Laypersons in the general public often have little information about, or low motivation to participate in, electoral politics.[15] Political voice and influence have, by contrast, often been produced through organized political activity. It is through

---

[13] Lawrence Lessig, *Republic, Lost: How Money Corrupts Congress – And a Plan to Stop It* (New York: Twelve, 2011); and Zephyr Teachout, *Corruption in America: From Benjamin Franklin's Snuff Box to Citizens United* (Cambridge, MA: Harvard University Press, 2014).

[14] Martin Gilens, *Affluence and Influence: Economic Inequality and Political Power in America* (Princeton, NJ: Princeton University Press, 2014); and Martin Gilens and Benjamin I. Page, *Democracy in America: What Has Gone Wrong and What We Can Do about It* (Chicago: University of Chicago Press, 2017), 38: "[e]conomic inequality begets political inequality, which, in turn, makes it harder to address economic inequality."

[15] Larry M. Bartels, "Uninformed Votes: Information Effects in Presidential Elections," *American Journal of Political Science* 40 (1996): 194–230.

6 *Civic Power*

civic association that many individuals gain knowledge, experience, and political efficacy.[16] Association not only increases the political efficacy of individuals and communities; associations themselves also can exercise direct influence on public policy through interest-group lobbying and politics. As a result, the changing balance between different civic associations has macro implications for the functioning of American democracy.

Recent political science scholarship has documented how business groups shifted their organizing strategies and advocacy goals in the 1970s and again in the 1990s.[17] The result has been a concerted effort to build a well-resourced and sophisticated system for lobbying, advocacy, and exerting influence on state and federal policymakers. Organized business advocacy groups outweigh labor organizations, public interest groups, and marginalized constituencies in their lobbying presence.[18] This influence is magnified by the close alignment between business interests and the Republican Party.[19] Business interests have also vastly outweighed other actors through lobbying and influencing regulatory bodies.[20]

This increase in political power on the part of business has in turn led to the pursuit of policies that further concentrate economic wealth and therefore political influence – for example through the promotion of tax cuts, "right to work" laws that fragment the ability of labor unions to exercise oppositional

---

[16] Robert D. Putnam, *Bowling Alone: The Collapse and Revival of American Community* (New York: Simon & Schuster, 2000); Theda Skocpol and Morris P. Fiorina, eds., *Civic Engagement in American Democracy* (Washington, DC: Brookings Institution, 1999); David Easton, *A Framework for Political Analysis* (Englewood Cliffs, NJ: Prentice-Hall, 1965); David Easton, *A Systems Analysis of Political Life* (Hoboken, NJ: Wiley, 1975); and Arthur H. Miller, "Political Issues and Trust in Government: 1964–1970," *American Political Science Review* 68 (1974): 951–72.

[17] Hacker and Pierson describe the shift within the business lobby from a focus on industrial interests that became dominant politically after the 1970s to a focus on financial interests starting in the 1990s (Jacob S. Hacker and Paul Pierson, *American Amnesia: How the War on Government Led Us to Forget What Made America Prosper* (New York: Simon & Schuster, 2017), 206.

[18] Martin Gilens and Benjamin Page, "Testing Theories of American Politics: Elites, Interest Groups, and Average Citizens," *Perspectives on Politics* 12 (2014): 564–81, 575: "business groups are far more numerous and active; they spend much more money; and they tend to get their way"; Kay Lehman Schlozman, Sidney Verba, and Henry E. Brady, *The Unheavenly Chorus: Unequal Political Voice and the Broken Promise of American Democracy* (Princeton, NJ: Princeton University Press, 2012), 442: "the weight of advocacy by organizations representing business interests ... in no case is ... outweighed by the activity of either organizations representing the less privileged or public interest groups."

[19] Hacker and Pierson describe links between these business interests and the Republican Party and the resulting rightward shift of the Republicans (*American Amnesia*, 166, 248–52).

[20] Jason Webb Yackee and Susan Webb Yackee, "A Bias towards Business? Assessing Interest Group Influence on the U.S. Bureaucracy," *Journal of Politics* 68 (2006): 128–39.

Democracy in Crisis

political power, and other similar shifts.[21] Indeed, business interests have focused on policy changes that – like the busting of unions – undermine the countervailing power of labor and other rival interest groups.[22] Meanwhile, the countervailing power of workers and other constituencies has been further undermined by the gradual shift away from mass-member organizations to professionalized nonprofit advocacy groups.[23] Scholars have documented the decline of organized labor and other mass-member civil society institutions in recent decades.[24] While these professionalized advocates can be more sophisticated in their lobbying campaigns, this shift has weakened the popular foundations that historically drove the political power of membership-based groups, from consumer leagues to labor unions.[25]

This disparity in political influence is further exacerbated by a growing class divide in political leadership. Fewer and fewer political leaders come from working-class backgrounds, leading to demonstrable skewing of policy outcomes in favor of wealthier groups.[26] Similarly, shared social and cultural ties between economic elites and regulators help explain subtle forms of "cultural capture," where regulators defer to industry interests and take a softer hand than they might otherwise.[27] As Nicholas Carnes puts it, the disparity of political influence is a product not just of who is doing the talking – with more (and more effective) advocacy coming from elite and business interests – but also of who is doing the listening: as the policy class becomes less representative themselves of the economic and social diversity of the country, these disparities in responsiveness become more pronounced.[28]

---

[21] See Brishen Rogers, "Libertarian Corporatism Is Not an Oxymoron," *Texas Law Review* 94 (2016): 1623–46, 1629–30; Kate Andrias, "The New Labor Law," *Yale Law Journal* 126 (2016): 2–100, 39–41.

[22] Alexander Hertel-Fernandez, "How the Right Trounced Liberals in the States," *Democracy: A Journal of Ideas* 39 (2016), http://democracyjournal.org/magazine/39/how-the-right-trounced-liberals-in-the-states [https://perma.cc/5Q6E-SY9W]. Hacker and Pierson also argue that much of the inequality crisis can be explained by the rise of business lobbying power, and the decline of organized labor. See Jacob S. Hacker and Paul Pierson, *Winner-Take-All Politics: How Washington Made the Rich Richer – And Turned Its Back on the Middle Class* (New York: Simon & Schuster, 2010).

[23] Theda Skocpol, *Diminished Democracy: From Membership to Management in American Civic Life* (Norman: University of Oklahoma Press, 2003).

[24] Hacker and Pierson, *American Amnesia*; and Hacker and Pierson, *Winner-Take-All Politics*.

[25] Ibid.

[26] Nicholas Carnes, *White Collar Government: The Hidden Role of Class in Economic Policy Making* (Chicago: University of Chicago Press, 2013).

[27] James Kwak, "Cultural Capture and the Financial Crisis," in *Preventing Regulatory Capture: Special Internet Influence and How to Limit It*, ed. Daniel Carpenter and David A. Moss (New York: Cambridge University Press, 2013), 71–98.

[28] Carnes, *White Collar Government*.

8   *Civic Power*

Additionally, a growing body of legal scholarship explores the ways in which concentrated wealth itself might represent a threat to the values and institutions of constitutional democracy.[29] The existing institutional structure of checks and balances in democratic politics in the American system depends on a dynamic interaction between institutions on the one hand and the political powers and interests that occupy those institutions at any given point in time on the other; changes in the configuration of these interest groups affect how the institutions themselves operate.[30] The Madisonian system of checks and balances requires self-interested political factions to leverage existing institutions to check rival factions – i.e., Congress checking the executive or states competing with one another. But when political interests and factions control multiple branches or operate to deliberately block some of these forms of accountability, the Madisonian system breaks down.[31] Furthermore, when one party or some group of factions deploys these forms of political blockage and hardball asymmetrically over other factions, it threatens long-term damage to institutions of responsiveness.[32] A similar dynamic manifests throughout our political system, as more wealthy interests are able to systematically skew policymaking to their favor, while other constituencies lack equivalent and countervailing political power.

---

[29]   See Joseph Fishkin and William E. Forbath, "The Anti-Oligarchy Constitution," *Boston University Law Review* 94 (2014): 671–98; Joseph Fishkin and William E. Forbath, "Wealth, Commonwealth, & the Constitution of Opportunity," public law research paper no. UTPUB632 (Austin: University of Texas School of Law, 2016), https://papers.ssrn.com/sol3/papers.cfm?abstract_id=2620920; Ganesh Sitaraman, *The Crisis of the Middle-Class Constitution: Why Economic Inequality Threatens Our Republic* (New York: Alfred A. Knopf, 2017); and Kate Andrias, "Separations of Wealth: Inequality and the Erosion of Checks and Balances," *Michigan Journal of Constitutional Law* 18 (2016): 419–504.

[30]   See Daryl Levinson, "Looking for Power in Public Law," *Harvard Law Review* 130 (2016): 31–143. Levinson suggests that we need to view both interests and institutions in relationship to one another by looking past the intrinsic powers that governmental institutions might possess on paper, and look instead to the configuration of interest-group powers that might currently occupy, influence, or lie behind particular institutions (40, 83–84).

[31]   Daryl J. Levinson and Richard H. Piles argue that constitutional checks and balances are more often driven by the conflict between parties, leveraging whichever branches they control, rather than following a pure tripartite process of legislative, executive, and judicial checks on one another. See "Separation of Parties, Not Powers," *Harvard Law Review* 119 (2006): 2311–86.

[32]   Joseph Fishkin and David Pozen argue that the problem of constitutional hardball is more a problem arising from one set of partisan actors than it is a universal or symmetrical problem. See "Asymmetric Constitutional Hardball," *Columbia Law Review* 118 (2018): 915–82).

Democracy in Crisis

Systemic Exclusion

These trends are compounded by deep, persisting problems of structural exclusion along lines of race and gender. The failure of American democracy is simply not a new phenomenon; it is built on a chronic legacy of antidemocratic exclusion. This form of democratic crisis lies not in the outsized political influence of some factions or constituencies, but in a more extreme and localized *exclusion* of some constituencies from political agency altogether. Historically, this has been a central feature of American democracy in the forms of legalized exclusion of enslaved persons, the legal system of Jim Crow, and the exclusion and subordination of women at common law. But even after the passage of the Thirteenth, Fourteenth, Fifteenth, and Nineteenth Amendments, abolishing slavery, assuring equal protection, and nominally protecting voting rights, indeed even after the civil rights movement of the 1960s, there remain often-hidden systems of exclusion from equal political power and participation.

Consider the extensive critiques of the institutionalized and systemic domination that communities of color face under the criminal justice system. The problems of mass incarceration and over-policing represent a modern system of racial subordination akin to the Jim Crow era of racial terror and inequality.[33] Over-policed and over-incarcerated communities of color do not, in a meaningful sense, live in a democratic polity marked by broad, equal, protected, mutually binding consultation. But similar patterns of structural exclusion appear in other contexts as well. Consider how precarious and insecure work is often racialized, leaving workers of color particularly vulnerable, or how the welfare bureaucracy treats mostly minority recipients and applicants, or how housing and zoning systems of many cities concentrate racial minorities and poverty in particular neighborhoods. These are all ways of constructing second-class citizenship for racial minorities, magnifying their economic and political inequality.[34]

This form of systemic racial exclusion is echoed in other contexts and with other constituencies as well. Legal and political assertions that certain spheres of life are apolitical "private realm[s]" have similarly operated at times to

---

[33] See Michelle Alexander, *The New Jim Crow: Mass Incarceration in the Age of Colorblindness* (New York: New Press, 2010).

[34] Andrea Flynn et al. map the ways in which different legal and policy systems from labor law to welfare bureaucracies to criminal justice to housing construct racial hierarchy today in *The Hidden Rules of Race: Barriers to an Inclusive Economy* (New York: Cambridge University Press, 2017).

Civic Power

shield the workplace, the market, or the family from publicly political claims aimed at addressing disparities of power and opportunity therein.[35] Similarly, legal regimes that immunize the inner workings of the firm from legal liability or political critique construct the workplace as a form of "private government" where workers are subject to the will of private managers and owners in ways that make them deeply unfree.[36]

These various issues, including racial and gender justice and labor law, involve "substantive" questions, that is, the substantive policy disputes that take place within ordinary democratic politics. Yet in the aggregate, these policies also construct implicit and explicit boundaries that limit who can make claims in public politics and what issues can be engaged in the first place.

***

Science fiction novelist William Gibson is often quoted (perhaps apocryphally) as having stated that, "The future is already here – it's just not very evenly distributed."[37] The aphorism is a useful articulation of the reality that places with high technological sophistication can coexist with others that are left behind by technological advances. The same observation applies to current concerns about democracy. Despite recent fears about a potential slide into authoritarianism, or at least, diminished democracy in the United States, the reality is that both democracy and authoritarianism are already present in America, they are just unevenly distributed. Both of the crises discussed here – the systematic inequalities in political power as fostered by the organized power of business interests as well as the systemic exclusions of communities and particular issues from the larger political and legal debate – represent important ways in which the ideal of a broad, equal, protected, mutually consultative democracy is violated. These more chronic and systemic crises of democracy persist beyond the depths of threats arising from the empowered

---

[35] For a classic statement of the ways in which appeals to a "private realm" have worked to immunize gender roles from political critique and reform, see Susan Moller Okin, "Justice and Gender," *Philosophy and Public Affairs* 16 (1987): 42–72. See also her "'Forty Acres and a Mule' for Women: Rawls and Feminism," *Politics, Philosophy and Economics* 4, no. 2 (2005): 233–48, 234: "Just as the freedom and equality proclaimed by the Declaration of Independence and the U.S. Constitution's Bill of Rights did not take account of the fact that the economy of half the country was based on slave labor, so the freedom and equality of most liberal political thought does not take account of the unpaid labor of women in the home."

[36] Elizabeth Anderson, *Private Government: How Employers Rule Our Lives (and Why We Don't Talk about It)* (Princeton, NJ: Princeton University Press, 2017), 39–42.

[37] Garson O'Toole, "The Future Has Arrived – It's Just Not Evenly Distributed Yet: William Gibson? Anonymous? Apocryphal?" *Quote Investigator* (blog), January 24, 2012, https://quoteinvestigator.com/2012/01/24/future-has-arrived/.

Democracy in Crisis

autocrat that is the focus of the backsliding literature. Furthermore, threats of autocracy can coexist, and even exacerbate chronic crises of inequality and exclusion. Democratization, and de-democratization, then, are "asynchronic" – that is, democracy as a form of mutually binding consultation between constituents and the state can thrive for some groups and in some spaces, while failing for others.[38]

What remains of our democratic institutions – from parties, to elections, to the mass media – appears almost laughably brittle. This chronic democratic weakness explains much of the loss of faith in contemporary American democracy. The 2016 election evinced a pervasive distrust of political institutions, which, already widespread in 2008, grew into a more corrosive and powerful current on both left and right, as the legitimacy of democratic institutions and the idea of democracy itself cratered.[39] The Pew Research Center found that less than a third of Americans expressed trust in the federal government in 2016,[40] while Gallup's polling revealed a similar finding, with trust in "the government's ability to handle domestic problems" at its lowest point since the 1970s.[41] Scholars have documented substantially the same trend in the United States and globally, as citizens have lost trust in governments and in their own sense of "political efficacy" – the sense of being able to exercise meaningful political power.[42] This justified disaffection represents for many scholars a "threat" to "the legitimacy and stability of the political system."[43] Indeed, the resurgence of exclusionary populisms and political instability in recent years has borne it out.

---

[38] Daniel Ziblatt suggests that, rather than evolving in lockstep, some institutional forms necessary for democracy might advance while others do not, in "How Did Europe Democratize?" *World Politics* 2 (2006): 311–38, 333.

[39] Roberto Stefan Foa and Yascha Mounk, "The Danger of Deconsolidation," *Journal of Democracy* 27, no. 3 (2015): 5–17; and Yascha Mounk, "Donald Trump Is the End of Global Politics as We Know It," *Foreign Policy*, November 11, 2016, https://foreignpolicy.com/2016/11/11/donald-trump-will-change-global-politics-as-we-know-it/.

[40] "Trust in Government: 1958–2015," chapter 1 in *Beyond Distrust: How Americans View Their Government* (Washington, DC: Pew Research Center, November 2015), www.people-press.org/2015/11/23/1-trust-in-government-1958-2015/.

[41] "Trust in Business vs. Government," *Wall Street Journal*, August 15, 2016, www.wsj.com/articles/trust-in-business-vs-government-1471304776.

[42] See Tina Nabatchi, "Addressing the Citizenship and Democratic Deficits: The Potential of Deliberative Democracy for Public Administration," *American Review of Public Administration* 40 (2010): 376–99; and C. H. Levine, "Citizenship and Service Delivery: The Promise of Coproduction," in *The Age of Direct Citizen Participation*, ed. Nancy C. Roberts (Armonk, NY: M. E. Sharpe, 2008), 78–92. Political efficacy was first defined in Angus Campbell et al., *The Voter Decides* (Evanston, IL: Row, Peterson, 1954), 187.

[43] Nabatchi, "Addressing the Citizenship," 377. See Archon Fung, "Putting the Public Back into Governance: The Challenges of Citizen Participation and Its Future," *Public Administration*

12   *Civic Power*

Yet for all its apparent failures, the ideal of a vibrant, responsive democratic polity remains the best weapon with which to counteract the deep, structural disparities of power, opportunity, and well-being that are at the heart of modern American society and shape its debates over economic inequality, racial discrimination, and more. Democracy at its core is about empowering a variety of constituencies to share in the project of self-governance, to exercise political agency, and to address shared problems in an inclusive and equitable manner. The solution to our current crisis is not to restore a mythical ideal of a democracy located in some vague rose-colored past; these chronic problems of inequality and exclusion along lines of race, class, and gender have perpetually afflicted American democracy to varying degrees and in varying forms. To put it another way, if the crisis of American democracy today is one of a *lack* of inclusion, accountability, and responsiveness, the solution must lie in deepening democratic institutions. Democracy reform must be about more than simply defending democratic institutions; it must be about radically reinventing them to better balance political power.

This orientation toward power – and this attention to the underlying social and political structures that shape the disparities of power in the first place – comprise what we term in this book the *civic power* perspective on democracy reform. This approach to democracy reform is critical to addressing the deep crises of inequality and exclusion undermining American democracy. And while this approach may deploy some familiar techniques of democracy reform – such as transparency, participatory governance, or grassroots organizing – we suggest in this book that there is a crucial difference between reforms that apply these techniques to shift power, in contrast to reforms that apply these techniques in order to optimize government in a power-neutral way. Indeed, too often democracy reform policies emphasize the need to optimize governmental functioning and to improve civility and rationality of politics, in ways that overlook – and therefore reify and further entrench – the deeper structural disparities of power.

Review 75, no. 4 (2015): 513–22: "According to many indicia, the bond between citizens and political institutions has weakened in the United States and other industrialized democracies." The United States reflects the broader global trend where citizens feel less and less trust in government or internal and external political efficacy. Virginia A. Chanley, Thomas J. Rudolph, and Wendy M. Rahn, "The Origins and Consequences of Public Trust in Government: A Time Series Analysis," *Public Opinion Quarterly* 64 (2000): 239–56; and Stephen C. Craig, Richard G. Niemi, and Glenn E. Silver, "Political Efficacy and Trust: A Report on the NES Pilot Study Items," *Political Behavior* 12 (1990): 289–314.

Democracy in Crisis

THE FAILURE OF CONVENTIONAL DEMOCRACY REFORM

Transparency, Technology, Deliberation

For scholars, reformers, and communities alike, the longer-term problem of American democracy is its declining responsiveness to the people themselves. For the democracy reform community, this problem stems from the corruption of the most foundational institution of democracy – the electoral system itself. Here the focus is on issues like the undue influence of wealthy campaign donors, the deliberate efforts by some political factions to inhibit access to the franchise through voter intimidation and barriers to registry, gerrymandered electoral districts, and the like.[44] Broader failures of democracy outside of the electoral arena have not gone unnoticed. The problem, however, is that many prevailing approaches to democracy reform overlook or avoid the deep structural crises of inequality, power, and exclusion.

The recent boom of interest in technology, transparency, and deliberative approaches to governance offer a telling example of how some of these techniques, while they have potential for redressing democratic inequities, can often be deployed in ways that do little to address the structural inequalities that inhibit real democratic agency and inclusion.

Shortly after winning the White House in 2008, Barack Obama's presidential campaign staff explicitly sought to build a grassroots movement through the creation of Obama for America (OFA), as a vehicle for participation, organizing, and advocacy.[45] Once in office, the Obama administration channeled much of the 2008 campaign rhetoric about reviving democracy into efforts aimed at expanding transparency, updating government bureaucracies for the modern era, and creating new modes of participatory input. The administration launched projects like the Open Government Initiative, which directed federal agencies to increase their transparency as well as to promote citizen participation in and civic engagement with their work;[46] Offices of Public Engagement, and of Social Innovation and Civic

---

[44] Ari Berman, *Give Us the Ballot: The Modern Struggle for Voting Rights in America* (New York: Picador, 2015); Lessig, Republic, Lost; Teachout, Corruption in America; and Richard Hasen, *Plutocrats United: Campaign Money, the Supreme Court, and the Distortion of American Elections* (New Haven, CT: Yale University Press, 2016).

[45] Paul Steinhauser, "'Obama for America' to Morph into 'Organizing for Action,'" *Political Ticker* (blog), CNN, January 18, 2013, http://politicalticker.blogs.cnn.com/2013/01/18/obama-for-america-to-morph-into-organizing-for-action/.

[46] Presidential Memorandum M-09-12, "President's Memorandum on Transparency and Open Government – Interagency Collaboration," February 24, 2009, https://obamawhitehouse .archives.gov/sites/default/files/omb/assets/memoranda_fy2009/m09-12.pdf.

14 *Civic Power*

Participation, to develop new modes of civic engagement with the White House; and a groundbreaking online site for citizen petitions, "We the People."[47] The administration also experimented with a variety of other, new federal offices all aimed at harnessing the power of data and technology and at hiring a new crop of public servants – designers, programmers, digital experts – who had not traditionally been engaged by government. These new departments included the Office of Citizen Services and Innovative Technologies (established 2010), 18F (established 2014), and the United States Digital Service (established 2014).

These approaches to renewing American democracy thus generally reflected the latest concepts about the best ways to reform democratic governance – through increased transparency, more efficient governance, and more public engagement. Transparency and openness have long been central themes for democracy reformers, and have shaped major reform efforts like the Freedom of Information Act (FOIA), which ensures the public has reliable and timely access to information,[48] and the Federal Advisory Committee Act (FACA) of 1972, which requires transparency in the use of outside advisors and experts to shape government policies.[49]

Similarly, the Obama administration's fascination with technology reflects a second, newer trend in democracy reform: the rise of the "civic tech" movement. Inspired by Silicon Valley and the explosion of new digital, technological, and data-analytics tools, a generation of "civic technology" or "civic tech" reformers began working to upgrade the bureaucracies that make public policy decisions, whether in cities, states, or federal agencies. Armed with big data, new modes of releasing public information and enhancing transparency, as well as new ways to leverage social media, these reformers sought to improve openness, civic engagement, and ultimately democracy. This effort to build "smart digital governance" has focused on revamping governmental processes to be more targeted, responsive, leaner, and more agile, often deploying data to drive real-time decisions while including crowd-sourcing funding and public feedback to improve public works projects.[50]

While this civic tech movement shares a rhetoric of improving democracy, the idea of democratic failure and reform animating this strain of activism is

---

[47] Office of the Press Secretary, "President Obama Launches Office of Public Engagement," White House, May 11, 2009, https://obamawhitehouse.archives.gov/the-press-office/president-obama-launches-office-public-engagement.

[48] 5 U.S.C. § 552.

[49] Pub. L. 92–463, 86 Stat. 770.

[50] Stephen Goldsmith and Susan Crawford, *The Responsive City: Engaging Communities through Data-Smart Governance* (San Francisco: Jossey-Bass, 2014), 62, 93.

Democracy in Crisis 15

often in practice different from the motivations of more radical campaign finance reformers. Many civic tech discussions take place within the walls of giant technology corporations or at special conferences like the annual World Economic Forum in Davos or TechCrunch Disrupt in San Francisco and are conducted between members of urban cosmopolitan elites.[51] These democracy reformers see the problems of special interests and democratic deficits as ones of *bureaucratic failure* and obsolete processes. If governing bodies can be made "smarter" – if democracy can be translated into some high-tech form ready for the twenty-first century – then perhaps it can survive in a new technological ecosystem, or at least maybe it will simply function better.

There is a third strand of democracy reform that has shaped contemporary efforts: the growth of interest in public engagement, participation, and "deliberative democracy." Deliberative democracy reforms have a long legacy aimed at facilitating good-faith dialogue between communities of citizens.[52] There is a vast scholarly literature on deliberative democracy and participatory governance, outlining different ways that constituencies can be engaged more directly in public policymaking.[53] Such proposals often aim to shift from a focus on "uninformed, superficial, and transient" public opinion[54] to institutions and processes that facilitate more thoughtful forms of "public

---

[51] Don Tapscott, "At Davos, Technology CEOs Discuss the Digital Economy," *Huffington Post*, January 24, 2015, www.huffingtonpost.com/don-tapscott/at-davos-technology-ceos-discuss-the-digital-economy_b_6537772.html.

[52] Derek W. M. Barker, Noëlle McAfee, and David W. McIvor provide a genealogy of the term and the movement in the introduction to their *Den* (Dayton, OH: Kettering Foundation, 2012), 4.

[53] Benjamin Barber, *Strong Democracy: Participatory Politics for a New Age*, 20th-anniv. ed. with a new preface (Berkeley: University of California Press, 2004); Jane Mansbridge, *Beyond Adversary Democracy* (New York: Basic Books, 1980); Jane Mansbridge, *Deliberative Systems: Deliberative Democracy at the Large Scale* (Cambridge: Cambridge University Press, 2013); Amy Gutmann and Dennis Thompson, *Democracy and Disagreement* (Cambridge, MA: Belknap Press of Harvard University, 1996); Amy Gutmann and Dennis Thompson, *Why Deliberative Democracy?* (Princeton, NJ: Princeton University Press, 2004); Archon Fung, "Recipes for Public Spheres: Eight Institutional Design Choices and Their Consequences," *Journal of Political Philosophy* 11, no. 3 (2003): 338–67; Joshua Cohen and Archon Fung, "Radical Democracy," *Raisons Politiques* 42 (2004): 23–34; Lisa Blomgren Bingham, Tina Nabatchi, and Rosemary O'Leary, "The New Governance: Practices and Processes for Stakeholder and Citizen Participation in the Work of Government," *Public Administration Review* 65 (2005): 547–58; Graham Smith, *Democratic Innovations: Designing Institutions for Citizen Participation* (Cambridge: Cambridge University Press, 2009); Nabatchi, "Addressing the Citizenship and Democratic Deficits"; and Carolina Johnson and John Gastil, "Variations of Institutional Design for Empowered Deliberation," *Journal of Public Deliberation* 11, no. 1 (2015), article 2.

[54] Edward C. Weeks, "The Practice of Deliberative Democracy: Results from Four Large-Scale Trials," *Public Administration Review* 60 (2000): 360–72, 361.

16   *Civic Power*

judgement."[55] Through novel institutional and process designs like the use of "minipublics" where smaller groups of citizens are convened to discuss and formulate public policy,[56] or citizens' juries where a random group of laypersons deliberate over major policy questions, deliberative democracy reformers have managed to provide a number of examples of what more participatory, engaged, and thoughtful forms of democracy might look like.[57]

The hope of these interventions is that through structured discussion, a wider array of voices will be taken into account, resulting in both the triumph of the better argument and a continually revitalized sense of civic identity.[58] Through small-group dialogue and deliberation, these minipublics foster consensus and collective problem-solving. In conventional participatory governance literature, such deliberative minipublics should be optimized to foster respect, inclusion, and quality participation.[59] Some practitioners have also developed more large-scale forms of deliberative and participatory publics, such as the AmericaSpeaks Citizen Summits that convened a representative and diverse group of 3,500 residents in Washington, DC to discuss citywide policy issues from education to public services to budgets, or the use of large-scale civic deliberations involving several thousand participants addressing similar budgetary battles over public service provision in cities like Eugene, Oregon, and Sacramento, California.[60]

Yet there are two major problems with these deliberative democracy experiments. First, much of this literature on deliberative and participatory democracy pays insufficient attention to underlying disparities of power. Small-scale participation in a minipublic is not the same thing as creating a deeply participatory democracy that genuinely expands the power of

---

[55] Daniel Yankelovich, *Coming to Public Judgment: Making Democracy Work in a Complex World* (Syracuse, NY: Syracuse University Press, 1991), 42.

[56] Bruce Ackerman and James S. Fishkin, *Deliberation Day* (New Haven, CT: Yale University Press, 2005); Fung, "Recipes for Public Spheres"; and James S. Fishkin, *The Voice of the People: Public Opinion and Democracy* (New Haven, CT: Yale University Press, 1995).

[57] Other deliberative processes include ChoiceWork Dialogues, deliberative polling, citizens juries, consensus conferences, study circles, and citizen assemblies. See Carolyn J. Lukensmeyer and Lars Hasselblad Torres, *Public Deliberation: A Manager's Guide to Citizen Engagement* (Washington, DC: IBM Center for the Business of Government, 2006), 24.

[58] Gutmann and Thompson, *Why Deliberative Democracy?*; Joshua Cohen, "Deliberation and Democratic Legitimacy," in *Debates in Contemporary Political Philosophy*, ed. Derek Matravers and Jon Pike (New York: Routledge, 2007), 342–60. This essay was originally published in 1989.

[59] See Mansbridge, *Deliberative Systems*; and Smith, *Democratic Innovations*.

[60] Fung, "Recipes for Public Spheres," 355–57; and Weeks, "The Practice of Deliberative Democracy."

individuals and communities to share in political authority. Informal networks of engagement benefit some communities, but not all. Political scientists Cathy J. Cohen and Michael C. Dawson have demonstrated that informal networks for political information and engagement are limited for African Americans who live in clusters of poverty.[61] This disparity even affects people who are not affected by poverty but live in dense areas of concentrated poverty.[62] In some instances, deliberation can actually exacerbate power differences between participants – making them feel frustrated with the system that made them deliberate together.[63] Furthermore, unless they substantively tie participation to direct changes in policy outcomes, deliberative and participatory spaces may use up citizens' valuable time only to give them an allure of empowerment.[64] This is especially problematic for already disadvantaged communities lacking resources and spare time with which to engage political processes.

Second, experiments in expanding deliberative democracy have been fairly limited in size, scope, and impact. Many deliberative democracy interventions focus on small-scale decision-making – modest and local issues of toilets and trees where the scale and focus of impact are limited, rather than addressing the more thorny and structural barriers that undermine communities' access to opportunity and well-being. These limitations have been exacerbated by the more recent phenomenon of corporate co-opting of the techniques of participatory democracy as an extension of their "corporate citizenship strategies."[65] These private companies have increasingly made grassroots engagement another public relations arm to support business interests with a patina of civic engagement, further distancing these engagement practices from the most glaring crises of inequality, exclusion, and power.

---

[61] Cathy J. Cohen and Michael C. Dawson, "Neighborhood Poverty and African American Politics," *American Political Science Review* 87 (1993): 286–302.

[62] Ibid.

[63] J. R. Hibbing and E. Theiss-Morse, *Stealth Democracy: Americans' Beliefs about How Government Should Work* (Cambridge: Cambridge University Press, 2002), 191.

[64] Caroline W. Lee, *Do-It-Yourself Democracy: The Rise of the Public Engagement Industry* (New York: Oxford University Press, 2015).

[65] See Edward T. Walker, "Legitimating the Corporation through Public Participation," in *Democratizing Inequalities: Dilemmas of the New Public Participation*, ed. Edward T. Walker, Michael McQuarrie, and Caroline W. Lee (New York: New York University Press, 2015), 69; Francesca Polletta "How Participatory Democracy Became White: Culture and Organizational Choice," *Mobilization: An International Journal* 10, no. 2 (2013): 271–88; and Edward T. Walker, *Grassroots for Hire: Public Affairs Consultants in American Democracy* (Cambridge: Cambridge University Press, 2014).

18 *Civic Power*

The Limits of Power-Neutral Reforms

Despite these limitations, there is no doubt that transparency, technology, and deliberation can play *some* role in the reinventing of modern democracy. While these efforts at promoting transparency, leveraging technology, and deploying deliberative techniques can be valuable, there is something missing in all of these different approaches. The problem with these conventional approaches to democracy reform is not so much a lack of commitment or effort, but rather a *conceptual* problem. Often, democracy reform is animated by one of four underlying hypotheses: civility, transparency, rationality, and hijacking. Each of these hypotheses has some persuasive force, but they all share a common gap in that they undersell the deeper structural disparities described above as key drivers of democratic failure.

- **The civility hypothesis.** In this view, the presumption is that American democratic failure stems from an excess of partisanship and polarization as well as a lack of civil or centrist dialogue. The hope here is that good citizenship, rooted in good-faith dialogue and common sense, can supplant gridlock, conflict, and division. If only partisanship could be brushed aside for a genuine dialogue, then our political problems would be more tractable. This is the account that lies beneath efforts to create centrist third-party candidates as on the open primary website Americans Elect, or efforts by foundations to sponsor bipartisan civic dialogue and deliberative democracy experiments of the sort noted earlier. Robert D. Putnam's famous (or infamous) call for people to bowl more and to socialize in communities is an example of this view.[66]

- **The transparency hypothesis.** A variant of the civility hypothesis is the view that the central problem is one of openness – if government were more transparent, this would bring key issues to the fore, subject them to public opinion and pushback, and also force policymakers to defend their positions in public. This conviction animates efforts by advocacy groups and reformers to push for greater disclosure, transparency, and openness on the part of governmental actors.

- **The rationality hypothesis.** Another strand of reform focuses less on democratic accountability than on assuring good governance – the ability of policymakers to make rational public policy. In this view, politics gets in the way of facts, knowledge, and expertise, all of which are vital to making government effective. To the extent that democracy is important to reformers of this ilk, it features in their thought as a way to

---

[66] Putnam, *Bowling Alone*, 178.

provide relevant information and citizen preferences to policymakers, communicating the needs of the public free of the contamination of interest group politics. This emphasis on rationality also underlies the optimism around new forms of "big data" analytics, or the appeal of social media and technology as means of aggregating citizen input.

- **The hijacking hypothesis.** A final conventional view focuses on the problem of "special interests." Closely related to the civility and transparency hypotheses, under this view our democratic systems – and the public as a whole – are actually quite functional and capable on their own, but special interest politics, money, and lobbying subvert the political system. The response, then, is to remove special interest influence, get money "out" of politics, and reform anti-lobbying, anti-corruption, and "revolving door" policies.

There is a common thread across these varieties of democratic reform. They all share to varying degrees a desire to purify policymaking of the vagaries of political disagreement or conflict. Implicitly, they all hold that deep down, the people are fundamentally capable of achieving agreement and driving the formation and execution of commonsense public policy – if only they are granted greater information and unmediated access to the levers of policymaking, free of the barriers of partisan and interest group politics.

As a result, many efforts at democracy reform rest on flawed theories of what we in this book call the *good governance ethos*. The good governance ethos focuses on trying to sterilize or insulate policymaking from undue influences of special interests and from the messiness of political conflict. Instead, governance, in this view, ought to be structured to maximize expertise, knowledge, rationality, and good-faith deliberation – all of which would obtain if only "politics" did not contaminate governance. The reforms that emerge from this mentality include efforts to prevent lobbying, to undo the "revolving door," to increase the barriers between interest groups and policymakers so as to make the latter more autonomous and independent, and to bind policymakers more directly to the public will through more aggressive transparency measures.[67] Empowered with technocratic expertise and unprecedented access to information, good governance efforts appear to offer a potential means for government to achieve its aim of generating public value.[68]

---

[67] See Lee Drutman, *The Business of America Is Lobbying* (New York: Oxford University Press, 2015); and Beth Simone Noveck, *Smart Citizens, Smarter State: The Technologies of Expertise and the Future of Governing* (Cambridge, MA: Harvard University Press, 2015).

[68] Mark Moore, *Recognizing Public Value* (Cambridge, MA: Harvard University Press, 2013).

20 *Civic Power*

This ethos has a deep intellectual pedigree. Eighty years ago, James M. Landis, one of the architects of the New Deal, saw the emergence of expertise-based regulatory bodies as a critical modernization of governance.[69] He envisioned that they would deploy science and rationality in their provision of governance, supplanting the chaos and ignorance of traditional legislative bodies who, in Landis's view, were deeply inadequate for the modern era.[70] More recently, proponents of greater expertise in governance – ranging from legal scholars like Cass R. Sunstein to civic technologists like Beth Simone Noveck – have made similar arguments regarding how expertise and technology alike can facilitate deliberation, making government both more responsible and more effective.[71]

But the view of democratic defect and remedy implicit in this ethos is problematic. Citizens and political associations are not disinterested, rationalistic, deliberative actors; they are, rather, necessarily subjective, partial, and themselves political. It is this partiality that motivates political action – and that is irreducibly at the heart of most normative disagreements in politics. Furthermore, attempts at sterilizing the policymaking process of such contestation, however well-intentioned, must be viewed with skepticism, for insulation of governance from the messiness of politics does little to redress the fundamental problem of disparate political power. More well-resourced and sophisticated individuals and groups are more likely to overcome whatever higher barriers to entry are used to shield governmental discretion; the groups most politically disempowered are more likely to be "screened out." The fundamental problem with the good governance ethos is that it rejects the value and importance of political disagreement and contestation. This is what is most structurally insufficient about the attempts to revive democracy through civility, transparency, rationality, or anti-corruption: these efforts at their core share a dislike of *politics itself*. In so doing, these accounts run the risk of ultimately being self-defeating in several respects.

First, unease with political disagreement leads to an incorrect diagnosis of what ails American democracy. On the surface, it may seem that the problem is the fact of political disagreement itself – and therefore the solution must lie in efforts to eliminate that disagreement. But lying beneath political disagreements are very real struggles taking place in American society between the

[69] James M. Landis, *The Administrative Process* (New Haven, CT: Yale University Press, 1938).
[70] Ibid.; and Archon Fung, Mary Graham, and David Weil, *Full Disclosure: The Perils and Promise of Transparency* (New York: Cambridge University Press, 2007), 15.
[71] Cass R. Sunstein, "Interest Groups in American Public Law," *Stanford Law Review* 38 (1985): 29–87, 30–32; and Noveck, *Smart Citizens, Smarter State*.

haves and have-nots – between the 1 percent and the 99 percent, to use the parlance of the brief Occupy movement. Put another way, America has vast disparities in economic wealth, opportunity, and power. In such a world, disagreement is not merely endemic, it is necessary. Social change of the sort capable of addressing these structural disparities cannot be achieved through an avoidance of politics, instead, it requires a form of politics in which different voices can actually operate on equal footing in the political realm. The problem, then, is not an *excess* of politics, but rather a *disparity in political power.*

Second, unease with political disagreement points to narrow visions of how best to reform democracy. Indeed, what is surprising about the civility, transparency, rationality, and hijacking hypotheses is that, if taken seriously, they each depict a very narrow vision of what role the people ultimately play in an ideal democracy. Each of these accounts implicitly envisions a sterilized democratic public – one bound by demands of centrism and civility, one where citizens simply provide preferences or informational inputs into policymaking. Unease with political conflict ultimately leads reformers operating within these frameworks to seek a neutered form of citizen engagement; in such proposals, citizens must be engaged, but only insofar as they do not generate more conflict. Yet such approaches ignore very real disparities in political capacity, organization, and power across different classes, genders, and demographic and interest groups. In light of these disparities, visions of genteel, apolitical civic engagement are a mirage obscuring an underlying institutional reality of political inequality.

Third, these limitations often manifest in affirmative proposals and experiments which, while valuable in their own right, are relatively marginal and small-bore, achieving participation or transparency in areas of decisionmaking that are modest and far removed from problems and policy decisions with higher stakes. Experiments in participatory governance are particularly susceptible to the problems of a lack of scale and a diminutive scope. Too often, such initiatives are focused on potholes or minipublics instead of the actual public and its structural issues.

This good governance ethos arises in part from a sociological difficulty – too often, democracy reform efforts are led by relatively elite reformers from privileged backgrounds, who tend to downplay problems of race, gender, religion, class, and power; this makes current attempts at democracy reform often quite problematic. Current disparities of power also pose problems at the level of organizations. Widening gaps in power, wealth, and well-being along various demographic indicators including political identity, income, education, and race, pose serious obstacles to equal participation within civic organizations.[72] System-level disparities of power are partially reflected in disparities among constituencies in their ability to mobilize and form durable, effective, influential organizations. Indeed, social movement research has demonstrated both a decline in traditional forms of social capital as well as an increase in organizational challenges to creating transformational leadership opportunities for individual participants.[73] Research has also demonstrated that the average person is not necessarily crunching the data provided by the efforts at more transparency or openness.[74] Rather elite opinion makers from journalists to academics and leaders of nongovernmental organizations (NGOs) are the ones most likely to use such information.[75]

The good governance ethos is also an expression of a deep tradition of what some democratic theorists have described as modern or liberal antidemocracy – a pattern among liberal thinkers, reformers, and activists of deep skepticism about the ability of the people to act rationally and effectively, and a resultant quest for efforts to hold the actual levers of political power at arm's length from the demos.[76] To be sure, there are such things as pathological expressions of public will, as evidenced by the revival of populisms on the right and left in recent years. But as we will argue in this book, these pathologies represent not an *excess* of democracy, but rather a *lack* of real democratic agency – or the *wrong kinds* of institutions to channel and structure democratic action.

RECLAIMING DEMOCRACY'S RADICALISM

If the good governance ethos points us in the wrong direction for democracy reform, it does so in large part because of its inability to grasp the deeper

---

[72] Schlozman, Verba, and Brady, *Unheavenly Chorus*; and Pietro S. Nivola and David W. Brady, eds., *Red and Blue Nation? Volume 2: Consequences and Correction of America's Polarized Politics* (Washington, DC: Brookings Institution, 2008).

[73] Putnam, *Bowling Alone*; Marshall Ganz, "Leading Change: Leadership, Organization, and Social Movements," in *Handbook of Leadership Theory and Practice*, ed. Nitin Nohria and Rakesh Khurana (Cambridge, MA: Harvard Business School Press, 2010), 1–42; and Hahrie Han, *How Organizations Develop Activists: Civic Associations and Leadership in the 21st Century* (New York: Oxford University Press, 2014).

[74] Francisca M. Rojas, *Recovery Act Transparency: Learning from States' Experience* (Washington, DC: IBM Center for the Business of Government, 2012), www.businessofgovernment.org/sites/default/files/Recovery%20Act%20Transparency.pdf.

[75] Archon Fung, Hollie Russon Gilman, and Jennifer Shkabatur, "Six Models for the Internet + Politics," *International Studies Review* 15 (2013): 30–47.

[76] Nadia Urbinati, "Unpolitical Democracy," *Political Theory* 38, no. 1 (2010): 65–92, 67; and K. Sabeel Rahman, *Democracy against Domination* (New York: Oxford University Press, 2017), 14, 113.

drivers of democratic failure – the systemic and chronic crises of inequality, exclusion, and disparities of power described above. The problem is not just about the efficacy and rationality of government action. For too many individuals and communities, our democratic institutions are not reflective, responsive, or representative; they are instead alien, arbitrary, and unaccountable. For democracy reform to be meaningful, it has to address these deeper, structural crises of exclusion and inequality. In the rest of this book, we sketch an approach to democracy reform that takes these structural problems of power as its core focus. We call this the "civic power" approach to democracy reform. Crucially, this attention to redressing disparities of power represents more than just a conceptual and policy shift; it is also a recognition of the already-existing sophisticated analyses that communities themselves have developed in recent years in response to these very crises of inequality and exclusion. Consider a few brief examples.

In August 2014, Michael Brown, an unarmed African American teenager, was fatally shot by police after a small-scale robbery.[77] The killing sparked a furor in the town of Ferguson, Missouri, which spread to social media, and accelerated the Movement for Black Lives (M4BL), which had initially begun after the death of another African American teenager, Trayvon Martin.[78] The movement continued to pick up steam during the torrent of police shootings of unarmed (and often lawful) African Americans. While much of the focus of M4BL has emphasized criminal justice reform and police misconduct, a formal policy agenda connected to the movement and released in the height of the 2016 electoral campaign is surprisingly broad, calling for, among other things, democracy reform and a shift to more participatory forms of local governance.[79] For M4BL activists, the reality is that disparities in racial justice, safety, and economic well-being are deeply entwined with disparities of political power – the deep alienation and exclusion of communities of color from formal systems of policymaking help drive the persistence of policies with racially disparate impacts, from criminal justice procedure to economic policy.[80]

---

[77] Rashawn Ray et al., "Ferguson and the Death of Michael Brown on Twitter: #BlackLivesMatter, #TCOT, and the Evolution of Collective Identities," *Ethnic and Racial Studies* 40 (2017): 1797–1813, 1802, doi:10.1080/01419870.2017.1335422.

[78] Ibid., 7.

[79] The Movement for Black Lives (website), "A Vision for Black Lives: Policy Demands for Black Power, Freedom, and Justice," https://policy.m4bl.org/.

[80] See Monica Bell, "Police Reform and the Dismantling of Legal Cynicism," *Yale Law Journal* 126 (2017): 2054–2150; Amna Akbar, "Policing 'Radicalization,'" *UC Irvine Law Review* 3 (2013): 809–83; and Keeanga-Yamahtta Taylor, *From #BlackLivesMatter to Black Liberation* (Chicago: Haymarket, 2016).

This sense of alienation – and the search for greater political power – is not limited to racial justice movements; rather, it inflects a growing range of social movements from a variety of constituencies and communities seeking greater economic, social, racial, and political equity. A common realization binds many of them; new labor groups organizing low-wage communities of color in the gig economy or service industries, community groups seeking to counteract gentrification and economic displacement, and activists organizing rural and deindustrializing communities – all recognize that they are pursuing aspirations for equity, inclusion, and justice, which cannot be achieved without first building the *political* power of these communities on the ground. Democracy, for these activists, is *not* a utopian vision of good-faith deliberation and comity; it is rather an urgent *necessity*, a critical weapon needed to counteract the power of elites, big business, and finance as well as a way to hold to account distant, unresponsive, and easily corrupted policymakers. When democracy works well, it enables effective channels for individuals to be empowered participants in decision-making, whether it is in the context of shaping city zoning and urban development policies, allocating public resources through participatory budgeting, or redressing structural racial discrimination in the criminal justice system.

The urgency of this vision of democracy reform is quite different from the good governance ethos. The task here is not to sterilize, rationalize, or purify democratic decision-making; rather it is to radically *open up* democratic politics to constituencies that are systemically disempowered and underprivileged. The key is not to promote some rationalized, apolitical view of civility, openness, rationality, or common sense; rather, it is to expand the ability of citizens themselves to mobilize, to organize, and to advocate for their views. Indeed, our alternative view emphasizes not good governance, but rather *countervailing power*. Building such countervailing power is critical to redressing the deeper structural drivers of democratic failure explored above: inequality, disparities of political power, and social exclusion. Furthermore, this view of democracy reform orients us toward a very different set of interventions and strategies – and links the project of democracy reform more closely to other efforts to tackle systemic injustices and inequalities.

Literatures on civic engagement, collaborative governance, and participatory governance have often been criticized for a rosy view of collaboration and participation, without addressing underlying questions of power, exclusion, and marginalization. The notion of power in democracy is often thought to be antithetical to productive participation and deliberation, but as we will argue, shifting power is actually essential to making participation real – and to making it effective. Social movement and community organizing conceptions of civic power and power building remain, however, to a large degree, mired in decades-old notions of mobilizing, organizing, and political power. Real democracy reform, in our view, requires interrogating, renewing, and reforming such theories of organizing and power building.

The reality is that while disagreement and power politics are here to stay, their tools also remain unequally distributed across groups and geographies. That being the case, the challenge for democratic institutional design is not to attempt to sterilize policymaking of these pressures, but rather to engage, manage, and balance them in ultimately productive ways. As James Madison famously observed, a central goal of his democratic institutional design for the United States was to counteract the dangers of "faction" and of "cabals of a few" by harnessing the countervailing power of rival factions and groups to prevent concentrations of political power:[81] "Ambition must be made to counteract ambition."[82] This is the core Madisonian insight: given realities of power and disagreement, institutional design should seek to *channel* such disagreement productively, creating institutions that facilitate the mutual checking of power and influence.[83]

Whether Madison himself was a true populist, or instead someone bent on preserving aristocratic rule[84] is somewhat tangential for this broader point. The key for our purposes is the shift to a specifically *power-balancing* view of institutional design and democratic politics.[85] The goal, then, is not

---

[81] "The Federalist, No. 10" (New York, 1787), in *The Federalist Papers*, ed. Ian Shapiro (New Haven, CT: Yale University Press, 2009).

[82] "The Federalist, No. 51" (New York, 1788), in *The Federalist Papers*; and Levinson, "Looking for Power," 33, 36.

[83] Levinson uses this Madisonian approach to frame the purposes of constitutional design as balancing power ("Looking for Power"). See also Jane Mansbridge et al., "The Place of Self-Interest and the Role of Power in Deliberative Democracy," *Journal of Political Philosophy* 18 (2010): 64–100, 93: "If, as we believe, the exercise of power is inevitable in human politics, then we must, like Madison, design democratic institutions that incorporate that power rather than ignore it."

[84] On the participatory strains of founding-era republicanism, see J. S. Maloy, *The Colonial Origins of Modern Democratic Thought* (New York: Cambridge University Press, 2008).

[85] The emphasis on countervailing power and contestation and its contrast to good governance understandings of democracy represents a running fault line in democratic theory, between accounts that prioritize consensus, deliberation, and collaboration on the one hand, and accounts that emphasize conflict, disagreement, and contest on the other. See Ian Shapiro, *The State of Democratic Theory* (Princeton, NJ: Princeton University Press, 2003). John P. McCormick, in *Machiavellian Democracy* (New York: Cambridge University Press, 2011), 141–69, contrasts his contestatory approach to the more aristocratic, deliberative view of other modern republican theorists like Philip Pettit. For an application of a similar Madisonian view of contestation to issues of legislative reform, see Lee Drutman, *The*

26 *Civic Power*

necessarily to prioritize institutional designs for their epistemic, deliberative, or technocratic values (though we may of course still hope to promote such values). Rather, this Madisonian view suggests that institutions must also focus on facilitating countervailing power and checks and balances. While we often associate Madisonian institutional design with the constitutional separation of powers, this focus on power building could take a variety of other forms.[86] Some scholars have highlighted the role of class-based institutions in empowering the powerless public against powerful economic elites as a major tradition in republican thought, from the Roman tribunes of the plebs to more modern consociationalist models.[87] Election law scholars have similarly appealed to Madisonian values of contestation and conflict to call for more competitive electoral systems that undo "lockups" of the electoral process from overbearing parties, political entrenchment, or even campaign finance overreach.[88]

Furthermore, the importance of this contestatory nature of mobilization provides an important amendment to existing discussions of participatory and collaborative governance in the administrative state. For almost twenty years now, scholars have offered a variety of suggestions for how stakeholders can be better empowered and engaged in regulatory policymaking, under the rubrics of "collaborative governance" or "new governance."[89] Many of the policy proposals in these accounts – for example, greater stakeholder representation and participatory monitoring of outcomes – can be leveraged to shift political power in more transformative ways. But conventional accounts of these reform techniques too often tend to gloss over the necessary role that power and conflict play in creating truly equitable and inclusive processes. In contrast to these accounts, the goal for a power-shifting institutional design should not be to optimize a policy process for efficiency, efficacy, or consensus; rather it

---

    Business of America Is Lobbying. See also Levinson, "Looking for Power," 33: "Constitutionalism is the project of creating, allocating, and constraining state power."

[86] Andrias, "Separations of Wealth," 423.

[87] See McCormick, *Machiavellian Democracy.* Sitaraman explores what a similar strategy for balancing class-based political power might look like in more formal "mixed-constitutional" methods (*The Crisis of the Middle-Class Constitution*).

[88] Samuel Issacharoff and Richard H. Pildes, "Politics as Markets: Partisan Lockups of the Democratic Process," *Stanford Law Review* 50 (1998): 643–717, 644; and Elizabeth Anderson and Richard H. Pildes, "Expressive Theories of Law: A General Restatement," *University of Pennsylvania Law Review* 148 (2000): 1503–75.

[89] Chris Ansell and Alison Gash, "Collaborative Governance in Theory and Practice," *Journal of Public Administration Research and Theory* 18 (2008), 543–71, 543; and R. A. W. Rhodes, "The New Governance: Governing without Government," *Political Studies* 44 (1996): 652–67, 655–56.

should be, in classic Madisonian fashion, to facilitate a productive form of contestation and disagreement.[90]

This focus on building countervailing power through which a wider range of constituencies can engage in political advocacy, and offset the pressures toward corruption, systemic exclusion, and deliberate de-democratization suggests an important broadening of focus for these emerging social movements. As Carole Pateman argues, genuine democratic transformation requires the creation of participatory mechanisms and accountability through structural changes to the way public policy operates at scale.[91]

CIVIC POWER

This focus on power and its institutional and social construction is the central theme of this book – what we call the *civic power perspective*. As we argue in this book, building such civic power requires two complementary and mutually reinforcing changes to our democratic ecosystem. First, it requires transforming the way we approach *organizing constituencies*. Second, it requires radical changes to how we structure *governing institutions* and the *process of policymaking*. Indeed, where inclusive economic and political arrangements have proven effective, transformative, and durable, they have depended not just on a durable coalition of organized civil society supporters;[92] they have also depended on the creation of powerful state *institutions* in which these policies are embedded, and through which they are enforced.[93] In each of these domains of organizing, institutional design, and policymaking, there is a pre-existing tendency to approach social change

---

[90] On the distinction between collaborative and contestatory forms of participation, see Rahman, *Democracy against Domination*, 105–09. For a critique of collaborative governance and its relative silence on disparities of power, see Amy Cohen, "Governance Legalism: Hayek and Sabel on Reason and Rules, Organization and Law," *Wisconsin Law Review* (2010); and Amy Cohen, "Negotiation, Meet New Governance: Interests, Skills, and Selves," *Law and Social Inquiry* 33 (2008): 503–62. Cristie Ford uses case studies in financial regulation to argue that conventional views of collaborative governance pay insufficient attention to the need to better institutionalize countervailing power in her article "New Governance in the Teeth of Human Frailty: Lessons from Financial Regulation," *Wisconsin Law Review* (2010): 441–89. David Super makes a similar argument in the context of poverty law in his "Laboratories of Destitution: Democratic Experimentalism and the Failure of Antipoverty Law," *University of Pennsylvania Law Review* 157 (2008): 541–616.

[91] Carole Pateman, "Participatory Democracy Revisited," *Perspectives on Politics* 10 (2012): 7–19.

[92] Jacob S. Hacker and Paul Pierson, "After the 'Master Theory': Downs, Schattschneider, and the Rebirth of Policy-Focused Analysis," *Perspectives on Politics* 12 (2014): 643–62, 652.

[93] Jane McAlevey, *No Shortcuts: Organizing for Power in the New Gilded Age* (New York: Oxford University Press, 2016), 7.

through a more thin, good governance framework. Thus new forms of online organizing risk prioritizing thin forms of engagement over more durable power-building approaches to organizing. Bureaucratic reforms may focus too narrowly on optimizing government efficiency rather than shifting power and increasing democratic accountability. Throughout the rest of this book, we argue for a power-shifting approach in each of these domains. In the rest of this chapter, we provide a brief preview of some of these arguments.

Organizing for Civic Power

Social movements can be understood as a larger network of individuals connected by shared experiences and commitments. These movements can be linked to a variety of formal organizations, and through organized political activity make claims on institutions and policymakers.[94] As sociologists Sidney Tarrow, Charles Tilly, and others have argued, the ability of movements to be successful in exercising political power and winning campaigns depends on a variety of conditions, including the presence of mobilizing narratives that can frame their values and demands, organizational resources and capacity, and "political opportunity structure" – the ways in which existing policymaking institutions create opportunities for movements to make effective claims on policymakers.[95]

Recently, new waves of organizing show that such movements face unique challenges and opportunities in the current democratic ecosystem. Take for example, recent efforts to organize low-wage and precarious workers in the on-demand economy. Jannette Navarro is a twenty-two-year-old Starbucks barista and single mother working toward her associate degree in business.[96] Moving from work at the Dollar Tree and a KFC franchise to Starbucks gave her the hope of opportunity and upward mobility. Starbucks, however, like most major restaurant and retail chains, uses software aimed at maximizing profits that can wreak havoc on the schedules and lives of employees by continually altering their assigned hours with limited notice.[97] This software subjects workers to last-minute changes in hours, reduced hours, and even

---

[94] See Charles Tilly, *Contentious Performances* (New York: Cambridge University Press, 2008).

[95] Sidney Tarrow and Charles Tilly, *Contentious Politics and Social Movements* (Boulder, CO: Paradigm, 2006); Sidney Tarrow, *Power in Movement: Social Movements and Contentious Politics*, 3rd ed. (New York: Cambridge University Press, 2011), 26–27, 80, 167–68.

[96] Jodi Kantor, "Starbucks to Revise Policies to End Irregular Schedules for Its 130,000 Baristas," *New York Times*, August 14, 2014, www.nytimes.com/2014/08/15/us/starbucks-to-revise-work-scheduling-policies.html.

[97] Ibid.

Democracy in Crisis

"clopening," closing late at night and opening again a few hours later. Although many white-collar workers desire greater scheduling flexibility, for low-income workers such flexibility can have nefarious implications by preventing predictable work schedules and impeding child care options. For Ms. Navarro, her unpredictable work schedule created turmoil in her life and for her four-year-old son, Gavin.[98]

In the current economic environment where corporations employ workers spread out across the globe, it can be challenging for labor to organize and have a collective voice or bargaining power. Without the traditional infrastructure of unions, how can these workers achieve the political power necessary to advocate for their needs? In 2015, Starbucks baristas, increasingly burdened by stressful just-in-time scheduling that made it impossible to have stable hours and wages, and to balance work and family commitments, organized a worldwide campaign that successfully forced the company to introduce more stable schedules.[99] Ms. Navarro's story, and similar stories of many across the country like her, were brought to public attention and highlighted in the *New York Times.*[100]

This is democracy in action: through collective action and organization, workers were able to advocate for their concerns, and exercise some degree of authority over the policies of a vast corporation. Yet this success did not emerge in a vacuum. The ability of the baristas to organize so effectively depended on a background infrastructure, particularly that of the online platform Coworker.org.[101] Coworker.org serves as an online forum and incubator of worker campaigns, enabling workers in a variety of industries to find one another, share ideas, and ultimately mobilize to defend their interests. Centralized support staff work with individuals to help organize and galvanize workers on the ground to form relationships around targeted issue campaigns. In an era of increasingly disempowered workers, Coworker.org is part of a new wave of alternative labor organizing groups seeking to build the power and

---

[98] Ibid.

[99] Noam Scheiber, "Starbucks Falls Short after Pledging Better Labor Practices," *New York Times,* September 23, 2015, www.nytimes.com/2015/09/24/business/starbucks-falls-short-after-pledging-better-labor-practices.html.

[100] Kantor, "Starbucks to Revise Policies"; Jodi Kantor, "Working Anything but 9 to 5: Scheduling Technology Leaves Low-Income Parents with Hours of Chaos," *New York Times,* August 13, 2014, www.nytimes.com/interactive/2014/08/13/us/starbucks-workers-scheduling-hours.html; and Jodi Kantor, "Times Article Changes a Starbucks Policy, Fast," *Times Insider* (blog), *New York Times,* August 22, 2014, www.nytimes.com/times-insider/2014/08/22/times-article-changes-a-policy-fast/.

[101] "Starbucks: Give Us a Fair Workweek!" Coworker.org (website), www.coworker.org/petitions/starbucks-employees-need-a-fair-workweek.

30   *Civic Power*

agency of workers and communities themselves. From the Domestic Workers' Alliance to the People's Action network, the latest wave of community organizing is increasingly shifting its focus from transient campaigns to the challenge of developing the kind of underlying *infrastructure* that builds long-term grassroots power and enables a more sustained, ongoing, and long-term capacity to exercise political influence. These new approaches to organizing address a deep structural problem in our democracy: the lack of opportunity for individual people to participate as active members in civic organizations that have actual political capacity.[102]

These movements must focus not only on mobilizing, but also on building long-term power for workers and grassroots communities themselves. As scholars of social movements have suggested, this means building mass-member, federated, civil society organizations driven by organic leaders developed from within the movement. It means converting people from newly mobilized supporters into long-term, committed members of the movement who deepen their knowledge, skills, and commitment over time.[103] Part of what makes membership-based advocacy groups' organizing so effective is that they build durable organizations that can exercise influence in a variety of ways and that persist beyond momentary flashpoints of controversy. Building long-term democratic inclusion, then, requires deep investments in building this kind of infrastructure for durable, grassroots organizing.

Linking Movements with Governance

For these movements to exercise meaningful influence, they must, at some point, embed their members and values within larger organizations and institutions that can exercise political power even more effectively than the movements themselves. Thus, where movements have "anchored" within mainstream political parties, they have exercised wider influence on public policy and institutional change.[104]

The literature on social movement theory gives a granular account of how institutional structures can incentivize and catalyze more specific forms of constituency voice and participation. This literature suggests that the ability of

---

[102]   Han, *How Organizations Develop Activists*; Ganz, "Leading Change"; Theda Skocpol, "Unravelling from Above," *American Prospect*, March/April 1996: 20–25.

[103]   See Han, How Organizations Develop Activists; Skocpol, Diminished Democracy; and Zeynep Tufekci, *Twitter and Tear Gas: The Power and Fragility of Networked Protest* (New Haven, CT: Yale University Press, 2017).

[104]   See Daniel Schlozman, *When Movements Anchor Parties: Electoral Alignments in American History* (Princeton, NJ: Princeton University Press, 2015), 2–3.

civil society groups to form durable, long-term organizations capable of exercising power depends a great deal on their internal organizational capacity, as well as the larger institutional context in which these groups operate. Additionally, the "political opportunity structure" in turn can inform the strategies and organizational capacities of movements, as movements tend to build a "repertoire" of expertise and skills specialized around the most effective methods of exercising real power and influence.[105]

Furthermore, other scholars suggest that beyond the constituency effects identified by political scientists like Andrea Campbell, Theda Skocpol, Suzanne Mettler, and others, there are more fine-grained ways in which institutional structures can catalyze movements and civil society organizations to build and exercise power *based on the types of institutional opportunities for influence*. Taken together, these insights suggest that institutional design can play a large role in shaping the terrain upon which movements and civil society actors operate. Institutions and processes for policymaking are not merely reflexively responsive to the external pressures of interest groups. Rather, they themselves shape the political terrain on which individuals and constituencies attempt to exercise political power. Thus, institutions and processes can be designed in ways that proactively catalyze and facilitate the ability of groups – particularly diffuse, under-resourced, marginalized, or traditionally overlooked groups – to be better able to exercise power and influence.

Expanding this capacity for influence, however, requires looking at both the nature of interest group organizing and the institutional context in which these organizations act. Much of the literature on social movements and organizing focuses on the ability of interest groups and organizations to exercise power in shaping a specific policy decision or outcome. Indeed, case studies often examine dynamics at this level of analysis, investigating especially how civil society groups mobilize and secure specific legal or policy victories.[106] But the likelihood and frequency of such policy victories is shaped by the distribution of power at deeper levels. Specific policy decisions are frequently themselves constrained by the power to set agendas to begin with; if an issue or option is not even considered "viable" or "on the table," no degree

---

[105] Han, *How Organizations Develop Activists*, 68–69, 74; Tilly, *Contentious Performances*, 10, 12, 148–49; and Tarrow, *Power in Movement*, 39–40.

[106] Scott Cummings describes how the law and social movements literature generally examines case studies of specific campaign mobilizations resulting in legal and policy change and further notes that this literature tends to focus on specific litigation strategies or mobilization efforts in his article, "Empirical Studies of Law and Social Change: What Is the Field? What Are the Questions?" *Wisconsin Law Review* (2013): 171–204, 184.

of influence on the policy decision itself will be effective. Furthermore, the ability to set agendas is similarly a function of even deeper background power structures about who can organize and exercise influence, and who has a seat at the table to begin with.[107]

To understand this focus on structural allocations of power, consider for example the battle for labor power in today's economy. Among the central challenges for worker organizing today are specific policy questions such as the minimum wage or fair workweek scheduling. But the ability of workers to drive such specific policy changes is a product of background structural conditions. Can labor groups mobilize a wide enough constituency of workers across different employers, sectors, and geographies? Can they organize such ad hoc mobilization into long-term, durable, movement groups that can maintain sustained advocacy pressure? Are there policymaking institutions to which these claims can be directed? Are such appeals one-off instances? Or can they be more deeply institutionalized, so that workers have a more sustained seat at the table? Will workers be able to attain a position that could allow them to shape policy on a forward-looking and ongoing basis, rather than battling for after-the-fact redress?

Labor law has been long criticized for imposing structural, historical constraints on the ability of labor to forge durable cross sector coalitions that can exercise ongoing power and influence on the policies of the workplace.[108] One of the most acute constraints is the historical exclusion of those performing many low-wage, precarious types of work – like domestic workers and farm workers – from protections for organizing.[109] These groups of workers now comprise a huge chunk of the modern labor force, and communities of color are also disproportionately represented within them. While some battles over labor organizing and policy are about specific surface issues like wages, other battles are about these deeper structural allocations of power. Indeed, these are the stakes of so-called "right to work" laws (and the contrast to the push for "card check" laws) that would undermine (or expand) the long-term capacity of labor to forge effective, mass civil society organizations.[110]

---

[107] See John Gaventa, *Power and Powerlessness: Quiescence & Rebellion in an Appalachian Valley* (Urbana: University of Illinois Press, 1982); and Archon Fung, "Understanding Power" (working paper, Gettysburg Project on Civic Engagement, June 2017), on file with authors.

[108] See Rogers, "Libertarian Corporatism," 1623–46; Andrias, "The New Labor Law," 2–100; Nelson Lichtenstein, *State of the Union* (Princeton, NJ: Princeton University Press, 2010); and Michelle Miller and Eric Bernstein, *New Frontiers of Worker Power: Challenges and Opportunities in the Modern Economy* (New York: Roosevelt Institute, February 15, 2017).

[109] Andrias, "The New Labor Law," 16.

[110] Rogers, "Libertarian Corporatism," 1629–30; Andrias, "The New Labor Law," 39–41.

Democracy in Crisis

From the standpoint of power, then, it is crucial to approach institutional design questions with a focus on the interactions between institutions and social movements and civil society organizing.[111] Thus, the project of redressing or balancing power disparities must approach the distribution of power at this deeper level. This is not to say that there exists a pure power-balancing process or institutional structure. Procedural protections are certainly susceptible to capture and influence by more well-resourced and sophisticated players.[112] Nevertheless, under conditions of already-existing disparities of capacity and influence, we can design bureaucracies and policies very differently in order to shift the terrain of power and influence in a more equitable and balanced direction.

Designing Institutions for Participation

In the drab, concrete brutalist building of Boston's City Hall, after two security checkpoints and down a long corridor next to the Mayor's office, lies a division of eclectic city officials who do not fit the traditional image of municipal bureaucrats. Their offices look more like those of a Silicon Valley start-up, with walls covered in whiteboards and post-it notes and a gray carpeted floor peppered with brightly colored cushions and chairs. This is the Mayor's Office of New Urban Mechanics (MONUM), staffed by "mechanics" with expertise in everything from sociology to business, ethnography, and technology. These officials are charged with tinkering and innovating new approaches to Boston's biggest public policy challenges.[113]

MONUM is part of a larger movement to create "innovation offices" in different levels of government. Other examples include the proliferation of city-based offices encouraged by philanthropies as well as the Obama administration's creation of the United States Digital Service, 18F, and tech-savvy digital service delivery offices in different federal agencies.[114] These offices aim to harness the creativity and technological know-how of a new generation of policymakers along the model of Silicon Valley start-ups. Yet while the innovation office movement tracks the good governance ethos with its goal

---

[111] Andrias, "Separations of Wealth," 497–99.

[112] Administrative law scholars Ganesh Sitaraman and Kevin Stack both refer to this as the "paradox of process." Sitaraman, "The Puzzling Absence of Power in Constitutional Theory," *Cornell Law Review* 101 (2016): 1445–1532, 1500.

[113] Garrett Quinn, "Former Boston Mayor Tom Menino Was City's Urban Mechanic" *MassLive*, October 30, 2014, www.masslive.com/news/boston/index.ssf/2014/10/boston-mayor-tom-menino-urban-mechanic.html.

[114] United States Digital Service (website), www.usds.gov/; 18F (website), https//18f.gsa.gov/.

34   *Civic Power*

of rationalizing public policy, in practice MONUM has operated quite differently than one might assume. Rather than focusing narrowly on upgrading the data and technological tools used in city government, the leaders of MONUM have quietly transformed the office into a vehicle for expanding the voice of often overlooked constituencies in the most critical city government decisions.

As Boston considers a major initiative to build affordable housing, for example, MONUM has used its position in government and its resources to seek out residents in traditionally marginalized communities such as Dorchester, to engage them in in-depth discussions about the proposed housing policies, and then to provide a vehicle for these communities to reshape the city's affordable housing agenda in significant ways. In fact, MONUM set up design "charrettes" all across Boston – deploying a 385-square-foot, one-bedroom unit on wheels everywhere from City Hall to Roslindale, Mattapan, Dorchester, Roxbury, and East Boston from August to November in 2016.[115] The goal was especially to reach parts of the city where people feel disconnected and not necessarily represented in city hall.[116] Residents were able to physically walk through the space and identify what are the most important housing principles for them. MONUM staff also sat down with eleven residents at their homes in Jamaica Plain for in-depth research to assess their housing needs. Importantly, the "mechanics" translate these diverse viewpoints directly back to city hall and have the political support of the mayor.

By serving as a "risk aggregator," according to one staffer, and absorbing risk from other city agencies, the mechanics enable city officials to operate in a more experimental, responsive, and participatory capacity. In a policy area more commonly associated with top-down, unaccountable government action that is often responsive to commercial developers over communities, such an outcome is remarkable. MONUM now works across city agencies and inspires others in government to be more open to experimentation and new forms of civic engagement.[117] MONUM is not alone in this approach to democratic governance. From the new Consumer Financial Protection Bureau in Washington, DC, to attempts at shifting institutional processes around urban economic development projects, to the spread of participatory

---

[115] Mayor's Office of New Mechanics, "Urban Housing Unit Road Show," last updated April 20, 2018, www.boston.gov/departments/new-urban-mechanics/urban-housing-unit-roadshow.
[116] New Urban Mechanics, "What We Learned from the UHU Roadshow," November 9, 2016, https://medium.com/@newurbanmechs/what-we-learned-from-the-uhu-roadshow-7b33caee d721#.jlopwk58g.
[117] Ibid.

Democracy in Crisis

budgeting across cities, government actors on the ground are experimenting with systems that could provide real authority for affected stakeholders.

***

These examples of new modes of community organizing on the one hand, and alternative approaches to the exercise of bureaucratic policymaking on the other, are indicative of the broader argument we advance in this book. Democracy, we argue, is best secured by practices, institutions, and interventions that *build the capacity of communities to exercise sustained political power*. Such "civic power" or "civic capacity" is in turn a product of different approaches to organizing on the one hand, and to institutional design and governance on the other – as well as how the two interact.

Thus, civic power first requires well-resourced, strategic, and locally rooted community organizations that can mobilize, organize, and engage individuals at the grassroots. From Tocqueville to modern theorists, political associations have long been viewed as "great free schools" that teach members how to participate and exercise agency in a democracy.[118] Durable associations are critical for more than their civic benefits; they are essential for building political power and influence. As Sherry Arnstein argued in her classic article, "A Ladder of Citizen Participation," in 1969, participation in the fullest sense of the term is actually about "citizen power," specifically, the "redistribution of power that enables the have-not citizens, presently excluded from the political and economic processes, to be deliberately included in the future."[119] In the face of the longer-term decline of unions and mass-member civic organizations,[120] there must be more variegated and innovative approaches to organizing citizens into lasting political associations, empowering them to advocate for their concerns, and enabling them to hold both government and private sector actors accountable. On the one hand, these associations must be built in ways that empower marginalized groups, while on the other, they must also defuse the dangers of racialized or gendered forms of exclusion and political subordination. Both of these challenges – building power and forging diverse coalitions and communal identities – suggest the need for a different approach to generating civic engagement and participation.

---

[118] Alexis de Tocqueville, *Democracy in America and Two Essays on America*, ed. Isaac Kramnick, trans. Gerald Bevan (London: Penguin, 2003), 606.

[119] Sherry R. Arnstein, "A Ladder of Citizen Participation," *Journal of the American Institute of Planners* 35, no. 4 (1969): 216–24, 216.

[120] Skocpol, *Diminished Democracy*; Han, *How Organizations Develop Activists*; and Ganz, "Leading Change."

Additionally, civic power of the type we advocate requires a radically different structure of governance institutions. In short, the key here is the combination of authority and accountability. Governance institutions need sufficient authority and capacity to be able to actually respond to the claims and needs raised by organized constituencies. If cities or regulators, for example, lack the basic resources, authority, and capacity to make meaningful policies in the first place, democratic engagement with these institutions does little good. MONUM is just one example of the kinds of developments that can help create more hooks and levers for civic participation, while expanding governmental capacity. Data and technology can be deployed to build governmental capacity, but they are not sufficient on their own to build civic power. Importantly, expanded governmental authority and capacity must be complemented by meaningful accountability. Constituencies need more direct and effective forms of leverage for holding policymakers accountable and spurring them to action. This means that those engaged in this project of democracy reform must look for ways that constituencies can interact with public policymaking beyond the localized and episodic engagement of elections and political campaigns. The ability of associations and organizations to exercise real influence and power depends largely on the hooks, levers, and points of entry that these groups have in the actual decision-making processes of ordinary governance.

There are of course many other dimensions to assuring a vibrant democracy, from questions about the changing nature of the modern public sphere and the role of online platforms in shaping the dynamics of democracy, organizing, and accountability,[121] to concerns about the changing nature of political parties,[122] and to continued debate over electoral system and campaign finance reform.[123] This book cannot address all of these issues. The focus here is on a crucial complementary set of concerns: how to expand the power and capacity of grassroots constituencies to shape day-to-day policymaking, and how to assure that such policymaking is both effective and responsive to the full range of affected interests.

---

[121] Tufekci, Twitter and Tear Gas; David Karpf, The MoveOn Effect: The Unexpected Transformation of American Political Advocacy (New York: Oxford University Press, 2012); and Frank Pasquale, Black Box Society: The Secret Algorithms that Control Money and Information (Cambridge, MA: Harvard University Press, 2015).

[122] Lee Drutman, "Donald Trump's Candidacy Is Going to Realign the Political Parties," Vox, March 1, 2016, www.vox.com/polyarchy/2016/3/1/11139054/trump-party-realignment.

[123] Hasen, Plutocrats United; Berman, Give Us the Ballot; Teachout, Corruption in America; and Lessig, Republic, Lost.

A ROAD MAP FOR RECONSTRUCTING OUR DEMOCRACY

The rest of this book develops this "civic power perspective" in more detail. Part I (Chapters 2 and 3) takes on the first set of implications of this civic power perspective, focusing on how power and democracy can be built (or undermined) through the operation of civil society associations. These chapters explore the centrality of civil society organizations in creating an equitable balance of power in democratic politics. Chapter 2 begins by exploring how social movements and social change are centrally dependent on the building of durable power through long-term community organizing. This power-building orientation in turn explains many of the shifts in American politics: as the power of progressive social movements like unions and the civil rights movement waned, the power of business interests and conservative civil society groups increased, in turn driving the shift in American political discourse and policy outcomes. Much of the contemporary sense of crisis in American democracy, including the ascent of business interests and the rise of exclusionary far-right populism, can be explained by this shift in the organizational balance of power. Chapter 3 then explores examples and mechanisms through which the countervailing power of *inclusive* new social movements might be built and expanded.

Part II (Chapters 4, 5, and 6) then shifts the focus from civil society to government. Chapter 4 outlines the limits of recent efforts to improve government through the promotion of innovation and new technologies. The book then turns to a discussion of how bureaucracies might be restructured internally to create a greater commitment to democratic participation and to offer a more robust and supportive counterpart to the kinds of social movement organizing described in Chapter 3. This shift toward more democratization of government should involve partly a shift in organizational culture and structure within bureaucracies to make them more friendly to democratic processes (Chapter 5), and partly a change in policy design to prioritize the institutionalization of countervailing power (Chapter 6).

Implications for Democratic Theory and Reform

In our approach, democracy is neither a utopian idyll of rational deliberation or of civic virtue nor an epistemically useful system for aggregating information and preferences. It is rather a project of balancing and equalizing political power. But at the same time, this focus on power is not exhausted by conventional appeals to the power of protest or the unruly mob. Rather, we suggest that the effective and balanced exercise of democratic power requires a larger ecosystem of organizations and institutions that both enable and structure contestation into effective and productive patterns. Through such organizations and institutions, constituencies can exercise real influence and power – at times, through disagreement with established authorities. This approach stands in stark contrast to the good governance ethos described above. Instead of seeking to sterilize policymaking of politics, the goal here is to catalyze, activate, and enable greater political engagement by a wider range of affected communities – and to create institutions that can structure such inclusion and contestation productively. This approach to democratic capacity offers several important contributions to the theory and practice of democracy reform.

First, we develop our theoretical account of democratic capacity and power building by engaging under-explored areas of contemporary democratic life. We suggest that the most critical yet overlooked sites of democratic action and renewal lie not within the headline politics of elections, campaigns, and national legislatures (although these are no doubt critical for longer-term democratic vitality), but in spaces of day-to-day governance that shape the more mundane yet important rules and policies that guide our economic, social, and collective lives. In particular, much of the most compelling innovations are arising from on-the-ground practitioners working in community organizing and local-level governance.

In developing this argument, this book employs original fieldwork highlighting the work of innovators in democratic governance as well as political theory to draw on the moral and institutional principles needed to expand and deepen these practices. We take a unique interdisciplinary approach that combines a variety of theoretical insights from scholarly literatures on democratic theory, participatory governance, political science, sociology, and social movements along with a survey of practices and innovations on the ground. We also put in common conversation the insights from several siloed domains of civic innovation, including civic tech, open government, community organizing, and bureaucratic reform. Too often, innovations in each of these arenas of technology, institutions, and civil society proceed in isolation. In order for the potential of these innovations for democratization to be realized, we need reform strategies that operate across all of these areas, empowering communities, reorganizing bureaucracies, and linking them through new technological tools and institutional procedures.

Second, we contribute to an emerging debate in democratic theory over the idea of power and institutional design. For classical democratic theorists, the idea of countervailing power was central to macro-scale institutional design

Democracy in Crisis

questions. Republican political thinkers from Niccolò Machiavelli to James Madison fundamentally concerned themselves with the productive structuring of contestation, through institutional designs like the separation of powers.[124] Madison envisioned a democratic institutional design reliant on a separation of powers where "[a]mbition must be made to counteract ambition."[125] Machiavelli outlines a more radical notion of populism and democratic participation facilitated by institutions that specifically empower representatives of the people as a check on economic elites.[126] Yet, this orientation toward catalyzing and channeling contestation has not been maintained in more modern discussions of institutional design, which tend to prioritize efficiency and expertise (e.g., in the design of regulatory and governance institutions) rather than the balancing of power. But in the twenty-first-century American economy, where so much authority resides in institutions of ordinary day-to-day regulation and governance, it seems vital to consider both how to create institutions where countervailing power has a built-in voice and how to structure productive and effective contestation in institutional structures that exist outside of the conventional domains of elections, parties, and the formal separation of powers. As noted above, this power orientation to institutional design also represents a distinctive shift to conventional approaches to deliberative and participatory governance literatures.

Third, this approach also offers an important alternative response to the growing debate in democracy reform about the role of intermediary organizations. Often, intermediary organizations – civil society groups, gatekeepers like media editors, and restrictive undemocratic institutions like the United States Senate – have been justified as aristocratic elements tempering the excesses of democracy. By contrast, many good governance reforms tend to pursue an illusory ideal of disintermediated politics – as if, by stripping away the influence of associations, parties, and politics, governance can be better structured through a *direct* connection between the mass public and decision-makers who can aggregate preferences and views via new technologies. The raw aggregation of public opinion or preferences is not the same thing as political power. Furthermore, such disintermediated democratic politics is, as a growing number of studies warn, more prone to pathological forms of

---

[124] Rahman, *Democracy against Domination*.

[125] "Federalist, No. 51."

[126] See John McCormack, in *Machiavellian Democracy* ; "Machiavelli against Republicanism: On the Cambridge School's Guicciardinian Moments," *Political Theory* 31 (2003): 615–43; and "Contain the Wealthy and Patrol the Magistrates: Restoring Elite Accountability to Popular Government," *American Political Science Review* 100, no. 2 (2006): 147–63.

polarization, disinformation, and demobilization.[127] By contrast, we suggest an approach to democracy that takes seriously the role of intermediating bodies, but casts them as *multipliers* of democratic capacity, not inhibitors. Note the importance, in our view, of civil society associations, face-to-face organizing, and institutional procedures for formulating decisions that include diverse (and often disagreeing) constituencies.

Implications for Practitioners

These theoretical shifts offer concrete implications for practitioners. For practitioners and scholars who are focusing on the work of social movements and community organizations, this book's engagement with the theory and practice of building democratic capacity and power offers a way of reinventing and updating social movement conceptions of civic power and power building for the twenty-first century. What does political power (and political power building) look like in the twenty-first century? What kinds of institutions, organizing strategies, and technologies are needed to generate genuine democratic empowerment? Through assessing power, our argument also sheds light on traditional notions of organizing to broaden the landscape of real power building to include more networked and diffuse opportunities provided by digital technology.

For community-based organizations, our approach to building democratic capacity suggests the importance of building organizations that are capable of participating effectively in these kinds of governance processes, from zoning decisions to regulatory enforcement and budgeting. This means developing a repertoire and skill set that goes beyond the articulation of grievance and advocacy toward one that includes the ability to share in the actual business of governing. This is not an automatic or costless transition, but it is essential to enabling civil society groups to make full use of the kinds of inclusionary strategies discussed above.[128]

By deliberately investigating cases of novel organizing strategies, we also engage with a parallel debate already under way among social movement

---

[127] Zeynep Tufecki, "Capabilities of Movements and Affordances of Digital Media: Paradoxes of Empowerment," Connected Learning Alliance (website), January 9, 2014, https://clalliance.org/blog/capabilities-of-movements-and-affordances-of-digital-media-paradoxes-of-empowerment/.

[128] On this shift from "grievance to governance," see Jodeen Olguin-Taylor, "From Grievance to Governance: 8 Features of Transformative Campaigns," LetsTalkMovementBuilding.org, January 26, 2016, http://letstalkmovementbuilding.org/grievance-governance-8-features-transformative-campaigns/.

Democracy in Crisis

scholars regarding the appropriate balance between online and offline modes of organizing. Indeed, the rise of digital tools not only offers the opportunity to mobilize more people with less resources, but also creates challenges for building civic power. For example, some civic associations, such as MoveOn.org, already rely primarily on internet technologies where the structure of activity is consistently shifting to react to current events.[129] Yet digital mobilizing, while it can enable a type of "fast, cheap, and low-cost ... [viral] engagement,"[130] also risks hindering the formation of a necessary leadership structure, which later enables people to exert power.[131]

In addressing questions at the level of organizations, we also make the point that organizational power is partly determined by the broader institutional context in which organizations operate. A growing body of research demonstrates that the choice to get involved in politics is embedded within complex social interactions.[132] As Sidney Tarrow argues, the impact of social movements in part depends on their own capacities, narratives, and the existence of permissive "political opportunity structure[s]."[133] Thus, this book also engages with a second area of scholarly literature on democratic theory and institutional design – specifically aiming to identify what kinds of macro-institutional structures are most conducive to catalyzing and deepening the ability of communities to organize and build power.

As a result, the arguments in this book also offer insights for institutional designers and reformers. Our view of democratic capacity shifts our reform orientation away from the conventional focus on elections and legislatures – although these remain critical sites of democratic action and engagement. So much of the day-to-day decision-making of public policy takes place outside of the electoral and legislative arenas, instead operating through the institutions of ordinary daily governance: regulatory agencies, municipal bodies, and the like. Thus, our approach to democratic capacity suggests that a need to be aware that policy design is in such institutions is not just about substantive and technical issues. Instead, policy design can be leveraged to build

---

[129] See Karpf, *The MoveOn Effect*.

[130] Archon Fung and Jennifer Shkabatur, "Viral Engagement: Fast, Cheap, and Broad, but Good for Democracy?" Max Weber Lecture no. 2013/04 (European University Institute, April 17, 2013), 13, http://cadmus.eui.eu/bitstream/handle/1814/27060/MWP_LS_2013_04.pdf.

[131] Tufecki, "Capabilities of Movements."

[132] Lisa Garcia-Bedolla and Melissa R. Michelson, *Mobilizing Inclusion: Transforming the Electorate through Get-Out-the-Vote Campaigns* (New Haven, CT: Yale University Press, 2012); and Todd Rogers, Alan Gerber, and Craig Fox, "Rethinking Why People Vote: Voting as Dynamic Social Expression," in *The Behavioral Foundations of Public Policy*, ed. Eldar Shafir (Princeton, NJ: Princeton University Press, 2013), 91–107.

[133] Tarrow, *Power in Movement*, 26–27, 80, 167–68.

constituencies, foster community organizing, and build countervailing power. In this book, we offer a theoretical framework with illustrative examples of policies that create what we call *interfaces, hooks, and levers* for organizations to grab onto. These interfaces, hooks, and levers are institutional design elements that provide an opportunity for communities to directly exercise and shape policy decisions. As a result, this approach to designing policies and institutions does more to expand agency and thicken democratic capacity than a policy that cuts off these avenues for engagement.[134] Thus, such democracy-building policy design requires more than simply making "submerged" policies visible and legible.[135] Rather, we suggest a very different approach to the design of the policies themselves to provide hooks and levers through which constituencies can shape or monitor the policies, and in so doing build and exercise meaningful political power.

Furthermore, to make these democracy-building processes work, we need to invest in governmental capacity, not just in the creation and administration of policies, but also in the facility to design, deploy, and manage inclusionary, representative, and participatory strategies. These approaches to inclusive governance and policymaking require significant investment and expertise on the part of procedural conveners,[136] who design representative and participatory mechanisms, provide briefings for the participants on relevant data and issues, and facilitate discussion to lead to concrete, usable recommendations. Policymakers tend not to invest in these skills or tasks. To fully harness the potential of institutional design and policymaking for building countervailing power, this will have to change.[137] Inside government institutions this includes investing in people's leadership development, both in current employees and in building a diverse talent pipeline. It will require making government an innovative and compelling place to work.

Finally, funders and reform advocates can help support alternative strategies for building democratic capacity. For example, philanthropy should work

---

[134] On "thick" versus "thin" democracy, see Tina Nabatchi and Matt Leighninger, *Public Participation for the 21st Century* (Hoboken, NJ: Jossey-Bass, 2015), 14–22; Karl Rogers, *Participatory Democracy, Science, and Technology: An Exploration in the Philosophy of Science* (New York: Palgrave Macmillan, 2008), 115; and Barber, *Strong Democracy*, xvi.

[135] See Suzanne Mettler, *The Submerged State: How Invisible Government Policies Undermine American Democracy* (Chicago: University of Chicago Press, 2011).

[136] Carolyn Lukensmeyer, *Bringing Citizen Voices to the Table: A Guide for Public Managers* (New York: John Wiley, 2012), 305–08.

[137] Charles Sabel and William Simon, "Minimalism and Experimentalism in the Administrative State" (unpublished manuscript on file with author, 2011), 27–30. See also Mariano-Florentino Cuéllar, "Rethinking Regulatory Democracy," *Administrative Law Review* 57 (2005): 411–99, 491–97.

Democracy in Crisis

with the government to create pathways for young people to serve in government or become organizers. This will require investing in diverse talent to ensure that people from all walks of life have the opportunity for meaningful work, career development, and mentorship support. In support for civil society, funding can be more flexible and move beyond project-specific deliverables to support cross collaboration and incubate new ideas. Funders can also support digital literacy trainings for public bureaucrats to learn how to leverage data, technology, and innovation to support democratic deepening.

OF, FOR, AND BY THE PEOPLE

In November 1863, Abraham Lincoln stood at the field of the bloodiest battle of the Civil War, and in his famous Gettysburg Address recast the Civil War as an epic battle for the very idea of democracy and freedom:

> Four score and seven years ago our fathers brought forth on this continent, a new nation, conceived in Liberty, and dedicated to the proposition that all men are created equal. Now we are engaged in a great civil war, testing whether that nation, or any nation so conceived and so dedicated, can long endure ... It is rather for us to be here dedicated to the great task remaining before us ... that we here highly resolve that these dead shall not have died in vain – that this nation, under God, shall have a new birth of freedom – and that government of the people, by the people, for the people, shall not perish from the earth.[138]

Lincoln's idyll – that "government of the people, by the people, for the people" has remained a distant reality. Whether through the systematic disenfranchisement and economic destruction of African Americans after the Civil War, or in the persisting systemic economic subjugation of workers despite the best efforts of the post-war labor movement, the realities of economic, political, and social inequity have undermined ideals of freedom and democratic self-government. Yet this aspiration for a genuinely inclusive and responsive democracy has been a central feature of economic and social justice movements over the centuries. It is not a coincidence that the push for abolition also involved a dramatic (if tragically failed) attempt to remake civil society and political institutions during Reconstruction. Critics of industrialization, corporate power, and economic inequality during the Progressive Era saw their substantive aspirations as closely tied to the remaking of democratic

---

[138] Abraham Lincoln, "The Gettysburg Address" (Bliss copy, 1864), as transcribed by the Smithsonian Institution, National Museum of American History, http://americanhistory .si.edu/documentsgallery/exhibitions/gettysburg_address_2.html.

institutions through new structures like mass-member movements, ballot initiatives, and the direct election of senators. The civil rights movement similarly and crucially connected voting rights and mass organizing to demands for economic and racial justice.

In many ways the upheavals of the early twenty-first century present another existential threat to the democratic experiment. Inequality, structural racial discrimination, and endemic political dysfunction have fueled an increase in the distrust of the democratic process to crisis levels. A growing body of research warns that the twentieth-century era of democratization and economic growth was perhaps not the "end of history" as some in the 1990s declared, but rather a highly contingent aberration.[139] Yet there are now new tools and techniques – from new technologies, to new modes of organizing, to new innovations in institutional design – that can be repurposed and expanded to create a new infrastructure of democratic practice. By highlighting these potentials and developing a framework for deeper democratic capacity, it is our hope that this book can speak to this urgent need.

[139] Compare Francis Fukuyama, *The End of History and the Last Man* (New York: Avon, 1992) with Thomas Piketty, *Capital in the Twenty-First Century* (Cambridge, MA: Harvard University Press, 2013).

PART I

CIVIC POWER THROUGH ORGANIZING

2

Democracy and Inequality as a Function of the Balance of Power

There is a paradox at the heart of the recent anxieties regarding democratic failure in America. As noted in Chapter 1, there is a pervasive sense that trust in democracy is eroding and American democracy may be collapsing. Yet there has been no shortage of democratic energy and mass-movement mobilization in recent years; it has been present in the Occupy movement, the Tea Party, the Movement for Black Lives, and more recently the Women's March, the March for Our Lives, Families Belong Together, and in the overall upsurge of protest activity since the election of 2016. At the same time, these instances of progressive mobilization under the rubric of popular "resistance" to the inequalities of the current moment feel very much outgunned by a parallel and terrifying upsurge of mobilization by white supremacists, the rise of "alt-right," the continued policy influence of big business, and the forces of "exclusionary populism" activated by Donald Trump's presidency. What enables movements to leap from momentary flashpoints of mobilization to exercising transformative power reshaping the political, economic, and social landscape? Why do some mobilizations and movements appear more powerful in some moments of time than others?

Chapter 1 argued that the current democratic crisis is a product of deep problems of unequal power and structural exclusion. The challenge for rebuilding our democracy, then, is one of rebuilding civic power – which means looking to both civil society organizations in building sustained social movements and durable forms of grassroots power capable of influencing policymaking and governance, and transformations to the institutions of governance themselves. In the next two chapters, we focus on this first set of questions. How can civil society organizations better organize to increase and strengthen grassroots power in ways that create a more inclusive democratic politics overcoming disparities of power and chronic exclusions particularly along racial, gender, and class lines?

In this chapter we focus on the challenges of civil society organizing, and in particular this underlying question of how movements acquire (or fall short of acquiring) meaningful political power. As we will argue in this chapter, democratic responsiveness does not simply occur automatically, nor does it react directly to public opinion or even mass protest alone. Rather, democratic politics is fundamentally shaped by the balance of organizational power. As a result, the dynamics of public policy debates, public identities, and coalitions are themselves products of organizational strategies and constructs.

This focus on civic power and organizational structure offers a better explanation of the pathologies of democratic politics today than more generic diagnoses of "crisis." Both the limitations of public protest and the specter of exclusionary populism can be better explained as products of disparities in organizational strength and power – shaping the limited impact of some forms of protest, and enabling the greater influence of other forms. As we argue in this chapter, the rapid increase in inequality, the erosion of civil rights, and the more recent boom of exclusionary far-right populism all came about not from some kind of "natural" political pendulum swing but rather from sustained and deliberate efforts to shift the balance of organizational power, such as through the rise of the modern business lobby, which accompanied the decline of voluntary, mass-member organizations like labor unions. Similarly, the rise of exclusionary far-right populism is not just an expression of raw emotion; it is rather made possible by sustained investment in an infrastructure of far-right organizing, stretching from grassroots groups to media infrastructures, to alliances with wealthy interests.

If this interpretation of the relationship between power, democracy, and inequality is correct, then this further underlines the need to rebuild durable grassroots organizational power rather than merely relying on narratives and persuasion of the median voter. Thus, in this chapter we also provide a sketch of major shifts in American democracy as driven by shifts in the organizational power of civil society groups. Many democratizing transformations in recent American history, like the rise of the New Deal social contract and modern civil rights, owe a great deal to the sustained building of grassroots power through organized labor and the civil rights movement. We examine how such mass-member organizing groups have built power and facilitated democracy in several ways, including by forging cross-cutting and inclusive identities and coalitions, building the civic capacities of individuals through collective action, and leveraging resources to exercise real political power and influence.

At the same time, however, restoring American democracy cannot be achieved by returning to a "golden era" of nineteenth- or twentieth-century mass-member organizing. Indeed, these nineteenth-century models of voluntary associations were often segregated by race and gender. Many relied on the productivity of upper- and middle-class women who were barred from middle-class professions in the formal economy, but had time to volunteer. Furthermore, racial minorities generally had their own separate associations, while multiracial coalitions were often violently suppressed. Meanwhile, the changing nature of work and the continued dismantling of organized labor now both suggest that the classic mode of twentieth-century labor organizing is not likely to return. Nostalgia for the voluntary associations of the past does not offer an effective blueprint for reengaging citizens in their democracy. Nor does it take seriously exclusionary identities around place, race, class, and religion. What we need, then, is a return to investing in the long-term infrastructure of grassroots organizing and grassroots power – but we must achieve these goals not by treating old organizational forms as idealized blueprints, but instead by adapting the underlying principles of power building to develop a modern approach to building civic power and organizing. After drawing out these principles in this chapter, Chapter 3 then turns to the contemporary prospects for democratizing and power-equalizing forms of organizing.

ORGANIZATIONS, POLITICAL POWER, AND ORGANIZING

In many scholarly and conventional accounts of politics, there is a presumption that the driving force behind democratic politics is mass public opinion, with political parties competing for voter support by pitching toward a mythical "center," in variations on the classic median-voter theorem developed by Anthony Downs and mid-century political science.[1] Public opinion research no doubt has grown tremendously sophisticated and has helped elucidate much about both contemporary American politics as well as the limitations or inconsistencies of voter opinions.[2] But from the perspective of political power, this focus on public opinion and voter behavior is at best incomplete. Democratic politics are fundamentally driven not only by raw public opinion, but also by *political organization*. By creating and deploying civil society organizations, different constituencies are able to exercise political influence on public policy and political discourse – as well as on public

---

[1] Anthony Downs, *An Economic Theory of Democracy* (New York: Harper, 1957).

[2] See Larry M. Bartels, *Unequal Democracy: The Political Economy of the New Digital Age*, 2nd ed. (Princeton, NJ: Princeton University Press/Russell Sage Foundation, 2016); and Christopher H. Achen and Larry M. Bartels, *Democracy for Realists: Why Elections Do Not Produce Responsive Government* (Princeton, NJ: Princeton University Press, 2016).

opinion itself.[3] Furthermore, it is in this contest between organized interest groups that we find a more complete explanation for the drivers of political outcomes – and a roadmap for rebuilding a more inclusive and responsive democratic politics.

As Jacob Hacker and Paul Pierson (among others) have powerfully argued, public policy is not a reflection of mass preferences; rather, it is a "prize" that organized interest groups win as a result of the contest for political power.[4] Those policy victories can take a myriad of forms. Sometimes it means getting the state to *do* something, either constructive or inhibitory, such as increasing funding for schools or imposing a tax on tobacco products. Other times it means *preventing* the state from doing something: promoting gridlock and "policy drift" as a way to change the de facto policy outcome by holding policy regimes steady in the face of external change in social and economic conditions.[5] Furthermore, such organized political contestation is a major force in entrenching some policy regimes. Organized interests can exercise outsize influence when they anchor their goals within the vessel of a political party, as organized labor did with the twentieth-century Democratic Party or the National Rifle Association has done more recently with the Republican Party.[6] As Hacker and Pierson point out, some policies, in turn, outlast even these interest group coalitions and party dynamics, for "[a]lthough often strongly connected to one party or another at the outset," some policy regimes "are sustained over time by supportive coalitions that have transcended and outlasted any specific electoral majority."[7] This is because of the "capacity of long-lived political actors to use government authority to refashion economies and societies in enduring ways."[8]

This centrality of organization is not in itself a problem, and the idea that democracy is a contest of interest groups is not a new one. Arguably, civil society associations and the mobilization of constituencies have been central to the self-image of American democracy since its founding, as evident in the First Amendment's implied protections for free association in civil society groups – and in the constitutional design of American democracy as a system where "the private interest of every individual may be a sentinel over the

---

[3] E. E. Schattschneider, *The Semisovereign People: A Realist's View of Democracy in America* (New York: Holt, Rinehart & Winston, 1960).

[4] Hacker and Pierson, "After the 'Master Theory,'" 643–62, 644–45.

[5] Hacker and Pierson, "Drift and Democracy: The Neglected Politics of Policy Inaction" (lecture, American Political Science Association Annual Meeting, September 2010).

[6] Schlozman, *When Movements Anchor Parties*.

[7] Hacker and Pierson, "After the 'Master Theory,'" 652.

[8] Ibid.

Democracy and Inequality as a Function of the Balance of Power 51

public rights."[9] And the concept of contestation between interest groups has shaped much of the late twentieth-century institutionalist political science literature.[10] The problem for democracy, however, arises whenever the balance of power between interest groups becomes so skewed as to structurally favor one set of interests over others. Indeed, much of the current crisis of inequality and exclusion in America politics can be traced to exactly such a disparity in organizational power and influence. Civil society organizations are not all morally equal between themselves or equally in need of checking. Nor does their influence arise automatically or in a vacuum. Understanding how organizations arise, build coalitions, and exercise power is crucial to diagnosing democratic dysfunction – and to achieving a more inclusive democratic alternative.

The political power of organizations depends on their ability to build what organizer and political scientist Marshall Ganz calls "strategic capacity" – the ability to mobilize a wide range of human, financial, discursive, political, and other resources and to translate them into influence on decision-makers.[11] Important tools include messaging and political framing that appeal to people's identities and provide incentives for them to participate.[12] Such framing is not just a matter of public relations and message testing; rather it requires a deep construction of new shared identities, narratives that articulate protagonists, villains, values, and a shared sense of the "we" activated by the organization or campaign in question.[13] Developing new political subjects is part of democratic contestation, but is constrained by the current structural inequities. But once mobilized and engaged, this engagement needs to be channeled into a form that can last beyond the campaign of the moment,

---

[9] "Federalist, No. 51."

[10] See Schattschneider, *Semisovereign People*; Robert A. Dahl, *Polyarchy: Participation and Opposition* (New Haven, CT: Yale University Press, 1971); and Charles E. Lindblom, *The Market System: What It Is, How It Works, and What to Make of It* (New Haven, CT: Yale University Press, 2001).

[11] See Marshall Ganz, "Resources and Resourcefulness: Strategic Capacity in the Unionization of California Agriculture, 1959–1966," *American Journal of Sociology* 105 (2000): 1003–62, 1005.

[12] David A. Snow and Robert D. Benford, "Ideology, Frame Resonance, and Participant Mobilization," in *From Structure to Action: Comparing Social Movement Research across Cultures*, ed. Bert Klandermans, Hanspeter Kriesi, and Sidney G. Tarrow (Greenwich, CT: JAI Press, 1988), 197–217; David A. Snow, "Collective Identity and Expressive Forms," in *International Encyclopedia of the Social and Behavioral Sciences*, ed. Neil J. Smelser and Paul B. Baltes (New York: Elsevier, 2001), 2212–19; and Daniel Kreiss, *Taking Our Country Back: The Crafting of Network Politics from Howard Dean to Barack Obama* (New York: Oxford University Press, 2012).

[13] See Jonathan M. Smucker, *Hegemony How-To: A Roadmap for Radicals* (Chico, CA: AK Press, 2017), 221–31.

becoming instead a foundation for longer-term political activism and influence. For many constituencies, one challenge with simply mobilizing members around specific issues is a resulting lack of investment in cultivating people's civic skills or civic muscles. Mobilizations that do not teach people capacities for civic life run the risk of producing only shallow issue-specific engagement that does not translate into transformed leadership opportunities or sustained civic involvement beyond the specific issue advocacy cause.

Building organizational power, in contrast, requires something more than simply transactional *mobilizing*; it also requires *organizing* that can build the skills and capacities of individual members over time, while simultaneously strengthening the relationships between them. It includes numerous opportunities for "thick" participation.[14] Instead of promoting individual behaviors connected to specific time-bound campaigns, organizing must provide opportunities to build genuine relationships and shared identities. Through this work, organizations derive new forms of commitment and activism as well as new resources from among their members, which in turn fuels long-term, durable organizational power and influence.[15] As political scientist Hahrie Han explains, "Organizers invest in developing the capacities of people to engage with others in activism and become leaders."[16] This is in contrast to "mobilizers," who "focus on maximizing the number of people involved without developing their capacity for civic action."[17] Organizations that possess such deeper capacity for action and influence can in turn forge more durable and effective political coalitions since they have real membership and power to deploy; this in turn expands their ability to exercise influence on public policy and public politics. Indeed, we can think of movements and communities as needing to build "civic capacity" – a durable capacity for engaging in collective action, building coalitions, mobilizing resources, and exercising influence through organization building.[18] More transient mobilizations and movements fall short in this regard, and thus are unable to achieve lasting, durable change – or to overcome the pressures of more organized and

---

[14] Ethan Zuckerman, "Beyond the 'Crisis in Civics' – Notes from My 2013 DML Talk," available at www.ethanzuckerman.com/blog/2013/03/26/beyond-the-crisis-in-civics-notes-from-my-2013-dml-talk/.

[15] Marshall Ganz, *Why David Sometimes Wins: Leadership, Organization, and Strategy in the California Farm Worker Movement* (New York: Oxford University Press, 2009); and Ganz, "Leading Change," 1–42.

[16] Han, *How Organizations Develop Activists*, 8.

[17] Ibid.

[18] Xavier de Souza Briggs, *Democracy as Problem Solving: Civic Capacity in Communities across the Globe* (Cambridge, MA: MIT Press, 2008), 13; and Clarence Stone, "Civic Capacity and Urban Education," *Urban Affairs Review* 36 (2001): 595–619.

Democracy and Inequality as a Function of the Balance of Power   53

powerful interests, particularly among business, the wealthy, and other elite constituencies. As Occupy protestor and social movement theorist Jonathan M. Smucker put it in his analysis of why progressive movements often fall short: "Social movements in the United States today do not have anywhere close to the capacity needed to mount sustained challenges to ... entrenched power structures."[19]

This focus on organizations, and on the sources of organizational power, offers both a way to diagnose the dysfunctions of American democracy today – and a starting point for redressing these dysfunctions. First, the formation of mass-member organizations was central to creating the political power needed to drive the major advances of equality and inclusion in American democracy from the late nineteenth to the mid-twentieth century. Second, the erosion and dismantling of these forms of organizational power has played a large role in the growing disparities of political power shaping contemporary American democracy. Third, the resurgence of exclusionary populism on the right can be explained as, in part, a product of precisely these same forms of organizational power building. The centrality of organization suggests that rebuilding American democracy requires building the *organizational* power especially among disempowered constituencies, including workers and communities of color.

THE DEMOCRATIZING FORCE OF PROGRESSIVE ORGANIZATIONAL POWER

In the late nineteenth century, the pressures of industrialization, immigration, and technological transformation created tremendous economic and social upheaval and inequality. These pressures manifested in, and were exacerbated by, the rise of new forms of concentrated private power, corruption, and institutional failure on the part of established state and federal legislatures and administrators. At the same time, these pressures drove new forms of social and political organization – which in turn proved crucial to the transformative social movements of the period.

As Theda Skocpol has argued, civic association in the United States emerged during the nineteenth century under a mass-member, federated organizational structure. From Elks Lodges to the Knights of Labor, to the Women's Christian Temperance Union and African American churches and fraternal orders, to religious networks clustering around the spread of Protestant evangelicalism, these organizations provided social spaces where

---

[19] Smucker, *Hegemony How-To*, 39–40.

54   *Civic Power*

communities could gather, combining both communal and self-help functions with political debate and advocacy. This provided members with community as well as a de facto training ground in public advocacy. Many of these organizations were themselves internally democratic, electing representatives and officers. Through these membership-based organizations, people across socio-economic backgrounds interacted and learned leadership skills. They were also often part of federated, national umbrella organizations, consisting of chapters in larger networks. These organizations ran annual conventions conferences and charged membership dues (in contrast to modern mass-mobilization techniques – a distinction discussed in more detail in Chapter 3). This structure provided these organizations with durable, sustained membership, as well as a steady stream of financial resources. But such civil society organizing was not merely good in its own right; it also formed an engine for *democratizing* social change movements that were able to force the kinds of policy and institutional changes needed to promote a more inclusive and egalitarian society.

Organizing and the Progressive Response to Industrialization

This kind of mass-member organizing became the foundational substrate upon which the massive reform movements of the late nineteenth century were built. From the rural Populist movement growing out of the Farmers' Alliance, to the urban Progressive movement of middle-class reformers, the late nineteenth century witnessed a remarkable push by diverse constituencies to transform the economic, social, and political institutions of the country. From an electoral perspective, these movements largely failed to capture significant elected office, and third-party efforts to create a People's Party and a Progressive Party led to high-profile but ultimately unsuccessful presidential candidacies like that of William Jennings Bryan in 1896 and Theodore Roosevelt in 1912. But from a policy perspective, these movements were remarkably successful, driving a major transformation in the discourse and public policy terms of the period, provoking everything from the rise of antitrust law, public utility regulations, and efforts to restrain the new corporate titans of the railroads and finance, to the creation of state and local administrative agencies designed to protect consumers and workers, and even increasing the public provision of key goods and services like municipal utilities.

While these movements covered a vast array of constituencies and issues, they shared some common organizational traits. Much of the activism around the Populist and Progressive movements clustered around mass-member

Democracy and Inequality as a Function of the Balance of Power   55

federated organizations. As Charles Postel has argued, the Farmers' Alliance, for example, was the germ for the national Populist movement, and it grew as a mass-member federated organization.[20] The backbone of the Populist movement was a network of pamphleteers and lecturers who helped make the organization a forum for civic education, discussing policy issues and mobilizing members for advocacy campaigns. These populists also sought to leverage new forms of business associations to generate funds for local communities and for the movement as a whole.[21] As Elisabeth Clemens has suggested, these late-nineteenth century movements – from the populists to the women's movement to organized labor – constructed the modern American understanding of "interest group politics," building civil society organizations as vehicles for political activism that, while related to partisan party organizations, were very much independent of them, committed to advocacy on behalf of the "people" themselves.[22]

The Rise of Organized Labor

Perhaps the most influential and critical of all of these movements that emerged in the late nineteenth century was organized labor. As industrialization radically transformed the nature of work, it created not just new pressures on workers but also a whole new generation of workers who had moved from the country into the factory. Labor organizers sought to advocate for better working conditions and support, but much of the history of the rise of labor centers around the efforts by worker organizations to overcome often violent efforts at suppression. Thus, major uprisings like the Haymarket Square riot in 1886 and the Pullman strike of 1894 were central to expressing and building the power of organized labor. Even as these strikes generated tremendous opposition and blowback, the ranks of organized labor grew in the late nineteenth century. The Federation of Organized Traders and Labor Unions of the United States and Canada formed in 1881, as a precursor to the American Federation of Labor (AFL), founded in 1886. While the AFL's trade union model focused on craft trades, the rise of an industrialized workforce in the late 1930s drove the formation of the Congress of Industrial Organizations (CIO), which crucially provided both a left flank to the New Deal coalition and a vital space for multiracial worker organizing.

---

[20]   Charles Postel, *The Populist Vision* (New York: Oxford University Press, 2009).

[21]   Postel, *Populist Vision*.

[22]   Elisabeth Clemens, *The People's Lobby: Organizational Innovation and the Rise of Interest Group Politics in the United States, 1890–1925* (Chicago: University of Chicago Press, 1997), 6–8.

56   *Civic Power*

Between 1840 and 1940, labor unions as well as professional and business groups grew across townships and cities in the United States.[23] By the mid-1940s, unions represented roughly a third of the workforce.[24] Union membership reached its peak in the 1950s with 34.8 percent of waged workers belonging to unions.[25] By the 1930s and 1940s, labor had risen to become a central player in national politics – at the heart of Franklin Delano Roosevelt's New Deal coalition.[26] In 1935 FDR passed the Wagner Act (the National Labor Relations Act of 1935), which protected the legal rights of workers to engage in organizing and collective bargaining.[27] The CIO in particular came to serve as not just part of the coalition but also as a critical voice from the left flank, countering some of the Roosevelt administration's efforts at moderating its New Deal policy agenda.[28]

Organizing in the Face of Racial Subordination

However, it is important not to overly valorize this apparent "golden era" of robust civil society organizations and mass organizing. While these movements produced some of the most transformative changes in American public policy during the late nineteenth and early twentieth centuries, it is also critical to note the degree to which they accepted, exacerbated, and reinforced deep structural inequities in American society, particularly along racial lines. Many Populists and Progressives either tacitly approved of or openly pursued white supremacist measures like the legal codification of Jim Crow segregation.[29] The cause of "reconciliation" between North and South proved more attractive than the project of post-Civil War racial equity.[30] Indeed, presumptions of racial hierarchy were foundational to many late nineteenth-century and early twentieth-century reform efforts, running right up to and through FDR's deal with Southern Dixiecrats in Congress to exclude from the

---

[23] For discussion see Skocpol, *Diminished Democracy*, chap. 2; and Robert H. Wiebe, *The Search for Order, 1877–1920* (New York: Hill & Wang, 1967).

[24] Gerald Mayer, "Union Membership Trends in the United States" (research report for Congress, Congressional Research Service, August 31, 2004), 11, https://digitalcommons .ilr.cornell.edu/key_workplace/174/; and Eric Schickler, *Racial Realignment: The Transformation of American Liberalism, 1932–1965* (Princeton, NJ: Princeton University Press, 2016).

[25] Mayer, "Union Membership Trends," 12.

[26] See Schlozman, *When Movements Anchor Parties*.

[27] 29 U.S.C. §§ 151–69.

[28] See Schlozman, *When Movements Anchor Parties*; and Schickler, *Racial Realignment*.

[29] Postel, *Populist Vision*, 175–76, 181–82.

[30] Ibid.

Democracy and Inequality as a Function of the Balance of Power 57

terms of the New Deal safety net and its labor protections farmworkers and guest workers as well as many other worker constituencies, where ethnic minorities were prevalent.[31]

The experience of the Colored Farmers' National Alliance and Co-Operative Union, better known as the Colored Farmers Alliance (CFA), is indicative.[32] For a time the CFA worked in parallel with the Farmers' Alliance, providing a vehicle for African Americans to engage in political advocacy and facilitating the rise of a generation of black political leaders. In some states, the CFA allied with white farmers to drive reformist policies and elect reformist candidates. But these instances of cooperation were short-lived. White farmers pushed for segregationist policies even as they sought grudgingly and opportunistically to ally with the CFA. Where black farmers and workers ultimately engaged in strikes, their white allies largely stayed on the sidelines, leaving black workers to be violently suppressed.

The exclusionary contexts of the Populist, Progressive, and later New Deal responses to industrialization are an important limitation to the legacy of these movements. But at the same time, these exclusions underscore our core concern here: the dynamics of civic power and the role of movement organization. Precisely because of how movement organizing can shape political outcomes and public understandings, the deliberate fragmenting of economic progressive movements along racial lines proved enormously consequential. At the same time, the expansions of the social contract to remedy historical exclusions on lines of race and gender have themselves turned on the ability of inclusionary movements to build and exercise similar forms of civic power through *organizing*.

Indeed, mass-member organizing was also critical to incubating and deepening African American political power, especially in the period between Jim Crow and the civil rights movement. As Theda Skocpol, Ariane Liazos, and Marshall Ganz argue, African American fraternal groups were key in the struggle for civil rights and racial integration, providing a space for building power, solidarity, and community despite legal and often violent pressure to break black civic power.[33] These organizations provided a base from which

---

[31] See Ira Katznelson, *Fear Itself: The New Deal and the Origins of Our Time* (New York: Liveright, 2013).

[32] Postel, *Populist Vision*, 61, 180–85.

[33] Theda Skocpol, Ariane Liazos, and Marshall Ganz, *What a Mighty Power We Can Be: African American Fraternal Groups and the Struggle for Racial Equality* (Princeton, NJ: Princeton University Press, 2008).

58 *Civic Power*

later civil rights organizing and lawsuits could emerge in the civil rights movement era.[34]

Take for example the battles over race and inequality in the labor movement. Organized labor's relationship with race has long been fraught – and a point of central contention. The AFL, for example, had been historically hostile to workers of color. But the CIO, as an industrial union, necessarily engaged more directly with workers of color – and became a central vehicle for the formation of a multiracial worker coalition. In its early days, the CIO worked explicitly to win over African American workers skeptical of unions on the one hand, and to leverage its multiracial constituency as a source of pressure on the Democratic Party on the other, thereby fusing racial inclusion with economic liberalism. This organized pressure from the CIO formed the left flank of the Roosevelt coalition. Although the New Deal codified problematic exclusions in the social contract, recent scholarship suggests that the CIO's organizing created a major shift in the rank and file of the Democratic Party.[35] As early as the 1940s, state Democratic parties and lower-level party officials began to take on board support for civil rights legislation.[36]

Similarly, the transformative impact of the civil rights movement of the 1960s and 1970s turned in large part on the organizational strategies, structures, and resources of social movement organizations. The struggle against Jim Crow segregation and the push for racial equality during this period depended greatly on the organizational capacity and structure of civil rights movement organizations, from the Congress of Racial Equality (CORE) to the Student Nonviolent Coordinating Committee (SNCC); it was this structure that enabled the movement to both plan deliberate flashpoints that became central to the larger civil rights struggle – like Rosa Parks's role in the Montgomery bus boycott – and to take advantage of more genuinely spontaneous or "emergent" opportunities for advancing the argument and winning greater support.[37] For example, in 1955 a yearlong boycott of the segregated bus system by the black population of Montgomery, Alabama served as an organizational strategy as well as a level of sustained mobilization that later enabled the 1963 March on Washington for Jobs and Freedom. In

---

[34] Ibid.

[35] See Schickler, *Racial Realignment*.

[36] Ibid.

[37] See Lewis Killian, "Organization, Rationality, and Spontaneity in the Civil Rights Movement," *American Sociological Review* 49 (1984): 770–83, 779; Doug McAdam, *Political Process and the Development of Black Insurgency* (Chicago: University of Chicago Press, 1982); and Aldon D. Morris, *The Origins of the Civil Rights Movement, Black Communities Organizing for Change* (New York: Free Press, 1984).

Democracy and Inequality as a Function of the Balance of Power   59

March 1955, prior to Rosa Parks getting arrested, Claudette Colvin was arrested for refusing to give up her seat and move to the back of the bus. Claudette was hardly alone. Underpinning decisions about how to execute on strategy were campaigns orchestrating behind the scenes. Sixty-eight African American groups in Montgomery including labor unions, church groups, and women's groups helped spread the word to ensure that people would join the boycott following Rosa Parks's arrest.[38] The presence of this level of underlying civic organization provided part of the foundation on which the civil rights movement was launched on a national scale.

Such organizing was also key in responding to the racialized and gendered gaps in the New Deal social contract. Marshall Ganz's account of the United Farm Workers of America under César Chávez, for example, highlights how immigrant laborers successfully organized a series of agricultural strikes, leveraging the shared identity of immigrant labor, strong interpersonal relationships, and the building of movement organizational capacity.[39] These approaches also inspired other movements for social inclusion including for women's equality, unionization of farm workers, LGTBQ rights, and the rights of nonwhite ethnic minorities.[40]

The Importance of Organizational Structure and Capacity

These social movements – from the Progressive Era to the civil rights movement – have justly been the subjects of deep scholarly investigation and public interest. The brief account here highlights one particular thread across these different time periods and movements: the transformative social change wrought by these movements did not just *happen,* nor were these movements carried forward by the sheer force or persuasiveness of their underlying ideas. Rather, the key developments during these periods of social change turned largely on the *organizational structure* of these social movements. By organizing members into constituencies capable of exercising political power over a long-time horizon, these movements were able to influence the trajectory of democratic politics.

Four dimensions of this organizational capacity stand out. First, these organizations forged common *identities among their members.* By creating

---

[38]   Tufekci, *Twitter and Tear Gas,* 69.
[39]   Ganz, "Resources and Resourcefulness."
[40]   J. Craig Jenkins and Charles Perrow, "Insurgency of the Powerless," *American Sociological Review* 42 (1977): 249–68; Debra C. Minkoff, *Organizing for Equality: The Evolution of Women's and Racial-Ethnic Organizations in America, 1955–1985* (Philadelphia: Temple University Press, 1995).

60   *Civic Power*

deep interpersonal relationships embedded within local communities and constituencies, these organizations helped strengthen ties between supporters and shaped the values and narratives through which members articulated their own values and formulated their own political aspirations. Second, these organizations created *pathways for members to build their own civic capacities.* Many of these movements drew their leadership from among their members and provided spaces in which members could gain ever-increasing responsibility and skills in organizing, leadership, and advocacy. Third, this membership-based orientation *allowed these organizations to leverage resources* – both the human resources of their members' energy, creativity, and talent as well as the financial resources that came with dues-paying members. Fourth, these factors combined to enable organizational strategies that in turn helped these *movements create political power and influence.*

As we will see in the rest of this chapter, these elements of organizational capacity and power manifest in a variety of contexts. Many of the pathologies of contemporary American democracy can be attributed, at least in part, to the ways in which such organizational power has been built more recently among constituencies on the right – particularly, the business lobby and the rise of exclusionary populist politics – while these same conditions have atrophied among countervailing constituencies.

INEQUALITY AS A PROBLEM OF ORGANIZATIONAL POWER

After a high-water mark of civic membership in the post-war period, the fabric of American civic life began to change in the 1960s.[41] The centrality of mass-member civic organizations gradually eroded. Civic groups and religious associations as variant as the Freemasons and the Women's United Methodist Association experienced a steep decline in membership, with some losing nearly 70 percent of their members.[42] The trend was not specific to an individual group, but rather can be seen across voluntary, membership-based organizations. Nowhere was this decline in membership more fraught, or more consequential, than in the case of labor unions.

The Decline of Union Power

The level of union power hardly proceeded along a linear course over the twentieth century. Indeed, efforts to secure the right to organize have always

---

[41] Putnam, *Bowling Alone.*
[42] Skocpol, *Diminished Democracy,* 154–56.

Democracy and Inequality as a Function of the Balance of Power   61

been contested. Even at the height of the New Deal era, the Taft-Hartley Act of 1947 represented a devastating blow to unions' abilities to organize and strike.[43] As a percentage of the overall workforce, union membership peaked in 1954 at 28.3 percent.[44] In absolute numbers, the volume of union workers peaked in 1979 with an estimated 21 million enrolled workers.[45] In 1983, the union membership rate had already dropped to 20.1 percent and enrolled workers to 17.1 million.[46] The collapse of labor since then has been stark. By 2017, only 10 percent of the workforce was unionized.[47] Furthermore, many of the sectors with the most unionized workforces are vulnerable to displacement by digital tools.[48]

This sea change in part reflects the shift away from manufacturing across the American economy. But it also reflects a concerted political attack on labor organizing, from the Taft-Hartley act of 1947 to Ronald Reagan's efforts to break the Professional Air Traffic Controllers Organization strike in 1981,[49] to the more recent efforts by states and courts to assert "right to work" laws that in the name of economic liberty of workers make it more difficult for unions to form and to secure dues contributions from members.[50] Indeed, it is not a coincidence that the decline of mass-membership organizations and the weakening of union power also accompanied the rise of inequality. Union benefits were not restricted to those with union membership; rather, unions provided an important countervailing power to corporate interests. Reductions in economic inequalities from the 1920s on benefited nonunion members as well.[51] During the middle of the twentieth century, a strong labor movement served as an effective countervailing power to the interests of business.[52] The decline in union membership since the 1970s has been linked directly to current vast disparities of income.[53] Comparative analyses also confirm this

---

[43] The Labor Management Relations Act of 1947, 29 U.S.C. §§ 141–97.

[44] Mayer, "Union Membership Trends," 12.

[45] Ibid., 10.

[46] "Union Members Summary," Bureau of Labor Statistics, January 19, 2018, www.bls.gov/news .release/union2.nro.htm.

[47] Ibid.

[48] Molly Kinder, *Automation Potential for Jobs in Indianapolis* (Washington, DC: New America, May 17, 2018), www.newamerica.org/work-workers-technology/reports/automation-potential-jobs-indianapolis/introduction.

[49] Joseph A. McCartin, *Collison Course: Ronald Reagan, the Air Traffic Controllers, and the Strike That Changed America* (New York: Oxford University Press, 2011).

[50] Rogers, "Libertarian Corporatism," 1629–30; and Andrias, "The New Labor Law," 39–41.

[51] Jack Orsenfield, *What Unions No Longer Do* (Cambridge, MA: Harvard University Press, 2014).

[52] Hacker and Pierson, *American Amnesia*.

[53] Steven Greenhouse, "Labor's Decline and Wage Inequality," *Economix* (blog), *New York Times*, August 4, 2011, http://economix.blogs.nytimes.com/2011/08/04/labors-decline-and-wage -inequality.

62   *Civic Power*

link, as countries with high union density tend to have lower income inequality and vice versa.[54]

Professionalized Advocacy and Its Limits

In some ways this decline of mass-member organizing seemed more than offset by the rise of the modern, professionalized public interest and nonprofit sector. Beginning in the 1960s, there was an "advocacy explosion."[55] Advocacy groups proliferated in a reinforcing cycle where "groups begot more groups."[56] From 1959 through the 1990s, civic organizations grew from 5,832 to over 23,000. All data indicate that their numbers are still growing. The number of organizations with Washington representation has doubled since the 1980s.[57] Part of why so many advocacy and interest groups exist is the sheer diversity in people, opinions, and contested political issues that have emerged since the 1960s. These organizations address a large range of issues including environmental concerns, social and racial justice, and women's issues. Furthermore, the earlier model of volunteer organizations was no longer tenable as those civic groups historically had often been segregated by race and gender. The new advocacy organizations were able to represent the growing American middle class and its concerns, while reducing the influence of the less educated and less affluent majority of ordinary citizens. These organizations have become effective at lobbying in Washington, DC, but much less effective at genuinely engaging ordinary people to serve as leaders.

Today's advocacy environment is highly focused on individual causes and organizations with headquarters in Washington, DC or New York City, although increasingly many have a West Coast presence as well. Day-to-day work is led by professionals and includes a significant level of fundraising by and from an educated class of professionals. Individual members do not have a leadership or governance role. For busy professionals, donating small amounts of money every once in a while, in contrast to ongoing organizing, works well for their busy lives. These "bodyless heads," as Marshall Ganz describes such advocacy groups, have a large media presence.[58] From the perspective of these organizations, engaging on-the-ground bodies is an

---

[54]   See Archon Fung, "It's the Gap, Stupid," *Boston Review*, September 1, 2017, http://bostonre view.net/class-inequality/archon-fung-its-gap-stupid.

[55]   Jeffrey M. Berry and Clyde Wilcox, *The Interest Group Society*, 5th ed. (New York: Routledge, 2016), 15–33.

[56]   Skocpol, *Diminished Democracy*, 202.

[57]   Schlozman, Verba, and Brady, *Unheavenly Chorus* (chap. 1, n. 30).

[58]   See Skocpol, *Diminished Democracy*, 163.

Democracy and Inequality as a Function of the Balance of Power 63

inefficient use of resources. People, as a result, became checkbook members.[59] People started giving small amounts of money to headquarters in Washington, DC, but did not donate their time.[60]

This shift from mass-member organizing to "thin" organizing through professional advocacy groups lacking in deep membership-based models has resulted in a decline in the political influence and capacity of many constituencies. The shift from membership-based organizing to memberless professional advocacy is a shift in power. Instead of ordinary people uniting their voices to amplify their power, now professionals and corporations increasingly consolidate *their* power in the political process via control of these advocacy organizations. As Skocpol describes, in these professionalized advocacy environments, "highly educated and privileged Americans and staff-led civic groups appeal to one another."[61] The result is a group of "members" in these advocacy organizations who no longer feel physically connected to one another. As Robert D. Putnam put it: "Their ties are to common symbols, commons leaders, and perhaps common ideals, but *not* to each other."[62]

Indeed, several aspects of civic capacity were lost during the transition from a unionized workforce and the decline of mass-member civic organizations. First and foremost, the decline of these organizations meant an erosion of the ability of many individuals to exert pressure on political actors to influence policy outcomes in favor of the broad swath of the citizenry – not just educated professionals, corporations, and elites. Second, these mass-member organizations also provided an important space for civic education, leadership development, and the equalizing of social status within communities. Within these organizations, individuals could develop leadership skills and learn about political issues and advocacy. These organizations connected people to their place and neighbors in a way that contemporary society makes more difficult.[63] Finally, the loss of the dues structure for funding creates different incentives around the perennial problem of raising money – and new roles for professional lobbyists, grant writers, large philanthropies, and corporate

---

[59] Putnam, *Bowling Alone*, 40, 52, 158; Theda Skocpol, "Associations without Members," *American Prospect*, July/August, 1999: 66–73, http://prospect.org/article/associations-without-members. See also Matthew A. Painter II and Pamela Paxton, "Checkbooks in the Heartland: Change over Time in Voluntary Association Membership," *Sociological Forum* 29 (2014): 408–28.

[60] Jeffry M. Berry, *The New Liberalism: The Rising Power of Citizen Groups* (Washington, DC: Brookings Institution, 1999); and Steven Shier, *By Invitation Only: The Rise of Exclusive Politics in the United States* (Pittsburgh, PA: University of Pittsburgh Press, 2000).

[61] Skocpol, *Diminished Democracy*, 218.

[62] Putnam, *Bowling Alone*, 52.

[63] Ibid.

64   Civic Power

interests.[64] Without large numbers of dues-paying members, advocacy groups
had to find other ways of raising revenue, becoming particularly dependent on
foundations and large donors. This has proven to be a central challenge that
skews the organizational efficacy and incentives of these advocacy
organizations.

The Rise of Organized Business Power

This shift in the civic associational landscape coincided with – and was in
some ways facilitated by – a parallel rise of business interests. During these
same decades since the 1970s, lobbying associations representing big business
have accumulated greater political power and influence. Some of this is
a product of a systematic orientation of policy outcomes toward the preferences of wealthier citizens.[65] As E. E. Schattschneider put it in his classic
work, *The Semisovereign People: A Realist's View of Democracy in America*,
"the heavenly chorus" of pluralism's participating citizenry "sings with
a strong upper-class accent"[66] – a finding further confirmed in more recent
scholarship.[67] But a central driver of this pattern is the rise of the *organizational* power of interest groups hostile to an economic equality agenda.

Historically, organized interests have been key to mobilizing sustained
efforts at dismantling economic regulations, restraints on business, and the
modern safety net, in the name of "liberty," starting with the American Liberty
League and its hostility to FDR's New Deal, yet extending to the modern
business lobby[68] and the backlash against organized labor in the post-war
era.[69] As several scholars have argued, in the modern era, this opposition
attained even greater power starting in the 1970s, through a combination of

---

[64] As we will discuss in the next section below, it is also notable that the collapse of dues- and
      membership-based organizing has accelerated with the concerted legal and policy attack on
      unions, as "right to work" laws and recent judicial rulings against compulsory union fees have
      further crippled the organizing capacity of labor.
[65] See Jeffrey Winters and Benjamin Page, "Oligarchy in the United States?" *Perspectives on
      Politics* 7 (2009): 731–51; and Bartels, *Unequal Democracy*.
[66] Schattschneider, *Semisovereign People*, 35.
[67] Schlozman, Verba, and Brady, *Unheavenly Chorus*; and Page and Gilens, *Democracy in
      America*.
[68] See Gillian Metzger, "1930s Redux: The Administrative State under Siege," *Harvard Law
      Review* 131 (2017): 1–95; and Kim Phillips-Fein, "Conservatism: A State of the Field," *Journal of
      American History* 98 (2011): 723–43.
[69] Elizabeth A. Fones-Wolf, *Selling Free Enterprise: Assault on Labor and Liberalism, 1945–60*
      (Urbana: University of Illinois Press, 1994); and Tami J. Friedman, "Exploiting the
      North-South Differential: Corporate Power, Southern Politics, and the Decline of
      Organized Labor after World War II," *Journal of American History* 95 (2008): 323–48.

Democracy and Inequality as a Function of the Balance of Power   65

more aggressive anti-regulatory attacks through lobbying vehicles like the Chamber of Commerce of the United States of America and the Business Roundtable[70] with a concerted effort by wealthy funders and foundations to build an intellectual critique of the New Deal social contract and to finance a larger shift in the public political discourse in favor of deregulated markets and unrestrained business.[71]

Starting in the 1970s, business interests and lobbying groups, from those representing big tobacco to those working on behalf of oil companies, proliferated.[72] Amidst the economic tumult of the 1970s, companies in the United States became more integrated into the global economy and more closely tied to the growing financial sector.[73] In 1972, a group of prominent chief executive officers (CEOs) formed the Business Roundtable to lobby for corporate profits and interests. As one business leader explained in the 1970s: "If you don't know your senators on a first-name basis, you are not doing an adequate job for your stockholders."[74] At this same time the U.S. Chamber of Commerce grew in influence. In a climate seeking to reduce regulation and raise corporate profits, the Chamber of Commerce increasingly became aligned with the Republican Party. According to Hacker and Pierson, the Chamber "combines first-rate lobbying and litigation capacities with the ability to fund campaigns and fight the trench warfare over popular and elite thinking on fundamental issues."[75] This political muscle acts as a key driver behind discourses and policies of deregulation, tax cuts, and growing pressures on labor unions – all of which contribute to economic inequality and undermine the countervailing political power of workers.[76] More recently, the internal politics of the business lobby has accelerated these trends, as the

---

[70]   Hacker and Pierson, *American Amnesia* (chap. 1, n. 24), 213; Hacker and Pierson, *Winner-Take -All Politics*; and Jacob S. Hacker and Paul Pierson, "Business Power and Social Policy: Employers and the Formation of the American Welfare State," *Politics and Society* 30 (2002): 277–325.

[71]   See Angus Burgin, *The Great Persuasion: Reinventing Free Markets since the Depression* (Cambridge, MA: Harvard University Press, 2012); Jon D. Michaels, *Constitutional Coup: Privatization's Threat to the American Republic* (Cambridge, MA: Harvard University Press, 2017); Nancy MacLean, *Democracy in Chains: The Deep History of the Radical Right's Stealth Plan for America* (New York: Penguin, 2017); and Jane Meyer, *Dark Money: The Hidden History of the Billionaires behind the Rise of the Radical Right* (New York: Anchor, 2017).

[72]   Jack L. Walker, *Mobilizing Interest Groups in America: Patrons, Professions, and Social Movements* (Ann Arbor: University of Michigan Press, 1991), 72.

[73]   Hacker and Pierson, *American Amnesia*, 168–200.

[74]   Ibid., 203. Hacker and Pierson draw this quote from Leonard Silk and David Vogel, *Ethics and Profits: The Crisis of Confidence in American Business* (New York: Simon & Schuster, 1976), 65.

[75]   Hacker and Pierson, *American Amnesia*, 225.

[76]   Hacker and Pierson, *Winner-Take-All Politics*.

66   *Civic Power*

industrial interests that dominated the Chamber and the Business Roundtable in the late twentieth century have given way to financial and investor interests, which have focused on even more extreme forms of rent seeking and profit maximization, to the detriment of not only government and labor, but also the real economy as well.[77]

The organizational muscle of business is reflected in the sheer scale of their lobbying operations. Business and industries have long had more representation than any other interested group in Washington.[78] In 2006, more than half of all the registered lobbying organizations represented corporations or business associations, while a bare 1 percent represented labor unions or poor people.[79] Business is disproportionately dominant in the pressure group system. This is especially apparent when their representation is compared with that of groups that lobby on behalf of the public interest causes or the interests of traditionally marginalized constituencies.[80] The result is a vicious cycle: with more clout, business interests are able to pursue policies that further accelerate inequality – and policies that directly attack the countervailing power of labor.[81]

One central channel for influence was the campaign finance system. From *Buckley v. Valeo* in 1976,[82] through the *Citizens United v. Federal Election Commission* decision in 2010,[83] the legal landscape has allowed campaign donations to become a massive lever through which corporate interests can curry favor with elected officials. Lobbying expenditures have grown roughly sixfold, holding for inflation, from \$200 million in 1983 to \$3.24 billion in 2013.[84] As scholars of the campaign finance system have argued, the result of this lobbying economy is not only blatant quid pro quo corruption, but also a softer form of informal influence.[85] Some studies, however, suggest that the decline in the share of elected officials with blue-collar backgrounds explains much of the policy skew toward wealthier interests, as more elite policymakers subconsciously respond more favorably to elite interests, and tend to

---

[77] Hacker and Pierson, American Amnesia; see also Rana Foroohar, *Makers and Takers: The Rise of Finance and the Fall of American Business* (New York: Crown, 2016).

[78] Frank R. Baumgartner and Beth L. Leech, *Basic Interests: The Importance of Groups in Politics and Political Science* (Princeton, NJ: Princeton University Press, 1998).

[79] Schlozman, Verba, and Brady, *Unheavenly Chorus*.

[80] Ibid.

[81] Hacker and Pierson, *Winner-Take-All Politics*.

[82] 424 U.S. 1 (1976).

[83] 558 U.S. 310 (2010).

[84] Lee Drutman and Steven Teles, "A New Agenda for Political Reform," *Washington Monthly*, March/April/May 2015, https://washingtonmonthly.com/magazine/maraprmay-2015/a-new-agenda-for-political-reform/.

[85] Lessig, *Republic, Lost*.

underestimate the popularity of more redistributive policies.[86] A similar form of "cultural capture" takes place in the context of regulatory policymaking, where regulators with a shared social background as business interests tend to treat those constituencies more favorably.[87]

Business interests exploit and further another trend as well – the erosion of public sector capacity. Lee Drutman and Steven Teles have documented in their work that the lobbying industry remains ever powerful, while the emaciated public sector cannot keep up.[88] Since the 1980s, government has reduced its capacity.[89] The modern Government Accountability Office (GAO) and the Congressional Research Service (CRS), which offer nonpartisan analysis to lawmakers, employ 20 percent fewer staffers now than in 1979.[90] This is in part a product of the rise of anti-government, deregulation-oriented, and cost-cutting viewpoints among lawmakers, which are heavily promoted by business interests.[91] At the same time, the roles and responsibilities of government have grown more complex. This complexity creates additional avenues for capture and business influence; armed with resources and a talent pool lured with big salaries, business lobbying organizations can offer regulators and elected officials access to data, analysis, and policy proposals they independently produce. In many cases, businesses themselves are the ones who possess the detailed and technical data necessary to shape regulations, providing them a lever through which to influence the policy process.[92]

These dynamics are even more pronounced at the state and local level, where state resources are even thinner, budgets are tighter, and business advocacy is more influential. Political scientist Alexander Hertel-Fernandez demonstrates that business interests take advantage of the particularly low policy capacity in state legislatures by providing private policy resources to the policy decision-makers among their legislators.[93] For example, the

---

[86] Carnes, *White Collar Government*, 12: "The shortage of people from the working class in American legislatures skews the policy-making process toward outcomes that are more in line with the upper-class' economic interests."

[87] Kwak, "Cultural Capture," 79–80.

[88] Lee Drutman and Steven Teles, "Why Congress Relies on Lobbyists Instead of Thinking for Itself," *Atlantic*, March 10, 2015, www.theatlantic.com/politics/archive/2015/03/when-congress -cant-think-for-itself-it-turns-to-lobbyists/387295/.

[89] Frank Baumgartner and Bryan Jones, *The Politics of Information: Problem Definition and the Course of Public Policy in America* (Chicago: University of Chicago Press, 2015).

[90] Drutman and Teles, "Why Congress Relies on Lobbyists."

[91] Michaels, *Constitutional Coup.*

[92] Kwak, "Cultural Capture"; and Nolan McCarty, "Complexity, Capacity, Capture," in *Preventing Regulatory Capture: Special Interest Influence and How to Limit It*, ed. Daniel Carpenter and David A. Moss (New York: Cambridge University Press, 2014), 99–123.

[93] Frank R. Baumgartner and Bryan D. Jones, *The Politics of Information.*

68 *Civic Power*

American Legislative Exchange Council (ALEC) is a business-backed conservative group that influences state legislatures by providing model bills on a variety of issues including elections. By providing pre-written bills, talking points, and capacity in the form of research assistance, business influence is magnified. Part of ALEC's influence is in specifically targeting state legislatures. Groups from pharmaceutical firms to Amazon and private prison operators have all worked through ALEC since it was started in 1973 by conservative activists, including Paul Weyrich, who was also a cofounder of the Heritage Foundation and the Moral Majority Coalition.

In some cases, business interests have mimicked and co-opted forms of membership-based organizing. Public companies increasingly have their own public affairs consultants, some of whom even are focused on mobilizing people on the grassroots level.[94] Increasingly, the language of deliberation or public participation has also been co-opted by corporate interests.[95] Major companies from Walmart and Wells Fargo to Pfizer and Best Buy have borrowed this discourse to drive their own lobbying agendas.[96] Walmart, for example, developed a "Community Action Network," which even won the Grassroots Innovation award from the Public Affairs Council in 2010; this network effectively advances the company's interest in the guise of civic engagement.[97] Corporations also increasingly pressure their own employees to vote and lobby on behalf of the corporate leadership's political interests, as Alexander Hertel-Fernandez has documented.[98] This can even extend into the realm of politics, with certain companies encouraging employees to support business-friendly candidates and the Republican Party.

ORGANIZING EXCLUSIONARY POPULISM

If inequality and the concentrated political power of business and wealthy interests represent major threats to American democracy, another set of concerns stems from the resurgence of openly exclusionary populist movements,

---

[94] Walker, *Grassroots for Hire*.

[95] Lee, *Do-It-Yourself Democracy*.

[96] Walker, "Legitimating the Corporation."

[97] Ibid.; Edward McClelland, "Is Walmart Sticking It to The People or Sticking It to The Man?" *Ward Room* (blog), NBCChicago.com, June 4, 2010, www.nbcchicago.com/blogs/ward-room/Is-Walmart-Sticking-It-to-The-People-or-Sticking-it-to-The-Man-95520589.html; and Kevin Robinson, "Wal-Mart Using Fake Community Group to Manufacture Support," *Chicagoist*, January 26, 2010, http://chicagoist.com/2010/01/26/wal-mart_using_fake_community_group.php#photo-1.

[98] Alexander Hertel-Fernandez, *Politics at Work: How Companies Turn Their Workers into Lobbyists* (New York: Oxford University Press, 2018).

Democracy and Inequality as a Function of the Balance of Power   69

particularly on the right. Donald Trump's election in 2016 cast into relief the rise of what we call an exclusionary populism, which draws on racialized, xenophobic, and misogynistic attitudes while glorifying a bygone era when mostly white men of means determined the fate of American politics. In many ways, the Trump moment is not wholly a new form of American politics; rather it draws on long-running traditions of exclusionary populism, most recently apparent in the Tea Party movement of the Obama era, but also readily evident in Richard Nixon's "Southern Strategy" and Barry Goldwater's mid-century conservatism, both of which appealed to white backlash against the civil rights movement.[99]

Much has already been written about the troubling nature of this exclusionary populism: its expression of racial resentment; its reassertion of traditional white, male identity roles; its connection to economic stagnation and dislocation.[100] But part of what makes exclusionary populism so troubling is it weaponizes and channels politicized anger through an already brittle and weak democratic ecosystem. The weakness of a broader civil society – characterized by a relative lack of membership-based advocacy organizations as noted above – is part of what makes a tendency to exclusionary populism more likely. The vehicles that used to channel the genuine voice of ordinary people – strong unions and voluntary membership-based organizations – have been replaced with weak unions and a professionalized ecosystem for advocacy. Furthermore, this exclusionary populism rests on a background of strategies for organizing and alliances with donors and media institutions that gives rise to its large political potency. Thus, exclusionary populism is both a reflection of the *weakness* of contemporary civic capacity, and the *potency* of civic capacity when built, repurposed and channeled toward dangerous ends, exclusionary ends. To put it another way, the very specter and threat of exclusionary populism arises not just from a hidden well of racial resentment, but also from the deliberate construction of organizations and infrastructures designed to harvest, amplify, and channel these attitudes into a political force.

---

[99] James Boyd, "Nixon's Southern Strategy," *New York Times*, May 17, 1970, www.nytimes.com /1970/05/17/archives/nixons-southern-strategy-its-all-in-the-charts.html; see also Rick Perlstein, *Nixonland: The Rise of a President and the Fracturing of America* (New York: Scribner, 2008); and MacLean, *Democracy in Chains*.

[100] See Katherine J. Cramer, *The Politics of Resentment: Rural Consciousness in Wisconsin and the Rise of Scott Walker* (Chicago: University of Chicago Press, 2016); and Arlie Russell Hochschild, *Strangers in Their Own Land: Anger and Mourning on the American Right* (New York: New Press, 2016).

70   *Civic Power*

Resentment and Reaction

Racial resentment and desires to reassert traditional racial and gendered hierarchies represent powerful undercurrents driving much of the contemporary right's anti-government political fervor.[101] There is a history of opposition to public spending that is tied to the perception that state-sponsored policies benefit racial and ethnic minorities.[102] Support for policy is often driven by ideas about the "deserving" poor that emphasize hard work and moral virtue.[103] These perceptions are tinged by racism.[104] This has particularly been evident in analyses of conservative opposition to Barack Obama's presidency and of hostility to his signature policies like the pursuit of health-care reform.[105] Even when opponents of government programs and safety-net provisions have not openly engaged in racial appeals, Republican politicians have proved adept at fusing business interests and anti-government critiques with more subtle (and perhaps not always intentional) appeals to racial sentiments.[106] Indeed, as Kathy J. Cramer notes, "support for small government is more about identity than principle."[107]

[101] Nicolas A. Valentino and David O. Sears, "Old Times They Are Not Forgotten: Race and Partisan Realignment in the Contemporary South," *American Journal of Political Science* 49 (2005): 672–88; and Hacker and Pierson, *American Amnesia*, 251: "[T]he case is strong that race is a major ingredient in the GOP's anti-government cocktail." See also Ian Haney Lopez, *Dog Whistle Politics: How Coded Racial Appeals Have Reinvented Racism and Wrecked the Middle Class* (New York: Oxford University Press, 2014).

[102] Martin Gilens, *Why Americans Hate Welfare: Race, Media, and the Politics of Antipoverty Policy* (Chicago: University of Chicago Press, 1999); Alberto Alesina, Edward Glaeser, and Bruce Sacerdote, "Why Doesn't the United States Have a European-Style Welfare State?" *Brookings Papers on Economic Activity*, no. 2 (2001): 187–254; Erzo F. P. Luttmer, "Group Loyalty and the Taste for Redistribution," *Journal of Political Economy* 109 (2001): 500–28; and Woojin Lee and John E. Roemer, "Racism and Redistribution in the United States: A Solution to the Problem of American Exceptionalism," *Journal of Public Economics* 90 (2006): 1027–52.

[103] Joe Soss and Sanford S. Schram, "A Public Transformed? Welfare Reform as Policy Feedback," *American Political Science Review* 101 (2007): 111–27, 121, 124–25.

[104] Nicholas J. G. Winter, "Beyond Welfare: Framing and the Racialization of White Opinion on Social Security," *American Journal of Political Science* 50 (2006): 400–20; Nicholas J. G. Winter, *Dangerous Frames: How Ideas about Race and Gender Shape Public Opinion* (Chicago: University of Chicago Press, 2008); and Christopher D. DeSante, "Working Twice as Hard to Get Half as Far: Race, Work Ethic, and America's Deserving Poor," *American Journal of Political Science* 57 (2013): 342–56.

[105] Michael Tesler, "The Spillover of Racialization into Health Care: How President Obama Polarized Public Opinion by Racial Attitudes and Race," *American Journal of Political Science* 56 (2012): 690–704; and Michael Tesler, *Post-Racial or Most Racial? Race and Politics in the Obama Era* (Chicago: University of Chicago Press, 2015).

[106] Alberto Alesina and Edward Glaeser, *Fighting Poverty in the US and Europe: A World of Difference* (Oxford: Oxford University Press, 2004).

[107] Cramer, *Politics of Resentment*, 145.

Democracy and Inequality as a Function of the Balance of Power   71

This engagement with deeper conceptions of communal identity – and the linking of identity with a mix of frustration at socio-economic decline and resentment of racial minorities – is particularly stark in the context of the Tea Party and other contemporary far-right movements that have a pervasive narrative of losing out to immigrants and racial minorities who in their view have "cut in line" to advance toward greater prosperity through unequal and unfair treatment.[108]

It is important here to distinguish between different gradations of these racialized appeals. Individuals may espouse attitudes their organizations do not endorse.[109] And there are gradations of tacit and explicit racial resentment. Tea Party members and staunch conservatives, for example, proclaim often vehemently that they are not explicitly racist and will often avoid using overtly racist language.[110] Instead, racial attitudes express themselves in other often more subtle ways. The policy and legal imagination of many conservative activists including Tea Party members often resorts to the idea of "color-blind" equality, in which individuals proclaim some degree of neutrality with respect to others' racial identities – but in so doing efface or systematically overlook deeper patterns of structural racism, including by criticizing policies like affirmative action that aim to redress historical and cumulative racial dispa-rities. Furthermore, racial resentments can often find greater expression in the context of some racial "others" more readily, given background social norms or taboos. Thus, many Tea Party members are much less sensitive about expressing racial resentments against immigrant groups and Muslims. And the gap between public expressions and private beliefs is also significant. There is often a disconnect between how people speak about African

---

[108]   Hochschild, *Strangers in Their Own Land*, ix, 135–39. See also Nils C. Kumkar, *The Tea Party, Occupy Wall Street, and the Great Recession* (New York: Palgrave Macmillan, 2018).

[109]   For example, as the Democracy Fund Voter Study Group explains in the executive summary to its 2016 VOTER survey data, "[S]ome will be tempted to conclude that people providing negative responses toward a group in survey responses are guilty of bigotry or prejudice. We want to be clear: this inference is not a fair reading of these data. Attitudes toward members of racial, ethnic, religious, or other social groups are complicated, and ... this survey is not designed to explain 'why' people reported these feelings. We will conduct further research in an attempt to understand the 'why' behind this 'what.'" Democracy Fund Voter Study Group, "Insights from the 2016 VOTER Survey," June 2017, 6, available at www.voterstudygroup.org/publications/2016-elections/executive-summary.

[110]   Theda Skocpol and Vanessa Williamson, *The Tea Party and the Remaking of Republican Conservatism* (New York: Oxford University Press, 2012), 69; Vanessa Williamson, Theda Skocpol, and John Coggin, "The Tea Party and the Remaking of Republican Conservatism," *Perspectives on Politics* 9 (2011): 25–43, 29; Cramer, *Politics of Resentment*; Hochschild, *Strangers in Their Own Land*; and Lydia Bean, *The Politics of Evangelical Identity: Local Churches and Partisan Divides in the United States and Canada* (Princeton, NJ: Princeton University Press, 2014).

Americans, Muslims, and immigrants on surveys and how they communicate in private. Data from Google trends also demonstrates racist behavior that surveys miss.[111]

In running for election, Donald J. Trump made an implicit and explicit link between these emotions of grievance, decline, and a sense of social and cultural threat from ascendant "others," in many ways removing prior social taboos on explicit racial resentment, amplifying these underlying attitudes and bringing them into an open political configuration. Quantitative data supports the ethnographic analyses of scholars like Katherine J. Cramer, Arlie Russell Hochschild, and others. White voters without a college education made up around two-thirds of Trump's supporters in the Republican primaries and around three-fifths in the general election. Survey data shows a strong correlation between negative assessments of Muslims and support for Trump both in the Republican primary and the general election.[112] Moreover, the survey results find the same relationship in the 2012 data on Muslims, suggesting Trump tapped into pre-existing attitudes.[113] Once engaged, these racial attitudes may have become even more toxic. In a recent study, Sean McElwee and Jason McDaniel analyzed the data of over 4,000 respondents in the American National Election Studies pre- and post-survey and found that Trump accelerated realignment in the electorate around racism.[114]

Indeed, although there were plenty of racist signs, slogans, and chants at events like Tea Party rallies and other ultraconservative events between 2010 and 2014, with some of this rallying rhetoric including calls for President Obama's birth certificate,[115] the rise of the alt-right after 2015 represents a distinct form of exclusionary populism, with the alt-right's more explicit and broad affirmation of violent terminology and explicit racism. The 2017 white supremacist rally in Charlottesville, Virginia – protesting the proposed removal of a statue of Robert E. Lee, and leading to the death of one

---

[111] Seth Stephens-Davidowitz, *Everybody Lies: Big Data, New Data, and What the Internet Can Tell Us about Who We Really Are* (New York: HarperCollins, 2017).

[112] Robert Griffin and Ruy Teixeira, "The Story of Trump's Appeal: A Portrait of Trump Voters," Democracy Fund Voter Study Group (website), June 2017, 4, www.voterstudygroup.org/pub lications/2016-elections/story-of-trumps-appeal.

[113] Ibid., 11, 22.

[114] Sean McElwee and Jason McDaniel, "Economic Anxiety Didn't Make People Vote Trump, Racism Did," *Nation*, May 8, 2017, www.thenation.com/article/economic-anxiety-didnt-make-people-vote-trump-racism-did/.

[115] Jonathan Raban, "The Tea Party and the Art of the Mean Joke," *New York Times*, January 7, 2017, www.nytimes.com/2017/01/07/opinion/sunday/the-tea-party-and-the-art-of-the-mean-joke.html. See also Skocpol and Williamson, *The Tea Party*, 45–82.

Democracy and Inequality as a Function of the Balance of Power 73

counterprotestor and nineteen other injuries[116] – underscores the renewed threat of far-right violence, particularly motivated against communities of color. American right-wing extremism has killed more American citizens than the Islamic State of Iraq and al-Sham (ISIS) in the last decade.[117] Research from New America demonstrates that right-wing extremists outnumber left-wing ones by a factor of seventeen to one.[118] In 2017, white supremacists and other far-right extremists were responsible for 59 percent of all extremist-related fatalities in the United States according to the Anti-Defamation League's (ADL) Center on Extremism.[119] The Southern Poverty Law Center has documented that young men who espouse alt-right rhetoric online have killed forty-three people and injured more than sixty others since the rise of the alt-right in 2015.[120]

But it is organizational capacity and muscle that make these exclusionary attitudes particularly powerful – and likely to persist even after the Trump moment passes. The Tea Party, for example, was not simply a spasm of organic grassroots sentiment. It also built many of the same organizational capacities that, as noted earlier, give rise to durable political power and influence. The Tea Party was able to connect elite conservative opinions and donor advocacy dollars to genuine bottom-up grassroots organizing. As Skocpol and Williamson put it in their study of the Tea Party:

> Men and women involved in Tea Party activism tend to be people who have held leadership positions in other community organizations, whether on the local library board or directing a community nonprofit. The Tea Party is simply a new venue to apply previously honed skills, just as it is yet another channel through which to express deep-seated conservative values.[121]

The Tea Party engaged with a conventional conservative intellectual agenda: promoting ideas of the free market, cutting taxes, and cutting red

---

[116] Hawes Spencer and Caitlin Dickerson, "Heather Heyer, Charlottesville Victim, Cannot Be Silenced, Mother Says," *New York Times*, August 16, 2017, www.nytimes.com/2017/08/16/us/charlottesville-heather-heyer-memorial-mother.html.

[117] Peter W. Singer, "National Security Pros, It's Time to Talk about Right-Wing Extremism," *Defense One*, February 28, 2018, www.defenseone.com/threats/2018/02/national-security-pros-its-time-talk-about-right-wing-extremism/146319/.

[118] Peter Bergen and David Sterman, "What Is the Threat to the United States Today?" in *Jihadist Terrorism 17 Years after 9/11* (Washington, DC: New America, updated September 10, 2018), www.newamerica.org/in-depth/terrorism-in-america/what-threat-united-states-today/.

[119] "Murder and Extremism in the United States in 2017," Anti-Defamation League (website), www.adl.org/resources/reports/murder-and-extremism-in-the-united-states-in-2017#the-incidents.

[120] Ibid.

[121] Skocpol and Williamson, *The Tea Party*, 42.

74   *Civic Power*

tape.[122] However, there has been a disconnect between Tea Party supporters who believe in free market ideals (especially for "undeserving others") but enjoy their own social service provisions including social security, veterans' pensions, and Medicare.[123] It also represented a new building of organizational capacity and political muscle. Many Tea Partiers had previously been civically active. Similar to other middle-income senior citizens, they can leverage prior expertise of community involvement to stay involved in retirement.[124] The Tea Party's rise parallels the decline of genuine grassroots membership organizations with leadership and governance opportunities.

The Tea Party is not unique in this regard. The political potency of racialized, exclusionary politics has historically been rooted in similar patterns of movement organizing and capacity building, as evident in the Barry Goldwater campaign of 1964 or the growing strength of conservative mobilization in the 1940s and 1950s, in particular across the Sun Belt.[125] The Tea Party is the latest reflection of such a pattern in the history of conservatism in the United States.[126] In fact, several Tea Partiers describe the Goldwater campaign as the awakening period of their activism.[127] Goldwater's slogan, "AuH$_2$O," borrowed from the periodic table with Au for gold and H$_2$O for water, even found a revival among younger Tea Partiers.[128] Scholars have argued that modern conservatism formed as a reaction to the liberal policy vision of the New Deal.[129] Historians have also documented similar distinctive features of post-World War I conservatism and movement organizing in the 1920s and 1930s. According to historian Kim Phillips-Fein, "The rise of black power, the

---

[122] Brian J. Glenn and Steven M. Teles, eds., *Conservatism and American Political Development* (New York: Oxford University Press, 2009); Steven M. Teles, "Conservative Mobilization against Entrenched Liberalism," in *The Transformation of American Politics: Activist Government and the Rise of Conservativism*, ed. Paul Pierson and Theda Skocpol (Princeton, NJ: Princeton University Press, 2007); and Jane Mayer, "Covert Operations," *New Yorker*, August 30, 2010, www.newyorker.com/magazine/2010/08/30/covert-operations.

[123] Skocpol and Williamson, *The Tea Party*, 93.

[124] Ibid., 42.

[125] Matthew D. Lassiter, *The Silent Majority: Suburban Politics in the Sunbelt South* (Princeton, NJ: Princeton University Press, 2007).

[126] See also Elizabeth Gillespie McRae, *Mothers of the Massive Resistance* (New York: Oxford University Press, 2018).

[127] Skocpol and Williamson, *The Tea Party*, 41, 81–82.

[128] Ibid., 81. See also J. William Middendorf II, *A Glorious Disaster: Barry Goldwater's Presidential Campaign and the Origins of the Conservative Movement* (New York: Basic Books, 2006).

[129] See George Wolfskill, *The Revolt of Conservatives: A History of the American Liberty League, 1934–1940* (Boston: Houghton Mifflin, 1962); and James T. Patterson, *Congressional Conservatism and the New Deal: The Growth of the Conservative Coalition in Congress, 1933–1939* (Lexington: University of Kentucky Press, 1967).

Democracy and Inequality as a Function of the Balance of Power 75

growing militancy of the antiwar movement, and the challenges of feminism and gay rights all provoked a sharp backlash from the mainstream of American society."[130]

Take for example the rise of the John Birch Society.[131] One of its core ideological practices was to protest the civil rights movement by aligning anti-communist forces through a common belief in small government as a protection against civil rights reforms. The John Birch Society argued that the Civil Rights Act of 1964[132] violated the Tenth Amendment and opposed the Equal Rights Amendment. Medicare was another hot button issue for the group, which saw it as a dual threat of communism and of racial integration.[133] Studies of the Ku Klux Klan and the more modern attempt to preserve the Jim Crow system from the threat of the civil rights movement as well as even more recent backlash against the movement's successes are also suggestive of how mass-member organizing and capacity building represented a key element in the political construction of racial inequality and the development of political coalitions over time. Indeed, racialized backlashes against the civil rights movement, the New Deal, and welfare rights all rest on the kinds of organizing that not only typified the Progressive Era but moreover drove the resurgence of racial hierarchy in the concurrent Jim Crow era.[134]

Indeed, it is notable that one of the most politically successful modern member-based organizations forms another central part of the contemporary conservative coalition – the National Rifle Association (NRA). The NRA has successfully built an organized network of grassroots power.[135] It has strategically fought for wins that do not necessarily impact the organization's day-to-day campaigns in order to build a broader culture and public narrative to support its goals. For example, the organization advocated against a policy that would have prevented minors from shooting on gun ranges on federal lands because it believes that unless children are socialized into gun culture early, they will be lost to video games and other distractions. Additionally, the NRA has been able reach out to many who may not necessarily agree with its principles. Peter Murray describes as "functional organizing" the way that the NRA provides accident insurance and a wide array of discounts on non-

---

[130] Phillips-Fein, "Conservatism," 726.

[131] See Adam Gopnik, "The John Birchers' Tea Party," *New Yorker*, October 11, 2013, www.newyorker.com/news/daily-comment/the-john-birchers-tea-party.

[132] Pub. L. 88–352, 78 Stat. 241.

[133] Gopnik, "The John Birchers' Tea Party."

[134] Phillips-Fein, "Conservatism," 737; and Linda Gordon, *The Second Coming of the KKK: The Ku Klux Klan of the 1920s and the American Political Tradition* (New York: Liveright, 2017).

[135] Hahrie Han, "Want Gun Control? Learn from the N.R.A.," *New York Times*, October 4, 2017, www.nytimes.com/2017/10/04/opinion/gun-control-nra-vegas.html.

76   *Civic Power*

gun related activities that strategically benefit members' everyday lives.[136]
Thus, unlike much of the professionalized advocacy of the center-left, the
NRA is not working in only an issues-based space. That is to say, the NRA has
helped people form a positive identity within and through the organization,
which is not limited to advocacy around specific issues, although the fact that
people who identify with the NRA often become fierce defenders of advocacy
issues is a useful and intentional by-product of this type of mobilization.
Recently scholars have suggested that a key to the NRA's political durability
has been its shift from an issue-based focus on guns to a larger cultural and
ideological emphasis on white resentment and opposition to multiracial,
egalitarian democracy.[137]

Amplifying the Anti-democratic Backlash: Conservative Dollars and Media Infrastructure

The political power of these right-wing organized movements to critique
government, promote business interests, and resist civil rights has been amplified through strategic alliances with financial donors and media conglomer-
ates. Starting when key figures at the DuPont company created the American
Liberty League in 1934 to fight FDR's New Deal and continuing with the mid-
century rise of the John Birch Society and its organizing of an infrastructure
across the country to protest the civil rights movement, corporate donors have
played a central role in bankrolling and fueling these organizing drives for
decades.[138]

While the Tea Party was a genuine grassroots movement that helped
successfully reshape the Republican Party, it has also benefited from conservative donors and dollars. For example, it was supported by the Americans for
Prosperity Foundation, which was founded in 2004 by philanthropists David
H. Koch and Charles G. Koch.[139] Indeed, the Kochs have played a key role in
funding a variety of conservative efforts. Between 1998 and 2008, foundations
they controlled gave $196 million to conservative causes.[140] In addition, their

---

[136] Peter Murray, "The Secret of Scale: How Powerful Civic Organizations Like the NRA and
AARP Build Membership, Make Money, and Sway Public Policy," *Stanford Social
Innovation Review*, Fall 2013: 32–39, 35.

[137] Carol Anderson, *White Rage: The Unspoken Truth of Our Racial Divide* (New York:
Bloomsbury, 2017).

[138] Kim Phillips-Fein, *Invisible Hands: The Businessmen's Crusade against the New Deal*
(New York: W.W. Norton, 2009).

[139] Mayer, "Covert Operations."

[140] Frank Rich, "The Billionaires Bankrolling the Tea Party," *New York Times*, August 28, 2010,
www.nytimes.com/2010/08/29/opinion/29rich.html.

Democracy and Inequality as a Function of the Balance of Power 77

firm, Koch Industries, spent $50 million on lobbying and $4.8 million in campaign contributions through its political action committee (PAC).[141] For the 2012 campaign the Koch network spent just shy of $400 million; they budgeted $889 million for 2016.[142] Organizations they fund include Freedom Partners (an independent expenditure-only political committee or super PAC), Americans for Prosperity, and Concerned Veterans for America.[143]

For the Kochs, politics was always a part of their life, and they grew up as ardent libertarians. Their father, Fred C. Koch, was a founding and distinguished member of the John Birch Society.[144] In 1980, David Koch ran for vice president as a Libertarian Party candidate.[145] After *Citizens United*, unchecked private dollars have enormous power, and the personas of oversized donors heavily influence the political system. For example, Robert Mercer and his daughter Rebekah have placed themselves front and center within the political ecosystem. Robert Mercer, a reclusive hedge-fund billionaire who made his money on algorithmic trading, gave $22.5 million in the 2016 campaign.[146]

In addition to short-term campaign funding, the Mercers, similar to the Koch brothers, have invested in long-term infrastructure on the right. Upon Steve Bannon's advice, they invested $10 million in Breitbart News in 2011.[147] Robert Mercer invested in Donald Trump and introduced him to key advisers, including Steve Bannon and Kellyanne Conway; Bannon went on to run Trump's presidential campaign.[148] Rebekah Mercer leads the private Mercer Family Foundation, which was operating on a budget of $24.5 million in 2015, giving out large sums to ultraconservative groups.[149] She has also taken an active role in the Republican Party, while Robert

---

[141] Mayer, "Covert Operations"; and Rich, "Billionaires Bankrolling the Tea Party."

[142] Nicholas Confessore, "Koch Brothers' Budget of $889 Million for 2016 Is on Par with Both Parties' Spending," *New York Times*, January 26, 2015, www.nytimes.com/2015/01/27/us/politics/kochs-plan-to-spend-900-million-on-2016-campaign.html.

[143] Ibid.

[144] Mayer, "Covert Operations."

[145] See Hacker and Pierson, *American Amnesia*, 201–38.

[146] Jane Mayer, "The Reclusive Hedge-Fund Tycoon behind the Trump Presidency," *New Yorker*, March 27, 2017, www.newyorker.com/magazine/2017/03/27/the-reclusive-hedge-fund-tycoon-behind-the-trump-presidency.

[147] Kyle Swenson, "Rebekah Mercer, the Billionaire Backer of Bannon and Trump, Chooses Sides," *Washington Post*, January 5, 2018, www.washingtonpost.com/news/morning-mix/wp/2018/01/05/rebekah-mercer-the-billionaire-backer-of-bannon-and-trump-chooses-sides/?nore direct=on&utm_term=.9bf5d31782b1.

[148] Mayer, "Reclusive Hedge-Fund Tycoon." Robert Mercer has since sold his share of Breitbart News. David Smith, "Major Trump Donor Robert Mercer to Sell Stake in Far-Right News Site Breitbart," *Guardian*, November 2, 2017, www.theguardian.com/media/2017/nov/02/billionaire-trump-donor-robert-mercer-breitbart.

[149] Mayer, "Reclusive Hedge-Fund Tycoon."

78   *Civic Power*

Mercer donated data analytics, via the services of Cambridge Analytica, which he has a large stake in, to Nigel Farage's Brexit campaign in the United Kingdom, so that it could better leverage data to influence people on Facebook.[150] Although the international dimensions of most of the phenomena we examine are beyond the scope of this study, it is worth noting that the Trump presidential campaign paid nearly $6 million dollars to Cambridge Analytica.[151] This data-analytics firm leveraged research at the University of Cambridge, which deployed personality tests on Facebook users, to determine the psychologies of different voters and build predictive algorithms to anticipate people's behavior.[152]

The combination of cutting-edge digital tools with unrestricted dollars and influence on the right emboldens the contemporary alt-right and has helped fuel the rise of exclusionary populism described above. The power of conservative media to amplify, reinforce, and create support for these viewpoints has been a key factor in the political impact of these movements – and this media megaphone has been financially supported by wealthy donors.[153] Breitbart News demonstrates this. But crucially this is not just a new technology phenomenon; rather the rise of the online alt-right represents the latest iteration of a strategy that goes back to the founding of Fox News. Fox is the brainchild of long-time Republican advisor Roger Ailes, whom Rupert Murdoch handpicked to develop the network in 1996,[154] and who was a key figure in the elections of both Richard Nixon and George H. W. Bush.[155] In contrast to traditional news outlets Fox has consistently used its coverage to amplify conservative movement ideas and leaders, from the initial rise of the

[150]   Carole Cadwalladr, "Revealed: How US Billionaire Helped to Back Brexit," *Guardian*, February 25, 2017, www.theguardian.com/politics/2017/feb/26/us-billionaire-mercer-helped-back-brexit.
[151]   There is much debate about the actual importance of Cambridge Analytica in the election of Donald Trump as president; see Issie Lapowsky, "What Did Cambridge Analytica Really Do for Trump's Campaign?" *Wired*, October 26, 2017, www.wired.com/story/what-did-cambridge-analytica-really-do-for-trumps-campaign/.
[152]   See Jamie Doward and Alice Gibbs, "Did Cambridge Analytica Influence the Brexit Vote and the US Election?" *Observer*, March 4, 2017, www.theguardian.com/politics/2017/mar/04/nig el-oakes-cambridge-analytica-what-role-brexit-trump; and David Gershgorn, "The Industry That Predicts Your Vote—and Then Alters It—Is Still Just in Its Infancy," *Quartz*, May 18, 2017, https://qz.com/977429/the-industry-that-predicts-your-vote-and-then-alters-it-is-still-just-in-its-infancy/.
[153]   Rich, "Billionaires Bankrolling the Tea Party."
[154]   Clyde Haberman, "Roger Ailes, Who Built Fox News into an Empire, Dies at 77," *New York Times*, May 18, 2017, www.nytimes.com/2017/05/18/business/media/roger-ailes-dead.html.
[155]   Alyssa Rosenberg, "Before Roger Ailes Created Fox News, He Made Richard Nixon the Star of His Own Show," *Washington Post*, May 18, 2017, www.washingtonpost.com/news/act-four/wp/2017/05/18/before-roger-ailes-created-fox-news-he-made-richard-nixon-the-star-of-his-own-show/.

Tea Party to the rise of Donald Trump.[156] Although Fox News provides the pre-eminent example of conservative media power, similar phenomena are true in radio. Conservative airtime minutes outnumber liberal ones by a ratio of ten to one. Of the six largest talk radio shows in the country, five are ultraconservative.

In key respects, then, Breitbart News should be seen as an online continuation of a pattern of partisan, conservative mobilization of media outlets by elite donors that was already well established on other platforms. Whether through cable TV or the Internet, the approach here is the same: building a mobilized and insulated right-wing core audience and political base through investment in a media infrastructure that creates an echo chamber to amplify and radicalize partisan (and racial) sentiments.[157]

***

It has become commonplace to lament the rise of exclusionary populism, but many such laments paint the problem as one of "too much democracy," that is, as an expression of why we really cannot trust "the people" to govern.[158] But as this brief account suggests, such views misrepresent the drivers of exclusionary populism. The ideological and identity-building forces of resentment have been buttressed, enhanced, and amplified by a set of organized, sustained institutional structures ranging from civil society organizing strategies to the financial resources of sophisticated donors as well as a favorable and equally strategic media infrastructure.

CONCLUSION

This chapter opened by arguing for the central importance of organizing and civic organizations in driving social and political change. While mass public opinion is no doubt an important substrate for politics, it is through organized political action that policies and institutions are changed, developed, and maintained. Furthermore, this focus on organization is distinct from more thin approaches to mass mobilization or public voice: the goal here is not to generate a momentary flash of public outrage or outcry; rather it is to channel

---

[156] Williamson, Skocpol, and Coggin, "The Tea Party," 27, 29; and Skocpol and Williamson, *The Tea Party*, 136.

[157] Kathleen Hall Jamieson and Joseph N. Cappella, *Echo Chamber: Rush Limbaugh and the Conservative Media Establishment* (New York: Oxford University Press, 2008).

[158] See Joshua Geltzer, "America's Problem Isn't Too Little Democracy. It's Too Much," *Politico*, June 26, 2018, www.politico.com/magazine/story/2018/06/26/america-democracy-trump-russia-2016-218894.

public activism into organizations that are durable, capable of strategic decision-making, and able to exercise long-term influence on policymaking.

This focus on organization and organizing in turn provides a better way to explain many of the macro shifts in the history of American democracy. As suggested in this chapter, organization and organizing infrastructure were crucial to the rise (and success) of progressive social change movements, from labor to civil rights. Organizing and organizing infrastructure, however, can also explain the rise of exclusionary populism and the power of the modern conservative movement. Conservative dominance in public policy and public politics today is not just a matter of anti-government and exclusionary public opinion; it is rather a product of sustained organized advocacy and investment in movement infrastructure, from the revival of the business lobby to the investment in conservative media infrastructure to the rise of the Tea Party and the weaponized racism of the Trump movement.

Crucially, these two stories are related. Right-wing organizing infrastructure emerged over the late twentieth century at the same time that progressive organizing infrastructure began to wane. This in turn suggests a way forward for rebuilding an inclusive democracy. To overcome the organized political power of big business and exclusionary populism, contemporary movements will have to invest in long-term organizing infrastructure that can exercise influence over political and social debates. This investment will also have to close the gap in organized strategic capacity between the far right and groups advocating for a more inclusive democratic polity. In Chapter 3, we explore some examples of how progressive, inclusive, intersectional movements are already being activated and organized by changemakers on the ground – and what lessons these experiences offer for the longer-term project of building civic power and achieving democratic inclusion.

3

Organizing for Power

As Chapter 2 suggests, disparities in organized advocacy and interest representation are central drivers of the more chronic crisis of American democracy this book investigates. Civic power rests on the ability of constituencies to organize into durable, and effective, mass-member organizations capable of exercising political power. The shift in the balance of power within the organizational landscape, particularly the decline of labor and the rise (and increased aggressiveness) of the organized business lobby, has been a key factor in policy changes that have contributed to increased inequality and further disparities in political voice. This dimension of organizational power and organizational capacity also helps clarify the origins and forces behind the rise of white nationalist, alt-right, and exclusionary populist movements on the right. While racial resentment has long been a motivating ideological force in American politics, it is the fusion of these motivations with financial resources, media infrastructure, and the formation of more organized movement building that makes it particularly powerful. This was true historically when groups like the Ku Klux Klan were mass-member organized associations, and it is equally true today in the context of the Tea Party and the alt-right with their linkages between media platforms, financial backers, and broader right-wing organizing in the Trump era.

Given the centrality of organizing to building and exercising political power – for good or for ill – *approaches* to organizing and civic action are of particular concern when thinking about the future of American democracy. Building democratic capacity involves, in part, a renewed investment in the capacity of civil society to engage communities, mobilize them, and organize them into groups capable of exercising democratic voice and political influence. This is why, for example, the shift from mass-member organizing to professionalized advocacy noted in Chapter 2 has been a matter of particular

82   Civic Power

concern for scholars of social movements as well as for movement activists.
The challenge for organizing today is twofold:

1) How can movements build durable countervailing power going
   forward?
2) How can they do so in a way that self-consciously forges more inclusive
   identities and communities rather than reinscribing historically deep
   cleavages along lines of race, gender, and class?

Today's populist moment calls for the creation of a genuinely responsive,
participatory democratic politics that is both empowered and inclusive. Think
of this as an "us populism," as opposed to a "them populism."

But such organizations and strategies do not arise spontaneously – and not
all organizational forms or strategies are equally effective in exercising political power. This chapter draws on some examples of organizations that are
working on both of these levels simultaneously, trying novel approaches to
building power, while also forging multiracial, often surprising coalitions
across identity groups. In particular, we suggest here that contemporary
fascination with technology platforms and online organizing offers a mixed
challenge: while digital tools offer tremendous possibilities, they must be
paired with sustained strategies for forging more durable identities and grassroots organizations. We also highlight examples of multiracial grassroots
organizing that attempts to forge new identities and coalitions capable of
exercising more sustained and impactful political power.

THE PROMISE AND PERIL OF "THIN" ORGANIZING

A central concern for scholars of social movements is the shift in recent
decades from mass-member organizing to professionalized advocacy groups
that engage "members" in a more superficial form through fundraising, petition, and publicity appeals.[1] Certainly professionalized Washington-based
advocacy organizations have their advantages, and the ability to field a more
formal, well-resourced effort for policy advocacy, communications, and lobbying is important for groups in exercising political power. But the concern arises
insofar as these tools displace, supplant, or otherwise erode the capacities of
advocacy organizations and movements to build deep ties with on-the-ground
constituencies and communities. A growing number of scholars – Yochai
Benkler, Frank Pasquale, Zeynep Tufecki, and Dave Karpf among many
others – have explored the democratic implications of a public sphere

---

[1] See Skocpol, *Diminished Democracy*, and the discussion in Chapter 2 of this volume.

Organizing for Power 83

premised on digital platforms like Facebook and Twitter; a comprehensive account of the emerging digital public sphere is beyond the scope of this volume. But for our purposes it is important to note the tension between the possibilities of online organizing and the need to build long-term durable social movements.[2]

Much of modern political organizing takes place at least partly online. The first wave of digital enthusiasts praised the ability of technology to reduce transaction costs of participation and make engagement "cheaper."[3] Expressing political views on the Internet may be more convenient and less intimidating for many people.[4] If so, online participation could be more inclusive than traditional forms of political engagement. Furthermore, as online platforms like Facebook and Twitter become focal points for public debate, they may enable new ways for groups to self-organize despite being geographically dispersed. Digital platforms also lower the costs of acquiring vast amounts of information and of creating and expressing all sorts of views, including political ones.[5] The explosion of small-dollar fundraising models – from email appeals to online "members" to crowdsourced funding platforms like GoFundMe and Kickstarter – has also provided movements with new tools for raising revenue. Indeed, some activist campaigns – such as Strike Debt, National Bail Out, and a viral fundraiser on behalf of the Refugee and Immigrant Center for Education and Legal Services (RAICES) during the Families Belong Together movement – have used the technique of online fundraising as a powerful focal point of their advocacy strategy.[6] Online platforms have also, at least in theory, offered the promise of more democratized and participatory internal discussions within movements.[7]

Social media in particular can accelerate in-person organizing. Social media was able to build upon on-the-ground organizing to build social

---

[2] See, e.g., Yochai Benkler, *The Wealth of Networks: How Social Production Transforms Markets and Freedom* (New Haven, CT: Yale University Press, 2006); Pasquale, Black Box Society; Tufecki, Twitter and Tear Gas; and Karpf, The MoveOn Effect.

[3] Clay Shirky, *Here Comes Everybody: The Power of Organizing without Organizations* (London: Penguin, 2008), 249; and Benkler, The Wealth of Networks.

[4] Ibid.

[5] Benkler, *Wealth of Networks*, 212–72; Yochai Benkler, "A Free Irresponsible Press: Wikileaks and the Battle over the Soul of the Networked Fourth Estate," *Harvard Civil Rights–Civil Liberties Law Review* 46 (2011): 311–97; and Shirky, *Here Comes Everybody*.

[6] Rob Aitken, "Everyday Debt Relationalities: Situating Peer-to-Peer Lending and the Rolling Jubilee," *Cultural Studies* 29 (2015): 845–68; Strike Debt (website), http://strike debt.org/; National Bail Out (website), https://nomoremoneybail.org/; and David Yaffe-Bellany, "A Viral Facebook Fundraiser Has Generated More than $20 Million for Immigration Nonprofit RAICES," *Texas Tribune*, June 27, 2018.

[7] Ethan Zuckerman, "New Media, New Civics?" *Policy and Internet* 6, no. 2 (2014): 151–68.

84 *Civic Power*

pressure during the Arab Spring and Occupy movements.[8] Popular unrest and economic factors played huge roles in the Arab Spring in Egypt.[9] Importantly, however, the Internet enabled like-minded activists across the Middle East and North Africa to connect with one another prior to the physical protests at the end of 2010 and in 2011. Many of the activists already had overlapping networks.[10] In Middle East authoritarian states, especially in Egypt and Tunisia, Facebook was able to serve as a counterweight to the tightly state-controlled media. Even though a small minority of households were online during this time, the connectivity of even a portion of the population had an exponential effect.

Similar dynamics have shaped American politics as well. In July 2018, the #BlackLivesMatter hashtag turned five years old, having taken off following the acquittal of George Zimmerman on criminal charges for his fatal shooting of Trayvon Martin, a black teenager.[11] What has been the lasting impact of this online movement and other social media campaigns? Use of #BlackLivesMatter has continued to spike in collaboration with major news events, typically connected to race, violence, and law enforcement. In 2017, the #MeToo hashtag generated significant media coverage. A recent survey also shows that 69 percent of adults in the United States find social media to be very or somewhat important for getting elected officials to pay attention to issues.[12] This is particularly true for communities of color, as black and Hispanic respondents viewed social media as an especially valuable tool for political engagement.[13] Roughly half of black social media users say these platforms are at least somewhat personally important to them as venues for expressing their political views or for getting involved with issues that are important to them.[14] In comparison, only around a third of white social media users feel this way.[15] Larger majorities of black Americans say sites promote important issues or give voice to under-represented groups.[16] While much further research is needed on how social

---

[8] W. Lance Bennett and Alexandra Segerberg, *The Logic of Connective Action: Digital Media and the Personalization of Contentious Politics* (Cambridge: Cambridge University Press, 2013).

[9] Lisa Anderson, "Demystifying the Arab Spring: Parsing the Differences between Tunisia, Egypt, and Libya," *Foreign Affairs* 90, no. 3 (2011): 2–7; and George Joffé, "The Arab Spring in North Africa: Origins and Prospects," *Journal of North Africa Studies* 16 (2011): 507–32.

[10] Tufekci, *Twitter and Tear Gas*, 12.

[11] Ray et al., "Ferguson and the Death of Michael Brown," 7.

[12] Monica Anderson, Skye Toor, Lee Rainie, and Aaron Smith, *Activism in the Social Media Age* (Washington, DC: Pew Research Center, July 2018), www.pewinternet.org/2018/07/11/acti vism-in-the-social-media-age/.

[13] Ibid.

[14] Ibid.

[15] Ibid.

[16] Ibid.

Organizing for Power

media use leads to in-person activity and sustained engagement, the experience of online organizing in recent years underscores its importance in generating large-scale movements for change.

But while digital tools create new organizing possibilities, the democratic implications of these online platforms and technologies are not at all unidirectional. These technologies enable "many-to-many" communication as opposed to the "one-to-many" infrastructure of twentieth-century media, where radio and television broadcast was ultimately controlled by insulated power brokers who could shape media narratives.[17] But it is unclear whether online tools can be effective forces to counterbalance business lobbying or rebuild civic power. It is also unclear what the precise relationship is between online tools and on-the-ground movement building.[18]

Indeed, some of the "beneficial inefficiencies" of in-person participation, as scholar David Karpf puts it, have been lost through these technologies.[19] With an emphasis on efficiency over building long-term engagement, digital tools run the risk of making engagement too shallow to be sticky and meaningful.[20] Scholars have raised concerns about whether online political participation may exclude certain groups from politics due to differential access to the Internet,[21] the technical skills required to participate online,[22] and the potential for rancorous debate and online harassment.[23] The rise of digital tools has only further made manifest the shallowness of online forms of engagement. Simply signing a petition, sending a text message, or clicking "like" on

---

[17] Shirky, *Here Comes Everybody*, 86–87.
[18] See Francesca Polletta and James M. Jasper, "Collective Identity and Social Movements," *Annual Review of Sociology* 27 (2001): 283–305.
[19] Karpf, *The MoveOn Effect*, 169.
[20] Eric Gordon and Stephen Walter, "Meaningful Inefficiencies: Resisting the Logic of Technological Efficiency in the Design of Civic Systems," in *Civic Media: Technology, Design, Practice*, ed. Eric Gordon and Paul Mihailidis (Cambridge, MA: Massachusetts Institute of Technology Press, 2016); Karpf, *The MoveOn Effect*; David Karpf, *Analytic Activism: Digital Listening and the New Political Strategy* (New York: Oxford University Press, 2016), 27–58; and Erhardt Graeff, "Evaluating Civic Technology Design for Citizen Empowerment" (PhD diss., Massachusetts Institute of Technology, 2018), https://dam -prod.media.mit.edu/x/2018/05/17/erhardt-phd-18.pdf.
[21] Kay Lehman Schlozman, Sidney Verba, and Henry E. Brady, "Weapon of the Strong? Participatory Inequality and the Internet," *Perspectives on Politics* 8 (2010): 487–509; Pippa Norris, *Digital Divide: Civic Engagement, Information Poverty, and the Internet Worldwide* (Cambridge: Cambridge University Press, 2001); and Anthony G. Wilhelm, *Democracy in the Digital Age* (New York: Routledge, 2000).
[22] Samuel J. Best and Brian S. Krueger, "Analyzing the Representativeness of Internet Political Participation," *Political Behavior* 27, no. 2 (2005): 183–216.
[23] Jennifer Stromer-Galley, "New Voices in the Public Sphere: A Comparative Analysis of Interpersonal and Online Political Talk," *Javnost/The Public* 9, no. 2 (2002): 23–42.

86   *Civic Power*

Facebook, is "thin participation."[24] Evgeny Morozov has warned about the threat of one-click "slacktivism," which obfuscates activism.[25] With cheap and instant communication, associations are less likely to continue long-standing events.[26] Zeynep Tufekci argues that digitally fueled social movements are sometimes stymied by a "tactical freeze" where they cannot pivot or change strategies because there is no underlying infrastructure for collective decision-making.[27] Tufekci analogizes the relationship of the Internet and networked protest in the twenty-first century to the relationship between Nepali Sherpas and climbers attempting to scale Mount Everest: "The assistance may have helped many under-experienced mountaineers to reach the summit, but Everest remains Everest: supremely dangerous and difficult, especially if anything goes even slightly wrong."[28] Digital technologies can obscure the "how" of organizing – the behind-the-scenes work that is especially key when rubber meets the road. As the line between online and face-to-face relationships seems to be getting blurrier, there may need to be, counterintuitively, even more emphasis on building lasting, in-person relationships.[29]

Furthermore, insofar as online and digital organizing depend on privately owned and operated platforms – like Facebook, Twitter, or other equivalents – these organizing techniques are deeply vulnerable to the background rules and algorithms that govern these digital public spheres. One of the challenges with digital tools is how they seek to become the intermediaries between which people communicate, discuss, and therefore organize. In the process, core components of deliberation and civic talk can be misinterpreted or lost.[30] The business model of many "free" platforms, including Google and Facebook, is to mine and sell ads based on people's data. While many civil society groups benefit from data-optimizing tools and the reach of platforms, honoring people's time, attention span, privacy, and data will continue to be a tension at the nexus of digital tools and organizing. Recent controversies over

---

[24]   Nabatchi and Leighninger, *Public Participation*, 17.
[25]   Evgeny Morozov, *The Net Delusion: The Dark Side of Internet Freedom* (New York: Public Affairs, 2011), 189–90.
[26]   Karpf, *The MoveOn Effect*.
[27]   Tufekci, *Twitter and Tear Gas*, xvi, 77–82, 270.
[28]   Ibid., xii.
[29]   Keith Hampton et al., *Social Isolation and New Technology* (Washington, DC: Pew Research Center, November 4, 2009), www.pewinternet.org/2009/11/04/social-isolation-and-new-technology/; and Eric Gordon, Jessica Baldwin-Philippi, and Martina Balestra, *Why We Engage: How Theories of Human Behavior Contribute to Our Understanding of Civic Engagement in a Digital Era* (Cambridge, MA: Berkman Center for Internet & Society, 2013), http://cyber.law.harvard.edu/publications/2013/why_we_engage.
[30]   Karpf, *The MoveOn Effect*; Karpf, *Analytic Activism*, 34–37.

Organizing for Power 87

Facebook's susceptibility to far-right propaganda and race-baiting misinformation campaigns – often with violent implications in not just the United States but other countries like Myanmar, where the platform has been weaponized to stir up ethnic conflicts – underscore how critical is the design of the platform itself to shaping what kinds of organizing strategies are more likely to prevail. If Lawrence Lessig is right and technologies are regulated by code, not only laws, the algorithmic code underpinning platforms contains manifold implications for civil society.[31]

The Obama Campaign of 2008 and the Limits of the Digital Revolution

The aftermath of the Obama campaign of 2008 offers a telling parable for the allure and limits of thin, digital organizing techniques. One of the central hallmarks of Barack Obama's campaign for the presidency in 2008 was its leveraging of online tools to build a scalable movement of supporters in a phenomenally rapid way. The campaign built a "Neighbor-to-Neighbor" program, where volunteers organized through the campaign's website portal signed up to speak to members of their community, to make phone calls on behalf of the campaign, and to host house parties.[32] The campaign leveraged Marshall Ganz's storytelling techniques of building narratives and shared community through a progressive combination of a "'Story of Self,' ... 'Story of Us,' ... and a 'Story of Now.'"[33] As Peter Levine noted, "Volunteers were encouraged and taught to share their stories, to discuss social problems, to listen as well as mobilize, and to develop their own plans. There was a rich discussion online as well as face-to-face."[34]

These organizing techniques helped the Obama campaign accelerate from its initial insurgent status to winning the Democratic nomination; they were then continued in the general election, helping to win several conventionally swing or conservative states for Obama.[35] The campaign had two million profiles created on the My.BarackObama platform (also known as "MyBO"), which enabled supporters to organize their own events, canvassing activities,

---

[31] Lawrence Lessig, *Code and Other Laws of Cyberspace* (New York: Basic Books, 1999).
[32] Elizabeth McKenna and Hahrie Han, *Groundbreakers: How Obama's 2.2 Million Volunteers Transformed Campaigns in America* (New York: Oxford University Press, 2014).
[33] Nabatchi and Leighninger, *Public Participation*, 62.
[34] Peter Levine, *We Are the Ones We Have Been Waiting For: The Promise of Civic Renewal in America* (New York: Oxford University Press, 2013), 156.
[35] David Talbot, "How Obama *Really* Did It," *MIT Technology Review*, August 19, 2008, www .technologyreview.com/s/410644/how-obama-really-did-it/.

88 *Civic Power*

and days of action.[36] By election day, the campaign had more than 13 million email addresses of supporters and had sent more than 1 billion emails.[37] Encouraged and organized through MyBO, volunteer supporters were active and engaged: 200,000 offline events were planned, roughly 400,000 blog posts were written, and 70,000 people raised $30 million.[38] The ability to combine grassroots support with sophisticated technology created unprecedented momentum for Obama's candidacy.

But the Obama administration, once in office, failed to translate the campaign energy into sustained engagement or governance opportunities for its supporters. Instead of turning Obama for America (OFA) into a sustained base of power in communities across the country, the Democratic Party tried to control it, and ultimately, decimated it.[39] As Micah L. Sifry has argued, drawing on internal campaign emails and interviews,[40] the dream of sustaining a genuine, grassroots Obama for America was subsumed by political higher-ups of the Democratic National Committee (DNC).[41] The result was a revised plan, with approval from the DNC to "affirmatively empower Barack Obama as the head of the Party, and in the process strengthen both him and the Party."[42] Practically, this meant that control over the online platform and the massive list of volunteers transferred to the DNC, who deployed it in a more conventional top-down approach relying on email solicitations for donations and petition drives. The grassroots, self-organized energy that had forged proto-chapters of a progressive organization in the making, with volunteers in towns all across the country, withered away.

The tragic lesson of OFA is that while digital tools allow for the possibility of mass organizing at scale, it is the interaction of digital and offline

---

[36] Jose Antonio Vargas, "Obama Raised Half a Billion Online," *The Clickocracy* (blog), *Washington Post*, November 20, 2008, http://voices.washingtonpost.com/44/2008/11/20/obama_raised_half_a_billion_on.html; and Micah Sifry, "President 2.0," *The Guardian*, June 25, 2008, www.theguardian.com/commentisfree/2008/jun/25/barackobama.internet.

[37] Vargas, "Obama Raised Half a Billion Online."

[38] Ibid.

[39] Although Obama for America has been converted into a platform for organizing, first under the moniker Organizing for America and now called Organizing for Action, this transformation was significantly delayed.

[40] Aaron Sharockman, "It's True: WikiLeaks Dumped Podesta Emails Hour after Trump Video Surfaced," *Politifact*, December 18, 2016, www.politifact.com/truth-o-meter/statements/2016/dec/18/john-podesta/its-true-wikileaks-dumped-podesta-emails-hour-afte/.

[41] Micah L. Sifry "Obama's Lost Army," *New Republic*, February 9, 2017, https://newrepublic.com/article/140245/obamas-lost-army-inside-fall-grassroots-machine.

[42] Ibid., quoting a Microsoft Word document titled "M20 New Plan 092608.doc" attached to an email found in a cache of John Podesta's emails, posted online by Wikileaks at https://wikileaks.org/podesta-emails/emailid/55032.

Organizing for Power

organizing that truly creates effective civic power. Furthermore, this inter-action must be fostered on a continuing basis if that power is to be durable. Indeed, studies suggest that individuals are more likely to be convinced by someone in their own community: as a result, door-to-door engagement can be more effective than phone calls or other mobilization efforts.[43] This dynamic interaction between two people is also a critical aspect of recruitment.[44] Some online-based movement organizations have absorbed this lesson and evolved accordingly. MoveOn.org, for example, has shifted from its origins as an online-organized advocacy group with a mass member-ship of email followers and donors to a model relying on investing in on-the-ground leadership and deepening membership.[45] Several scholars have noted the blurring between online and face-to-face relationships is getting more, not less, complex.[46]

There is another lesson in the OFA story: that movements, once catalyzed, need to retain some degree of autonomy, flexibility, and decentralization in order to continue to thrive. While some degree of coordination and centrali-zation is necessary to fuse disparate constituencies and ideas into a coherent political agenda, the heavy-handed, top-down approach taken by the DNC was not able to foster a continuation of the power ignited by OFA. As Manuel Castells has argued, digital social networks offer possibilities for action, delib-eration, and movement building that require retaining a degree of autonomy, "free from the control of those holding institutional power."[47] To the extent that movements can fuse some of the sense of nonhierarchical freedom of online spaces with the tangible and personal impacts that can be created by using physical spaces for interacting, organizing, and community building, they will be able to channel movements for inclusive change via deeper bonds into more effective organizations.[48]

---

[43] Alan S. Gerber and Donald P. Green, "The Effects of Canvassing, Telephone Calls, and Direct Mail on Voter Turnout: A Field Experiment," *American Political Science Review* 94, no. 3 (2000): 653–63; and Donald P. Green and Alan S. Gerber, *Get Out the Vote: A Guide for Candidates and Campaigns* (New Haven, CT: Yale University Press, 2004).

[44] Gerber and Green, "The Effects of Canvassing"; and Donald P. Green and Alan S. Gerber, *Get Out the Vote: How to Increase Voter Turnout* 3rd ed. (Washington, DC: Brookings, 2015).

[45] Karpf, *The MoveOn Effect*.

[46] See Nabatchi and Leighninger, *Public Participation*, 195–237; Gordon, Baldwin-Philippi, and Balestra, "Why We Engage."

[47] Manuel Castells, *Networks of Outrage and Hope: Social Movements in the Internet Age* (Cambridge: Polity, 2012), 9.

[48] Ibid., 11.

90   *Civic Power*

TOWARD INCLUSIVE, EMPOWERED CIVIC CAPACITY

If digital tools offer at best only a partial solution to the challenges of disparate civic power and exclusionary populism, what then would a more empowered, inclusive alternative approach to building civic capacity look like? In the rest of this chapter, we explore some examples of organizations taking innovative approaches to building power and to forging new, inclusive coalitions and identities. As we will see in each of these case studies, the selected organizations have been highly self-conscious and strategic in both of these dimensions. They have sought to leverage some online and professional advocacy and mobilization tools in the service of deep, member-based organizing. Additionally, they have approached their work in ways that deliberately seek to forge coalitions across constituencies that are conventionally – and in our exclusionary populist moment in particular – often pitted against one another: urban versus rural residents, workers of different races and occupational backgrounds, and different faith communities.

First, we present a pair of case studies on the Center for Rural Strategies (CRS) and the Partnership for Working Families (PFWF). These case studies offer a window into how the geographic realities of place and infrastructure can form a basis for forging new coalitions as well as building a locally based form of political power.

Second, we look at how the decline of organized labor, combined with the growing precarity of many workers in the service economy and the online-based "gig" economy, has provided a crucial catalyst for creative new forms of worker organizing. From the online organizing platform Coworker.org to organizations like the National Domestic Workers Alliance (NDWA), this "alt-labor" movement offers lessons of its own in its approach to forging a multiracial worker coalition aimed at building durable worker power outside of the Wagner Act model of formal trade unions.[49]

Third, the example of Faith in Texas (FIT), a multi-faith progressive movement in deeply conservative Texas, combines some elements from the other cases, focusing both on the experience of economic precarity and also on geographic linkages between urban and suburban constituencies as a way to tackle a growing partisan divide between urban communities of color and suburban white voters. FIT suggests ways in which economic inequality, faith, and creative urban–suburban organizing can create new coalitions and

---

[49] Josh Eidelson, "Alt-Labor," *American Prospect*, January 29, 2013, http://prospect.org/article/alt-labor.

Organizing for Power

effective forms of political power that can operate not just at the local but also at the state level.

These examples are by no means exhaustive of the extraordinary state of on-the-ground innovation in progressive and mass-member organizing being driven by a wide array of grassroots organizations and leaders. But they are illustrative of how novel approaches to building durable organizing infrastructure are crucial not only to forging multiracial coalitions and powerful new identities, but also to tackling some of the deep structural inequities that cripple our current democratic polity. Indeed, the focus of these case studies on key features like geographic exclusion, urban inequality, worker precarity, and predatory lending is illustrative as well of how organizing and power building can be targeted toward tackling deep systemic drivers of inequality and exclusion – and not just the thin aspirations for generic "participation." As such these examples offer a contrast to the limits of thin organizing of the sort described earlier in this chapter – and a hopeful counterpoint to the rise of big business and exclusionary populist political power described in Chapter 2.

Organizing Around Place and Infrastructure

Geographic and physical spaces are central to constituting social and economic experience. Socially lived experience is intimately shaped by the physical realities of urban, suburban, and rural places. Economically, one's place of origin shapes one's economic opportunities, health, and income over one's lifetime.[50] Crucially, some of the most compelling experiences of powerlessness are tied to loss of control over the politics of place. Place and the distribution of power over it are also both central to the construction of identity. In this section we highlight two different examples of how movements draw on the politics of place to construct new forms of power – and, importantly, new solidarities that cut across conventional divisions.

The Infrastructure of Rural America: The Case of the Center for Rural Strategies

Rural America faces particular social and economic pressures. While some accounts of rural communities characterize them as places with high social capital and strong communal ties,[51] many rural communities suffer from

[50] Raj Chetty, Nathaniel Hendren, and Lawrence Katz, "The Effects of Exposure to Better Neighborhoods on Children: New Evidence from the Moving to Opportunity Project," *American Economic Review* 106 (2016): 855–902.

[51] Sandra L Hofferth and John Iceland, "Social Capital in Rural and Urban Communities," *Rural Sociology* 63, no. 4 (December 1998): 574–98.

chronic poverty, poor health, and disproportionate burdens from climate change.[52] One of four rural children live in poverty; rural places also show growing rates of opioid addiction and suicide.[53] The increasingly urbanized and information-based modern economy poses further challenges: economic opportunity has increasingly centralized in cities, leading to a powerful migratory pull away from rural communities into urban spaces. These social and economic challenges have also shaped a common rural political consciousness that sees rural communities as ignored by decision-makers, neglected in the allocation of social and economic resources, and disrespected by mainstream culture.[54] "Rural America," writes Wendell Berry, "is a colony and its economy is a colonial economy. The business of America has been largely and without apology the plundering of rural America, from which everything of value – minerals, timber, farm animals, farm crops, and 'labor' – has been taken at the lowest possible price."[55] Basic needs are front and center in rural America, as residents worry about access to health, education, and uncontaminated land and water along with the opioid crisis.[56]

Yet progressive movements have not entirely abandoned rural areas; indeed, some organizations are seeking to address the gaps in organizing across rural America and are working to build real solutions to economic decline, while also trying to counteract racism, prejudice, xenophobia, and anti-government zeal. People's Action, a national federation of forty-eight membership-based organizations with 600 local staff in thirty states, recently launched a "Rural and Small Town Organizing Strategy" across seventy-two counties in ten states – including twenty-eight "pivot counties" that voted for Obama in 2008 and 2012, before swinging to Trump in 2016.[57] One aspect of the initiative is to build multiracial, multiethnic coalitions reflecting the reality that both

[52] See *Rural Climate Dialogues: State Convening* (St. Paul, MN: Jefferson Center, September 2016), www.ruralclimatenetwork.org/sites/default/files/RCD%20State%20Convening%20Report.pdf.

[53] USDA (website), "Rural Poverty & Well-Being," Economic Research Service, last updated April 18, 2018, www.ers.usda.gov/topics/rural-economy-population/rural-poverty-well-being/; USDA (website), "Opioid Misuse in Rural America," www.usda.gov/topics/opioids; and CDC (website), "Suicide in Rural America," last updated May 2, 2018, www.cdc.gov/ruralhealth/Suicide.html.

[54] Cramer, *Politics of Resentment*, 12.

[55] Wendell Berry, "Southern Despair," *New York Review of Books*, May 11, 2017, www.nybooks.com/articles/2017/05/11/southern-despair/.

[56] *The Promise of a Progressive Populist Movement: Building a Multiracial, Race-Conscious Movement for Bold Change in Rural and Small-Town America* (Chicago: People's Action, April 2018), https://peoplesaction.org/wp-content/uploads/2018/04/PA_Report_Final_digital.pdf.

[57] Ibid., 3.

Organizing for Power 93

rural and small-town America are ethnically diverse. In order to empower rural residents to tell their own stories, People's Action member organization Down Home North Carolina piloted a listening project with residents.[58] People's Action state partners across Michigan, Pennsylvania, Minnesota, Wisconsin, Iowa, Missouri, New Jersey, New Hampshire, and Alabama talked with residents from seventy-two counties via phone and door-to-door conversations, helping to build relationships and a shared sense of vision across these constituencies.[59]

The Center for Rural Strategies (CRS), a community organization based in Whitesburg, Kentucky, provides another compelling example of local, rural organizing. Situated in the central Appalachian coalfields, CRS not only advocates directly on key issues but also organizes and manages the National Rural Assembly, a coalition of over 400 organizations.[60] A key focal point for CRS has been building a durable mass-member organization that can exercise political power. At the same time, CRS has focused on the on-the-ground problems of communications infrastructure as a way to build long-term political power, and to forge new bonds across different constituencies.

Throughout the last twenty years, there has been a systematic disinvestment in these regions on the part of mainstream media, with newspapers and broadcasters pulling out of rural areas. Filling that gap is Christian radio, as well as politicized church sermons. The CRS is working to create a more inclusive and representative narrative around rural communities. One aspect of this is the Daily Yonder, a digital news platform for rural issues as experienced by rural residents.[61] Another aspect of the center's work involves publishing information on rural issues and serving as a liaison between rural organizations and mainstream media in order to help with a more accurate and diverse portrayal of rural perspectives – for example, rural communities much more diverse than the mainstream media portrayal, which does not reflect this diversity. Roughly one-fifth of rural residents are people of color.[62] These new forms of narration and communication are central to both building

---

[58] Ibid., 16.

[59] Ibid., 17.

[60] Center for Rural Strategies (website), "Rural Assembly," www.ruralstrategies.org/national-rural-assembly/; and Hollie Russon Gilman and K. Sabeel Rahman, *Building Civic Capacity in an Era of Democratic Crisis* (Washington, DC: New America, September 2017).

[61] Center for Rural Strategies (website), "The Daily Yonder: Keep It Rural," www.ruralstrategies.org/the-daily-yonder/.

[62] Sean Illing, "'Rural America' Doesn't Mean 'White America' and Here's Why That Matters," *Vox*, April 24, 2017, www.vox.com/conversations/2017/4/24/15286624/race-rural-america-trump-politics-media; and Mara Casey Tieken, *Why Rural Schools Matter* (Chapel Hill: University of North Carolina Press, 2014).

94   *Civic Power*

identities and building power. The lack of a rural media infrastructure has led many rural communities to rely on more ideologically driven media corporations like Fox News and Breitbart. By creating a new media infrastructure, CRS hopes to create new narratives and political possibilities in rural communities.

This focus on communications infrastructure has also included a prolonged investment in campaigns around broadband and internet access. CRS advocates for improved broadband connectivity in rural America.[63] Many rural communities lack high-speed internet access. Existing internet service providers and telecom companies tend to bypass expensive investments in rural fiber and broadband networks.[64] Lack of competition among telecom firms means that the few carriers like AT&T, Comcast, and Verizon can charge high prices for access.[65] Local officials have tended to downplay broadband as a policy issue, viewing it as less important than clean water, safe highways, or education. The result, however, is a growing digital divide between rural America and the rest of the country – which magnifies the economic stagnation and sense of removal from the mainstream of popular culture and communication.[66]

Additionally, CRS has built its own robust online platform, RuralAmerica .org, which provides new tools to inform advocacy and power-building strategies, particularly for partner organizations that are members of its National Rural Assembly. CRS's National Rural Assembly is designed to bring rural organizations from over thirty-five states together specifically around shared themes of longer-term narrative, a shared communications structure, and power building.[67] Importantly, it is also a physical assembly – with an annual conference. The 2018 Rural Assembly in Durham, North Carolina addressed the feelings of despair facing many rural communities and the opportunities provided by communities of faith. In another example of work to build solidarity across traditional boundaries, one session of the Rural Assembly called "Building Civic Courage" was focused on the question: "How do we

---

[63] Center for Rural Strategies (website), "Broadband Advocacy," www.ruralstrategies.org/broad band/.

[64] Edward Carlson and Justin Goss, "The State of the Urban/Rural Digital Divide," National Telecommunications and Information Administration, United States Department of Commerce, August 10, 2016, www.ntia.doc.gov/blog/2016/state-urbanrural-digital-divide.

[65] Marguerite Reardon, "Are AT&T and Verizon Fleecing Rural America?" CNET, August 3, 2018, www.cnet.com/news/are-at-t-and-verizon-fleecing-rural-america/.

[66] Lauren Gibbons, "Rural Communities Suffer the Most without Access to the Web," *Government Technology*, June 29, 2018, www.govtech.com/network/Rural-Communities-Suffer-the-Most-Without-Access-to-the-Web.html.

[67] National Rural Assembly (website), home page, http://ruralassembly.org.

Organizing for Power   95

reckon with overall rural marginalization while at the same time acknowl-
edging inequities within our own communities?"[68] Thus, although CRS
provides a centralized infrastructure for the Rural Assembly, it does not simply
have top-down control over it.

In addition to the RuralAmerica platform, CRS deploys other communications tools to assist Rural Assembly members, including advanced big data and
analytics tools to document trends in economics, health, demographics, and
other relevant rural topics; mapping software; and social media to develop
a more reliable and authentic voice for rural Americans. It is notable that
a focus for the Daily Yonder and RuralAmerica.org lies in the deliberate
linking of rural narratives with urban audiences, in an attempt to create
a new mutual understanding. Policy needs in urban and rural areas are
often similar, but politically separated. Rural and urban communities may
not realize that they have similar interests; the CRS uses technology to create
different kinds of content and show how urban and rural areas share
a common purpose. The CRS media and communications infrastructure
also focuses on first-person accounts, with the goals of having rural communities narrate their own stories, providing a sense of empowerment, shifting the
public understandings of rural America, and enabling more effective political
advocacy. If the CRS strategy proves durable and powerful, it will show that
creating a different kind of communications infrastructure can engender
a broader discourse and make possible novel political coalitions, identities,
and alignments.

The CRS experience highlights an important lesson about building grassroots organizing capacity. The ability of civil society groups to successfully
engage, mobilize, and organize constituencies depends on an underlying
communications and media infrastructure. But that communications infrastructure is neither neutral nor automatically provided. Rather, groups are
dependent on relationships between physical communications infrastructure
and the infrastructure of content generation. Communities need to be connected to these physical communications infrastructures (e.g., assuring internet access for rural and disinterested urban communities). At the same time,
the content that flows through these channels must speak to the experiences,
values, and concerns of communities themselves. Furthermore, physical, in-
person organizing is important in making sure that a coordinating network
remains accountable to its goal of empowering community voices through the

---

[68] National Rural Assembly (website), "National Rural Assembly 2018: Building Civic Courage,
May 21–23, Durham, NC," http://ruralassembly.org/2018-rural-assembly/.

Civic Power

channels it supports. In short, communications infrastructure should not be taken for granted; it has to be built, defended, and broadened.

Power, Infrastructure, and the Fight for the City

As several scholars working on the revived interest in local government law and urban inequality suggest, questions about participation and power have long shaped local battles over economic development, zoning, and housing policy.[69] The porousness and relative informality of local level administrative governance offer an array of opportunities for civil society participation, organizing, and influence.[70] At the same time, urban politics have long been fraught, skewed by persisting disparities of power – such as those among and between developers, party machines, and local communities – as well as by fractured political identities and coalitions that break down particularly along racialized lines in conflicts over housing, development, and zoning.

The Partnership for Working Families (PFWF), headquartered in Oakland, California, is a national network of nineteen permanent coalitions in different metropolitan regions.[71] These regions often cross multiple municipal boundaries and can extend across urban, suburban, and exurban divides. PFWF was started in 2006 with the goal of rebuilding regional organizing with the breadth and depth of a national network.[72] PFWF and its affiliate organizations focus on issues pertinent to working families, and they advocate for policies to support economic growth, civic engagement, and innovative solutions for economic and environmental concerns. PFWF makes power building central to its work – including through novel strategies that leverage the politics of place to both build power and forge new, more inclusive and effective coalitions and solidarities.

For example, Pittsburgh United, the Pittsburgh, Pennsylvania, affiliate, has been deploying a carefully constructed experimental model for testing

---

[69] See Richard Schragger, *City Power: Urban Governance in a Global Age* (New York: Oxford University Press, 2016); Nestor Davidson, "Localist Administrative Law," *Yale Law Journal* 126 (2016); and Nadav Shoked, "The New Local," *Virginia Law Review* 100 (2014): 1323–1403. For classic accounts of democracy, power, and inequality in the city, see Gerald E. Frug, *City Making: Building Communities without Building Walls* (Princeton, NJ: Princeton University Press, 2001); and Gerald E. Frug and David Barron, *City Bound: How States Stifle Urban Innovation* (Ithaca, NY: Cornell University Press, 2008).

[70] See Davidson, "Local Administrative Law."

[71] Partnership for Working Families (website), "National Network of Affiliates," www.forworkingfamilies.org/about/affiliates.

[72] Partnership for Working Families (website), "History," www.forworkingfamilies.org/about/history.

different outreach strategies and then adapting its practice based on results. In the last campaign cycle, Pittsburgh United conducted a field test comparing voter turnout among low-propensity voters.[73] As a control group, Pittsburgh United engaged voters through a conventional civic engagement outreach strategy that emphasized the importance of voting and general values of civic engagement.[74] Another group of voters was approached through an issue-specific appeal seeking support for an affordable housing trust fund.[75] Pittsburgh United found that when reaching out to citizens with a low propensity to vote, engagement about specific issues was more successful in persuading them to vote. Indeed, the issue-specific appeal proved far more powerful in motivating turnout: it yielded a 30 percent greater participation rate compared to the control group.

Across the country, PFWF has deployed a similar focus on issues – such as affordable housing and the privatization of urban infrastructure – as a way to develop deeper ties across racial lines and to link urban, suburban, and exurban constituencies.[76] This broader conception of the metropolitan region, linked together by a shared set of concerns on housing affordability, privatization, and infrastructure, is increasingly essential to exercising effective political power. By foregrounding the lived experience of urban inequality, Partnership organizers can help activate members and channel these interests into longer-term organizing and movement building. Furthermore, by highlighting issues that cut across neighborhoods and involve the larger metro region, the Partnership can help forge a multiracial and regional set of movements that link communities in different neighborhoods and cut across urban/exurban/suburban boundaries. This coalition- and identity-building approach is particularly powerful given the legal context of most American cities: because urban policies can be relatively easily pre-empted by state legislatures, coalitions between urban and suburban constituencies are key to pressuring state legislatures to embrace – or at least refrain from pre-empting – urban policy innovations.[77]

---

[73] Pittsburg United (website), www.pittsburghunited.org/. Conversation at New America, Washington, DC, 2017.

[74] Ibid.

[75] Ibid.

[76] See the "We Make This City" campaign, 2018, http://wemakethiscity.org/.

[77] Roxana Tynan discusses this issue from the organizing perspective in a recent blog post, "Unmasking the Hidden Power of Cities," *Medium*, June 14, 2018, https://medium.com/@rox anatynan/unmasking-the-hidden-power-of-cities-dbc9f1f724c8. For a scholarly treatment of these issues around city power and state pre-emption, see Schragger, *City Power*; and Frug and Barron, *City Bound*.

Civic Power

Organizing and the Future of Work

If place presents one central fault line for problems of inequality, power, and identity, another is the changing nature of work and labor. In recent decades, the increasing "fissuring" of the workplace has meant that more and more workers are placed in precarious, insecure positions with little protection and few benefits.[78] Through outsourcing, franchising, and the rise of the "gig" economy, large employers in sectors as diverse as retail, restaurant work, and domestic work have shed labor costs – in the process depressing wages and placing more workers outside of the reach of employer-provided benefits.[79] This growth in worker insecurity is both exacerbated by and fueled by the shift in power noted in Chapter 3, as the power and influence of business interests have grown and that of organized labor have concurrently eroded, fractured, and been corroded by the legal attacks on trade unions, collective bargaining, and through the proliferation of "right to work" statutes. Yet, even if mid-century forms of labor organizing could be restored, they would be of limited use. With more workers increasingly working outside of the formal confines of the conventional firm, the traditional model of employer–employee bargaining is even less well suited to representing worker interests. Meanwhile, the politics of labor have remained fraught along lines of race and gender; historically, the New Deal's social contract protections of labor rights and providing safety net protections for workers included exceptions that were racialized and gendered, leaving domestic workers, farmworkers, and other such groups out of the legal structure of the safety net.[80]

Yet the sheer political and economic pressures facing workers today have led to some compellingly novel forms of worker organizing that seek to build power and forge multiracial, inclusive coalitions in potentially transformative ways. New worker movements have clustered around social movement organizations and worker centers rather than around conventional trade unions; these worker centers organize workers and provide a range of support services like childcare and training.[81] The social movement organizations that run

---

[78] David Weil, *The Fissured Workplace* (Cambridge, MA: Harvard University Press, 2014), 122.

[79] Ibid., 120; Sarah Kessler, "Pixel & Dimed On (Not) Getting by in the Gig Economy," *FastCompany*, March 18, 2014, www.fastcompany.com/3027355/pixel-and-dimed-on-not-getting-by-in-the-gig-economy; and T. J. McCue, "57 Million U.S. Workers Are Part of the Gig Economy," *Forbes*, August 31, 2018, www.forbes.com/sites/tjmccue/2018/08/31/57-million-u-s-workers-are-part-of-the-gig-economy/#285ba9ae7118.

[80] Caroline Frederickson, *Under the Bus: How Working Women Are Being Run Over* (New York: New Press, 2015); and Katznelson, *Fear Itself*.

[81] Janice Fine, *Worker Centers: Organizing Communities at the Edge of the Dream* (Ithaca, NY: ILR Press, 2006).

Organizing for Power 99

them in turn aim to build worker power at both the sector level as well as at larger political levels. Thus, organizations like the Restaurant Opportunities Centers United (ROC), the National Domestic Workers Alliance (NDWA), the National Guestworker Alliance, and the Coalition of Immokalee Workers (CIW) have been at the forefront of more recent worker organizing.

It should be no surprise that these multiracial and multisector worker movements have emerged from precisely those worker constituencies cut out of the mid-century labor law regime – nor that they speak directly to the experience of precarious, insecure, contingent work that marks the modern fissured workplace and the "gig" economy.[82] As labor law scholars have argued, we need a new legal and institutional regime for this new form of worker power, for example through codifying sectoral rather than employer-based forms of organizing, and institutionalizing labor voice through administrative commissions.[83] Where conventionally unions combined collective bargaining in the workplace with political mobilization and power, these new worker movements represent the hope of an "unbundled union," where workers can exercise political power and influence outside of the conventional strictures of collective bargaining.[84] But the front lines lie in converting these new approaches to organizing modern workers into durable forms of bottom-up civil society power. To take but one example, consider the case of Coworker.org and its approach to building worker power in the new economy.

Building Organizing Capacity

Here, we return to and expand on the case of Coworker.org, briefly discussed in Chapter 1. There we recounted how Jannette Navarro, a twenty-two-year-old Starbucks barista and single mother working toward her associate degree in business, was able to use the Coworker.org platform to launch a movement against last-minute scheduling.[85] In recent years, major retail chains have been deploying software that adjusts worker schedules in nearly real time,

---

[82] See David Rolf, *Fight for Fifteen: The Right Wage for a Working America* (New York: New Press, 2015); Andrias, "The New Labor Law," 47–56; and Michelle Miller, "The Union of the Future" (thought brief, Roosevelt Institute, July 2015), http://rooseveltinstitute.org/wp-content /uploads/2015/10/Miller-The-Union-of-the-Future.pdf.

[83] See Rogers, "Libertarian Corporatism"; and Andrias, "The New Labor Law." See also Chapter 6 of this volume, on power-building institutional and policy designs.

[84] See Ben Sachs, "The Unbundled Union: Politics without Collective Bargaining," *Yale Law Journal* 123 (2013), 1–265, 182.

[85] Portions of this section reproduce work published in our earlier report, *Building Civic Capacity in an Era of Democratic Crisis* (Washington, DC: New America, 2017). These passages are adapted with permission of New America.

according to demand at individual stores.[86] The results for workers are wrecked personal schedules, taking a physical toll on workers' health, family lives, and ability to succeed in educational endeavors.[87]

Algorithmic scheduling is aimed at increasing efficiency. Software that combines sales patterns and analyzes large data sets decides precisely when and where Starbucks's 130,000 baristas are needed across thousands of locations.[88] Some are given as little as one day notice for their shifts.[89] As Zeynep Ton has argued, on-demand scheduling practices are creating unpredictability and instability in workers' lives: workers cannot reliably plan their lives, whether in terms of coordinating childcare or pursuing additional education.[90] But Ms. Navarro was able to get her story featured in the *New York Times*.[91] Through the support of Coworker.org, Ms. Navarro became a leader for more humane scheduling practices; she declared, "I want to surprise everyone ... because no one is expecting anything of me."[92]

Coworker.org offered her a platform where she could connect with other baristas around the world, who would otherwise have found it hard to have collective power. In 2015, these baristas organized a worldwide campaign against last-minute scheduling at Starbucks – and won.[93] Yet this victory did not emerge in a vacuum. Background infrastructure, particularly the online platform, Coworker.org, was key. Coworker incubates worker campaigns online, by connecting workers to each other and offering them a "place" to discuss their problems, explore solutions, and build momentum for campaigns.[94] Coworker.org staff also work directly with workers to help them build communities of support on the ground. Coworker aims to empower workers and to strengthen their agency and their communities.

Cofounder Jess Kutch explained the impetus behind founding Coworker.org:

---

[86] Kantor, "Working Anything but 9 to 5."

[87] Ibid.

[88] Ibid.

[89] Ibid.

[90] Zeynep Ton, *The Good Jobs Strategy: How the Smartest Companies Invest in Employees to Lower Costs and Boost Profits* (New York: Houghton Mifflin, 2014).

[91] Kantor, "Starbucks to Revise Policies"; and Kantor, "Times Article Changes a Starbucks Policy."

[92] Kantor, "Starbucks to Revise Policies."

[93] Coworker.org, "Starbucks: Give Us a Fair Workweek!"

[94] Ben Schiller, "Where There Aren't Unions, Can Online Platforms Organize Workers?" *FastCompany*, July 6, 2015, www.fastcompany.com/3047759/where-there-arent-unions-can-online-platforms-organize-workers.

Organizing for Power

We built Coworker.org to be a laboratory for workers to access information and peer support, pool resources, and experiment with ways to build power together and improve the quality of their work.[95]

Coworker.org was born out of hostile battles over union power in Wisconsin. In the spring of 2011, collective bargaining and unionizing were hot buzzwords there, thanks to a proposed budget bill in the state legislature. The governor, Scott Walker, a Tea Party favorite, promoted the budget as preventing layoffs caused by strict union regulations.[96] As Katherine J. Cramer documented:

Scott Walker arrived at the right place at the right time. His candidacy and programs have tapped into the economic anxiety and dread that mark this point in history. Walker's platform has also made use of the desire for people to make sense of their world, to figure out who is to blame and identify boundaries that clearly show that those who are to blame are not one of us.[97]

In response to Walker's budget proposal, public unions argued that the bill denied them the ability to negotiate their pay, pensions, and healthcare, inciting huge protests.[98] The demonstrations lasted for approximately four months and gained national media attention. After months of chaos and political drama, the budget eventually passed with amendments, but the protests brought unionizing and collective bargaining back into public attention and common discourse.

At the time, Michelle Miller had already been working at the Service Employees International Union (SEIU) for ten years as an organizer to engage both workers and the public, including through worker campaigns leveraging art, culture, and media. Watching the events surrounding Wisconsin, Miller realized that people across the country were intrigued about the idea of being able to negotiate for changes in their workplaces – but they did not know how to begin organizing.[99] Inspired, Miller and her SEIU co-worker Jess Kutch had the idea of developing an online platform to put skills and resources in the hands of employees who wanted them. In effect, Miller and Kutch created a new model of twenty-first-century labor organizing to match not only the

---

[95] Aspen Institute, "An Interview with Job Quality Fellow Jess Kutch," February 20, 2018, www.aspeninstitute.org/longform/job-quality-fellows-profile-series/jess-kutch/.

[96] Dave Umhoefer, "For Unions in Wisconsin, a Fast and Hard Fall since Act 10," *Journal Sentinel*, November 27, 2016, https://projects.jsonline.com/news/2016/11/27/for-unions-in-wisconsin-fast-and-hard-fall-since-act-10.html.

[97] Cramer, *Politics of Resentment*, 207.

[98] Ibid., 1.

[99] MobLab (website), "Coworker.org to Give Deep Support to Mobilize Workers," March 11, 2013, https://mobilisationlab.org/new-organization-to-give-deep-support-to-mobilize-workers/.

interests that employees have, but also the changing realities of the modern workplace, which traditional unions were not addressing.

Coworker.org meets potential organizers where they are and takes a build-it-and-they-will-come approach. Instead of hosting community organizing workshops or trying to promote institution building, Miller and Kutch give employees the means for organizing online, where people already expect to find answers to their questions. The platform is an educational resource and launch pad for anyone interested in starting a campaign in his or her own workplace. It also serves as a leadership development tool. While workers can learn about current campaigns happening across the country and connect with like-minded individuals, the platform also helps identify creative and driven workers who have leadership potential – and offers them a conduit for developing those skills.[100] Thus, it not only provides resources but also seeks out emerging talent who can take on more leadership in the organizing work.

Yet, it must be noted that Coworker.org is not involved in workplace research and does not search for cases where their services could be useful. Instead of going out to their target community, the organization waits for employees to come to them. When employees do get involved, Coworker.org encourages their participation and development by actively investing in people to show employees how to become leaders in their community.[101] It flips the traditional union model on its head. Instead of presupposing to know the solution for an individual worker in her workplace, Coworker.org lets workers self-identify and self-organize.

A key feature of Coworker.org's model involves creating subnetworks within campaigns. For example, if a user is particularly active in commenting on a campaign on the Coworker.org platform, staff will invite the user to join that campaign's media committee. Similarly, if a user shows leadership skills by running a campaign well, staff will work with that user to develop his or her leadership skills further and to identify new potential campaigns for that community. Additionally, "data contributors" collect data by polling people in the workplace; Coworker.org aggregates the data and reports back to users to provide an overview of the campaigns themselves.

This approach necessarily means that the content of each Coworker.org campaign is highly specific to its context and community. But what the Coworker.org model offers is a powerful tool for identifying, training, and building locally rooted leaders. In essence, Coworker.org's model is more designed for

---

[100] J. M. Kaplan Fund (website), "Michelle Miller & Jess Kutch: Project Overview," www.jmkfund.org/awardee/michelle-miller-and-jess-kutch/.

[101] Aspen Institute, "An Interview with Job Quality Fellow Jess Kutch."

Organizing for Power   103

building up the capacities and underlying movement infrastructure of its user base than for pursuing specific campaigns. The theory is that, by building leadership, skills, and – over time – shared identities of users as workers, Coworker.org is multiplying the power and capacity of workers themselves, which may enable more far-reaching economic justice campaigns and democratic mobilization in the future.

The platform thus creates an infrastructure that allows people to self-organize and self-advocate in the workplace based on decentralized networks of employees. Most users are in the retail and on-demand sectors, and most are low-income or people of color. In terms of issues, the platform has also shown a focus on workers managed by algorithms (i.e., in scheduling) or workers who deal with workplace surveillance technology that track keystrokes.

For example, Starbucks barista Kristie Williams initially started a Coworker .org campaign to protest Starbucks's inflexible ban on showing tattoos, even when covering them might result in severe discomfort, after the air conditioning at her Atlanta franchise broke.[102] Coworker.org helped her campaign by connecting her with other baristas as well as journalists, ultimately creating a network that spanned seventeen countries.[103] The campaign also included social media activism, such as Facebook ads and a hashtag-commandeering tactic where protesters repurposed one of Starbucks's own tags on social media.[104] By the end, Kristie had not only created a change in company policy, but she had over 25,000 signatures.[105] This group kept working to improve Starbucks's environment by tackling practices and procedures on hair dye, wage increases, recycling, lies in corporate public statements, and scheduling policies.[106]

Starbucks baristas have run fifty campaigns using the platform; it's also being used by workers at other large organizations such as Wells Fargo.[107] Coworker.org has also begun working with large technology companies on behalf of workers who want to have a stake in how companies are run and how technology is deployed as well as in the political consequences of the

---

[102] Coworker.org (website), "To: Starbucks: Let Us Have Visible Tattoos!!!," www.coworker.org /petitions/let-us-have-visible-tattoos.

[103] Coworker.org, "Grounds for Change: How Baristas Won Visible Tattoos at Starbucks," *Medium*, February 20, 2018, https://medium.com/@TeamCoworker/grounds-for-change-how-baristas-won-visible-tattoos-at-starbucks-a1b578e3a417.

[104] Ibid.

[105] Alexander C. Kaufman, "Starbucks Baristas Fight to Show Tattoos," *Huffington Post*, September 13, 2014, www.huffingtonpost.com/2014/09/12/starbucks-tattoos_n_5811888.html.

[106] Ibid.

[107] Coworker.org (website), "Coworker.org Victories," https://home.coworker.org/victories/.

information that technology companies are collecting.[108] Critically, most campaigns are in places where no labor structure and organizing exist. In its relatively short lifespan, Coworker.org has been used by nearly half a million workers across hundreds of campaigns.[109] Those campaigns resulted in successful changes at Starbucks, Recreational Equipment, Inc. (REI), Wells Fargo, FIFA, Publix, and more.[110]

Coworker.org also has begun organizing tech employees themselves, as part of the Tech Workers Coalition. Workers in Silicon Valley have started to deploy this coalition to put pressure on their employers to oppose certain practices that curb civil liberties or do not empower workers, such as hiring part-time contractors.[111] For example, one campaign includes employees of tech companies supporting a petition to show solidarity for security officers seeking to negotiate a fair contract with the agencies that employ them.[112] By investing in an underlying infrastructure that enables new forms of worker organizing, Coworker.org is thus helping to catalyze novel new worker movements in a range of sectors.

Multiracial Organizing and Economic Insecurity:
Faith in Texas

After years of conservative rule, the social justice infrastructure in Texas was weak. Social justice organizing struggled to connect with faith communities and also faced difficulties linking faith communities across racial lines. But for Lydia Bean, founder of Faith in Texas (FIT), a key challenge to progressive politics in Texas lay in the organizing strategies – or limitations thereof – that progressives conventionally employed. In particular, Bean, the granddaughter of a Baptist minister and a long-time organizer, who holds a PhD in sociology from Harvard University, saw an untapped potential to forge new solidarities

---

[108] Coworker.org (website), "Tech Workers Coalition," www.coworker.org/partnerships/tech-workers-coalition; and Tanvi Misra and Sarah Holder, "Workers' Rights, Silicon-Valley Style," *City Lab*, August 31, 2018, www.citylab.com/equity/2018/08/workers-rights-silicon-valley-style/568189/.

[109] Aspen Institute, "An Interview with Job Quality Fellow Jess Kutch."

[110] Coworker.org, "Coworker.org Victories."

[111] Coworker.org (website), "Tech Workers Coalition"; Michael J. Coren, "Silicon Valley Tech Workers Are Talking about Starting Their First Union in 2017 to Resist Trump," *Quartz*, March 24, 2017, https://qz.com/916534/silicon-valley-tech-workers-are-talking-about-starting-their-first-union-in-2017-to-resist-trump/.

[112] Coworker.org (website), "Tech Workers Stand with Our Security Officers," www.coworker.org/petitions/solidarity-with-tech-security-officers.

Organizing for Power 105

and new forms of political power on the basis of religious faith as well as in shared experiences of economic insecurity.[113]

Faith in Texas was created in 2015 with the goal of shifting the dominant narrative of faith in Texas to reflect a more inclusive, multiracial future. Headquartered in Dallas, FIT now has a staff of nearly ten employees, with a mix of people from different faiths, races, and socio-economic backgrounds. A managing director, previously a conservative, was originally an evangelical youth pastor at Concord Church in Dallas. The FIT model focuses on training and coaching leaders as well as providing them assistance with strategy. It encourages organizing through the existing infrastructure in place in congregations and stresses issues like payday lending, criminal justice reform, and immigration.

The key to FIT's unique approach, however, lies in its emphasis on building a novel interfaith coalition that cuts across traditional urban–suburban, racial, and left–right divides. The long-term goal for FIT is to change the narrative of "what it means to be Texan," by securing tangible campaign wins on small issues chosen to thicken a shared sense of solidarity among its key constituencies. Indeed, FIT is focused on knitting together a coalition of four very distinct, and often at-odds communities: Hispanic millennials, African American millennials, white working-class women, and white moderate people of faith.[114] This coalition necessarily challenges prevailing divides between white, suburban Republicans and mostly Democratic urban communities and communities of color. Yet it does not reduce to a least-common-denominator form of bipartisanship. There are inherent challenges to this work. For, example getting the black and Hispanic communities to identify with one another is very difficult. Similarly, getting working-class white people to identity with working-class people of color is another obstacle, particularly as Texas has been the petri dish for the Republican Party, which developed key political narratives in Texas to realign white working-class voters through ideals centered on free enterprise, moral traditionalism, and faith.

Consider FIT's campaign against payday lending in the greater Dallas area. A key part of the campaign involved working with white suburban women by gradually making them comfortable in admitting, and ultimately narrating publicly, what was for many a *private* matter of shame and suffering – experiences with payday lending.[115] In contrast to urban communities of color where

---

[113] See Gilman and Rahman, *Building Civic Capacity in an Era of Democratic Crisis*.
[114] Faith in Texas (website), home page, https://faithintx.org/.
[115] Matthew Choi, "Texas Payday Lenders Face Tougher Standards with New Federal Rules," *Texas Tribune*, October 12, 2017, www.texastribune.org/2017/10/12/texans-hope-for-better-protections-from-payday-loans-following-federal.

106   *Civic Power*

the problem of debt and payday lending was already a matter of common knowledge and concern, for these suburban white families it was a hidden experience. Once brought out into the open, it could be leveraged to build a wider multiracial urban–suburban coalition.

Furthermore, as this shared narrative developed, it involved a heavily moralized and religious narrative dimension that helped bond the different key constituencies together. Many faiths, from evangelical Christianity to Islam, include theological concerns about debt and usury that offer rich moral language upon which FIT could draw to build this common conversation. During the campaign, some groups, like white veterans, were engaged directly through their evangelical church communities to discuss how payday lending directly impacted their lives and their faith. Through organizing, FIT was able to leverage words in the Bible and connect them to words in the Quran. In the process, these divergent constituencies generated new forms of understanding that cut against prevailing political currents of racism and Islamophobia.

While the payday lending community had wielded significant power over the city council of Dallas, FIT was able to demonstrate in a practical way how it was predatory. The payoff of this type of hard work is not just in the creation of new political coalitions and shared narratives. It is also in the novel forms of political power that such new identities can make possible. The payday lending campaign is telling in this regard as well. By local ordinance, a city government in the Dallas-Fort Worth area imposed limits on payday lending. But the heavily Republican Texas state legislature then threatened to pre-empt those local policies.[116] FIT was able to mobilize its new urban–suburban coalition to put pressure on the state legislature, helping swing enough votes to block the pre-emption drive.

The issue of pre-emption is important nationwide. Many organizations are working to pass progressive ordinances in "blue" cities, yet these face significant hurdles in states where legislatures have broad pre-emptive powers.[117] Furthermore, one of the significant challenges with reform approaches that focus on municipal government and local ordinances as sites of opportunity lies in facing the pressure corporate lobbyists put on state-level legislation to pre-empt city ordinances, for example on payday lending or paid sick leave. A progressive strategy that is primarily focused on the local level must engage

[116]   Jackie Wang, "Bills Would Undo Cities' Efforts to Rein in Payday Lenders, Advocates Warn," *Texas Tribune*, April 27, 2017, www.texastribune.org/2017/04/27/texas-bills-would-override-local-regulations-on-payday-lending/.
[117]   Schragger, *City Power*; and Frug and Barron, *City Bound*.

with the broader structures and politics, yet many such reform efforts have not fully embraced this reality.

Meanwhile, FIT has worked to pass progressive ordinances in "purple" and "red" cities. Part of its strategy was to leverage the city council in places where there was not a well-defined economic justice agenda. But the real key to its success was the incorporation of traditionally conservative white suburban voters into a broad coalition with urban communities of color – thus gathering additional support in the legislature to defend the city of Dallas's policy autonomy.

CONCLUSION

The case studies above by no means exhaust the field of ongoing innovations in bottom-up organizing. Further, many of the organizations profiled here engage in similar strategies; leadership development animates not only Coworker.org, for example, but also the work of PFWF, Faith in Texas, and CRS. The urban–suburban coalition building of FIT is similar to that of PFWF. All of these organizations share an emphasis on narrative. These examples do, however, highlight some important themes for our question of how to build democratic capacity through civil society organizing.

First, civic engagement must be understood as a constant, sustained practice that outlives election cycles and stretches beyond voting or other formal, governmental channels for citizen input. The motivation, skills, organizational support, and capacity to engage in sustained civic action all need to be constructed as well as maintained over time. Individual policy issues and campaigns are crucial ways to activate communities, but they must be conducted in ways that help build this longer-term capacity for civic participation. Organizing around a particular short-term goal is not enough. Civil society organizations must toggle between immediate goals and larger visions, showing concretely that participatory methods and active engagement can deliver results, while at the same time orienting their work toward building those skills, leaders, and capacities that will enable more – and more effective – mobilizations in the future.

Importantly, electoral politics is not the primary focus of these organizations. Engagement within electoral politics is highly partisan. These case studies offer instead an alternative vision of engagement focused on longer-term movement building. The locus of power for these organizations is in day-to-day governance and policy decisions, many of which are occurring outside the purview of the federal government. In many cases, it is the state government or private-sector actors that are engaged.

The organizations described above are all strategic in how they deploy people. A common theme in the examples above is that certain organizing strategies can construct durable power and membership over time. On the one hand, individuals are motivated to participate by specific issues that speak to their experience, rather than broad campaigns. On the other hand, over time, these experiences with mobilization and participation start to create broader conceptions of belonging, identity, and community. Such solidarity and shared bonds of trust and inclusion must be built thoughtfully, in particular when organizing across racial, gender, class, and geographic lines.

Second, a key aspect of long-term civic capacity stems from the identities and solidarity that are given voice through the types of civic action that it enables and promotes. In this process, public engagement is not disassociated from the emotions, struggles, and identities of real communities. Certain styles of civic engagement can exacerbate or further emphasize divisions. Yet alternative narratives can build across conventional community boundaries, if such new identities and solidarities are actively constructed over time.

The shared identities that the different organizations in this chapter struggled to build – from the reframing of "rural" identities by CRS to the forging of new conceptions of worker power in Coworker.org to the linking of urban–suburban multiracial coalitions in PFWF and FIT – all represent a radically different vision of identity and politics than the specter of exclusionary populism. Identity remains a motivating feature in these coalitions, yet it functions very differently than in exclusionary populism, where identity is central – and centered on anger and resentment manifest along racialized lines, backed up by media narratives and existing organizational infrastructures, as noted in previous chapters. Here, however, movements and organizations are focused on using identity in order to connect strategic wins with building new power bases and developing new leaders. These models are trying to build their own type of positive feedback loop that reinforces new relationships and solidarities by connecting small wins to larger narratives built around shared and often new identities. For example, many of the workers organizing through Coworker.org do not self-identify as "organizers" or "leaders." Yet through the process of engagement, they learn something new about themselves while fighting for tangible wins in their workplace. They learn how to organize and, often times, lead.

Third, these movements balance between the immediate and urgent needs of their constituencies on the one hand and more structural, longer-term diagnoses of power, inequality, and disempowerment on the other. Their seemingly small policy targets – like algorithmic scheduling in the barista campaign or household debt in Texas – are certainly important and address

Organizing for Power
109

real needs and concerns. But these movements make sure to connect these campaigns to deeper diagnoses about structural drivers of inequality and marginalization: the power of corporate actors, the ways in which state power undercuts worker and grassroots power, and above all the need to build durable forms of bottom-up political power to counteract such forces.

Policy wins are therefore crucial in these case studies; they provide examples of short-term success that give these movements, organizations, and solidarities vital energy and impetus. Importantly, the success of these organizations in attaining such wins depends on more than their ability to build grassroots power and new solidarities – it also depends crucially on the institutional levers they can deploy to translate political organization into political influence. As Sidney Tarrow, Charles Tilly, and others have argued, successful movements need not just mobilizing narratives to frame their demands, but, importantly, they must have the capacity to make the best of the "political opportunity structure,"[118] as discussed in Chapter 1. How they respond to this structure further shapes the movements themselves.[119] In the examples above, the key techniques deployed in the relevant political opportunity structures included voting, lobbying, and forming public narratives. But could the structures themselves offer other levers that could provide both greater *power* for these kinds of movements and a further institutional *foundation* for these new solidarities and identities? That is the subject of the next three chapters.

[118] Tarrow and Tilly, *Contentious Politics*; Tarrow, *Power in Movement*.
[119] Han, *How Organizations Develop Activists*, 68–69; and Tilly, *Contentious Performances*, 148–49.

PART II

CIVIC POWER THROUGH GOVERNANCE

4

From Governance to Power – Rethinking
Democracy Reform

In the previous chapters we explored how grassroots organizations could build bottom-up power and new coalitions. The ability of civic groups to exercise political influence turns not only on their strategies for building power, but also on the larger institutional contexts within which these organizations operate. In these next few chapters we shift focus from grassroots to government. What kinds of institutional structures and governance mechanisms are necessary to create a more inclusive and equitable power balance in policymaking? We argue that the ability of grassroots movements to exercise power depends on more than their ability to build durable organizations and new coalitions and identities. It also depends on an institutional policymaking context that provides points of entry and leverage for these movements. We suggest that democratic inclusion requires radical changes to institutional design and policymaking within government bodies. In particular, we suggest that democracy requires bureaucracies that are designed (and acculturated) to engage with grassroots actors. It also requires the implementation of what we call institutional *hooks and levers* through which grassroots groups can exert influence on policymakers.

Conventional views of civil society's levers on policymakers center on voting and public opinion. Both exert a powerful influence on policymakers' decisions and incentives. Both are vital for democracy to thrive, and battles over access to the ballot, voter suppression, districting, and campaign finance, as well as over the future of the media and public sphere, are all essential front lines for the future of democracy. But here we take a different focus. Even in a well-functioning electoral system and public sphere, there remain structural disparities of influence and power in day-to-day processes of governance. Indeed, as noted in Chapters 1 and 2 this is precisely where some of the most troubling forms of disparate influence and democratic failures take place. Even after an election is won or a bill passed, the bureaucratic

implementation of a policy can still be skewed by the disproportionate influence of more sophisticated and well-resourced groups including business
lobbies.

Administrative institutions and day-to-day governance are often overlooked in broad accounts of democracy and power. Yet agencies, more so
than legislatures, are the front line of governance in the modern era,
where decisions about policy enforcement and design are made.[1] Agencies
also have the ability to house a more dynamic form of representation,
based not just on geography – which is often the basis of electoral
accountability – but rather on forms of participation that can be tailored
to cut across and engage different types of constituencies, often along
lines of race, ethnicity, class, gender, substantive interests, or regional
affiliation.[2]

The centrality of governance institutions is not just procedural; these
institutions are key in addressing substantive questions of inequality and
exclusion. Without powerful civil rights enforcement agencies and offices,
racial and gender discrimination and exclusion cannot be undone.
Without an administrative regime to protect workers, or to provide universal access to public goods and the safety net, inequality increases.[3]
Given the importance of governance institutions in addressing the substantive, chronic, and structural dimensions of inequality and exclusion, it
should be unsurprising that the *dismantling* of these institutions has been
central to the political and policy strategy of the kinds of business interests
and exclusionary politics described in Chapters 1 and 2. The business
lobby – and thus the political power of corporate interests – has focused
much of its agenda in recent decades on blocking, slowing down, or
dismantling regulatory bodies, from the Environmental Protection
Agency (EPA) to the Consumer Financial Protection Bureau (CFPB).[4]
The backlash against the civil rights movement has similarly fueled the

---

[1]   Christopher K. Ansell, *Pragmatist Democracy: Evolutionary Learning as Public Philosophy*
(New York: Oxford University Press, 2011), 3.
[2]   Mark Warren, "Governance-Driven Democratization," *Critical Policy Studies* 3 (2009): 3–13,
3, 5.
[3]   See Desmond King, "Forceful Federalism against American Racial Inequality," in
"Democracy without Solidarity: Political Dysfunction in Hard Times," special issue,
Government and Opposition 52 (2017): 356–82; K. Sabeel Rahman, "Reconstructing the
Administrative State in an Era of Economic and Democratic Crisis," *Harvard Law Review*
131 (2018): 1682–89; and K. Sabeel Rahman, "Constructing and Contesting Structural
Inequality," *Critical Analysis of Law* 5 (2018): 99–126.
[4]   Michaels, *Constitutional Coup*, 82–98; Hacker and Pierson, *American Amnesia*.

From Governance to Power – Rethinking Democracy Reform 115

dismantling of civil rights enforcement regimes, accelerating under the Trump administration.[5]

Robust governance agencies – with sufficient personnel, funding, and authority – are essential to redressing problems of inequality and exclusion. Yet in a democracy characterized by highly disparate political power, the egalitarian and democratic potential of these agencies is fragile and precarious. Building civic power to remedy these disparities of influence thus necessarily involves changes to the structure and internal dynamics of policy-making institutions. Recall in Chapter 1 we argued for the need to institutionalize countervailing power as a key to building a more inclusive democratic system. The investment in organizing infrastructure described in Chapter 3 offers one important way of building grassroots power. But organizing alone is insufficient to redress the deep disparities of political power that undermine our current democratic politics. Instead of putting all the pressure for democratic power on grassroots organizing, institutional configurations must enable empowered participation. Creating more hooks and levers through which constituencies can exercise influence will likely deepen democratic capacity, creating feedback loops as constituencies exercise more power, and policymakers grow more accustomed to engaging with these groups.

Our approach also represents a radically different approach to democracy reform and institutional design. It recommends focusing governance reform not on the efficient and rational execution of policy, but in actually balancing power and in creating more inclusive and democratic forms of policymaking. This emphasis on participation and democracy may feel risky to some – a departure from the safer confines of technocratic, insulated decision-making. In some ways it is. But it also requires more than simply opening up policymaking to the masses. It requires the creation of more and better structured forms of democratic policymaking. The alternative is not neutral governance by experts, but rather the persistence of nefarious power imbalances in sites of governance that are hard to contest.

The rest of this chapter provides a critical analysis of three waves of governance reform: (1) the proceduralization of the modern administrative state; (2) the move to "reinvent government" through greater privatization and deregulation; and (3) the rise of the "civic tech" movement to rationalize government through the use of big data and new technological platforms. Each of

---

[5]   Sherrilyn Ifill, "President Trump's First Year Was an Affront to Civil Rights," *Time*, January 17, 2018, http://time.com/5106648/donald-trump-civil-rights-race/.

116 *Civic Power*

these movements has promised to enhance government by making it more rational and efficient as well as, in some ways, by improving accountability to the public. But as this chapter will argue, each of these approaches to governance reform falls short insofar as they bracket, and thereby reinforce, problems of disparate power.

These conventional approaches to governance reform are manifestations of the "good governance" ethos critiqued in Chapter 1. Indeed, there is a way in which these familiar discourses of governance reform too often *take as given* existing disparities of power and assume them as fixed, severe resource constraints on government. The best these discourses can hope for, then, is more "efficient" and "user-friendly" government – rather than more *empowering* government. Having established a critique of these conventional "good governance" approaches to reform, Chapters 5 and 6 then turn to outline an alternative vision of institutional design and reform within policymaking institutions. Chapter 5 looks at examples for alternative approaches to the internal reform of government bureaucracies to facilitate this kind of empowered participatory policymaking. Chapter 6 explores new approaches to creating hooks and levers for increasing participation in policymaking.

ADMINISTRATIVE PROCEDURE AND THE LIMITS OF GOOD GOVERNANCE

As discussed in Chapters 2 and 3, power disparities and interest group capture play a major role in skewing the outcomes of democratic policymaking. The structures of policymaking institutions are a key part of why some groups have outsize influence. What would a more accountable and responsive approach by administrative institutions look like? Concerns about administrative accountability and capture have fueled waves of legal and institutional reform within the administrative state.[6] But as we shall see, these reform efforts are flawed, operating on a "good governance" model emphasizing expertise in, as well as the insulation and rationality of, policymaking.

The early battles over the constitutionality of the New Deal administrative state eventually produced foundational case law confirming the constitutional status of agencies as well as the landmark Administrative Procedure Act of 1946

---

[6] See Robert Rabin, "Federal Regulation in Historical Perspective," *Stanford Law Review* 38 (1986): 1189–1326; Reuel Schiller, "Enlarging the Administrative Polity: Administrative Law and the Changing Definition of Pluralism, 1945–1970," *Vanderbilt Law Review* 53 (2000): 1389–1453; and Reuel Schiller, "The Era of Deference: Courts, Expertise, and the Emergence of New Deal Administrative Law," *Michigan Law Review* (2007): 399–441.

From Governance to Power – Rethinking Democracy Reform   117

(APA).[7] In the 1970s, a new wave of public interest legislation in areas like environmental law and consumer protection created another wave of expanded agency authorities and responsibilities.[8] This expansion of agency authority came with parallel efforts to deepen agency accountability through transparency measures like the Freedom of Information Act (FOIA) as well as the rise of "interest representation" in the regulatory process.[9] These accountability regimes notably evinced a growing skepticism on the part of reformers about the public interestedness of agencies; these later efforts sought to prevent special interest influence and regulatory capture, even as they concurrently sought to expand agency authority. While concerns about agency authority and capture grew in the late 1970s and into the 1980s, driving a shift toward deregulation,[10] regulatory reform in the 1990s and early 2000s took on a different valence, seeking not to expand external forms of accountability through participation or transparency, but rather to invest in *internal* forms of rationalization and oversight of agency action, through the institutionalization of mechanisms for cost–benefit analysis and a deeper commitment to presidential control of administration.[11] These new measures absorbed "Chicago School" critiques of regulatory capture and market efficiency in an attempt to make regulation smarter, more rational, and more effective.[12]

These prior waves of reform have by and large tended to focus on the goal of rationalizing and improving governance; even the reforms of the 1970s and 1980s did not do much to address the background problems of disparate political power and influence. To the extent that measures enhancing expertise, insulation, transparency, and the like can address disparities of power,

---

[7] Pub. L. 79–404, 60 Stat. 237. See Mark Tushnet, "Administrative Law in the 1930s: The Supreme Court's Accommodation of Progressive Legal Theory," *Duke Law Journal* (2011): 1565–1637.

[8] American Bar Association (website), "Public Interest Law Community," www.americanbar.org/groups/public_services/public_interest_law1/.

[9] See Richard B. Stewart, "The Reformation of American Administrative Law," *Harvard Law Review* 88 (1975): 1667–1813, 1760–89; and Thomas Merrill, "Capture Theory and the Courts: 1967–1983," *Chicago-Kent Law Review* 72 (1997): 1039–1117, arguing that judicial review in the 1960s and 1970s worked to push agencies to expand representation and participation of stakeholder interests in shaping regulatory policies.

[10] See Jodi Short, "The Paranoid Style in Regulatory Reform," *Hastings Law Journal* 63 (2012): 633–94.

[11] See Elena Kagan, "Presidential Administration," *Harvard Law Review* 114 (2001): 2245–2385; Lawrence Lessig and Cass R. Sunstein, "The President and the Administration," *Columbia Law Review* 94 (1994): 1–123.

[12] Lawrence Lessig, "The New Chicago School," *Journal of Legal Studies* 27 (1998): 661–91, 665–72.

Civic Power

they do so by prioritizing a streamlined and conflict-free vision of "good governance."[13] The overarching focus here is to make governance more streamlined, more based on expertise, and more efficient. This vision of good governance animated approaches to the building of legal regimes for transparency, participation, and regulatory oversight. Each of these regimes has its benefits. But by doing relatively little to address deeper disparities of power, they fall short in terms of deepening democracy. Indeed, many of the standard frameworks for civil society participation in the administrative process are either not sufficiently powerful to fully balance rival forms of power and influence, or they are themselves easily co-opted by existing loci of political power, exacerbating rather than balancing power disparities.[14]

Consider for example, the conventional focus on transparency as a form of accountability. There is no question that transparency is essential to hold governmental authority accountable. However, what is often overlooked is how limited transparency regimes can be in relation to problems of power or more robust ideals of democratic inclusion. While transparency measures, notably the FOIA regime, have become touchstones for norms of transparency and accountability, the day-to-day operation of FOIA falls far short of these aspirations. FOIA itself is characterized by many exemptions, and use of the FOIA system tends to favor sophisticated industry and business interests.[15] Rather than facilitate inclusive decision-making, FOIA can often be a harmful distraction and imposition on regulators. Perhaps most perniciously, FOIA facilitates an ethos of distrust and skepticism toward government, rather than deepening norms that encourage more productive forms of engagement. In this light, FOIA is furthering the government as problem rhetoric of the deregulatory right, which has systematically pushed to discredit governance institutions. FOIA at times can reaffirm mistrust of government, instead of providing a window into its core operating functions.[16]

---

[13] For a longer critique of the good governance framework and regulatory reform, see Rahman, *Democracy against Domination*, especially chapters 5 and 7.

[14] Andrias offers a similar take on this argument in her "Separations of Wealth," 475–76.

[15] David Pozen, "Freedom of Information beyond the Freedom of Information Act," *University of Pennsylvania Law Review* 165 (2017): 1097–1158.

[16] For a recent critique of FOIA and its harmful implications, see Pozen, "Freedom of Information beyond the Freedom of Information Act," at 1101: "Given FOIA's many limitations and drawbacks, a forward-looking legislative approach must do more than refine the Act's request-driven strategy: it must look beyond the FOIA strategy altogether." Pozen continues his critique in "Transparency's Ideological Drift," *Yale Law Journal* 128 (2018): 100–65. See also Jameel Jaffer and Brett M. Kaufman, "A Resurgence of Secret Law," *Yale Law Journal Forum* 126 (2016): 242, examining the decline of the FOIA "working law" doctrine developed by the Supreme Court.

From Governance to Power – Rethinking Democracy Reform   119

A second conventional area of governance reform emphasizes participation through existing mechanisms, such as through public comments on proposed regulations or through advisory bodies. Indeed, on the federal level there are several blunt instruments deployed to engage citizens. But these offer less than compelling foundations for a more democratic and accountable form of policymaking. For example, the Administrative Procedure Act (APA) enables citizen input in rulemaking. However, even with fifty years of provisions in the APA on citizens' right to participate in regulatory processes, the reality is that very few non-elites participate.[17] Thus, while the administrative state already possesses a variety of mechanisms for participation, from notice-and-comment procedures to negotiated rulemaking to advisory committees and more,[18] the efficacy of these mechanisms and the degree to which they serve to counterbalance power disparities depend a great deal on presumptions about *who* makes use of these vehicles and *how* influential those uses actually are.

Several studies have highlighted that public comments on proposed regulations are often dominated by established and sophisticated business interests.[19] More recently, the advent of electronic rulemaking via online commenting platforms like Regulations.gov has enabled a mass flooding of comment dockets by a much wider range and quantity of commenters.[20] While this is a potentially positive development, there is still much work to be done both technologically and normatively to enable regulators to manage mass-comment dockets.[21] Scholars and administrators also express significant skepticism with regard to whether or to what degree such mass comments are in fact useful to or influential on rulemaking.[22]

A third key focal point of conventional approaches to good governance is an emphasis on rationality and expertise in policymaking. As with

[17]   See Noveck, *Smart Citizens, Smarter State*, 237, for her critique of tools such as the Federal Advisory Committee Act (FACA), the Paperwork Reduction Act (PRA), and the Administrative Procedure Act (APA).

[18]   Miriam Seifter, "Second-Order Participation," *UCLA Law Review* 63 (2016): 1300, 1308–10.

[19]   See Jason Webb Yackee and Susan Webb Yackee, "A Bias towards Business? Assessing Interest Group Influence on the U.S. Bureaucracy," *Journal of Politics* 68 (2006): 128–39.

[20]   For a discussion of this phenomenon, see Noveck, *Smart Citizens, Smarter State*; and Beth Simone Noveck, "The Electronic Revolution in Rulemaking," *Emory Law Journal* 53(2) (2004): 433–519.

[21]   For a discussion of new computational tools to assist in synthesizing mass comment dockets, see Michael Livermore, Vladimir Eidelman, and Brian Grom, "Computationally Assisted Regulatory Participation," *Notre Dame Law Review* 93 (2018): 977–1034.

[22]   See Cynthia Farina et al., "Rulemaking 2.0," *University of Miami Law Review* 65 (2011): 395, 477: "The true potential of Rulemaking 2.0 is unknowable at this point because e-rulemaking has not tried systematically to address the barriers of stakeholder unawareness, process ignorance, and rulemaking information overload."

120 *Civic Power*

transparency and participation, the problem here is not the concept of expertise itself, but rather the way in which it operates to narrow, rather than expand, the scope of governmental action – and how little it does to redress deeper disparities of political power and influence. Thus, a central feature of modern administrative governance is the legal and political pressure on agencies to justify their proposed regulations through appeals to expertise and cost–benefit analyses. Regulatory agencies face these incentives as a matter of administrative law, arising from judicial doctrine and the APA's own provision against "arbitrary [and] capricious" agency action.[23] But these requirements are easily susceptible to manipulation by business interests, who are able to deploy their greater resources to generate the kinds of studies and data that can be persuasive, creating a kind of epistemic or complexity capture.[24] Furthermore, the ethos of rationalizing government has often been leveraged to instantiate skepticism of government and its more normatively egalitarian and inclusionary aspirations.[25]

THE LIMITS OF "INNOVATING GOVERNMENT"

Recent decades have also witnessed a bipartisan move to "reinvent" how government works, in an effort to innovate new approaches to government policymaking.[26] This effort has involved public administration scholars, government officials, and politicians of both parties. Innovation is a nebulous term that can mean many different things. At times, the idea of reinventing government has taken its cue from the private sector, seeking to make government agencies more adaptive, responsive, and accountable. At other times, the focus has instead been on the possibilities afforded by new technologies. But, like earlier waves of reform – and in parallel to the power-neutral approach of civic tech described in Chapter 3, the reality is that efforts to bring innovation to government have rarely focused on building civic voice or expanding access to civic power.

One common approach has tended to emphasize a model of innovation drawn from private-sector for-profit businesses and to position these

---

[23] 5 U.S.C. § 706; see Jody Freeman and Adrian Vermeule, "*Massachusetts v. EPA*: From Politics to Expertise," *Supreme Court Review* 2 (2007): 51–110.

[24] See McCarty, "Complexity, Capacity, Capture," 99–123.

[25] See Rahman, *Democracy against Domination*, 42–44.

[26] The term took off especially after David Osborne and Ted Gaebler's *Reinventing Government: How the Entrepreneurial Spirit is Transforming the Public Sector* (Reading, MA: Addison-Wesley, 1992).

businesses as partners for governmental policymaking.[27] Starting in the 1980s, such new public management (NPM) concepts started to become more mainstream. In this approach, public managers are encouraged to steer not row, utilizing a range of tools from privatization to incentives to private sector-style management techniques to deliver better services to citizens as customers. This would help unburden public managers from bureaucracies so that they could be entrepreneurial and part of a new, leaner, and increasingly privatized government. But in practice the turn to the apparent efficiencies of private sector-style management has been less about making government better and more about accepting a more limited vision of what government is for – thus mainstreaming conservative attacks on government into a new management philosophy essentially premised on government's very dismantling.[28]

This turn to privatized government has cut across recent presidential administrations, both liberal and conservative. The Clinton administration embraced this ethos in its reinventing government movement and the National Performance Review to make government "work[] better and cost[] less."[29] David Osborne and Ted Gaebler's book, *Reinventing Government: How the Entrepreneurial Spirit is Transforming the Public Sector*, meanwhile, became a definitive text after it was published in 1992.[30] President George W. Bush created initiatives that focused on innovation and entrepreneurship.[31] The Obama administration continued the trend with a particular focus on digital technology.

During the Obama administration, leveraging private-sector expertise often took the form of bringing technologists into government. For example, the Presidential Innovation Fellows (PIF) program brought personnel with innovative skills into government.[32] In the aftermath of the fraught launch of the Healthcare.gov website, the Obama administration launched the United States Digital Service (USDS), a special technology office inside of the

---

[27] See Hollie Russon Gilman, "Government as Government, Not Business," *Stanford Social Innovation Review*, October 5, 2017, https://ssir.org/articles/entry/government_as_government_not_business.

[28] Michaels, *Constitutional Coup*, 103–17.

[29] Al Gore, *From Red Tape to Results: Creating a Government That Works Better and Costs Less; Executive Summary*, National Performance Review (Washington, DC: United States Government Printing Office, 1993).

[30] Osborne and Gaebler, *Reinventing Government.*

[31] "E-Government Act of 2002," 107th Cong., 2nd sess., *Congressional Record*, January 23, 2002, www.congress.gov/107/plaws/publ347/PLAW-107publ347.pdf.

[32] Presidential Innovation Fellows (website), home page, https://presidentialinnovationfellows.gov/.

government to help agencies with high-level priority policy areas.[33] The stated goal of USDS is to bring top private-sector talent, including designers, engineers, product managers, and digital policy experts, into the government to help transform and deliver critical digital services for American citizens.[34] Another late feature of the Obama administration's digital service delivery in the federal government was 18F, which sought to build internal digital services talent, as opposed to relying on external contractors. This fee-for-service digital consultancy launched in the spring of 2016, as part of a broader new unit of the General Services Administration (GSA) named Technology Transformation Services (TTS).[35] TTS housed 18F,[36] the Office of Citizen Services and Innovative Technologies, and the PIF program. In addition, the Social and Behavioral Sciences Team focused on using behavioral insights or what Richard Thaler and Cass Sunstein call "nudge" techniques for policymaking.[37] While each of these initiatives represents an important first step in making government more *efficient*, they were not institutionalized within a structure that also provided more *effective* opportunities for engaging diverse types of people in more collaborative governance.

More recently in March 2017, President Trump unveiled his Office of American Innovation, led by his son-in-law Jared Kushner, which seeks to apply business practices to the business of government.[38] The Trump Administration waited nearly 560 days, double the longest of any other modern president, to name a director of the understaffed Office of Science and Technology Policy.[39]

---

[33] Robinson Meyer, "The Secret Startup That Saved the Worst Website in America," *Atlantic*, July 9, 2015, www.theatlantic.com/technology/archive/2015/07/the-secret-startup-saved-healthcare-gov-the-worst-website-in-america/397784/.

[34] The U.S. Digital Service (website), home page, www.usds.gov/.

[35] U.S. General Services Administration (website), "Technology Transformation Services," www.gsa.gov/about-us/organization/federal-acquisition-service/technology-transformation-services.

[36] Jason Shueh, "The Case for 18F: Why Federal IT Procurement, Contracting Need to Change," *Government Technology*, July 12, 2016, www.govtech.com/data/The-Case-for-18F-Why-Federal-IT-Procurement-Contracting-Need-to-Change.html.

[37] See Executive Office of the President, National Science and Technology Council, *Social and Behavior Sciences Team: 2016 Annual Report* (Washington, DC: Office of Science and Technology Policy, September 2016), https://sbst.gov/download/2016%20SBST%20Annual%20Report.pdf; and Richard Thaler and Cass Sunstein, *Nudge: Improving Decisions about Health, Wealth, and Happiness* (New Haven, CT: Yale University Press, 2008).

[38] "Presidential Memorandum on the White House Office of American Innovation," White House, March 27, 2017, www.whitehouse.gov/the-press-office/2017/03/27/presidential-memorandum-white-house-office-american-innovation.

[39] David Malakoff, "Trump's Pick to Head White House Science Office Gets Good Reviews," *Science*, July 31, 2018, www.sciencemag.org/news/2018/07/trump-s-pick-head-white-house-science-office-gets-good-reviews.

On a day-to-day level, turns to privatization can take a number of different forms. Decentralization of government services can often mean their privatization: as resource-strapped localities and states have become increasingly responsible for policy implementation, they also devolved their responsibilities to private and non-private organizations.[40] This "hollow state" has led to new governance networks, including the interweaving of public and private hands.[41] Meanwhile, governmental bodies increasingly defer to private actors either in setting regulatory standards adopted into law by federal agencies or in some cases, even leaving such private actors to enforce their own codes of conduct through industry self-regulation. More explicit forms of privatization can arise when government outsources its key activities by contracting with private vendors and service providers or increasingly leaning on private sources of funding for public projects.[42]

There are a number of limitations with this approach to governmental reform. A customer service orientation sounds good but is often vague and misleading as an organizing concept.[43] At times NPM has involved a devotion to output metrics that can undermine regulatory discretion, incentivizing outputs over results.[44] Ultimately, the challenge with the citizen-as-consumer model is that it provides a shallow analysis of the roles and responsibilities of citizens. Being a member of a democracy is more nuanced than purchasing goods or chatting with your friends online. People expect things from government – and those things, like public utilities, disaster relief, clean drinking water, and universal social policies covering education, healthcare, and so on, are not always driven by a bottom line.

Furthermore, the delegation of ever more vital governmental functions to private actors supposedly in the name of efficiency makes accountability more difficult. The result of such outsourcing is a complex network of local

---

[40] H. Brinton Milward and Keith G. Provan describe this change as a move to a hollow state in their article, "Governing the Hollow State," *Journal of Public Administration Research and Theory* 10 (2000): 359–80, 360.

[41] Ibid. See also D. F. Kettl, "Managing Boundaries in American Administration: The Collaboration Imperative," in "Symposium on Collaborative Public Management," supplement, *Public Administration Review* 66, no. S1 (2007): 10–19; and D. F. Kettl, "The Job of Government: Interweaving Public Functions and Private Hands," *Public Administration Review* 75, no. 2 (2015): 219–29.

[42] Michaels, *Constitutional Coup*, 104–16.

[43] Donald F. Kettl, *Reinventing Government? Appraising the National Performance Review* (Washington, DC: Brookings Institution, 1994).

[44] John J. DiIulio, *Deregulating the Public Sector: Can Government Be Improved?* (Washington, DC: Brookings Institution, 2011); and Carolyn Heinrich, "Outcomes-Based Performance Management in the Public Sector: Implications for Government Accountability and Effectiveness," *Public Administration Review* 62 (2002): 712–25.

124 *Civic Power*

nonprofits, states, cities, and private-sector organizations responsible for governance. Without government responsible for centralized policy outcomes, who precisely is held accountable? This problem of "fuzzy boundaries" undermines, rather than enhances, democratic values.[45] Private actors are not subject to the statutory and constitutional limits that structure governmental action and make government accountable – including public commenting and transparency requirements. Privatization is thus essentially a shift in *power*, away from formal democratic processes to the whims of private parties.[46]

THE RISE – AND LIMITS – OF THE "CIVIC TECH" MOVEMENT

These tensions around the ideas of privatization and innovation are exacerbated in the modern boom of interest in "civic tech." With the revolution in online, internet-based software and the proliferation of big data and sophisticated algorithms in the technology sector, the push to innovate government has increasingly centered not on privatization per se, but rather on technology. Like the NPM wave, civic tech reformers have sought to emulate private-sector practices in data integration, analysis, and optimization as a way to streamline government and make it more efficient. And as in earlier waves of reform, civic tech reformers saw themselves as assuring more public transparency and enhancing participation – this time by publishing data and tracking governmental actions along public metrics and through the magic of online portals connecting the state and its citizens. But as described in Chapters 1 and 3 above, this application of civic tech ideals to bureaucracy reform shares the presumptions and limitations of "good governance" approaches to reform noted earlier: by focusing on optimizing and rationalizing government, rather than redressing deeper disparities of power, these approaches have tended to accomplish less than they promise.

Defining Civic Tech

There is a threshold difficulty to assessing the democratizing impact of civic tech: there are so many definitions of civic tech with disparate metrics and indicators and the sector is so diverse and diffuse, that it can be difficult to even

---

[45] For more on the fuzzy boundary problem, see H. Brinton Milward et al., "Managing the Hollow State" (lecture, American Political Science Association Annual Meeting, 1991).
[46] Michaels, *Constitutional Coup*, 126–30.

define the scope of the field.[47] Some see civic tech as synonymous with government technology, while others argue that the term applies more narrowly, restricted to technologies that strengthen the connection between the public and the government.[48] Yet others debate about whether for-profit entities such as Airbnb or Waze should be classified as civic tech.[49] For many civic tech innovators, the central focus of the field is to develop "technology that enables greater participation in government or otherwise assists government in delivering citizen services and strengthening ties with the public" – in a view that promotes civic tech as a salve for democracy's woes.[50] In 2016, Micah L. Sifry, Matt Stempeck, and Erin Simpson generated an open source civic technology field guide with the following definition: "Civic Tech is the use of technology for public good."[51] As mySociety, a prominent civic tech organization, explained: "Civic technology tools, rather than representing citizens at the very end of a policy development process, provide motivation to public bodies to develop better policies and services in concert with citizens throughout the legislative, policy and service delivery cycle."[52]

In the words of Candace Faber, a civic technology advocate from Seattle, "[T]he reason civic tech exists is because, so far, technology has not fulfilled its promise to make society more equitable."[53] Reflecting the zeitgeist of the times, Faber was appointed the City of Seattle's first ever Civic Technology Advocate to serve as a bridge between city hall, technologists, and civic leaders.[54] Buoyed by leaders like Faber, civic technology has boomed as a field, backed by both philanthropic funds from foundations like Ford Foundation, Mozilla Foundation, Open Society Foundation, Knight

---

[47] David Tannenwald and Hollie Russon Gilman, *A 21st Century Town Hall?* (Washington, DC: New America, July 27, 2017), www.newamerica.org/oti/policy-papers/21st-century-town-hall/.

[48] Ibid., 4.

[49] See Nathaniel Heller, "The Sharing Economy Is Not Civic Tech," *Global Integrity* (blog), www.globalintegrity.org/2013/12/the-sharing-economy-is-not-civic-tech/.

[50] Colin Wood, "What Is Civic Tech?" *Government Technology*, August 16, 2016, www.govtech.com/civic/What-is-Civic-Tech.html.

[51] See Erhardt Graeff, "Evaluating Civic Technology Design for Civic Empowerment" (PhD diss., MIT, June 2018); and Micah L. Sifry, Matt Stempeck, and Erin Simpson, "Civic Tech Field Guide" (Google sheet, 2016), https://docs.google.com/spreadsheets/d/1FzmvVAKOOFdixCs7oz88cz9g1fFPHDlg0AHgHCwhf4A/edit#gid=895533063, See "The Civic Tech Timeline: 1994–2018," https://civictech.guide/timeline/.

[52] Rebecca Rumbul and Emily Shaw, *Civic Tech Cities* (London: mySociety, May 16, 2017), 13, www.mysociety.org/files/2017/05/civic-tech-cities.pdf. This report was funded by Microsoft.

[53] Wood, "What Is Civic Tech?"

[54] Amber Cortes, "Person of Interest: Candace Faber, Civic Technology Advocate for the City of Seattle," *The Stranger*, February 1, 2017, www.thestranger.com/features/2017/02/01/24853520/person-of-interest-candace-faber.

Foundation, Bloomberg Philanthropies, and the Omidyar Network (including Luminate) as well as by direct private investment by and through partnerships with technology companies including Microsoft and Google.[55] By some estimates (which are themselves fraught by definitional disagreements), the field grew at an annual rate of 23 percent from 2008 through 2012, while from 2013 to 2015, actions and affiliations involving civic technology rose by 39 percent and 107 percent, respectively.[56] Financial support for civic technology has steadily risen, for example from $225 million in 2013 to $493 million in 2015, according to the Omidyar Network.[57] In its analysis, the Omidyar Network outlined three broad categories of civic tech including citizen to citizen technologies, citizen to government technologies, and government technologies.[58] In 2013, the Knight Foundation released a report showing that the number of civic tech organizations had grown 23 percent in 2008, with a total investment of more than $431 million.[59]

Meanwhile, governments have increased their expenditures on information technology (IT); President Trump's 2018 budget includes roughly $45.6 billion in civilian federal IT.[60] The IT boom has in part fueled the rise of new public-sector roles including chief information officers, chief technology officers, chief innovation officers, and chief data officers, in federal, state, and local government agencies. For example, companies working on purely government technology, or "gov tech," as opposed to the broader realm of civic tech, received $185 million in fresh funding in 2016 and a total of $949 million cumulatively.[61]

Civic technology also has expanded its geographic reach, establishing a significant presence not only in the federal government and major American metropolises such as San Francisco and New York City, but

[55] Microsoft funding for research at organizations like mySociety is one example of this.

[56] Tannenwald and Gilman, *21st Century Town Hall?*, 4.

[57] *Engines of Change: What Civic Tech Can Learn from Social Movements* (Washington, DC: Omidyar Network, 2016), 7, www.omidyar.com/sites/default/files/file_archive/Pdfs/Engines%25200f%2520Change%2520-%2520Final.pdf. Omidyar provided $870 million in venture capital funding for civic projects between 2013 and 2015 (13).

[58] See Heller, "Sharing Economy Is Not Civic Tech."

[59] Mayur Patel et al., *The Emergence of Civic Tech: Investments in a Growing Field* (Miami, FL: Knight Foundation, December 2013), www.knightfoundation.org/media/uploads/publication_pdfs/knight-civic-tech.pdf.

[60] Aaron Boyd, "Trump Budget Calls for Slight Increase in IT Spending," *Nextgov*, February 12, 2018, www.nextgov.com/cio-briefing/2018/02/trump-budget-calls-slight-increase-it-spending/145914/.

[61] See *Scaling Civic Tech: Paths to a Sustainable Future* (Miami, FL: Knight Foundation / Rita Allan Foundation, October 31, 2017), https://knightfoundation.org/reports/scaling-civic-tech; and "GovTech 100: 2018," *Government Technology*, www.govtech.com/100/.

From Governance to Power – Rethinking Democracy Reform   127

also smaller cities, including Virginia Beach and Kansas City.[62] Since 2011, at least fifteen cities, including Chicago, Boston, Louisville, Los Angeles, and Nashville, hired chief data officers to manage and propel data usage, with the majority of the new positions being appointed in the last four years.[63] In 2010, Colorado became the first state to appoint a chief data officer.[64]

Civic tech skeptics have tended to question the field's true potential to transform governance for the public good. This is in part because the field remains nascent, which makes it difficult to gauge impact.[65] In addition, critics lament that civic technology lacks a "shared identity."[66] As Sifry – the cofounder of Civic Hall, a physical meeting space for civic tech innovators in New York City, and the founder of Personal Democracy Forum, a central civic tech and democracy reform convention[67] – put it in 2014, "It's not enough to assume that, ... we know good civic tech when we see it. And if we can't say why something is good (or even great), how can we know what to design for? Indeed, how do we even know if we're after the same design goals?"[68]

In our view, the central problem of the civic tech movement has been that, like previous efforts to rationalize and streamline government, its efforts have fallen short precisely because they bracket or ignore questions of power. These limitations are apparent in the three major areas where civic tech reforms have been most prevalent: (1) in integrating advanced data management techniques to streamline the inner workings of government agencies; (2) in creating more open access to governmental data and greater transparency; and (3) in expanding public participation in

---

[62] Zack Quaintance, "What's New in Civic Tech: Bloomberg's What Works Cities Honors Best at Using Data to Improve Residents' Lives," *Government Technology*, January 25, 2018, www.govtech.com/civic/Whats-New-in-Civic-Tech-Bloombergs-What-Works-Cities-Honors-Best-at-Using-Data-to-Improve-Residents-Lives.html.

[63] Jane Wiseman, *Lessons from Leading CDOs: A Framework for Better Civic Analytics* (Cambridge, MA: Ash Center for Democratic Governance and Innovation, Harvard Kennedy School, January 2017), 26–27, https://ash.harvard.edu/files/ash/files/leasons_from_leading_cdos.pdf.

[64] Ibid., 4; and Jake Williams, "Colorado Appoints New Chief Data Officer," StateScoop (website), July 16, 2015, https://statescoop.com/colorado-appoints-new-chief-data-officer/.

[65] Wood, "What Is Civic Tech?"

[66] "Engines of Change," 26–27.

[67] Personal Democracy Forum 2018, "How We Make Good" (meeting home page, New York Law School, June 7–8, 2018), www.pdf-18.com/.

[68] Micah L. Sifry, "Civic Tech and Engagement: In Search of a Common Language," *Tech President* (blog), September 5, 2014, http://techpresident.com/news/25261/civic-tech-and-engagement-search-common-language.

128   *Civic Power*

policymaking through the use of online platforms. Within each of these areas, it is essential that technology is used to supplement, not replace, in-person engagement.

Civic Tech in Action

The first major focus of the civic tech movement was on optimizing the use of government data and making it more open to the public. Governmental entities both produce and collect a vast amount of data. That data has always been a valuable foundation for major public and private uses; for example, the federal government's decision to release geospatial data collected by the National Oceanic and Atmospheric Administration (NOAA) led to a $90 billion industry ranging from precision crop farming to location-based apps such as Google Maps and Waze.[69] These data, in turn, created the modern weather industry.[70] The cornerstone argument underlying the modern push for open data and open government is that by releasing and integrating previously locked or siloed data sets, government can unleash more efficient public services and provide the foundation for whole new forms of public- and private-sector innovation.

Making data sharable, usable, and accessible is no small feat. For example, data "locked" in older portable document formats (PDFs) may not be easily readable by machines. There are often challenges of interoperability between data sets even within departments as well as competing ideas of *how* data should be used. Non-interoperable systems create decentralized standards, methods, and descriptions of data. Data silos emerge in the absence of a common language to describe, interpret, and use data collaboratively within organizations and across sectors. Individuals face harsh penalties for sharing data incorrectly, and organizations lack strong data trust agreements, removing incentives for effective collaboration to take place. Even if data is accessible to policymakers, it is rarely made available to the lay public in a transparent and actionable way.

In 2013, the Obama administration released Executive Order 13642, setting a new data standard: federal government information should be open and machine-readable by default.[71] There are currently over 300,000 data sets

---

[69] Tim Cashman, "The Economic Impact of Open Data," Socrata (website), February 27, 2014, https://socrata.com/blog/economic-impact-open-data/.

[70] Ibid.

[71] "Making Open and Machine Readable the New Default for Government Information," Exec. Order No. 13642, 78 Fed. Reg. 28111 (May 14, 2013; signed May 9, 2013).

available on Data.gov.[72] As the order put it, "Openness in government strengthens our democracy, promotes the delivery of efficient and effective services to the public, and contributes to economic growth."[73] Cities around the country also have adopted their own open-data standards.[74] The launch of federal data portals like Data.gov or Cloud.gov, combined with the development of new application program interfaces (APIs), theoretically makes that data far more usable by both public and private actors by setting data-usage norms and more accessible interfaces.

A second major focal point for civic tech reformers has been to enhance participation. Indeed, many civic tech tools are aimed at optimizing the current relationship between citizens and the state. For example, issue-reporting platforms such as SeeClickFix have enhanced the ability of residents to report and resolve nonemergency infrastructure defects, such as potholes, by making 311 requests on their smartphones. Other tools also seek citizen input to identify key governance issues that perpetually go unaddressed, with petition-gathering platforms and electronic town halls as paradigmatic examples of such efforts.

The SeeClickFix platform is free for users and charges municipalities for residents' reports – as of 2017, it worked with over 300 local governments globally and had over 1 million users.[75] As of September 2018, the site identified over 4 million issues as having been resolved.[76] As a result of the platform, mid-tier and small municipalities have increased capacity to address public concerns: it is not just bigger, more resourced cities that can afford the tool.[77] One of its functionalities is alerting a resident if someone else makes a submission in his or her community, with the goal of deepening community engagement. Although Erhardt Graeff's study of the relationship between participation in SeeClickFix and a community's political efficacy showed no boosting effect,[78] such work offers a potential future area of research for civic technology, especially because the application of digital technology to local governance is expanding. Boston's StreetBump provides an interesting

---

[72] See Data.gov, "Datasets Published per Month," www.data.gov/metric/federalagency/dataset-published-per-month.

[73] Exec. Order No. 13642.

[74] Meta S. Brown, "City Governments Making Public Data Easier to Get: 90 Municipal Open Data Portals," *Forbes*, April 29, 2018, www.forbes.com/sites/metabrown/2018/04/29/city-governments-making-public-data-easier-to-get-90-municipal-open-data-portals/.

[75] "SeeClickFix Year in Review 2017," Fixer Stories (blog), SeeClickFix, January 2, 2018, https://blog.seeclickfix.com/seeclickfix-year-in-review-2017-f95f78619d30.

[76] SeeClickFix (website), home page, https://seeclickfix.com/.

[77] SeeClickFix (website), "About SeeClickFix," https://seeclickfix.com/pages/about.html.

[78] Graeff, "Evaluating Civic Technology Design."

130   *Civic Power*

contrast; instead of soliciting subjective reports from citizens, it uses sensors and networked devices – in short, innovations connected to Internet of Things (IoT) technology – to recognize when someone passes over a pothole. The integration of IoT technology into public services raises many normative questions surrounding privacy, vulnerability to security risks, and the further submergence of "visible" effects of government when "invisible" sensors are helping deploy service delivery. One argument behind IoT is that it will help provide fairer services, insulated from power disparities and enhance account-ability. While we lack the space to engage with this argument, we note the many challenges to the future of IoT, including ensuring public-sector capa-city, training, and resources to ensure that the private sector does not control service provision and people's data. In the early stages of IoT deployment there is the risk of further acerbating disparities in municipalities as some cities have the investment to become "smart" while no cities want to become "stupid."[79]

Initiatives for electronic town halls, meanwhile, work to integrate digital tools into the traditional town hall meeting paradigm. Take for example the platform Peak Democracy, which offers a tool called an "open town hall" to city governments, which was acquired by Open Gov.[80] Another example of digital tools being deployed to try to supplement but not upend an existing process is the Obama administration's signature e-petitions platform "We the People."[81] Petitions are a popular form of online engagement. For example, Change.org is a petition site that enables anyone worldwide to create and write a petition.[82] More than 177 million people across 196 countries have used the platform.[83] "We the People" was based on petitions websites such as Change .org and the similar Downing Street E-petitions for Tony Blair's government; its goal was to make good on the promise of a more open and accountable federal government.[84] In December, 2016 the Obama administration reported

---

[79] Homi Kharas and Jaana Remes, "Can Smart Cities Be Equitable?" Brookings (website), June 11, 2018, www.brookings.edu/opinions/can-smart-cities-be-equitable/.

[80] "OpenGov Acquires Citizen Engagement Leader Peak Democracy," Cision PR Newswire, October 20, 2017, www.prnewswire.com/news-releases/opengov-acquires-citizen-engagement -leader-peak-democracy-300540434.html.

[81] "We the People," White House, https://petitions.whitehouse.gov/.

[82] See also Jonathan Mellon et al., *Gender and Political Mobilization Online: Participation and Policy Success on a Global Petitioning Platform*, Ash Center Occasional Paper (Cambridge, MA: Harvard Kennedy School, July 2017), https://ash.harvard.edu/links/gender-and-political-mobilization-online-participation-and-policy-success-global.

[83] Change.org reports on its main page that over 250 million people have taken action through its platform as of September 2018.

[84] Open Government Partnership (website), "01.1A Launch 'We the People,'" www.opengovpartner ship.org/commitment/o11a-launch-we-people.

that "We the People" had over 29 million users, 40 million total signatures, and 480,793 petitions.[85]

For some reformers, like Clay Shirky in his account *Here Comes Everybody*, the main promise of digital tools and civic technology was their potential for producing data that could be leveraged to enhance governance.[86] One of the implied promises of civic tech was that digital interfaces would enable citizens to serve as coproducers to work directly with institutions to solve public challenges. A difficulty with this approach is that public problems often require resources, time, capital, and power – things that everyday people simply do not have. Furthermore, "coproduction" is not necessarily the same thing as "equal power" over decisions. Indeed, as these civic tech tools have been put in place, the reality is that, in contrast to Shirky's account, everyone may *not* be coming; well-resourced elites, however, do. For example, the federal government launched the website Recovery.gov to make public and transparent most of the data on the allocation, pursuant to the American Recovery and Reinvestment Act (Recovery Act), of more than $275 billion in federal contracts, grants, and loans.[87] Part of the rationale behind the project was that armchair citizens would crunch the numbers, be engaged, and hold the government to account.[88] In reality, it was NGOs, journalists, and other elites who had the capacity, resources, and wherewithal to dissect and analyze the disclosed materials.[89] Perhaps civic tech is opening the aperture of what defines political elites – such that the term can no longer be confined to policymakers, legal figures, and members of academia – but broadening the composition of elites is not true democratizing. But even if a wider group of individuals participate, it is not clear that such access to information would change in any meaningful way the structural disparities of power and influence that separate regular citizens from well-connected advocacy groups.

The "We the People" online petition platform provides another instructive warning. "We the People" continually raised its threshold for receiving a response.[90] When it was launched, the platform required 5,000 signatures

---

[85] Jason Goldman, "What Happens Next for We the People," *Medium*, December 21, 2016, https://medium.com/@Goldman44/what-happens-next-for-we-the-people-b55da1309d2c.

[86] Shirky, *Here Comes Everybody*, 12.

[87] This website is no longer active, however.

[88] Francisca M. Rojas, *Recovery Act Transparency: Learning from States' Experience*, Assessing the Recovery Act Series (Washington, DC: IBM Center for the Business of Government, 2012), 11, www.businessofgovernment.org/sites/default/files/Recovery%20Act%20Transparenc y.pdf.

[89] Ibid.

[90] Graeff, "Evaluating Civic Technology Design," 19–24.

before triggering an official response from Obama administration officials.[91] Rather than responding to the petitions themselves, the administration increased the threshold for response first to 25,000 signatures and then 100,000 signatures within thirty days.[92] Critiques ensued, including concerns that only those with social media savvy would meet the petition threshold.[93] The majority of petitions do not cross the threshold for a response, and even the ones that do, receive a cursory answer that has been sanitized for a wide audience.

But as the platform grew in popularity many petitions quickly crossed that threshold – and did so raising issues that may have been a departure from what the creators envisioned. For example, the famous "Death Star" petition tried to secure the resources to begin construction of the Death Star from the movie *Star Wars*.[94] Other petition topics included calling for a state animal to be a Pokémon character, wanting Beyoncé barred from singing the national anthem at President Obama's inauguration, and requesting a reality TV series with Vice President Biden.[95] David Karpf, when arguing that "We the People" lacked enough independence from the administration to truly have an impact on it, noted that "vibrant online publics have to be curated and supported."[96]

In 2015, the Obama administration made changes to integrate "We the People" with Change.org and to make data about the site publicly available on GitHub, in an effort to demonstrate how petitions were transferred to an inter-agency task force, leading thence to new law.[97] Responding to criticism that petitions were not answered in a timely fashion, the administration promised to answer them within sixty days.[98] It made changes to the *mechanics* of engagement via "We the People" but such changes were merely cosmetic

---

[91] Dave Karpf, "How the White House's We the People E-Petition Site Became a Virtual Ghost-Town," *TechPresident* (blog), June 20, 2014, http://techpresident.com/news/25144/how-white-houses-we-people-e-petition-site-became-virtual-ghost-town.

[92] Ibid.

[93] Nick Judd, "With 'We the People,' White House Promises to Go E-To-The People," *TechPresident* (blog), September 1, 2011, http://techpresident.com/blog-entry/we-people-white-house-promises-go-e-people.

[94] Asawin Suebasaeng, "'My God, What Have We Done?' White House Staffers React to Insane Online Petitions," *Mother Jones*, January 18, 2013, www.motherjones.com/politics/2013/01/we-the-people-white-house-petitions-obama-administration/.

[95] Ibid.

[96] Karpf, "How the White House's We the People E-Petition Site Became a Virtual Ghost-Town."

[97] "WhiteHouse/petitions," GitHub, https://github.com/WhiteHouse/petitions; and Alexander Howard, "White House Responds to Remaining 'We The People' E-Petitions," *Huffington Post*, July 28, 2015, www.huffingtonpost.com/entry/white-house-clears-the-backlog-of-we-the-people-epetitions_us_55b788dde4b0074ba5a6165a.

[98] Howard, "White House Responds."

From Governance to Power – Rethinking Democracy Reform 133

and did not mitigate the core challenge as to what the platform could deliver *substantively*: the structure of "We the People" still did not seek to genuinely empower people in any fundamental way. As with the initial promise of open data, this online platform did provide a new mode of participation, yet it did little to change the underlying dynamics of power and who decides governmental policy.

Furthermore, these initiatives have been left at the mercy of the executive branch itself. After closing and reopening the platform, the Trump administration has demonstrated the true weaknesses of a government-run e-petitions website.[99] The "We the People" platform did not build in any countervailing checks and balances of its performance to external organizations. Even though under the Obama administration there was an open data API, that open data itself cannot hold government to account for either answering petitions or changing outcomes. Thus, the site has been manipulated by the Trump administration. While selectively providing generic answers to citizens on some petitions – and not adhering to the prior petition threshold rules – the Trump administration has pushed the full limits of this initiative.[100] "We the People" ultimately has little external power to generate incentives to put pressure on presidential administrations.

More broadly, the deployment of civic tech has not necessarily created new opportunities for previously marginalized communities, tending instead to favor participation by predominantly male, white, and well-resourced constituencies.[101] As Tina Nabatchi and Matt Leighninger describe:

> The "civic technologists" who have pioneered most of the new online forms of thin participation have repeated some of the same mistakes made by the inventors of face-to-face deliberative processes, producing innovative apps and tools that often falter because they are not anchored in a larger plan or infrastructure for participation.[102]

Any efforts by public administrators to deploy digital tools must acknowledge these potential biases and address questions surrounding digital access, literacy, and equity. It is critical that these projects be approached in ways that ensure they will be inclusive and community driven. The underlying problem here is that civic tech has yet to innovate credibly on the core problem of disparities of political power. Tools for optimizing current processes create

---

[99] Rosenberg, "White House Takes Down."
[100] Ibid.
[101] Rebecca Rumbul, *Who Benefits from Civic Technology?* (London: mySociety, 2015), https://research.mysociety.org/publications/who-benefits-from-civic-technology.
[102] Nabatchi and Leighninger, *Public Participation*, 320.

134 *Civic Power*

little feedback or accountability mechanisms. Without teeth, these tools create few accountability structures to produce new outcomes.

GOVERNANCE REFORM AS POWER SHIFTING: AN ALTERNATIVE TRADITION

Enhancing administrative procedures or deploying technologies that facilitate transparency and participation are not in and of themselves bad approaches to governance, but, as we have seen, they do relatively little to create genuine shifts in political power. Their overarching impact instead lies, at best, in making government a more "efficient" deliverer of services to "citizen-consumers." But there is a real need for institutions that expand citizens' political *agency*, their ability to exercise political influence, and their power over matters of public consequence. What would a governance reform agenda look like if it actually focused on such power shifting and power building?

Indeed, there is a more optimistic and potentially more democratic version of democracy reform, one committed to engaging stakeholders in collaborative, deliberative, democratic decision-making. In the realm of public administration, this has included scholarship that pushes beyond the concepts invoked by the reinventing government movement toward methods of "new governance" including terms such as new public management, new public service, collaborative governance, networked governance, and public engagement.[103] Several scholars focus on the need to leverage citizen expertise in the process of governance – and on the opportunity to thereby make citizens into coproducers of decision-making.[104] In this conception, citizens are able to move beyond their role as clients, voters, or customers to become more active problem-solvers and cocreators of policy.[105] Relying on citizen expertise fits into deliberative norms for participation, and it can build government trust in

---

[103] Lester M. Salamon, *The Tools of Government: A Guide to the New Governance* (New York: Oxford University Press, 2002); Nabatchi, "Addressing the Citizenship and Democratic Deficits," 376–99; John M. Bryson, Barbara C. Crosby, and Laura Bloomberg, "Public Value Governance: Moving beyond Traditional Public Administration and the New Public Management," *Public Administration Review* 74, no. 4 (2014): 445–56; and Janet V. Denhardt and Robert B. Denhardt, *The New Public Service: Serving, Not Steering*, 3rd ed. (New York: Routledge, 2015).

[104] Carmen Sirianni, *Investing in Democracy: Engaging Citizens in Collaborative Governance* (Washington, DC: Brookings Institution, 2009).

[105] Kettl, "The Job of Government"; Noveck, *Smart Citizens, Smarter State*; Nabatchi, "Addressing the Citizenship and Democratic Deficits"; Nabatchi, "Putting the 'Public' Back in Public Values Research"; and Briggs, *Democracy as Problem Solving*.

citizens.[106] The literature on collaborative governance focuses on types of institutional arrangements designed to engage citizens in decision-making. Collaborative governance at its core "aims to empower, enlighten, and engage citizens in the process of self-government."[107] A key characteristic of collaborative governance is that it ensures that diverse stakeholders engage in a "collective decision-making process that is formal, consensus-oriented, and deliberative and that aims to make or implement public policy or manage public programs or assets."[108]

Certainly, there is potential for improving accountability and responsiveness by implementing collaborative and new governance frameworks more widely. As Robert Agranoff has argued, despite the proliferation of these ideas, the vast majority of public managers still spend their time working within conventional bureaucratic processes.[109] Furthermore, there is a real question about whether and to what extent such collaborative processes actually alter background disparities of power. In the emphasis on collaboration, consensus, and problem-solving, there is a risk that these collaborative governance frameworks may downplay the realities of power and the need to address those disparities.[110] Indeed, as Caroline W. Lee has shown, the rise of an industry of deliberative democracy and public engagement professionals creates a veneer of civic engagement and enhanced responsibility for citizens without radically changing either the resource constraints on government or the existing disparities of power that shape policymaking.[111] Lee argues that the "public engagement industry" is fueling a toxic combination of high-production, one-off events that leave citizens feeling hollow, frustrated, and ultimately disaffected from civic life – particularly in the face of pressing and urgent concerns in an era of economic upheaval.[112]

Fully implementing a participatory vision of governance, however, requires a more radical transformation of existing bureaucratic institutions, processes, cultures, and politics. The scholarship on new governance has not fully

---

[106] See Kaifeng Yang, "Public Administrators' Trust in Citizens: A Missing Link in Citizen Involvement Efforts," *Public Administration Review* 65, no. 3 (2005): 273–85.

[107] Carmen Sirianni, "Can a Federal Regulator Become a Civic Enabler? Watersheds at the U.S. Environmental Protection Agency," *National Civic Review* 95, no. 3 (Autumn (Fall) 2006): 17–34, 39.

[108] Ansell and Gash, "Collaborative Governance," 544.

[109] Robert Agranoff, "Inside Collaborative Networks: Ten Lessons for Public Managers," *Public Administration Review* 66 (2006): 56–65.

[110] See Rahman, *Democracy against Domination*, 107–08.

[111] Caroline W. Lee, *Do-It-Yourself Democracy: The Rise of the Public Engagement Industry* (New York: Oxford University Press, 2015), 27–28.

[112] Ibid.

136 *Civic Power*

grappled with this. As Tina Nabatchi argues, further research is needed on the "democratic implications of networked governance, how the structures and patterns of new governance affect the balance of bureaucratic and democratic ethos, and how this balance affects, both positively and negatively, the citizenship and democratic deficits."[113]

There has been scholarly attention to networks for public management but not enough research into how networked government impacts practice – who is responsible for what.[114]

What is needed, then, is a look at what a truly power-shifting approach to governance and policymaking requires. The rest of this chapter – and the following two chapters – picks up this charge. The emphasis on neutral procedure, privatization, and technology are not the only traditions of governance reform in American politics. Indeed, we often overlook a much more radical tradition where grassroots reformers have sought to reshape governance institutions, specifically with the purpose of creating more durable levers of power. What is particularly striking about these alternative approaches to governance reform is how they leverage many of the similar tools described above – for example, transparency, participation, information, and technology – in ways that actually *shift* political power, rather than accepting or legitimizing power disparities.

Power Shifting in the Federal Administrative State

Consider some examples from the history of federal governance reform. In the 1940s, even at the peak of top-down wartime administrative planning, the emerging consumer rights movement used wartime administrative price setting of consumer goods to spark organizing, eventually shaping the structure and operation of the Office of Price Administration (OPA) itself.[115] This is an example of what historian Meg Jacobs calls "build[ing] the state from the bottom up": the OPA was formed out of a dynamic interplay between grassroots consumer movement activists on the one hand, and policymakers on the other.[116]

---

[113] Nabatchi, "Addressing the Citizenship and Democratic Deficits," 390.

[114] Laurence J. O'Toole, Jr., "The Implications for Democracy in a Networked Bureaucratic World," *Journal of Public Administration Research and Theory* 7 (1997): 443–59.

[115] Meg Jacobs, "'How about Some Meat?' The Office of Price Administration, Consumption Politics, and State Building from the Bottom Up, 1941–1946," *Journal of American History* 84, no. 3 (1997): 910–41, 931.

[116] Ibid., 918.

From Governance to Power – Rethinking Democracy Reform   137

Similarly, the formation of a federal welfare bureaucracy in the 1930s and 1940s created policymaking spaces wherein movements representing marginalized constituencies from poor people to Native Americans could navigate in search of levers of influence, playing some offices off of others to try to shift the implementation of poverty programs in a more equitable direction.[117] As historian Karen Tani argues, the shift to a modern regime of welfare rights arose out of this negotiation between creative bureaucrats within the Social Security Administration and movements from below demanding greater procedural protections and more equitable administration of poverty laws.[118] To the extent that these demands were successful, such success depended not just on the movement organizing of civil society groups, but also on their ability to interface with the bureaucracy, and the presence of creative, responsive bureaucrats who were socialized into administering welfare programs through an entitlement and rights mentality rather than through a punitive, charity-based mentality.[119]

The story of equal access to Medicare is similar. In the early days of the Medicare program, there was a very real likelihood that the program would be administered in racially discriminatory ways, or at least in ways that were blind to the racial disparities of public health facilities, like hospitals, that were still shaped by the realities of Jim Crow segregation. By 1966, however, the federal bureaucracy administering Medicare had shifted its position dramatically, declaring that it would enforce civil rights requirements of desegregation and antidiscrimination by conditioning Medicare grants on the racial integration of hospitals. The government created an Office of Equal Health Opportunity and even began training grassroots organizers, many of them veterans of the civil rights movement, as inspectors for this new regime.[120] This policy shift arose out of sustained bargaining between civil rights movement organizations like the National Association for the Advancement of Colored People (NAACP), the Southern Christian Leadership Conference (SCLC), the Student Nonviolent Coordinating Committee (SNCC), and the Congress

---

[117] Karen M. Tani, "States' Rights, Welfare Rights, and the Indian Problem: Negotiating Citizenship and Sovereignty, 1933–1954," *Law and History Review* 331, no. 1 (February 2015): 1–40.

[118] Ibid.

[119] Karen M. Tani, "Welfare and Rights Before the Movement: Rights as a Language of the State," *Yale Law Journal* 122, no. 2 (November 2012): 314–521.

[120] CMS.gov (website), "Office of Equal Opportunity and Civil Rights," last modified September 5, 2018, www.cms.gov/About-CMS/Agency-Information/CMSLeadership/Office_OEOCR.html.

138   *Civic Power*

of Racial Equality (CORE), and bureaucratic entrepreneurs within the Department of Health, Education, and Welfare.[121]

What these examples highlight is the following: even well-organized movements that have built sustained membership and organizational power along the lines discussed in Chapters 2 and 3 face uphill battles in trying to exercise political influence, but creative institutional design and government reform, along with the presence of favorable and responsive individuals *within* policy-making bodies, can create a radically different balance of power. With favorable counterparts in government, and with institutions designed to facilitate real engagement with movements providing actual levers of influence on policy design and implementation, governmental bodies can play a major role in balancing disparities of political power.

Power-Shifting Institutional Design at the Local Level

These are brief examples of what productive power-shifting relationships between grassroots movements and government bodies can look like. This alternative approach to governance reform, emphasizing shifts in power, need not be limited to the federal level. Local administration exhibits similar dynamics: it is not only an arena where power can be exercised and contested – but also a domain where existing power disparities tend to reassert themselves with troubling ease.

Consider, as intertwined examples, the welfare rights movement of the 1960s and 1970s and the local activism aspect of the War on Poverty. Though often dismissed as failures, these efforts involved a number of attempts to create very real avenues for empowering African Americans, the urban poor, and other minority groups. The Economic Opportunity Act of 1964 (EOA) developed new programs to tackle poverty through job training, work-study, and access to legal services.[122] But the most radical innovations of the War on Poverty lay in experiments with policies and institutions to mobilize community groups themselves as a political force to hold the bureaucracy accountable to its poverty-reduction mandate. The EOA provided funding for community organizing; created local boards consisting of local government officials and representatives from business, local community

---

[121] David Barton Smith, *The Power to Heal: Civil Rights, Medicare, and the Struggle to Transform America's Health Care System* (Nashville, TN: Vanderbilt University Press, 2016); see also Vann R. Newkirk II, "The Fight for Health Care Has Always Been about Civil Rights," *Atlantic*, June 27, 2017, www.theatlantic.com/politics/archive/2017/06/the-fight-for-health-care-is-really-all-about-civil-rights/531855/.

[122] Pub. L. 88–452.

groups, and minority and low-income stakeholders; and involved community organizations in implementing poverty-reduction programs such as training centers and legal services clinics.

For advocates of this "maximum feasible participation" approach, power was a central animating concept.[123] These policymakers saw poverty as a problem of political disempowerment, not just of insufficient income. Therefore, the way to combat poverty was to empower poor people with a direct voice in the shaping, governing, and implementing of poverty programs. Only through such direct empowerment could the poor hold the bureaucracy accountable – and redress traditional disparities of political influence in local government. This political strategy for reducing poverty proved remarkably effective. By creating institutionalized sources of political power and leverage, the community action approach inspired many local community organizations to channel funds toward expanding membership, providing services, and mobilizing constituencies as a political force in defense of poverty-reducing policies. Even where local groups were denied representation on community action boards by local elites, the institutional commitment to representation created an important foundation for exerting political pressure on policymakers.[124]

As some recent historical accounts suggest, the collapse of the War on Poverty owes much to a backlash against this community empowerment – in a sense, proving just how potent these new institutional structures could be in shifting the balance of power at the local level. As community action programs catalyzed the mobilization of grassroots constituencies to advocate for more accountable and equitable economic policies, the backlash from local power elites – from the political establishment to business interests – led to systematic efforts to defund and dismantle community action.[125] Ultimately, the problem was a lack of alignment over the importance of community action itself. Federal officials saw participation as a surface-level strategy to generate cooperation and consensus among stakeholders, whereas the civil rights and welfare rights movements saw it as a mechanism for reclaiming greater political power over economic policymaking. State and local governments, meanwhile, saw the directive for formal representation of the poor as a categorical threat to their own authority and control of patronage

---

[123] Lillian B. Rubin, "Maximum Feasible Participation: The Origins, Implications, and Present Status," *Annals of the American Academy of Political and Social Science* 385, no. 1 (September 1969): 14–29, 14.

[124] See Annelise Orleck and Lisa Gayle Hazirjian, eds., *The War on Poverty: A New Grassroots History, 1940–1980* (Athens: University of Georgia Press, 2011).

[125] Orleck and Hazirjian, *The War on Poverty*.

networks.[126] Even the founders of the program in the Johnson administration often operated under vastly different motivations and visions for how the program should invest in poor people's *political power*, as opposed to merely providing welfare services.[127] As a result of these tensions, while more than 1,600 community action boards were established by 1968, covering two-thirds of the nation's counties, by 1974 most of the funding for the most active programs had been withdrawn, with Congress placing new restraints on those remaining and dismantling the Office of Economic Opportunity, the federal office charged with creating and coordinating community action across the country.[128]

The experience of the War on Poverty underscores lessons similar to those made manifest in the histories of the earlier power-shifting reforms in the federal regulatory context. First, local-level administrative processes and institutions, such as the allocation of economic development funds and the administering of poverty programs, represented a valuable political arena that grassroots constituencies could target, mobilize around, and seek to leverage to make substantive claims. In so doing, the processes of local administration became a key battleground not just over substantive policies, but over the background distribution of local political power. Indeed, it was this threat to the existing power hierarchy that generated harsh counterreaction by local mayors and power elites against welfare rights activists. Second, the critical challenge for such models, however, is in securing buy-in and cooperation both from government officials and from community groups. As the War on Poverty's failure indicates, where officials themselves reject the core premise of participation, it is difficult to sustain procedures that enable it. Yet where communities are not organized and mobilized through advocacy and membership-based organizations, there is no countervailing voice that can exert effective pressure and credibly claim to speak on behalf of affected communities when policies are made.

FROM CITIZEN AS CONSUMER TO CITIZEN AS AGENT

This alternative tradition of more radical governance reform focused on balancing power contrasts sharply with the more genteel but ultimately less

---

[126] Tara J. Melish, "Maximum Feasible Participation of the Poor: New Governance. New Accountability, and a 21st Century War on the Sources of Poverty," *Yale Human Rights and Development Journal* 13, no. 1 (2010): 28.

[127] See Michael L. Gillette, *Launching the War on Poverty: An Oral History*, 2nd ed. (New York: Oxford University Press, 2010).

[128] Melish, "Maximum Feasible Participation," 26–27.

From Governance to Power – Rethinking Democracy Reform 141

transformative traditions of "good governance" discussed earlier. If a central problem in modern democracy is the disparity of political power, then it follows that, as discussed in Chapters 1 and 2, governmental institutions must be better designed to remedy those disparities of power. Prevailing approaches to governance reform, emphasizing transparency, efficient procedures, privatization, and civic tech are not enough; governance must be reconceived along new lines, by adopting an approach that, like the War on Poverty, takes as its central premise a need to shift power over policymaking. Where movements and grassroots communities have more institutionalized forms of representation, participation, and actual *leverage*, they can exercise more power. Where policymaking bodies are staffed by personnel who view their mission in part as *responding* to these constituencies on fair and equal terms rather than avoiding or subjugating them, the result is a more genuinely democratic and participatory policymaking process. This alternative approach to governance reform thus suggests a very different view of institutional design, and even of the personnel and internal characteristics of policymaking bureaucracies themselves.

In many ways, this is a controversial proposition. The War on Poverty, like the other historical examples of power-shifting institutions mentioned above, was relatively short-lived and eventually undermined by fluctuating views about the desirability of such power shifting. Yet today some of the most potentially transformative, exciting, and *necessary* developments in democracy reform represent modern-day attempts to follow in this more radical tradition, by bodybuilding institutions and bureaucracies oriented toward the problem of power and the goal of democratic participation. As we will see in Chapters 5 and 6, contemporary examples suggest some common institutional design and governance approaches that can do a better job of establishing a more equitable balance of power in policymaking.

5

Bureaucratizing Participation

In Chapter 4 we argued that conventional approaches to governance reform, particularly legalistic reforms to the administrative process and the rise of the modern civic tech field, have tended to focus on a "good governance" framework that does relatively little to address deeper disparities of power and inequality. Yet we also saw that there is a different tradition of governance reform that takes the problems of power seriously. From mid-century experiments with institutionalized countervailing power to battles over participation in the War on Poverty, these alternative approaches to governance reform sought to remake bureaucracies and public policies alike to redress power imbalances, creating genuine democratic agency for individuals and communities. Chapters 6 and 7 explore what this power-shifting approach to governance reform looks like in the context of today's battles over democracy, inequality, and governance.

This chapter focuses on the inner structure, organization, and culture of bureaucracies themselves. We suggest that building civic power and democratizing government cannot be achieved just by building external advocacy power through social movements that demand policy change. Civic power and deep democracy require a more thorough transformation *within* government itself, including at the level of organizational structure and culture and personnel. Indeed, while social movements are often adept at positioning themselves in an oppositional mode, in the long run building a new democracy will require that outsider, adversarial, and oppositional frame to be supplemented by a focus on the actual, day-to-day mechanics of governing.[1]

---

[1] See Smucker, *Hegemony How-To*; and Jodeen Olguin-Taylor, "From Grievance to Governance: 8 Features of Transformative Campaigns," *Let's Talk: At the Heart of Movement Building* (blog), January 26, 2016, http://letstalkmovementbuilding.org/grievance-governance-8-features-transformative-campaigns/.

Indeed, the decline of trust that is unraveling American democracy runs in both directions: communities distrust government, but often government officials also distrust the knowledge, rationality, and good faith of communities. Some communities view government, at best, as incompetent, and at worst, as malignant. Community mistrust of government is a challenge. Many communities, especially racial minorities, immigrants, and others already face pervasive discrimination and state surveillance, making them understandably distrustful of the state and of participation. For marginalized communities, forging deeper ties with government can come with considerable risk. What mechanisms exist to repair these mistrusting relationships?

On the other side, some public officials fear engaging the public will lead to unrealistic expectations with attendant criticism and increased burdens. With declining budgets, public servants across the country are being asked to do more with less. Without higher-level support for engagement, bureaucrats are left with limited ability to engage the citizenry on an array of issues. Yet absent robust forms of consultation, engagement, and accountability, policies themselves will be flawed, based on mistaken assumptions about goals, users, and priorities. Furthermore, engagement with communities that are marginalized or excluded from policy discussions entails its own form of risk. Policies might create expectations for government responsiveness that institutions and officials may be ill-equipped to meet. This chapter looks inside administrative bodies at how they might better create internal culture and develop personnel to be supportive and *capable* of engaging in more participatory and inclusive forms of governance.

BUREAUCRATIZING ENGAGEMENT: THE CASE OF THE CFPB

As discussed earlier, for most federal regulatory bodies, enabling laws along with practices and norms of "good governance" require some systems for transparency and public engagement, often in the forms of notice-and-comment rulemaking procedures and federal advisory committees. Yet the prevailing focus of administrative governance tends to be on assuring the rationality, expertise, and efficiency of government policymaking. Agencies are vast institutions, with significant inertia and well-established internal cultures. Instilling a greater commitment to, and capacity for, more robust participatory governance would require a major shift in the internal structure and culture of these agencies. But we do have some telling examples of what this might look like.

The Consumer Financial Protection Bureau (CFPB), created in the aftermath of the 2008–9 financial crisis, is the most recent and ambitious attempt to forge a brand-new federal regulatory agency in decades. It is also one of the most controversial, posing a central target for business interests, congressional Republicans, and now the Trump administration, all seeking to dismantle and neuter it.[2] As this book was going to press, the Trump administration had appointed new leadership to the CFPB, and drastically curtailed its enforcement actions and the kinds of stakeholder engagement practices described below. But this controversy over the CFPB in many ways proves our central point. The CFPB as an institution has been threatening to its opponents precisely because it represents a novel and highly impactful institutional innovation that alters the power landscape in economic regulation. Furthermore, the CFPB as an institution represents a valuable experiment in forging a regulatory system and culture more oriented toward participation and engagement than is common for federal agencies. Future regulatory reforms can do much by learning from – and expanding on – the innovations of the CFPB.

First, consider the unique institutional design of the CFPB itself, which is distinctive in the context of conventional financial regulatory bodies. Despite the vast implications financial regulation has on the economy and society as a whole, financial regulatory agencies have traditionally been relatively insulated from broad-based participation by constituencies outside of financial industry interests. The relative insularity of financial regulatory agencies has made it challenging for the views and concerns of marginalized, vulnerable, and diffuse constituencies to be heard alongside the demands of firms with business interests at stake.[3] The Dodd-Frank Wall Street Reform and Consumer Protection Act of 2010, a key financial reform statute, created two new regulatory bodies, the Financial Stability Oversight Council (FSOC) and

---

[2] Richard Cordray, "The Trump Administration Is Trying to Undermine the CFPB. It Will Fail," *Washington Post*, February 14, 2018, www.washingtonpost.com/opinions/the-trump-administration-is-trying-to-undermine-the-cfpb-it-will-fail/2018/02/14/cab18f18-10d2-11e8-8ea1-c1d91fcec3fe_story.html.

[3] Gillian E. Metzger, "Through the Looking Glass to a Shared Reflection: The Evolving Relationship between Administrative Law and Financial Regulation," *Law and Contemporary Problems* 78 (2015): 129–56. She writes, "[A]lthough financial regulation agencies engage in notice-and-comment rulemaking, their regulatory mode is often more informal, ad hoc, and hidden from public view. Protecting vulnerable groups and preventing externalities are important concerns, but an overriding regulatory goal is ensuring the stability of the financial system, which often means protecting profitable lines of business" (130–31). See also Saule T. Omarova, "Bankers, Bureaucrats, and Guardians: Toward Tripartism in Financial Services Regulation," *Cornell Law Faculty Publications*, paper 1010 (Spring 2012), noting the chronic lack of public representation and participation in financial regulation – especially when macro questions of systemic risk are at stake.

the CFPB.[4] The contrast between these bodies highlights the distinctiveness of the CFPB – and its orientation toward greater participation.

From a policy perspective, the central problem the FSOC was designed to solve was the fragmentation of the financial regulatory landscape. Prior to the 2008 financial crisis, no single regulator was charged with the responsibility for systemic financial stability concerns. As a result, the risks of mortgage-backed securities and toxic assets fell through the cracks in the gaps between regulators with jurisdiction over securities, commodities, and banks.[5] But this fragmentation represented more than just a policy problem; it was also an accountability problem. In a highly fragmented regulatory ecosystem, established players like financial firms can navigate accordingly, exploiting gaps for regulatory arbitrage, and thus exercise outsize influence on individual regulatory agencies.[6]

In the debate over regulatory fragmentation, the idea of consolidating all our financial regulatory institutions into a "single peak" regulator similar to the United Kingdom's Financial Services Authority was quickly dismissed.[7] Nevertheless, the FSOC as created represents a major attempt at consolidating systemic risk regulation authority in a single body as well as at coordinating between different financial regulatory agencies like the Securities and Exchange Commission (SEC), the Commodity Futures Trading Commission (CFTC), and more.[8] Creating a centralized regulator of systemic risk transformed the dynamics of power and influence in financial regulation, enabling not only policy coordination, but also protecting against undue industry influence. The FSOC is insulated from interest group pressure; it is politically accountable directly to the president through the treasury secretary's role as chair of the FSOC.[9] But what is telling about the FSOC is that even as it attempted to rationalize and coordinate regulation, closing off

---

[4] For a preliminary take on this comparison see Rahman, "Policymaking as Power-Building," 156–60.

[5] See Michael S. Barr, "The Financial Crisis and the Path of Reform," *Yale Journal on Regulation* 29, no. 1 (2012): 91–119, 94–95.

[6] On the facility of interest groups in exercising influence on regulators in fragmented and complex regulatory environments, see generally Dan Awrey, "Complexity, Innovation, and the Regulation of Modern Financial Markets," *Harvard Business Law Review* 2, no. 2 (2012): 235–94; and John C. Coffee, Jr., "Political Economy of Dodd-Frank: Why Financial Reform Tends to be Frustrated and Systemic Risk Perpetuated," *Cornell Law Review* 97, no. 5 (July 2012): 1019–82.

[7] See Michael S. Barr, "Comment: Accountability and Independence in Financial Regulation: Checks and Balances, Public Engagement, and Other Innovations," *Law and Contemporary Problems* 78, no. 3 (2015): 119–28, 122–25.

[8] Ibid.

[9] Metzger, "Through the Looking Glass," 146–47.

146 *Civic Power*

gaps for financial firms to arbitrage, it did little to expand the direct representation and voice of affected but often less influential constituencies. As Saule Omarova has noted, to make macro financial policy more democratically accountable and responsive would require institutionalizing greater representation of more diverse constituencies from workers to consumers to student debtors and others in the policymaking process.[10] Omarova's proposal is the creation of a "Public Interest Council" with representatives of these diverse constituencies charged with overseeing and holding financial regulators accountable.[11]

Like the FSOC, the CFPB was partly created to respond to the problems of capture and fragmentation of banking and financial regulators.[12] But in contrast to the FSOC, the CFPB was designed not just for insulation from political pressure, but rather to be more democratically accountable; first, through a substantive mission of consumer protection, and second, through a greater commitment to engagement with grassroots constituencies and affected communities.[13] As a result, the success of the CFPB is arguably a product of the agency's de facto role as a "proxy advocate" of consumer interests in the financial regulatory ecosystem.[14]

First, the CFPB possesses a newly consolidated and empowered decision-making authority. This makes it more visible to lay citizens as a target for airing grievances and seeking redress. This aspect of CFPB authority also makes the agency more responsive and accountable, by centralizing consumer protection and watchdog functions. A consolidated CFPB undoes some of the prior fragmentation of its policy space, which had been confusing to lay constituencies and easily navigated by financial sector firms. Instead, the CFPB centralizes authority in one agency, clarifying lines of accountability and responsibility and providing a clear target against which stakeholder groups can make claims.

At the same time, the CFPB has a culture that enables it to act not only as a neutral policymaker, but as a *representative* of consumer interests. The

---

[10] Omarova, "Bankers, Bureaucrats, and Guardians."

[11] See Omarova, "Bankers, Bureaucrats, and Guardians," 659–69, for details of her proposed Public Interest Council.

[12] See Adam J. Levitin, "The Consumer Financial Protection Bureau: An Introduction," *Review of Banking and Financial Law* 32 (2013): 321–69.

[13] Metzger, "Through the Looking Glass," 148, 152; and Barr, "Comment: Accountability and Independence," 127.

[14] See Daniel Schwarz, "Preventing Capture through Consumer Empowerment Programs: Some Evidence from Insurance Regulation," in *Preventing Regulatory Capture: Special Interest Influence and How to Limit It*, ed. Daniel Carpenter and David A. Moss (New York: Cambridge University Press, 2013), 366.

CFPB contains designated offices for outreach to and engagement with constituencies that may have particular needs, but are often overlooked in financial regulation policy, such as veterans, students, and pensioners.[15] The agency's orientation is also a product of its personnel: many individuals working in the CFPB are themselves veterans of the consumer rights movement.

Through public hearings and town halls set up around the country,[16] CFPB staff leverage public engagement to identify priorities for new rules and enforcement actions. The agency has also experimented with online platforms to engage broader participation, from its launching of a new centralized consumer complaint database to trying out innovative online platforms like Regulation Room to engage more diverse groups in commenting on ongoing rulemakings.[17] The CFPB also runs a complaint database,[18] compiling millions of grievances and concerns from the general public, in a publicly searchable and accessible system.[19] The database enables the CFPB to set priorities based on its analysis of the real problems facing ordinary Americans.[20] The public nature of the database also helps shame and hold industry actors accountable, while simultaneously holding the CFPB itself to account.

The agency also operates an office of community affairs charged with organizing outreach to consumer advocacy groups and seeking input from constituencies like minorities, students with debt, and homeowners.[21] Through town halls, focus groups, online engagements, and other strategies, the office carries out its core mission – building trust and relationships with affected constituencies – in hopes of channeling these grassroots concerns into the core work of the agency itself.[22] This office invested significant staff time and resources into identifying grassroots stakeholders, lay citizens, and community organizations who can speak for different segments of the population,

---

[15] Dodd-Frank Act § 1013(c) (to be codified at 12 U.S.C. § 5493).

[16] See Consumer Financial Protection Bureau (website), "Field Hearing on Debt Collection in Sacramento, Calif," last updated July 28, 2016, www.consumerfinance.gov/about-us/events/a rchive-past-events/field-hearing-debt-collection-sacramento-calif/.

[17] See Farina et al., "Rulemaking 2.0." Regulation Room is no longer being maintained, however.

[18] Consumer Financial Protection Bureau (website), "Consumer Complaint Database," www .consumerfinance.gov/data-research/consumer-complaints/.

[19] Ibid.

[20] See Barbara Kiviat, "The CFPB Is Making Government More Accountable. The GOP Wants to Stop It," *Washington Monthly*, June 8, 2017, http://washingtonmonthly.com/2017/06/08/th e-cfpb-is-making-government-more-accountable-the-gop-wants-to-stop-it/.

[21] Consumer Financial Protection Bureau (website), "The Bureau," www.consumerfinance.gov /about-us/the-bureau/.

[22] Ibid.

148   *Civic Power*

thereby actively working to build the trust and relationships it needs to engage and empower these grassroots voices in shaping the agency's direction by identifying problems and weighing in on open policy questions.

The CFPB's complaint database offers another example of its functioning as a conduit for traditionally disempowered constituencies to exercise more effective leverage on economic regulations. The bureau operates a publicly accessible complaint database where consumers can register complaints about financial firms and products. In addition to publicizing the platform to encourage online submissions, staff have analyzed public complaints and input when identifying enforcement priorities and topics for future agency rulemakings. A complaint database is not as radical as the kinds of citizen audits described more fully in Chapter 6 below. But the combination of even a modest form of participatory monitoring with a proactive commitment to that participation on the part of agency staff has made it surprisingly powerful. Indeed, it is unsurprising that this complaint database has been a central target for CFPB critics; under the Trump administration, the agency's new leadership has worked to dismantle this system.

Viewing the FSOC and the CFPB in comparison is instructive; both radically reshaped the relationships between industry and regulators by creating a new consolidated, centralized regulatory authority.[23] This consolidation of authority changed existing power dynamics, disrupting relationships between industry and agencies, and closing off gaps firms could exploit through regulatory arbitrage. But it is the CFPB that has generated the most vitriolic pushback from financial interests, in large part because it can serve as a powerful advocate on behalf of constituencies ordinarily overrun in financial reform decisions. The fact that the CFPB combined both a consolidation of authority and power on the one hand with a greater connection to grassroots constituencies on the other made it a more radical threat to existing distributions of power and influence over financial regulation. The FSOC by contrast, while powerful in its own right, has been regarded by financial sector interests like any other regulator – indeed, from the implementation of the Volcker

---

[23] Metzger, "Through the Looking Glass," 148. See also Leonard J. Kennedy, Patricia A. McCoy, and Ethan Bernstein, "The Consumer Financial Protection Bureau: Financial Regulation for the Twenty-First Century," *Cornell Law Review* 97, no. 5 (July 2012): 1141–75, 1158–59, 1164–65. In particular, these authors argue that the CFPB is fulfilling its statutory obligations through four principles: "(1) a market-based approach, (2) a focus on evidence-based analysis, (3) a commitment to encouraging and enabling robust public participation through transparency and innovative uses of technology, and (4) a recognition that history and other agencies' experience can provide invaluable guidance" (1143).

Rule to other major initiatives,[24] financial sector interests have proven adept at lobbying the FSOC to influence its new systemic risk regulations.[25]

By combining these institutional features with internal practices that invest in civic engagement and outreach efforts, the CFPB has made itself a trusted intermediary for many constituencies who would otherwise find it difficult to exercise political influence. The CFPB has invested significant financial resources and technological expertise into building a complaint database and into proactively engaging constituencies across the country through town halls and outreach efforts. These investments also allow it to operate as a hub for a version of the kind of participatory monitoring more fully described in Chapter 6. The CFPB thus operates in part as a conduit for complaints, offering a macro structure that facilitates the engagement of a diffuse and disorganized constituency – consumers – in a form of the participatory monitoring described in the next chapter. Indeed, this is arguably what makes the CFPB so powerful – and so threatening. The combination of participatory and representative mechanisms with the independent funding of the CFPB, as well as its status as an agency operating alongside other financial regulation agencies, makes it an extremely effective channel for countervailing power. Thus the "representativeness" or depth of constituency linkage within an agency is something of a fractal phenomenon, potentially existing at levels ranging from the individual policymaker, to the office, to the agency as a whole. Here too, the lesson is one of institutional flexibility: there are many routes toward facilitating these linkages and thereby toward rebalancing power relationships within a particular sector or policy area.

This approach has its limits, of course; in some ways the CFPB remains a conventional regulatory agency that develops policy through its expertise – and while its practices for civic engagement are far more proactive and committed than those of most agencies, these practices remain largely

---

[24] § 619 of the Dodd–Frank Wall Street Reform and Consumer Protection Act of 2010 (12 U.S.C. § 1851).

[25] See generally *Metlife, Inc. v. Fin. Stability Oversight Council*, 177 F. Supp. 3d 219 (D.C. Cir. 2016), on reversing FSOC's determination that MetLife constituted a significant financial institution; Hilary J. Allen, "Putting the 'Financial Stability' in Financial Stability Oversight Council," *Ohio State Law Journal* 76 (2015): 1087–1152, arguing that the influence of the Federal Reserve and Treasury Department handicaps FSOC's ability to perform its duties; Cary Martin Shelby, "Closing the Hedge Fund Loophole: The SEC as the Primary Regulator of Systemic Risk," *Boston College Law Review* 58, no. 2 (2017): 639–701, describing FSOC's failure to classify hedge funds as Systematically Important Financial Institutions and arguing that the SEC should be the primary agency tasked with financial stability; and Christina P. Skinner, "Regulating Nonbanks: A Plan for SIFI Lite," *Georgetown Law Journal* 105 (2017): 1379–1432.

dependent on the instigation of agency staff themselves. This dedication remains vulnerable to changes in organizational personnel and culture. Indeed, under the Trump administration, the business lobby's long-running campaign to dismantle the CFPB has effectively gained a foothold within the agency itself. In February 2018 the Trump administration stripped a unit in the CFPB, the Office of Fair Lending and Equal Opportunity, of its enforcement powers in discrimination cases.[26] Trump's appointee Mick Mulvaney is also strategically dropping crucial, high-profile CFPB cases, including a lawsuit against payday lenders.[27] The White House is also working to sharply reduce the CFPB budget through a "restructuring period."[28] The budget plan includes cutting the budget by one-third, capping it at $485 million for FY 2019, equivalent to the 2015 funding level, and $610 million for 2020.[29] By way of contrast, the CFPB's budget request under the Obama administration was $630.4 million for FY 2018.[30]

CULTIVATING INTERNAL SUPPORT FOR PARTICIPATORY GOVERNANCE

The limitations of the CFPB point to another key area of concern for the design of more institutionalized forms of participation and countervailing power. A lot turns on the *internal* dynamics of governance bodies themselves: who is in charge, what skills and values and orientations line officers have, and the degree to which agencies actually have the normative commitment and tangible skills needed to manage policymaking in a more participatory fashion. Part of the CFPB's run of success was a result of its ability to bring in

---

[26] Renae Merle, "Trump Administration Strips Consumer Watchdog Office of Enforcement Powers in Lending Discrimination Cases," *Washington Post*, February 1, 2018, www .washingtonpost.com/news/business/wp/2018/02/01/trump-administration-strips-consumer-watch dog-office-of-enforcement-powers-against-financial-firms-in-lending-discrimination-cases/?utm_ term=.dfc7f9619e42.

[27] Cordray tried to instill his chief of staff, Leandra English, as acting director; however, the Trump White House argued it had power to name an acting director, with which a federal judge agreed, though to date the case is still in the courts.

[28] Yuka Hayashi, "Trump Administration Overhauls CFPB's Mission, Proposes Budget Cuts," *Wall Street Journal*, February 12, 2018, www.wsj.com/articles/trump-administration-overhauls-cfpbs-mission-proposes-budget-cuts-1518480377.

[29] Dave Boyer, "Trump Plan Cuts CFPB's Budget by One-Third," *Washington Times*, February 13, 2018, www.washingtontimes.com/news/2018/feb/13/trump-plan-cuts-cfpbs-budget-by-one-third/.

[30] Yuka Hayashi, "Trump Budget Plan Cuts CFPB's Budget, Restricts Its Enforcement Power," *Wall Street Journal*, February 12, 2018, www.wsj.com/livecoverage/trumps-2019-budget-proposal-live-analysis/card/1518471424.

Bureaucratizing Participation 151

diverse new talent with a wide range of skill sets, from lawyers to tech-savvy user-experience (UX) designers. This is what made it possible for the agency to develop new systems for analyzing and responding to masses of public comments on proposed regulations as well as to design more effective forms of civic engagement and public outreach. Similarly, as we will see in Chapter 6 with the example of participatory budgeting (PB) in New York, successful participatory processes require a significant investment of *internal* personnel and resources within government.

These examples thus highlight an important, often overlooked dimension of building civic power. Civic power is not just the province of building up power by civil society groups *external* to government. It also requires a change in the culture and structure of governance *internal* to government bureaucracies. Indeed, some of the most valuable experiments in civic power today revolve around the efforts by reformers to create new cultures, talent pipelines, and internal organizational forms within governmental bureaucracies aimed at better supporting and enabling more participatory governance models throughout the government.

Boston's New Urban Mechanics

Deep within the hulking brutalist building that is Boston City Hall, there is an unusual department that instantly stands out as distinct. Marked by post-its and whiteboards along the walls, and marked by a staff that hails from a much more diverse range of racial, economic, and occupational backgrounds than one might expect for a government office, lies the novel Mayor's Office of New Urban Mechanics (MONUM). Launched in 2010 by Boston's long-serving mayor Thomas Menino, MONUM is charged with a unique mandate. Substantively, MONUM was given a portfolio encompassing major urban planning projects, from streetscapes to affordable housing. But it was MONUM's approach to these problems that was designed to be distinctive: MONUM was to address these policy issues through a deliberately experimental, innovative, and participatory approach aimed at creating "pilot experiments that aim to improve the quality of life for Boston's residents."[31] But more than its substantive agenda, MONUM is instructive for us as an example of a newly created bureaucracy that has committed itself structurally and culturally to facilitating participation and engagement and to

---

[31] City of Boston (website), "New Urban Mechanics," www.boston.gov/departments/new-urban-mechanics.

approaching policymaking with an eye toward empowering traditionally dis-empowered constituencies.

Innovation and Governance Reform

MONUM is not the only city innovation office. In recent years cities across the country have been creating "innovation" departments, often housed under chief technology officers or chief data officers, to focus on novel uses of big data and sophisticated technology, often managed through public–private partnerships and backed by philanthropic investments.[32] These innovation offices have been key hubs for the larger civic tech movement described earlier. Many of these innovation units are focused on agile development and user-centric design. On the federal level, the Obama administration created several new roles and offices including the United States Digital Service (USDS, established in 2014) under the Office of Management and Budget (OMB), agency digital service teams, and 18F, a fee-for-service digital consultancy within the General Services Administration (GSA). Although these innovation units have proliferated, they have not yet been able to translate their lessons back to the wider public.[33] But even among these innovation offices, MONUM has been notable for its commitment not just to generic "innovation" and technology, but specifically to acting as an institutional home for the pioneering of more participatory approaches to public policy.

According to Nigel Jacob, a computer scientist who cofounded MONUM along with Chris Osgood, a Harvard Business School alumnus, the broader aim of the initiative is to create an office that can carry on Mayor Menino's legacy while injecting a start-up mentality into Boston's government, dedi-cated to inventing the future of city services. The first initiative Jacob and Osgood developed was a 2009 project to create an app, Citizens Connect, through which residents could report issues to city agencies directly from their smartphones.[34] The initiative was renamed Commonwealth Connect and now is called BOS:311, and it has been used by over 70,000 Massachusetts

---

[32] Ruth Puttick, Peter Baeck, and Philip Colligan, *I-teams: The Teams and Funds Making Innovation Happen in Governments around the World* (London: Nesta, 2014), http://theiteams .org/system/files_force/i-teams_June%202014.pdf.

[33] David Eaves, "The End of the Beginning of Digital Service Units," *Medium*, June 11, 2018, https:// medium.com/digitalhks/the-end-of-the-beginning-of-digital-service-units-cfifcce8aa57.

[34] BOS: 311 (app/website), https://311.boston.gov/.

residents and has led to over 35,000 individual projects of nonemergency infrastructure improvement.[35]

Since Boston's new mayor took office, MONUM has moved from a pilot initiative to become more embedded and institutionalized within the government. Where MONUM initially focused on developing technologies and applications that could help it gather data to serve people more effectively, as the office evolved it has shifted toward exploring ways to use technology to engage citizens in a more sophisticated fashion. As Stephen Walter, a program director at MONUM, explained, Urban Mechanics staff challenged themselves to think "about more deliberative interactions as part of democracy" and asked themselves, "How can technology create more nuanced conversations?"[36]

Much of the work of other municipal innovation units is focused on performance management, delivery models, and data analytics. MONUM, however, is interested in a much broader definition of innovation, which includes changing the opportunities for residents to have a say in policymaking. In fact, Boston already has a separate data innovation initiative run by its Department of Innovation and Technology (DoIT), overseen by the city's chief information officer.[37] Boston is taking part in the What Works Cities initiative, funded by Bloomberg Philanthropies, and is one of only nine cities to achieve a "Silver" certification by the initiative for its use of evidence and data analytics in decision-making.[38] Some of these projects are more like conventional civic tech and open-government projects, focused solely on improving data interoperability, access, and use across city government so that government will be more driven by data and evidence, including in procurement.[39] MONUM, by contrast, is freed from having to deliver solely

---

[35] City of Boston (website), "BOS:311 App," www.boston.gov/departments/new-urban-mechanics/bos311-app; and Susan Crawford and Dana Walters, *Citizen-Centered Governance: The Mayor's Office of New Urban Mechanics and the Evolution of the CRM in Boston* (Cambridge, MA: Berkman Klein Center for Internet and Society, July 30, 2013).

[36] Stephen Walter, personal communication, June 29, 2016, previously cited in Tannenwald and Gilman, *A 21st Century Town Hall?*, 12.

[37] City of Boston (website), "Innovation and Technology," www.boston.gov/departments/innovation-and-technology.

[38] Angel Quicksey, "What Works Cities Blog Post: Better Procurement, Better Outcomes: Technology and Design Interventions in Boston," Bloomberg Philanthropies (website), December 2, 2016, https://whatworkscities.bloomberg.org/better-procurement-better-outcomes-technology-design-interventions-boston/; and City of Boston (website), "Boston Recognized by Bloomberg Philanthropies for Excellence in Government Services," January 25, 2018, www.boston.gov/news/boston-recognized-bloomberg-philanthropies-excellence-government-services.

[39] See Bloomberg Philanthropies (website), "Where We've Worked," https://whatworkscities.bloomberg.org/cities/; and Travis Andersen, "Boston Hopes Data Can Aid Its Efforts in Fighting Fires," *Boston Globe*, April 4, 2016, www.bostonglobe.com/metro/2016/04/04/city-

154 *Civic Power*

on data improvements and increased analytics, and can instead focus on testing new policy experiments.

As a result, MONUM had been focused from the start on going beyond simply modernizing government performance and instead working on deepening civic engagement. MONUM is now much more than simply an app creator. The team is focused on several core municipal concerns, which include: (1) education, (2) housing, and (3) streets and street infrastructure.[40] It is now comprised of core staff who are based out of city hall full-time as well as staff who shuttle between other agencies, such as housing and education departments, while spending part of their time in MONUM itself. The team leverages an iterative approach to explore, experiment, and evaluate to meet specific goals such as a welcoming city hall, transparent government, and empowered residents.

The launch of MONUM's Housing Innovation Lab provides a telling example of MONUM's unique approach. Funded through Bloomberg Philanthropies, the Housing Lab creates a participatory forum aimed at codesigning – with residents – novel approaches to the affordable housing crisis and to chronic problems of economic inequality for communities who are priced out of Boston's rapidly accelerating housing market.[41] The Housing Lab is deeply integrated into a larger effort by city hall to invest heavily in new affordable housing construction, with a target of over 50,000 new units built by 2030.[42] MONUM's contribution to this larger effort, however, echoes the kinds of participatory processes described in Chapter 6.

As one staffer put it, MONUM's first step was to engage residents in a sophisticated, structured process of consultation eventually leading to policy codesign aimed at resolving issues raised by residents. For example, in the fall of 2016, staffers took a 385-square-foot, one-bedroom model unit on wheels from city hall to minority communities in neighborhoods like Roslindale, Mattapan, Dorchester, Roxbury, and East Boston.[43] Residents were given the opportunity to physically explore a space and answer questions about their own priorities. Housing Lab staff also sat down with other residents at their

---

> boston-using-data-improve-firefighting-and-other-services-report-says/vCspAKEgRYkAB4mM xz7qwN/story.html#comments.

[40] City of Boston (website), "New Urban Mechanics," www.boston.gov/departments/new-urban-mechanics.

[41] City of Boston (website), "Housing Innovation Lab," www.boston.gov/departments/new-urban-mechanics/housing-innovation-lab.

[42] City of Boston (website), "Housing a Changing City: Boston 2030," www.boston.gov/depart ments/neighborhood-development/housing-changing-city-boston-2030.

[43] City of Boston (website), "Urban Housing Unit Roadshow," www.boston.gov/departments/n ew-urban-mechanics/urban-housing-unit-roadshow.

homes in Boston's Jamaica Plain neighborhood for deep dialogues about housing needs and concerns.[44] These consultations were admittedly small in scale – a reflection of MONUM's budgetary constraints. But these conversations convinced MONUM staffers to push for more transformative affordability strategies, such as offering incentives for developers to make affordable units, launching a framework to simplify the home-buying process, and developing an intergenerational homeshare pilot program.[45]

Analysis: The Importance of Staff and Structure

The structure of MONUM illustrates how governments can be redesigned to become proactive and sustained drivers of participatory governance, so that innovation not only exists on the margins of governance, but also gets baked into the most high-profile and high-stakes policy issues of the day.

First, MONUM is integrated with the centers of city hall power. The head of MONUM reports directly to the mayor, and even the physical office is located near the mayor's office. MONUM is a member of the mayor's weekly cabinet meetings, allowing it to interface with both the mayor and other agencies at multiple points in the policymaking process. As a result, MONUM can connect its experimentation directly to mayoral priorities, bring results back to agencies, and leverage data for better services that directly impact communities through field experiments and civic research. Furthermore, having the buy-in of the mayor provides MONUM with critical political air cover as well as the political capital to experiment and have the room to fail.

Second, this deep integration in city hall is combined with staff attention to the lived experiences, expertise, and policy needs of other agencies. MONUM is cautious not to step on the toes of others in government. The Urban Mechanics spend time working directly with agency partners to assess needs and understand an agency's culture, priorities, and constraints. Several of the staff split their time between city hall and other government agencies. This allows MONUM to tailor its experiments not only for residents and constituencies on the ground, but also for *internal* stakeholders within the city bureaucracy, securing crucial buy-in and support. Furthermore, as experts in experimentation and participatory policymaking, MONUM can absorb the

---

[44] Ibid.
[45] See City of Boston (website), "Simplifying the Home Buying Process," www.boston.gov/dep artments/new-urban-mechanics/simplifying-homebuying-process; "Urban Housing Unit Roadshow," www.boston.gov/departments/new-urban-mechanics/urban-housing-unit-roadshow; and "Intergenerational Homeshare Pilot," www.boston.gov/departments/new-urban-mechanics/housing-innovation-lab/intergenerational-homeshare-pilot.

risk from other agencies. The task of running a civic engagement pilot project is daunting to most bureaucrats, beyond their bandwidth, resources, or expertise; MONUM can take those risks, and do so in ways that are sensitive to the needs and orientation of the agency itself. MONUM staffers try to not get stuck in "analysis paralysis" and instead, and the orientation of staff is to remain entrepreneurial in approach.

Third, resources are crucial to making MONUM possible. Boston's significant resources (as city governments go) and multiple philanthropic grants have permitted more narrow tech initiatives to be channeled instead to DoIT, leaving MONUM free to focus on genuinely participatory policy innovation. Similarly, having a well-funded, well-staffed, high-prestige office like MONUM dedicated to more participatory governance, and a mayor willing to embed these approaches in the most high-profile policy issues like affordable housing, represents a significant commitment of human, financial, and political resources to the idea of participation.

MONUM is not without its limitations, however. MONUM's structure, which emphasizes actionable policy outcomes, runs the risk of being co-opted by elites or watering down citizen voices. At its core, MONUM is still a government office and is therefore constrained by the limits of city hall policy. By design, it is not a movement-building organization. Rather, it is beholden to bureaucratic realities, which may be frustrating for external constituencies who may not understand why precisely their interests cannot be channeled more directly into policy outcomes. They may question, for example, why some issues, such as middle-income housing, are being prioritized over others, such as inequality or climate change. While MONUM is more focused on experimentation and genuine civic empowerment than many other urban innovation offices, its priorities are still constrained by bureaucratic realities (e.g., policy preferences) and the funding environment (e.g., philanthropic priorities). With some of MONUM's positions funded by fellowships from philanthropy, there is a perceived risk that external donors can influence the agenda. While MONUM has now weathered one mayoral transition, it could still be terminated by another mayor.

In Philadelphia, for example, an experimental New Urban Mechanics office modeled on MONUM was not able to have the institutionalized impact of Boston and did not survive a mayoral transition. Nonetheless, Philadelphia has continued to grow its innovations cohort within city hall, including through the Office of Innovation & Technology and the PHL Participatory Design Lab (which leverages human-centered design and evidence-based decision-making), and through philanthropic support from the regional William Penn Foundation as well as the Knight Foundation, suggesting that

Bureaucratizing Participation

its Urban Mechanics were one component of a larger trend to innovate and change culture within Philadelphia's city hall.[46] Additionally, as with any innovation with government, there are vulnerable populations who may not want to engage with government for a variety of reasons.

Staffing, resources, and internal capacity can be particular challenges when an office like MONUM is tasked with tackling such a diverse range of issues. Its staffing model maximizes creativity and capitalizes on the benefits of multisector actors including universities and philanthropies.[47] The MONUM staff includes people with backgrounds not typically associated with city government – from ethnography to product management – alongside policy experts. The city has leveraged philanthropy to bring in external talent and to offer fellowship rotations.[48] These funding streams allowed MONUM to grow from an initial staff of three to a modern staff of nearly a dozen. For example, some staff have remained after arriving as a part of Code for America, a philanthropic initiative that places technologists in city halls across the country on fellowships.[49] Indeed, the cofounder of MONUM, Chris Osgood, was on a Harvard Business School fellowship to serve at Boston City Hall when he first started working on the ideas that led to the creation of the office.[50] Yet injecting fellowship dollars into city hall requires both time to apply for grants as well as an internal plan to ensure resources for continued operations. MONUM has created a culture of innovation that is appealing to external talent. As a result, it is able to retain people after fellowships end and to leverage their diverse perspectives into improved policy processes for the residents of Boston. But this resourcing model may not be sustainable in the long run.

---

[46] City of Philadelphia, "PHL Participatory Design Lab Announces Project Partners and Fellows," November 9, 2017, https://beta.phila.gov/2017-11-09-phl-participatory-design-lab-announces-project-partners-and-fellows/; Shawn McCaney, "A New Path for Urban Philanthropy," William Penn Foundation blog, November 29, 2017, https://williampennfoun dation.org/blog/new-path-urban-philanthropy; Knight Foundation (website), "Philadelphia," https://knightfoundation.org/communities/philadelphia/; and Chayenne Polimedio, Elena Souris, and Hollie Russon Gilman, *Where Residents, Politics, and Government Meet: Philadelphia's Experiments with Civic Engagement* (Washington, DC: New America, November 2018).

[47] Mitchell Weiss, "New Urban Mechanics," Harvard Business School Case 315–075, January 2015 (revised March 2017), www.hbs.edu/faculty/Pages/item.aspx?num=48429.

[48] Susan Crawford and Dana Walters, *Citizen-Centered Governance*.

[49] City of Boston, "Mayor's Office of New Urban Mechanics and Code for America Partner to Build Nation's First Backpack Apps," news release, February 15, 2011, www.cityofboston.gov /news/default.aspx?id=4988; and City of Boston (website), "Housing Innovation Lab Now a Permanent Office," July 19, 2017, www.boston.gov/news/housing-innovation-lab-now-permanent-office.

[50] Crawford and Walters, *Citizen-Centered Governance*.

158   *Civic Power*

The Mayor's Public Engagement Unit in New York City

Like MONUM in Boston, the Mayor's Public Engagement Unit (PEU) in New York City represents another novel experiment in forming a government body dedicated to proactively catalyzing grassroots participation.

Mobilizing Communities from City Hall

Whereas MONUM has a technology start-up's vibe, PEU feels more like a grassroots campaign office. Its offices in downtown Manhattan are teeming with young people at computer stations wearing headsets, cycling through calls with constituents. The image is revealing, for the team is structured very much like a political campaign. The staff skews young and tends to be comprised of individuals with expertise in data, operations, policy, community engagement, and community affairs. Furthermore, the office is staffed by roughly 150 campaign "specialists" who, like canvassers, go door-to-door to connect with residents and proactively seek to generate "cases" – specific complaints or potential enrollees for the city's major programs, such as the Get Covered NYC health insurance enrollment assistance program.[51] PEU has been dubbed a "proactive version of the city's 311 help line."[52] It is worth noting that 311, a one-stop interface for residents to report problems or to enroll in city services, itself fields more than 50,000 calls a day.[53]

PEU was created by Mayor Bill de Blasio and officially opened in 2015 with a budget of $4.7 million.[54] It was built out of a campaign to get New Yorkers to sign up for universal pre-K – i.e., government-funded preschool – in the largest such initiative in the country.[55] Having demonstrated its capacities in this effort – along with the necessity of this approach – the office was born. The first director of the office, Regina Schwartz, has a background in city hall as well as expertise in behavioral psychology and policy design; additionally, she was involved in building digital tools for progressive campaigns and organizations through the Analyst Institute, which has worked with groups including the

---

[51] NYC (website of City of New York), "Mayor de Blasio's GetCoveredNYC Campaign Announces over 150 Upcoming Health Insurance Enrollment Events Citywide," March 27, 2018, www1.nyc.gov/office-of-the-mayor/news/163-18/mayor-de-blasio-s-getcoverednyc-campaign-over-150-upcoming-health-insurance-enrollment.

[52] Ben Chapman and Lisa L. Colangelo, "NYC Rolling Out New Unit To Connect Residents in Need with Social Services," *New York Daily News*, September 20, 2015, www.nydailynews.com/new-york/exclusive-nyc-creates-unit-connect-needy-nyers-article-1.2366942.

[53] Steven Johnson, "What a Hundred Million Calls to 311 Reveal about New York," *Wired*, November 1, 2010, www.wired.com/2010/11/ff_311_new_york/.

[54] Chapman and Colangelo, "NYC Rolling Out New Unit."

[55] Kate Taylor, "New York City Will Offer Free Preschool for All 3-Year-Olds," *New York Times*, April 24, 2017, www.nytimes.com/2017/04/24/nyregion/de-blasio-pre-k-expansion.html.

Obama campaign, the AFL, and the SEIU.[56] From the beginning, de Blasio aspired to incorporate campaign field tactics from community organizing into government practice in order to bring resources to vulnerable New Yorkers. Similarly, campaigns for elected office, especially on presidential, gubernatorial, mayoral, and congressional levels, deploy sophisticated data analytics and organizing strategies. But once in office, candidates rarely deploy such measures to serve constituents.

The concept behind PEU is simple, yet powerful. Instead of following a usual model in which city officials wait for residents to reach out to them, PEU goes out to vulnerable communities and builds face-to-face relationships to engender trust while signing people up for vital city services. Some of the issues on which PEU is working to connect people to services include health insurance, anti-eviction legal counsel, financial assistance for the homeless, workforce training, and access to rent freeze programs.

PEU both generates new cases and works directly with constituents until their policy issues are resolved. When new issues arise that affect New Yorkers, the administration leverages PEU as a frontline unit to spread awareness about new key services or service changes, such as new Deferred Action for Childhood Arrivals (DACA) renewal deadlines, or free summer meals.[57] Indeed, PEU's first major undertaking was the outreach for signing up constituencies for universal pre-K, a signature program of the de Blasio administration offering universal, free early childhood education to every three-year-old regardless of income.[58] As Schwartz puts it:

> We serve as a connector and a case manager. If we meet you at your door, or at an elected official's office hours and you're about to be evicted, we'll connect you with a legal service provider to help you fight your case in court. If you need health insurance, we'll schedule an in-person appointment with a certified enroller and help you go through the process of collecting the paperwork and scheduling a wellness visit.[59]

---

[56] Analyst Institute (website), "Our Mission," https://analystinstitute.org/our-mission/.

[57] NYC (website of City of New York), "Find a Summer Meals Program," www1.nyc.gov/nyc-resources/service/4061/find-a-summer-meals-program.

[58] NYC (website of City of New York), "Mayor de Blasio Announces 3–K for All," news release, April 24, 2017, www1.nyc.gov/office-of-the-mayor/news/258-17/mayor-de-blasio-3-k-all#/o.

[59] Elena Souris and Regina Schwartz, "Case Study Highlight: Q&A with NYC's Regina Schwartz," Participatory Democracy Project blog post, New America, October 24, 2017, www.newamerica.org/political-reform/participatory-democracy-project/civic-engagement/case-study-highlight-q-nycs-regina-schwartz/; see also Gilman and Rahman, *Building Civic Capacity in an Era of Democratic Crisis.*

160   *Civic Power*

The day-to-day operation of PEU reflects this mentality, combining campaign tactics with social work, service delivery, and intake techniques. For example, PEU fieldworkers, fluent in multiple languages, go door-to-door, armed with iPads set up with sophisticated customer relationship management software on the back end. When they meet residents, they input their information and then work with them to enroll them in city services that might be useful for them. Staff then follow up on each in-person visit by phone, calling from headquarters to offer appropriate support services ranging from confirming a legal service provider appointment to ensuring that someone is now properly enrolled in a health insurance program. The average staff specialist has roughly forty active cases at any given time and spends most of the week out knocking doors and one day in the office every week for follow-ups.

Take, for example, PEU's role in efforts to address New York's worsening homelessness crisis. PEU field staff serve as frontline responders,[60] working with the city to move homeless individuals out of expensive and often poorly maintained hotels or cluster apartments and into more stable shelters, where they can receive city services such as drug treatment and be entered in programs that provide an on-ramp to permanent housing.[61] PEU caseworkers have also been central to homelessness prevention efforts by identifying residents on the cusp of eviction and enrolling them in city services aimed at protecting those vulnerable residents, such as the city's newly funded program for housing defense lawyers.

Analysis: Building Agency Capacity

While the frontline, proactive service delivery aspect of PEU's work represents a major improvement in connecting vulnerable populations to needed support services, PEU is also notable for how it is effectuating an *internal* cultural shift within city bureaucracy. Because of the impact of its field operation, PEU is being called on by city agencies for thorny issues. For example, when the Department of Consumer Affairs wanted to get the word out to immigrants about new benefits and programs, they reached out to the team. In another instance, there was a disease being carried by rats, and the de Blasio administration needed a trusted source to conduct the knowledge and outreach campaign, so it turned to PEU. PEU is thus increasingly serving as an in-

---

[60] Nikita Stewart and William Neuman, "De Blasio Calls for 'Blood and Guts' War on Homelessness. Is His Plan Gutsy Enough?" *New York Times*, February 28, 2017, www .nytimes.com/2017/02/28/nyregion/bill-de-blasio-new-york-homelessness-plan.html.

[61] Nikita Stewart, "De Blasio Seeks to Turn Homeless 'Cluster Sites' into Affordable Housing," *New York Times*, December 12, 2017, www.nytimes.com/2017/12/12/nyregion/homeless-shelter-cluster-nyc-de-blasio.html.

house mayoral infrastructure that all city agencies can engage and deploy to reach residents on different issues. PEU is building both internal tools to manage constituencies as well as external tools to foster better engagement by sharing its best practices with other interested cities of varying size. By designing better systems for tele-townhalls, hotlines, and face-to-face engagement – and by building new digital apps and interfaces that can be used across government – PEU is also moving the frontier of "civic tech" beyond expensive, commercially marketed products that governments might otherwise pursue.

Part of why PEU has been successful is that, like MONUM, it complements an already robust municipal ecosystem for technology and innovation. As of 2017, in addition to PEU, New York City has a Mayor's Office of Technology and Innovation (MOTI) that oversees the Mayor's Office of Data Analytics (MODA); the latter has housed both the Chief Digital Analytics Office and the Mayor's Office of the Chief Technology Officer, which works across city agencies.[62] MOTI has focused on a range of issues from smart-city technology and IoT technology to the LinkNYC project, which is transforming New York City's unused pay phone infrastructure into a network of Wi-Fi hotspots equipped with information screens and cell phone charging ports.[63] MODA is working to ensure data is effectively deployed across government and proactively thinking about the future of digital tech policy, including cyber resilience.[64] New York City's Office of the Chief Technology Officer has launched NYCx Co-Lab Challenges, which include experimentation hubs to leverage technology to improve residents' lives in certain previously underserved neighborhoods.[65] The first test site launched in 2017 in Brownsville, which has one of the highest poverty rates in the city, with 45 percent of Brownsville residents living in poverty compared to 21 percent citywide.[66] In other cities with fewer resources and a smaller pipeline of talent, it would be harder to have a dedicated services outreach office such as PEU. Nonetheless, PEU is building its tools with an eye toward transferability to other cities and municipalities.

---

[62] www1.nyc.gov/site/analytics/about/meet-team.page; https://tech.cityofnewyork.us/; https://tech.cityofnewyork.us/; and NYC Mayor's Office of the Chief Technology Officer (website), "Making Tech Work for All New Yorkers," www.nyc.gov/html/innovation/.

[63] LinkNYC (website), home page, www.link.nyc/.

[64] NYC Analytics (website), "Open Data," www1.nyc.gov/site/analytics/initiatives/open-data.page.

[65] NYC Mayor's Office of the Chief Technology Officer (website), "NYCx Co-Labs," https://tech.cityofnewyork.us/projects/nycx-co-labs/.

[66] Yasmeen Kahn, "Poverty and Hardship Make Life Shorter in Brownsville," WNYC News, March 28, 2017, www.wnyc.org/story/poverty-and-hardships-make-life-shorter-brownsville/.

PEU, like MONUM, also draws much of its power and efficacy from its direct line to the city mayor. The head of PEU reports directly to de Blasio, and the mayor's commitment to the office has given it a greater degree of influence and integration among the various city agencies than might otherwise be expected for a new office. PEU's focus on deploying campaign tools and canvassing techniques has led to a distinctive staffing model and culture, as most of the office's personnel are younger workers with direct grassroots organizing experience who also have in-depth expertise in the major policy issues and programs that the city is implementing.

It is important to view these strengths of PEU in light of what PEU is *not*. As a city-originated project – and as a top-down outreach institution – PEU cannot substitute for the kind of independent, community-based power building discussed earlier in Chapter 4. But as a novel creation within the ecosystem of city agencies, PEU offers an institutionalized home for a civic engagement function – and a valuable shift in orientation away from conventional technocratic policymaking toward a greater focus on engaging with residents and, crucially, meeting residents where they are.

PEU is also a part of the Mayor's Office – a set of executive branch agencies in New York City that can be described as a political wing of the city administration, directly under the mayor's control and thus serving a mayor's personal political purposes – and even campaign efforts – in addition to serving a civic use. The political purposes, and the civic and policy uses, are clearly not mutually exclusive. However, the use of the Mayor's Office for political purposes does raise normative questions about the repurposing of campaign tactics for day-to-day governance as well as the tricky balance between inherently politicized executive powers and the ideals of a neutral bureaucracy. Additionally, the close ties of the Mayor's Office to de Blasio's interests and politics may make PEU more vulnerable to termination by another mayor. PEU, like all executive offices, is not immune to changing political tides.

***

Each of these initiatives has limitations; furthermore, they are both located in wealthy, progressive, coastal cities that are not necessarily representative of the broader country. Having a strong mayoral system helps. Yet despite important limitations and critiques, these examples offer promising models for governance. Each, respectively, has been picked up in different places across the country, with cities such as Philadelphia and Salt Lake City having experimented with their own offices of New Urban Mechanics, and several other communities, including cities in the South, beginning to explore the opportunities for their own Public Engagement Units.

DEMOCRATIZING GOVERNMENT FROM WITHIN

The institutional designs explored in this chapter are not silver-bullet blueprints. But they offer glimpses of what might be possible under a radically different approach to institutional design and governance reform. In place of a "good governance" focus on expertise, rationality, and efficiency, what these examples instead offer is a commitment to building the kinds of governance institutions needed to achieve a better balance of political power, and to make government more genuinely inclusive, accessible, and responsive to constituent demands. Thus, institutionalized support for engagement, whether at the level of federal agencies as in the case of the CFPB or in the creation of city agencies like MONUM or the PEU, suggests that the *internal* expertise and culture of bureaucracies themselves can be shifted to a more constituent-centered orientation, cultivating the skills and tools necessary to proactively engage residents, and respond to their needs.

Some of these experiments are more radical than others. Importantly, some of them are radical in very different ways. The power-shifting institutional designs discussed in Chapter 6, including the institutionalizing of bargaining power in community benefits agreements (CBAs), particularly in Oakland, California, arguably represent a more aggressive push to equalize disparities of power in urban development than those discussed so far in this chapter. The formation of MONUM does not represent a strong challenge to external power disparities between different constituencies. But by its centrality within Boston City Hall, and its distinctive culture and orientation, MONUM is radical in its own way and offers a very distinctive vision of "reinventing government."

Unlike initiatives that simply offer lip service to the idea of engagement but are really focused on making government operate more like the private sector or use public engagement as a public relations wing of government, PEU and MONUM are examples of engagement being used to transform the traditional relationship between citizens and the state. In contrast, the Obama administration's Office of Public Engagement was primarily focused on engaging individual constituency groups in time-bound events.[67] While individual, targeted outreach campaigns were able to engage specific communities, in

---

[67] Indeed, this office continues the work typically called public affairs under previous presidential administrations.

aggregate their impact neither shifted power nor the relationship between citizens and the state. It was a move in the right direction but did not change the bureaucratic structures or internal culture toward engaging people in a robust way.

Similarly, for many innovation units within government a large portion of their focus is on internal innovation – how to make internal processes more efficient, data driven, and agile – without necessarily connecting internal decision-making to external community members. The public sector has recognized the need to modernize, yet the political appetite for internal transformation to lead to external transformation is not always there. Political election cycles, in particular, make elected officials concerned about creating external innovation too quickly, which can open up an administration to public critique. These examples highlight a number of key principles for better institutionalizing democratic inclusion within governmental bureaucracies. Innovation requires internal change to drive external results and provide better outcomes.

First, institutional design is central, particularly in creating *visible targets* for mobilization, advocacy, and participation. American governance is highly fragmented: political authority is divided vertically, between federal, state, and local bodies as well as horizontally between legislative, executive, and judicial branches – and then further fragmented across a confusing multiplicity of different regulatory and enforcement agencies. This makes it extremely difficult for constituencies, even well-organized and durable ones, to participate and exercise political influence. While it is true that some degree of fragmentation can be helpful in providing more arenas for countervailing views,[68] there is a trade-off between such fragmentation and actual policy-making impact. Furthermore, it is more likely that in an extremely fragmented and complex terrain, more well-resourced, sophisticated, and well-connected groups will be able to navigate their way and make themselves heard, while less-resourced groups may fall short, appealing to the wrong office or not even knowing where to appeal in the first place. By contrast, creating highly *visible* institutions can significantly overcome this opacity and fragmentation, making it clear where to go for making particular claims.

Second, these governmental institutions must combine *authority* and *accountability*. The issue of the scope of institutional authority is closely related to the question of its scope of jurisdiction. Where institutions lack

---

[68] See Heather K. Gerken's argument that decentralization is valuable precisely because it allows minority views to be tested out in practice through local- or state-level bodies, in "Dissenting by Deciding," *Stanford Law Review* 57 (2005): 1745, 1759–60.

the actual authority and capacity to shape social or economic conditions, they are less useful levers through which interests and constituencies can exercise power. Stated another way, the promise of actual "influence over a slice of state power" creates "powerful incentives" for participation.[69] This facilitates the capacity of constituencies to mobilize, organize, and exercise power.[70] At the same time, this *authority* must be complemented by institutionalized points of leverage that assure the accountability and responsiveness of policy-makers, whether in the form of dedicated representation as described above, or in the form of more participatory processes as described in Chapter 6.

All three of these elements – *visibility, authority, and accountability* – must be present together. Visibility of an institution alone, without real authority or accountability, may help make clearer to constituents where they can go with a claim or concern, but it offers little leverage for those constituents, and it thus has little impact on the ground. Where an institution has authority without visibility and accountability it is likely to be a powerful but relatively hidden and unresponsive body. Meanwhile, institutions with accountability that lack authority may be more "participatory" but they are simply not powerful enough to affect the most important issues or areas of concern.

Third, in addition to these institutional design principles, the examples above suggest that the presence of governmental institutions dedicated to assuring participation by affected constituencies leads to more structured forms of civic engagement and more sustained processes that convert participation into impact. In particular, the expertise and dedication of participation-oriented bodies like MONUM or PEU make participation much more meaningful, valuable, and impactful. Offices like PEU or MONUM are literally meeting people where they are and ensuring that the very people most affected by a policy are given a seat at the table. Furthermore, part of demonstrating that the community's participation is being taken seriously must involve moving from pilot, ad hoc programs to structured, sustained institutional processes that can be relied upon by communities as ongoing

---

[69] Fung, "Recipes for Public Spheres," 346. See also Archon Fung, "Varieties of Participation in Complex Governance," *Public Administration Review* 66 (December 2006): 66–75, 69.

[70] Archon Fung, *Empowered Participation: Reinventing Urban Democracy* (Princeton, NJ: Princeton University Press, 2006), 71. He writes that participants "must believe that there is some benefit to participation: that meetings are not just talk shops or venting sessions"; Carole Pateman, *Participation and Democratic Theory* (New York: Cambridge University Press, 1976), says that the motivation to engage in political participation stems from a "sense of political efficacy" (46); and Gerald E. Frug, "The City as a Legal Concept," *Harvard Law Review* 93, no. 6 (1980): 1057–1154, says that "power and participation are inextricably linked: a sense of powerlessness tends to produce apathy rather than participation, while the existence of power encourages those able to participate in its exercise to do so" (1070).

spaces for dialogue and contestation. Creating legitimacy and buy-in from communities themselves requires efforts by government officials to show what government can do – and to show that the community's participation is being taken seriously. Without providing such emotionally satisfying forms of engagement and without going beyond mere service delivery or passive forms of input, governmental efforts at civic engagement will fail to generate the necessary buy-in. Moving from pilot programs to institutionalized processes further embeds civic voice in decision-making, signaling to communities that their participation matters and is taken seriously. This in turn makes participation more worthwhile and legitimate *within* the bureaucracy, as a real and important part of policymaking, rather than merely an extra layer of work.

Fourth, these examples suggest a radically different way to approach the internal organization and culture of bureaucracies. If participation and civic power are taken seriously, democracy reforms must move beyond the focus on expertise, efficiency, and conventional understandings of improving and modernizing government. A truly democratic institutional ecosystem requires governmental bodies that do more than simply provide services efficiently. They must also create meaningful points of leverage and mechanisms for participation through which communities can exercise a share of decision-making power.

The restructuring of government agencies that these approaches require is not cosmetic. All of the examples in this chapter required significant investments of staffing resources and internal capacity – and even then, often faced tough resource constraints. In an era where governments at all levels are facing pressures to cut staff and budgets, the realities of the limited bandwidth of public officials as well as the external disparities of power and influence across different constituencies together suggest a need for a radical *reinvestment* in government itself. In such resource-constrained environments, civic engagement cannot be viewed as an ad hoc or auxiliary process. Rather, engagement must be viewed as integral to the core functioning and goals of city hall, from education to housing and transportation.

Relatedly, the more such participatory institutions can be directly connected to core leadership and to central matters of policy concern, the more they will be able to shift power and deepen civic capacity. Because of the time-intensive and potentially politically risky nature of civic engagement, such strong connections to power centers are necessary rather than paradoxical: they reduce the risk that the new power-shifting mechanism will be a one-off endeavor or a vague aspiration. In order to really change the realities of power or policy, these initiatives cannot feel like "island[s] off the mainland" –

Bureaucratizing Participation

marginal and isolated efforts not likely to gain lasting traction.[71] Therefore, although the goal of these institutions is to shift power to generally excluded constituencies, political air cover and commitment from the top are essential. Furthermore, engagement efforts must be deeply integrated into the day-to-day work of governmental policymaking.

Fifth, this approach to participation necessarily requires personnel who view themselves as not only efficiently delivering public services, but also as enthusiastically applying new methods of governance from digital tools to ethnography to civic engagement and organizing. This reorientation requires a very different approach to recruiting, training, and retraining personnel.[72] There are already a variety of programs that focus on expanding and deepening the pipeline of talent moving into public service, from a city manager learning exchange organized by the Kettering Foundation and the National Civic League that brings together public managers from across the country to share lessons and build skills,[73] to federal government fellowships and prestigious civil service honors programs,[74] to Code for America, which has successfully placed tech experts and coders within government bureaucracies,[75] to the efforts by cities like Kansas City and San Francisco to create their own data academy training programs for public employees.[76] The International City/County Management Association (ICMA) is also working to expand its focus to include an exploration of ways that city managers can better implement civic engagement strategies.[77]

But much more can and must be done to train and invest in existing staff while creatively bringing in a crop of new public servants. Outreach to traditionally marginalized communities – for example, through dedicated training and recruitment programs, moving staff from unpaid to paid internships, and creating more diverse "on-ramps" to government service – will be crucial. These measures also must be adapted for recruiting top talent, offsetting the pull of more remunerative and sophisticated recruiting on the part of private-sector companies, particularly at top universities and professional

---

[71] This section is adapted, with permission, from Hollie Russon Gilman and Jessica Gover, *The Architecture of Innovation: Institutionalizing Innovation in Federal Policymaking* (Washington, DC: Beeck Center for Social Impact and Innovation at Georgetown University, 2016), section 7, available at http://beeckcenter.georgetown.edu/wp-content/uploads/2016/10/The-Architecture-of-Innovation_BeeckCenter.pdf.

[72] Ibid.

[73] National Coalition for Dialogue & Deliberation, "Community Blog," http://ncdd.org/27766.

[74] One example is the Presidential Management Fellows, www.pmf.gov/.

[75] Code for America (website), home page, www.codeforamerica.org/.

[76] DataSF (website), "Data Academy," https://datasf.org/academy/.

[77] ICMA (website), home page, https://icma.org/.

168   *Civic Power*

schools. Expanding the pipeline of public service workers is critical not only for expanding the possibilities of institutionalized participatory governance, but also for ensuring the future of government more broadly. The average civil servant today is older than the average civil servant a decade ago.[78] Statistics show that the percentage of government employees under the age of thirty hit an eight-year low of 7 percent in 2013, compared with about 25 percent of the private-sector workforce.[79] By contrast, in 1975, more than 20 percent of the federal workforce was under thirty.[80] Over a third of federal employees are eligible to retire. Indeed, many are leaving the civil service under the combined pressure of budget cuts and deliberate regulatory dismantling under the Trump administration.[81]

This chapter has focused on the ways in which bureaucracies can be created, reformed, and restaffed to orient toward the need to redress disparities of democratic participation and power, and to bake this orientation more deeply into the day-to-day work of governing. But as these various case studies above suggest, much of the concrete work of shifting power through institutional (re)design turns on remaking existing policymaking processes themselves, from the new ways the CFPB sought to make financial regulations to the approach MONUM took to affordable housing in Boston. But as suggested above, these efforts are dependent on the goodwill of policymakers – and on the support of executives running these administrations. A more durable approach to civic power requires not just favorable agencies; it also requires more codified and institutionalized forms of power and influence for grassroots constituencies. In Chapter 6, we focus more specifically on the policymaking process itself, to outline specific institutional designs and approaches that can better institutionalize leverage and influence for traditionally disempowered constituencies.

---

[78] OPM.gov (website), "Profile of Federal Civilian Non-Postal Employees," September 30, 2017, www.opm.gov/policy-data-oversight/data-analysis-documentation/federal-employment-reports/rep orts-publications/profile-of-federal-civilian-non-postal-employees/.

[79] Dann Vinik, "America's Government is Getting Old," *Politico*, September 29, 2017, www .politico.com/agenda/story/2017/09/27/aging-government-workforce-analysis-000525.

[80] Rachel Feintzeig, "US Struggles to Draw Young, Savvy Staff," *Wall Street Journal*, June 10, 2014, www.wsj.com/articles/u-s-government-struggles-to-attract-young-savvy-staff-members -1402445198.

[81] Joe Davidson, "Top Civil Servants Leaving Trump Administration at a Quick Clip," *Washington Post*, September 9, 2018, www.washingtonpost.com/.

6

Power-Oriented Policy Design

The ideas of "public participation" and "civic engagement" call to mind many different well-worn images, like that of the classic public forum, where laypersons gather to hear from and offer comments to policymakers, or the paper version of the public forum, notice-and-comment procedures to gather public input as part of administrative rulemaking. Yet most of these images represent particularly thin forms of participation. Such fora or comment procedures fall short of ideals of civic power in myriad ways. The participants are necessarily limited to a self-selected, and therefore often more well-resourced or well-connected, constituency. Many participants in public fora are passive spectators. Those who do show up to speak may not have the expertise or language to make their arguments persuasive to decision-makers. Even if they do, the decision-makers have little accountability to respond to or follow the requests of the public. When the meeting or comment period ends, there is rarely any follow-up.

As we saw in the previous chapters, the good governance approach to reform does little to alter the fundamental *lack* of power that participants experience in these kinds of conventional civic engagement episodes. But as we noted earlier, alternative reform traditions include attempts to create more structural and empowered forms of participation, where participants have real power and are more representative of affected constituencies. Power, as we have argued, is contextual; it is not just a product of the capacities of social movements and civil society organizations, but rather a result of the interactions between civil society groups and the larger institutional contexts in which advocacy and organizing takes place. Where there are greater institutional points of leverage, constituencies can exercise actual influence on, if not outright control over, policymaking outcomes. Where those levers are connected to decisions of actual consequence and import, participation becomes meaningful, tangible, and *worthwhile*. In this chapter, we explore some

Civic Power

strategies and mechanisms for achieving such participation, and examples of how policymaking processes and institutions can be designed with a focus on shifting power – in stark contrast to the kinds of "good governance" bureaucratic reforms described in Chapter 4.

Social science scholars have argued that policy designs can create political feedback loops, helping to shape political identities and to activate constituent mobilization, thereby making policies more durable and sustainable against attempts at rollback, capture, or drift. The classic example here is Social Security: as a universal benefit, Social Security over time proved formative in shaping American identities, becoming so embedded that it has proven very difficult to dismantle due to the depth of public support for it.[1] Such accounts suggest that, by contrast, policies that are "submerged" and less visible to beneficiaries are more easily dismantled as they command less public support.[2] Opaque or hidden regulatory schemes and policy designs exacerbate pre-existing disparities of political power and organizational capacity: such submerged policy designs "easily capture and hold the attention of organized interests" but "fail to make themselves apparent as social programs to most citizens who use them," exacerbating the difficulties of organized, countervailing collective action.[3] The feedback literature thus offers a starting point for thinking about how policy and institutional design might better balance disparities of power – by making some benefits more visible, less opaque, we might make it easier for the lay public to form political opinions and exercise influence on policy debates.

But power-shifting policy design can and should go much further. The "political opportunity structure" that helps define civil society influence and power extends beyond policy visibility and its feedback effects.[4] It is important to design institutions with power in mind, focusing particularly on how those institutions will interact with social movements or civil society organizations.[5]

---

[1] See generally, Jacob S. Hacker, *The Divided Welfare State: The Battle over Public and Private Social Benefits in the United States* (New York: Cambridge University Press, 2002); Paul Pierson, *Dismantling the Welfare State? Reagan, Thatcher and the Politics of Retrenchment* (New York: Cambridge University Press, 1994); Theda Skocpol, *Protecting Soldiers and Mothers* (Cambridge, MA: Belknap Press of Harvard University, 1992); and Andrea Louise Campbell, "Self-Interest, Social Security, and the Distinctive Participation Patterns of Senior Citizens," *American Political Science Review* 96, no. 3 (September 2002): 565–74.

[2] Mettler, *Submerged State*, 32.

[3] Ibid., 46.

[4] Sidney G. Tarrow, *Power in Movement: Social Movement and Contentious Politics*, 3rd ed. (New York: Cambridge University Press, 2011), 26–27, 80, 167–68.

[5] Andrias, "Separations of Wealth," 497–99.

We do not suggest there is any guaranteed method for balancing power in administrative institutions. Procedural protections can be captured by well-resourced actors or turned into methods of abuse by unsympathetic officials.[6] Still, while taking such factors into account along with pre-existing disparities in civic capacity, we can nonetheless identify key ways to improve the design of institutions and policymaking processes so that they can better balance and shift power.

If the classic town hall or notice-and-comment procedures represent "thin" participation, what would "thick" participation look like?[7] Thin participation is often marred by problems of limited access; a focus on matters that are ultimately marginal or trivial, rather than on the more game-changing decisions that tend to take place prior to the moment of public engagement; and a lack of public power to actually alter policy decisions. When designing institutions and policy processes to create more empowered participation, three dimensions of concern are key.[8] First, who participates – and how is that participation structured? Is it through selected representatives, through delegation to experts, through a random panel of laypersons, or through some engagement with the mass, diffuse public? Second, what is the form of power or authority that the participatory engagement carries? Is it merely advisory? Or do participants actually co-govern alongside policymakers? Third, what is the specific design mode for the participatory moment? Is it a conventional town hall or notice-and-comment rulemaking? Are people merely listening as spectators? Or does it involve processes of deliberation, aggregation, bargaining, and negotiation?

A huge number of design decisions shape a particular policymaking process or attempt to structure participation. But for our purposes, four design principles stand out. First, participation must be not only *structured* – channeled through an actual procedure or institutional form rather than through a process that simply holds a discursive space out as open to the public, as in open town hall meetings or during public comment periods – but also *contestatory*, open to disagreement, negotiation, and bargaining, rather than focused on consensus. Second, this structured contestation has to be centered around real institutional levers of influence. Third, the participation should be focused on a set of questions that actually matter; when participation is localized to the latter stages of a policymaking process there is less and less room for actual influence, as so much has already been decided. Finally,

---

[6] Ganesh Sitaraman "Puzzling Absence," 1500.
[7] Nabatchi and Leighninger, *Public Participation*, 14–22.
[8] Archon Fung, "Varieties of Participation," 66–75.

participation cannot be ad hoc or one-off; it must have an institutional home that can sustain the participation over time, serve as an interface between constituents and policymakers, and function as a visible forum or target for future mobilization.

In this chapter we explore three specific strategies for institutionalizing greater power and leverage by *designing public policies differently*, providing examples and analyses for each. First, we explore the value of structured contestation and participation in the *policymaking* stage, through the example of participatory budgeting. Second, we explore the impact of structured contestation and participation that occurs further "downstream" in the *monitoring and enforcement* phase of *policy implementation*, when engagement can influence how policies are applied, and therefore, made real on the ground. Third, we explore models that *institutionalize stakeholder representation* in day-to-day governance, at both the federal and local levels.

These examples demonstrate the value of considerations far beyond the traditional cost–benefit analysis of efficiency in neoliberal policymaking. Indeed, these strategies have little to do with analyzing the impacts of *particular* policy outcomes, as they focus on transforming policy itself as a process. Furthermore, instead of simply structuring low-cost interactions for citizens, many of these examples equip and empower communities with real decision-making authority. The value proposition offered to citizens in exchange for their investment of their *resources* (including time, insights, and trust) in such processes is that through structured engagement they can truly influence policy outcomes.

PARTICIPATORY POLICYMAKING: THE CASE OF PARTICIPATORY
BUDGETING

Participatory budgeting (PB), is a process that empowers citizens to make binding, rather than merely advisory, recommendations on spending public money.[9] While other participatory and deliberative processes involving budgeting exist, the form of participatory budgeting discussed here harkens back to a specific process that first originated in Brazil. Following the collapse of a twenty-year military dictatorship, the socialist Workers Party (Partido dos Trabalhadores, PT) developed PB in an attempt to genuinely empower citizens and bring enhanced legitimacy to democratic governance. Thirteen Brazilian cities introduced PB programs in 1989. PB

---

[9] See Fung, "Putting the Public Back into Governance," 2.

Power-Oriented Policy Design

represented an experiment in "radical democracy,"[10] offering a way to "relegitimate the state by showing that it could be effective, redistributive, and transparent."[11] At the height of Porto Alegre's PB experience, between 1991 and 1994, upward of 15 percent of the entire municipal budget was allocated through PB; during 1995 and 2000 that portion ranged between 8 and 9 percent.[12] During this time the World Bank found that nearly 20 percent of the population was participating.[13] This was the high-water mark, however, and the power of PB dissipated in Porto Alegre after 2005 and in other large Brazilian cities and culminated in the suspension of the process in Porto Alegre in 2017. It became much more common to allocate 1 to 3 percent of the entire municipal budget to PB.[14] Nonetheless, by 2013 this model of PB had spread to more than 2,700 municipalities worldwide.[15]

In practice, PB in Brazil has been a success – both substantively and procedurally. Substantively, PB has led to decreases in corruption and in infant mortality rates as well as increases in the numbers of civil society organizations (CSOs) and the size of spending allocations for healthcare.[16] Procedurally, although most forms of public participation activate wealthier and more well-resourced constituencies, PB in Brazil has been able to effectively attract low-income, less-educated people.[17] PB in Brazil has a redistributive effect with respect to lower-income neighborhoods with

[10] Benjamin Goldfrank, "Lessons from Latin America's Experience in Participatory Budgeting," in *Participatory Budgeting*, ed. Anwar Shah (Washington, DC: World Bank, 2007), 91–126, 95.

[11] Ibid.

[12] Adalmir Marquetti, "Participação e redistribuição: O orçamento participativo em Porto Alegre" in *A inovação democrática no Brasil: O orçamento participativo*, ed. Leonardo Avritzer, Zander Navarro, and A. Marquetti (São Paulo, Brazil: Cortez Editora, 2003), 129–56.

[13] *Brazil: Toward a More Inclusive and Effective Participatory Budget in Porto Alegre* (Washington, DC: World Bank, 2008).

[14] Ibid.

[15] Benjamin Goldfrank, "The World Bank and the Globalization of Participatory Budgeting," *Journal of Public Deliberation* 8, no. 2 (2012): 1–18, http://blogs.worldbank.org/ic4d/mobile-enhanced-participatory-budgeting-in-the-drc"; and Yves Sintomer, Carsten Herzberg, and Anja Röcke, "Transnational Models of Citizen Participation: The Case of Participatory Budgeting," in *Hope for Democracy: 25 Years of Participatory Budgeting Worldwide*, ed. Nelson Dias (São Brás de Alportel, Portugal: In Loco Association, 2014), 28–44.

[16] Brain Wampler and Michael Touchton, "Brazil Let Its Citizens Make Decisions about City Budgets. Here's What Happened," *Washington Post*, January 22, 2014, www.washingtonpost.com/news/monkey-cage/wp/2014/01/22/brazil-let-its-citizens-make-decisions-about-city-bud gets-heres-what-happened/.

[17] Carole Pateman, "Participatory Democracy Revisited"; Michael Touchton and Brian Wampler, "Improving Social Well-Being through New Democratic Institutions." *Comparative Political Studies* 47, no. 10 (2014): 1442–69.

poorer locales now receiving more spending per capita than wealthier areas.[18] Looking at census data over ten years of PB, however, shows that redistribution becomes visible only several years after the implementation of PB.[19] In Brazil, PB has been shown to improve governance, reinforce democracy, and contribute significantly to the well-being of the poorest citizens.[20] Michael Touchton and Brian Wampler connect the presence of PB in a given locality with increased municipal spending on sanitation and health, increased numbers of CSOs, and decreased rates of infant mortality.[21] Similarly, Sónia Gonçalves found that Brazilian municipalities that implemented PB channeled a larger fraction of their total budget to investments in sanitation and health services, with a pronounced reduction in infant mortality.[22] However, as the process in Brazil has been going on for decades, there is no consensus on how long it takes for well-being effects related to PB to appear.[23]

Following its success in Brazil,[24] PB experienced a boom in global popularity. Parisian mayor Anne Hidalgo has turned over € 426 million over six years to a version of PB that combines online and in-person voting options.[25] The World Bank dubbed PB a "best practice" in democratic innovation and has supported its use across several developing countries.[26] PB has been used at the district, city, or state level in Peru (2002); the Dominican Republic (2007); Kenya (2010); South Korea (2005); Indonesia (2000); and the Philippines (2012); and in the first national process, in Portugal (2017).[27]

---

[18] Marquetti, "Participação e redistribuição: O orçamento participativo em Porto Alegre."
[19] See also Brian Wampler, "A Guide to Participatory Budgeting." In *Participatory Budgeting*, edited by Anwar Shah (Washington, DC: World Bank, 2007), 21–53.
[20] Touchton and Wampler, "Improving Social Well-Being."
[21] Ibid.
[22] Sónia Gonçalves, "The Effects of Participatory Budgeting on Municipal Expenditures and Infant Mortality in Brazil," *World Development* 53 (January 2014): 94–110, doi: 10.1016/j.worlddev.2013.01.009.
[23] Brian Wampler, Stephanie McNulty, and Michael Touchton, *Participatory Budgeting: Spreading across the Globe*, Transparency Initiative, January 2018, www.transparency-initiative.org/uncategorized/2094/participatory-budgeting-spreading-across-globe/.
[24] Touchton and Wampler, "Improving Social Well-Being."
[25] Pauline Véron, "Why Paris Is Building the World's Biggest Participatory Budget," NewCities (website), https://newcities.org/why-paris-is-building-the-worlds-biggest-participatory-budget/.
[26] Goldfrank, "The World Bank and the Globalization of Participatory Budgeting," 2.
[27] See Wampler, McNulty, and Touchton, *Participatory Budgeting*, 31; Touchton and Wampler, "Improving Social Well-Being"; and Aaron Schneider and Ben Goldfrank, *Budgets and Ballots in Brazil: Participatory Budgeting from the City to the State*, IDS Working Paper 149 (Brighton, UK: Institute of Development Studies, 2002).

PB in the United States

PB's absorption into American politics has been more tentative, but its successes and failures are instructive in highlighting ways that participatory policymaking can be designed to rebalance power, whether at small or larger scales. The Participatory Budgeting Project (PBP), a nonprofit organization that champions PB in the United States and Canada, has worked to adapt the Brazilian process to the municipal ward level in the United States by providing education, technical assistance, research, and evaluation.[28] PB got its American start in Chicago in 2009, when Alderman Joe Moore began to employ PB for the allocation of $1.32 million in neighborhood discretionary funds, leveraging funds that had previously been dispersed at the discretion of each alderman.[29] This "menu money" is viewed as a "perk" of the job.[30] Some have critiqued the process as being less than transparent about how decisions are made.[31] Chicago's Office of Inspector General has recommended that the Chicago Department of Transportation take over the allocation of these resources because it has centralized knowledge of infrastructure needs.[32]

From Chicago, PB has spread across the United States to a number of other cities including Vallejo, California; Seattle, Washington; and Greensboro, North Carolina.[33] Since 2009, PBP has helped residents

---

[28] Josh Lerner and Donata Secondo, "By the People, for the People: Participatory Budgeting from the Bottom Up in North America," *Journal of Public Deliberation* 8, no. 2 (2012): 1–9; and Josh Lerner, *Everyone Counts: Could "Participatory Budgeting" Change Democracy?* (Ithaca, NY: Cornell University Press, 2014).

[29] A more detailed description of how Alderman Moore and other American municipal officials came to adopt PB in the first place is offered by Josh Lerner, a key actor in PB's arrival in America and cofounder of the PBP, in *Everyone Counts*.

[30] See City of Chicago, "Capital Improvement Program," www.cityofchicago.org/city/en/depts/obm/provdrs/cap_improve.html.

[31] Orlando Ortiz, "Money in Politics: What Funds Do Elected Officials Have at Their Disposal?" Project Six (website), November 29, 2016, https://thesecretsix.com/2016/11/29/money-in-politics-what-funds-do-elected-officials-have-at-their-disposal/.

[32] Editorial board, "Chicago's 'Menu' Program for Aldermen: 50 Ways to Waste Your Money," *Chicago Tribune*, April 20, 2017, www.chicagotribune.com/news/opinion/editorials/ct-menu-chicago-aldermen-cdot-infrastructure-city-council-0421-jm-20170420-story.html.

[33] See City of Vallejo, California (website), "Vallejo's PB Program," www.ci.vallejo.ca.us/cms/One.aspx?pageId=52101; Greensboro, North Carolina (website), "About Participatory Budgeting," www.greensboro-nc.gov/departments/budget-evaluation/participatory-budgeting/about; Oscar Perry Abello, "Participatory Budgeting Fans Say State DOT's Embrace Is 'Revolutionary,'" Next City (website), September 20, 2017, https://nextcity.org/daily/entry/california-transportation-participatory-budgeting-process; and Participatory Budgeting Buffalo (website), www.pbbuffalo.org/. The Vallejo project has not been sustainable, and the Greensboro project began in 2015 with a total allocation of $500,000. The Buffalo project was $150,000 until it was cut down to $10,000; see Participatory Budgeting Process (website), "PB Network Partners," www.participatorybudgeting.org/participate.

176   *Civic Power*

allocate roughly $200 million through PB processes across the United States and Canada.[34] Localities including Oakland, California, are beginning to allocate federal community development block grants (CDBGs) from the Department of Housing and Urban Development (HUD) toward PB.[35] Boston launched the first youth-driven PB in which people between the ages of twelve and twenty-five can allocate a $1 million in mayoral discretionary funds.[36]

New York City, meanwhile, has become one of the most prominent municipalities to embrace PB, in large part because PB has been endorsed with enthusiasm and high-level support from the city council and city hall. By 2015, PB became an official practice, and many council members ran the process in their districts. In the 2017–18 cycle, twenty-seven (out of fifty-one) city council members allocated a portion of their discretionary funds to PB and over 99,250 New Yorkers (more voters than the previous mid-term elections) voted on how to allocate over $36 million in capital funds. Thirty-two city council members pledged to each allocate at least $1 million during the 2018–19 process.[37] The current process includes an online voting option, and residents as young as eleven may vote.[38] In 2018, New York City Mayor Bill de Blasio expanded PB through a parallel program in all of the city's 400 public high schools, where each school will have $2,000 of public dollars to allocate through a participatory process.[39] In the 2018 midterm elections, PB was approved as a wider ballot initiative in New York City, along with the creation of a new

---

[34]   Public Agenda (website), "Research and Evaluation of Participatory Budgeting in the U.S. and Canada," February 20, 2015, www.publicagenda.org/pages/research-and-evaluation-of-participatory-budgeting-in-the-us-and-canada; and Kristine Wong, "Participatory Budgeting Is Gaining Momentum in the US. How Does It Work?" *Shareable*, March 20, 2017, www.shareable.net/blog/participatory-budgeting-is-gaining-momentum-in-the-us-how-does-it-work.

[35]   Oscar Perry Abello, "Oakland Lets Residents Decide How to Prioritize Federal Grant Money," Next City (website), May 3, 2017, https://nextcity.org/daily/entry/oakland-participatory-budgeting-residents-decide-spend-cdbgs.

[36]   City of Boston, "Youth Lead the Change," www.boston.gov/departments/boston-centers-youth-families/youth-lead-change.

[37]   New York City Council (website), "Participatory Budgeting: Winning Projects," https://council.nyc.gov/pb/cycle-7-results/; New York City Council (website), "Participatory Budgeting," https://council.nyc.gov/pb/participate/; and New York City Council (website), "Speaker Corey Johnson and the New York City Council Kickoff Participatory Budgeting Cycle 8," August 20, 2018, https://council.nyc.gov/press/2018/08/20/1633/.

[38]   Ibid.

[39]   Lauren Cook, "City Council Program Lets You Choose What Public Projects to Fund in Your Neighborhood," amNewYork (website), updated April 13, 2018, www.amny.com/news/participatory-budgeting-nyc-1.17864253.

Civic Engagement Commission. The ballot measure includes expanding participatory budgeting across every council process.[40]

Crucially, high-level support from within city government has enabled PB in New York City to have a more centralized and streamlined process with dedicated staff and access to resources. Indeed, successful PB implementation involves a highly structured – and very resource-intensive – process, underscoring the degree to which genuinely inclusive and empowered participation requires more strategic process design beyond the conventional town hall model.

In many PB experiments across the United States the process begins with "idea assemblies," where residents gather to learn about the available budget as well as brainstorm different possible projects. Following an initial brainstorm, neighborhood residents break into smaller groups to brainstorm possible projects to fund with the neighborhood budget.[41] In Chicago and New York City, organizers from the sponsoring alderman's or city council member's staff assemble the results of these discussions. Individual participants then select "budget delegates" to take on leadership roles in the next stage. Here, the delegates are at the center. As a smaller group, they can engage more deeply in deliberation and debate over different proposals. During this time other participating residents – not just the budget delegates – are also briefed by city officials on guidelines for expenditures; there are also technical briefings from engineers and other experts on issues that might be relevant for implementing, or deciding between, different projects. Residents and delegates then often form thematic subcommittees (such as "Parks," "Streets and Sidewalks," "Public Housing"), each focused on a different set of proposals or issues. This phase is time intensive, often requiring a significant commitment to attend in-person meetings over several weeks or months; as a result there is often attrition among attendees during this phase. But it also reflects a sustained process where participants have multiple opportunities to deliberate over project selection and implementation.

---

[40] Christina Veiga, "Haven't heard of participatory budgeting? Voters approved it on Tuesday – and here's how it can bring millions to New York City schools," Chalkbeat (website), November 7, 2018, https://chalkbeat.org/posts/ny/2018/11/07/havent-heard-of-participatory-budgeting-voters-approved-it-on-tuesday-and-heres-how-it-can-bring-millions-to-new-york-city-schools/; and Amy Plitt, "NYC's ballot measures all receive decisive approval," NYC Curbed (website) November 7, 2018, https://ny.curbed.com/2018/11/7/18071574/election-2018-new-york-results-ballot-proposals.

[41] The process is more fully laid out in Hollie Russon Gilman, *Democracy Reinvented: Participatory Budgeting and Civic Innovation in America* (Washington, DC: Brookings Institution, 2016), 37–107.

178   *Civic Power*

There is a concern that although PB in the United States has been effective at inclusion, in particular at ensuring that people from diverse racial, economic, immigrant status, and gender backgrounds are included, nonetheless this diversity has not, in turn, led to projects that promote racial or gender equity or larger social justice outcomes.[42] PB in the United States has also suffered from low rates of participation. One PB district in New York City had a turnout rate of only 4.7 percent in 2018. In this district, which includes the relatively well-educated and affluent citizens of Gowanus, Cobble Hill, and Park Slope, out of roughly 127,650 eligible voters over the age of ten, only 6,000 voters participated. A nearby district, however, which includes the much more working-class neighborhoods of Sunset Park and Red Hook, had the highest voter tally with 11,600.[43]

That said, in practice, New York and Chicago have been generally successful in mobilizing a wide cross section of residents to engage as participants – wider even than in Brazil.[44] While higher-income residents are still overrepresented in some districts, city officials have engaged in proactive efforts to engage low-income and minority households, for example by targeting distinct communities such as public housing residents, youth, and seniors.[45] Roughly a third of the idea assemblies in both cities included multilingual interpretation and translation support.[46] In New York City, 51,000 residents voted in the 2014–15 PB cycle.[47] The

[42] Wampler, McNulty, and Touchton, *Participatory Budgeting*; Celina Su, "Whose Budget? Our Budget? Broadening Political Stakeholdership via Participatory Budgeting," *Journal of Public Deliberation* 8, no. 2 (2012): 1–16, www.publicdeliberation.net/cgi/viewcontent.cgi?art icle=1227&context=jpd; and Madeleine Pape and Josh Lerner, "Budgeting for Equity: How Can Participatory Budgeting Advance Equity in The United States?" *Journal of Public Deliberation* 12, no. 2 (2016): 1–15, www.publicdeliberation.net/cgi/viewcontent.cgi? article=1435&context=jpd.

[43] Mary Frost, "NYC's 'Participatory Budgeting' Procedure Doles Out Millions, Though Few Actually Vote," *Brooklyn Daily Eagle*, updated May 16, 2018, https://brooklyneagle.com/articles/ 2018/05/15/nycs-participatory-budgeting-procedure-doles-out-millions-though-few-actually-vote/

[44] Hollie Russon Gilman and Brian Wampler, "The Difference in Design: Participatory Budgeting in Brazil and the United States," *Journal of Public Deliberation*, forthcoming.

[45] See Gilman, *Democracy Reinvented*; Ron Hayduk, Kristen Hackett, and Diana Tamashiro Folla, "Immigrant Engagement in Participatory Budgeting in New York City," *New Political Science* 39, no. 1 (2017): 76–94.

[46] Community Development Project at the Urban Justice Center and the Participatory Budgeting in New York City Research Team, *A People's Budget: A Research and Evaluation Report on Participatory Budgeting in New York City* (New York: Urban Justice Center, 2015); and "Participatory Budgeting Chicago: Rulebook 2017," 2017, www.pbchicago.org/uploads/1/ 3/5/3/13535542/2017_pbchi_rulebook.pdf .

[47] New York City Council (website), "Speaker Melissa Mark-Viverito and New York City Council Launch 2015–2016 Participatory Budgeting Cycle," September 21, 2015, https://coun cil.nyc.gov/press/2015/09/21/180/.

majority of these voters, 57 percent, identified as people of color, in comparison to 47 percent for local election voters.[48] Initial data from PB in the United States, including in New York City, demonstrates that PB is an effective gateway for getting people to vote in more conventional elections.[49] Comparing data from two city council districts in New York City, District 39 and District 23, researchers compared PB voters with similar people in the voter files who could not participate in PB because their council district was not participating.[50] The researchers matched people from neighborhoods with similar racial composition, income, education, and voting patterns.[51] Through this matched-pair analysis, they demonstrated that people who vote in PB are on average 7 percent more likely to vote in subsequent elections (not related to PB).[52]

The New York City process has been particularly successful at galvanizing typically marginalized communities, in part because of a combination of strong internal (governmental) and external (community) support. In New York City, Melissa Mark-Viverito – one of the original four bipartisan city council members to launch the PB process – was later elected speaker of the city council. PB then became integrated into a wider set of reforms aimed at making discretionary funding more transparent and equitable.[53] Overall, these reforms offer a formulaic, needs-based model of disbursement.[54] Having strong external, community support for PB in New York City has also been key to its success. The technical lead, the Participatory Budgeting Project (PBP), is located in Brooklyn. Another key partner is Community Voices Heard (CVH), a grassroots, membership-based, multiracial community organization that organizes low-income populations to influence policy change; it has rich ties to community members.[55] PBP and CVH have advocated for broader PB adoption and have deployed their networks to

---

[48] Community Development Project at the Urban Justice Center and the Participatory Budgeting in New York City Research Team, *A People's Budget*.

[49] Josh Lerner, "Participatory Budgeting Increased Voters Likelihood 7%," Participatory Budgeting Project (website), June 28, 2018, www.participatorybudgeting.org/participatory-budgeting-increases-voter-turnout-7/.

[50] Ibid.

[51] Ibid.

[52] Ibid.

[53] Gloria Pazmino, "'Long Overdue:' Mark-Viverito Introduces New Rules," *Politico*, April 30, 2014, www.politico.com/states/new-york/city-hall/story/2014/04/long-overdue-mark-viverito-introduces-new-rules-012586.

[54] Council of the City of New York, Office of Communications, "Council to Vote on Landmark Rules Reform Package," press release, May 14, 2014, http://council.nyc.gov/html/pr/051414sta ted.shtml.

[55] Community Voices Heard (website), "Mission & Vision," www.cvhaction.org/what-we-do/.

180 *Civic Power*

mobilize participants.[56] Where civil society groups like PBP and CVH play a stronger role, there is a notable increase in representation of traditionally marginalized communities in the PB process.[57] Yet even in New York City, the presence of such civil society groups is unevenly dispersed throughout districts employing PB. Some communities have a strong support network of civil society organizations that, in turn, can lift and amplify PB, while other communities have less well-established civic infrastructure.

Furthermore, the success of PB turns on the significant allocation of public resources in the form of expenditures, personnel, and staff time. Indeed, given the intensity and multifaceted nature of the process, the resource commitment required of public administrators in a successful PB project is significant. This is especially true *because* PB in the United States has not been more institutionalized; for example, in Brazil PB has been adopted at the municipal level, which allows the PB process there much greater access to resources.[58] By contrast, in the United States PB efforts are typically carried out by elected officials representing single-member districts; therefore the process hinges upon the goodwill of public administrators across agencies who often volunteer to work closely with volunteer residents over the course of several months during hours that they would normally not expect to work and without additional compensation.

In some cases, elected officials have been able to officially allocate staff time to PB, but there is wide variation among districts. For example, in New York City each city council member has a set amount of dollars for his or her operating budget but rental costs for district offices can vary widely, as in some districts real estate is much more expensive than in other places. As a result, not every council member has the same budgetary resources to dedicate to paying to staff PB. The result is an uneven process. Similar phenomena exist across the country in other localities that are implementing PB. Smaller cities are especially vulnerable to obstacles in properly supporting PB because of limited staff bandwidth and capacity to engage.

The American experience with PB is thus promising, but not perfect. Most glaringly, PB remains a piecemeal practice, and where it has taken root in places like New York City it nonetheless remains focused on capital neighborhood budgets, rather than on more far-reaching and transformative policy decisions over larger budgets or other issues of macro-scale impact. Yet the

---

[56] Nancy Baez and Andreas Hernandez, "Participatory Budgeting in the City: Challenging NYC's Development Paradigm from the Grassroots," *Interface* 4, no. 1 (2012): 316–26.

[57] Gilman, *Democracy Reinvented*.

[58] Gilman and Wampler, "The Difference in Design."

Power-Oriented Policy Design 181

experience of PB is crucial, for it illustrates both the challenges and potential of participatory policymaking. PB highlights that diverse, grassroots constituencies can be engaged in complex policy decisions, which while necessarily involving debate and disagreement, can nevertheless yield tangible, legitimate, and effective governance decisions. Through its involved structure for participation, contestation, and decision-making, PB allows for grassroots control without chaos. But to pull this off, PB requires not only a sophisticated *process design*, but also significant investment of time and resources from community organizations and civil society groups that can facilitate resident engagement as well as engagement from public officials whose staff are needed to guide the process.

Lessons for Participatory Policymaking

PB offers several instructive lessons for participatory policymaking. The very expansion of PB from Brazil across the globe with varying mutations and forms illustrates the portable lessons of the model. It is important to note first that the outcomes of PB in the United States are more constrained than in other prominent deliberative exercises. Yet these constraints are by design. As scholars including Caroline W. Lee, Edward T. Walker, and Francesca Polletta have noted, there are strong reasons to be concerned that common forms of public engagement are nothing more than public relations campaigns to mask actual power.[59] However, unlike other forms of deliberation that run the risk of co-opting civic time without offering tangible benefits, PB leads to tangible outcomes. This is an inherent compromise of its process design – because PB is *not* open-ended, tangible outcomes are guaranteed.

Second, although theorists have articulated norms for increased participation in a broad variety of political interactions, budgets are sometimes missed as opportunities for meaningful civic engagement. In their work, Archon Fung and Erik Olin Wright articulate a concept of "empowered deliberative democracy," in which Brazilian PB is given as one compelling example among others that include: neighborhood governance in Chicago to check urban bureaucratic power over public schools and policing; WRTP/BIG STEP, a merger of the Wisconsin Regional Training Partnership and the Building Industry Group Skilled Trades Employment Program that enables organized labor, firms, and government to assist workers in employment transitions; and panchayat reforms in West Bengal and Kerala, India that have created both

---

[59] Walker, *Grassroots for Hire*; Lee, *Do-It-Yourself Democracy* ; and Polletta, "How Participatory Democracy Became White."

182 *Civic Power*

representative and direct channels to empower local villages.[60] Fung and Wright's concept of "empowered deliberative democracy" places PB in dialogue with diverse initiatives meant to give citizens an additional voice in decision-making and offers models for deepening engagement. Similarly, Lisa Blomgren Bingham, Tina Nabatchi, and Rosemary O'Leary place participatory budgeting within a broader category of "quasi-legislative new governance processes" that "include deliberative democracy, e-democracy, public conversations, citizen juries, study circles, collaborative policy making, and other forms of deliberation and dialogue among groups of stakeholders or citizens."[61]

Third, PB throws both the paradigm of good governance as well as the move to create a more seamless digital democracy on their heads. Many technological innovations are designed to streamline processes, removing the human touch. In our increasingly automated society, participatory budgeting provides an alternative approach. By design, the process is high touch or labor intensive, requiring elected officials to devote resources and time to encouraging face-to-face engagement. Its innovation is in bringing people back in – not through a groundbreaking technology but through a deliberative mechanism that seeks to marshal civic and political will to reinvent the current budgeting process and to reengage citizens in democracy.

The participatory budgeting process is effective in part because it is not as efficient as these less transparent or hands-on approaches. PB is both labor intensive and time intensive because it involves the hard work of coalition building and direct dialogue. Ultimately, it is the process itself, and the experience of participation, that makes PB such an important phenomenon. PB provides opportunities for civic knowledge, strengthened relationships with elected officials, greater community inclusion, and leadership combined with skill development. It is a reminder that participatory governance cannot simply overlook the benefits of in-person, "slow democracy."[62]

Fourth, unlike reforms to insulate policymaking from politics, PB is an inherently political process. There is contestation by design. Residents need to actively grapple with shrinking budgets, bureaucratic constraints, and competing interests. Time and time again in a PB process people need to make tough compromises and sacrifices. In a PB process, elected officials are turning over

---

[60] Archon Fung and Erik Olin Wright, "Deepening Democracy: Innovations in Empowered Participatory Governance," *Politics and Society* 29, no. 1 (2001): 5-42.

[61] Bingham, Nabatchi, and O'Leary, "The New Governance," 552.

[62] Susan Clark and Woden Teachout, *Slow Democracy: Rediscovering Community, Bringing Decision Making Back Home* (White River Junction, VT: Chelsea Green Publishing, 2012), xxii.

Power-Oriented Policy Design

decision-making power – and this is perhaps the most political act of all. Typically, definitions of new governance or collaborative public management "emphasize the role of the public in collaborative management processes."[63] Yet PB also includes a powerful role for public administrators themselves, making it important for researchers to continue studying how to identify and assist public managers and elected officials in deploying new governance models.[64]

DOWNSTREAM PARTICIPATION: MONITORING AND ENFORCEMENT

Participatory budgeting exemplifies the kinds of power shifting and participation that can be achieved in the initial moment of policy formation. Another strategy for institutionalizing structured, empowered participation and balancing disparities of power involves a very different domain of policymaking: rather than focusing "upstream" on the formation of policy, these strategies emphasize the shifting of power in "downstream" decisions around monitoring and enforcement of government conduct.[65]

Consider two brief examples first. In the years following the protests in Ferguson, Missouri, activists coalesced around the Movement for Black Lives Policy Table, developing an aggressive and powerful policy agenda focused on shifting political power to communities of color. As the Movement for Black Lives has continued to reshape the political and policy landscape around the United States, activists have helped pioneer radical new experiments in participatory, community control over key areas of policymaking. For example, as Jocelyn Simonson has argued, the Movement for Black Lives has helped inspire the rise of "copwatching" groups in cities across the country, focused on holding police officers accountable and counteracting systemic racial biases in law enforcement.[66] These groups organize neighborhood "patrols" of residents to monitor police activity and ultimately prevent abuses

---

[63] Terry L. Cooper, Thomas A. Bryer, and Jack W. Meek, "Citizen-Centered Collaborative Public Management," *Public Administration Review* special issue 66 (2006): 76.

[64] Tina Nabatchi has been in the forefront of this new research area. See her "Putting the 'Public' Back in Public Values Research: Designing Public Participation to Identify and Respond to Public Values," *Public Administration Review* 72, no. 5 (2012): 699–708.

[65] Much of this section is based on an earlier essay, K. Sabeel Rahman, "From Civic Tech to Civic Capacity: The Case of Citizen Audits," *PS: Political Science & Politics* 50, no. 3 (2017): 751–57.

[66] For an excellent documentation and analysis of copwatching as part of a broader movement for criminal justice reform from below, see Jocelyn Simonson, "Copwatching," *California Law Review* 104, no. 2 (2016): 391–445.

of police power.[67] Copwatching patrols have helped shift the calculus of many police officers on the beat, leading to reduced instances of aggression or stop-and-frisk activities, even in the absence of a formal policy change.[68] As Simonson argues, while copwatching is made easier by the availability of technology that can record and disseminate citizen videos of police activity broadly and rapidly – such as smartphones, YouTube, and social media – nonetheless, copwatching is about more than technology. Rather, it represents a concerted strategy that leverages residents' ability to monitor and observe governmental conduct as a way both to organize constituencies for broader battles over public policies, including especially criminal justice reform, and to exercise leverage on policymakers.

Meanwhile, in slums around the world, affiliates of Shack/Slum Dwellers International (SDI) organize landless residents to conduct pavement censuses, documenting informal uses of land, property lines, and provision of public services. These monitoring techniques are also used to hold city government officials accountable to promises made but rarely kept regarding investments in the slums and protections for the land rights of current slumdwellers.[69] These activists use the data as an advocacy tool, giving the lie to public officials' promises of investing in poor neighborhoods, and revealing patterns of corruption or neglect. The collection of data also helped identify local needs that the community could then advocate for in city budget decisions. SDI activists then leverage this data and local knowledge to elevate themselves into necessary – and therefore, powerful – partners for governments seeking to construct infrastructure and development projects. This local knowledge in turn has enabled SDI chapters to gain the support of individual bureaucrats, thus building greater political influence over time – a tactic that one SDI leader describes as "picking off the state one person at a time."[70]

In both of these cases, grassroots civil society groups have organized to monitor the conduct of public officials, to generate information about their communities, and to direct these efforts toward activities intended to both goad policymakers and hold them accountable. These are examples of what we can call "citizen audits," the *organized, strategic use of participatory monitoring techniques to hold government actors accountable*. As Tara

---

[67] Ibid., 394.
[68] Ibid., 412–17.
[69] See Xavier de Souza Briggs, *Democracy as Problem Solving: Civic Capacity in Communities across the Globe* (Cambridge, MA: MIT Press, 2008), 95–96; and Anni Beukes, "Know Your City: Community Profiling of Informal Settlements," *International Institute for Environment and Development (IIED) Briefing*, June 2014, http://pubs.iied.org/pdfs/17244IIED.pdf.
[70] Briggs, *Democracy as Problem Solving*, 95–96.

Melish has argued, this strategy of oppositional, adversarial, yet constructive engagement that leverages grassroots monitoring and data collection represents a new pattern of human rights advocacy, emphasizing a shift away from "nonnegotiable material demands and mass confrontation" toward "participatory and process-oriented" approaches that attempt to create institutional frameworks that encourage accountability.[71]

Through participatory monitoring of public standards and goals – for example via "report cards," citizen auditing, development of alternative proposed budgets, and monitoring of performance indicators – grassroots groups can track public policy outcomes, diagnose failures and slowdowns, and advocate for policy changes.[72] Such participation can check the manipulations of private actors by facilitating regulatory enforcement, while also protecting against potentially lax enforcement by regulators themselves. Communities engaged and mobilized in this way can devise their own performance goals, indicators, or targets, which may be used to evaluate the performance of policymakers in implementation through audits, report cards, and diagnoses of blockages, slowdowns, or implementation failures.[73] These monitoring activities can further build power through two related channels: (1) by enabling advocacy and influence on government officials through a combination of political pressure and policy-relevant data; and (2) by thickening the connections and relationships between different grassroots organizations and between organizations and affected communities.

Such models have proliferated in an international human rights context, documented in instances like India's right to information movement and in its impact on worker and farmer organizing around anti-corruption efforts[74] as well as in the use of digital participatory mapping tools in holding service delivery accountable in Kenya.[75] In the United States, similar forms of participatory monitoring and countervailing power have been set up through the proliferation of state and local human rights enforcement bodies. These bodies serve as institutional targets and focal points for community

---

[71] Tara J. Melish, "Maximum Feasible Participation of the Poor: New Governance, New Accountability, and a 21st Century War on the Sources of Poverty," *Yale Human Rights and Development Journal* 13, no. 1 (2010): 1–133, 55, 68, 73–74.

[72] Ibid., 76–99.

[73] Ibid., 89–98.

[74] See Rob Jenkins and Anne Marie Goetz, "Accounts and Accountability: Theoretical Implications of the Right-to-Information Movement in India," *Third World Quarterly* 20, no. 3 (1999): 603–22.

[75] See Molly K. Land, "Democratizing Human Rights Fact-Finding," in *The Transformation of Human Rights Fact-Finding*, ed. Philip Alston and Sarah Knuckey (New York: Oxford University Press, 2015).

186   *Civic Power*

mobilization, while monitoring outcomes offers a way for affected communities to exercise influence and leverage.[76] Policies can be made amenable to
such participatory monitoring through further design features: (1) providing
the means for citizens to monitor outcomes, such as through the articulation
of standards that outline the goals of the policy and the collecting of data or
other metrics on outcomes; (2) providing citizens with real leverage by
empowering them to trigger actual policy and enforcement proceedings;
and (3) making these findings and activities public.[77] It is notable that these
approaches deploy some of the same transparency techniques that we criticized in earlier chapters; but crucially, transparency here is paired with
institutional levers that meaningfully shift power, rather than simply relying
on the passive act of disclosure to drive policy change. Consider as another
example the case of the Community Reinvestment Act (CRA).

Designing Power Shifts through Monitoring: The Community Reinvestment Act

The community reinvestment movement was one of the last major victories of
the civil rights era, arising out of a push to address racial disparities in housing
and lending; it also attempted to address the deindustrialization and decline of
major urban areas.[78] Following the passage of the Fair Housing Act in 1968,

---

[76] See Melish, "Maximum Feasible Participation," 68–110 for examples in state and local
contexts.

[77] Deploying this type of countervailing power through monitoring of policy implementation
and enforcement is somewhat akin to conventional legal accounts of the "private attorney
general" in that it deputizes civil society and private actors to proactively facilitate enforcement, incentivized in part by their own self-interest. This can expand the enforcement
capacity of the government agency itself. But where private attorney general models have
raised concerns about potentially sapping the capacity of the state, the models described here,
such as the CRA and the Oakland Army Base CBA, are institutional structures that actually
expand state capacity – and provide an independent lever through which civil society actors
can hold both private third parties (like banks or developers) as well as lax regulators to
account. On the private attorney general and its potential limits, see Stephen Burbank,
Sean Farhang, and Herbert Kritzer, "Private Enforcement," *Lewis & Clark Law Review* 17,
no. 3 (2013): 637–722, on the benefits of private enforcement regimes (662) and on the
disadvantages of private enforcement (667); Pamela S. Karlan, "Disarming the Private
Attorney General," *University of Illinois Law Review* 2003, no. 1 (2003): 183–209; and
William B. Rubenstein, "On What a Private Attorney General Is – And Why It Matters,"
Vanderbilt Law Review 57, no. 6 (June 2005): 2129–77, on mapping the different forms of
private attorney general lawyers and distinguishing them from public law enforcement
officers.

[78] Prepared for the Gettysburg Project by K. Sabeel Rahman and Archon Fung. This case was
developed from published sources and excerpts from Archon Fung, Mary Graham, and
David Weil, *Full Disclosure: The Perils and Promise of Transparency* (New York: Cambridge

Power-Oriented Policy Design

this push for community reinvestment centered around the growing efforts of community groups to make private lending more transparent and equitable.[79] The Home Mortgage Disclosure Act of 1975 (HDMA) required financial institutions to publicly disclose the geographic, racial, gender, and income-level distributions of mortgage applications, origins, and purchases.[80] The Community Reinvestment Act (CRA) of 1977, meanwhile, required lenders to meet the credit needs of local communities, subjecting these financial institutions to inspections by federal regulators.[81]

These statutes have had a major impact on lending practices and community development. Under HMDA, in 2004 as many as 33.6 million loan records were reported by nearly 9,000 financial institutions.[82] The CRA has increased lending for home mortgages, small businesses, and community development to low- and moderate- income borrowers and communities by over $600 billion, reducing racial and income disparities in homeownership. The evidence suggests that banks have changed their behavior in many ways as a result of the CRA, including: forming multibank community development corporations (CDCs), investing in locally based community development financial institutions (CDFIs), and dedicating special units to focus on meeting the needs of local low- and moderate-income borrowers within the geographic area of the bank branch.[83] More importantly, in 1989 the Federal Reserve Bank rejected a merger request by Continental Illinois National Bank and the Trust Company of Chicago, for the first time issuing a request denial grounded on a bank's violation of its CRA responsibilities to provide credit to local communities. As merger activity increased during the late 1980s and early 1990s,[84] so too did the sophistication of advocacy groups, which tracked

---

University Press, 2007), and Kazi Sabeel Al-Jalal Rahman, "Governing the Economy: Markets, Experts, and Citizens" (PhD diss., Harvard University, 2013).

[79] 42 U.S.C. §§ 3601–31, Title VIII of the Civil Rights Act of 1968.

[80] Pub. L 94-200, 89 Stat. 1124.

[81] Pub. L. 95-128, 91 Stat. 1147, title VIII of the Housing and Community Development Act of 1977, 12 U.S.C. § 2901 et seq.

[82] See Federal Financial Institutions Examination Council (FFIEC) (website), "Home Mortgage Disclosure Act," www.ffiec.gov/hmda; and Fung, Graham, and Weil, *Full Disclosure*.

[83] Barr, "Credit Where it Counts," 147–48. See also Jill Littrell and Fred Brooks, "In Defense of the Community Reinvestment Act," *Journal of Community Practice* 18, no. 4 (2010): 417–39; and Raymond H. Brescia, "Part of the Disease or Part of the Cure: The Financial Crisis and the Community Reinvestment Act," *University of South Carolina Law Review* 60 (2009): 617–77, 639–40. It should be noted that the evidence also indicates that the CRA is not a cause of the subprime lending crisis. The CRA covers only a small percentage of subprime loans, while the CRA itself has gradually eroded into more of a rubber stamp of approval.

[84] Barr, "Credit Where it Counts," 113.

188   *Civic Power*

the performance of particular banks and often petitioned regulators to turn down merger requests if a bank's performance indicated unfair lending practices.

What is most noteworthy about this community reinvestment movement, however, is how lending disclosure and CRA enforcement depended on a confluence of mobilization and institutional structure. The policy was pushed by community organizations, but elements of the policy design itself made possible a more participatory form of monitoring, which in turn radically altered the power dynamics between minority communities, banks, and (often lax) federal regulators.

Under the CRA, banks were required to meet the credit needs of local neighborhoods, in an effort to reduce racial discrimination in access to credit. Federal agencies were empowered to inspect banks on their CRA performance and could veto proposed mergers if the banks involved did not score highly enough on metrics of lending to local, and especially minority, communities.[85] Furthermore, civil society groups could request or trigger a federal inspection of banks suspected of failing to meet these credit needs. The result was a significant shift in power and responsiveness. Community groups in Philadelphia and elsewhere were able to pressure government regulators who might otherwise be lax in enforcing the CRA. These inspections in turn created incentives for banks to proactively engage representatives of local community groups. In effect community members had gone from marginalized to centrally empowered in local lending policies.

Indeed, advocacy groups used HMDA data to document constraints on credit in their communities and to negotiate new mechanisms for low-income lending with individual banks. Broad-based community reinvestment task forces in Washington, Rhode Island, New Jersey, and Michigan forged partnerships among community organizations, lending institutions, and state and local governments to address access problems. Investigative reporters, financial analysts, and other third parties used the information to document pervasive patterns of discriminatory lending and the exodus of banks from low-income neighborhoods. In 1988, for example, the *Atlanta Journal-Constitution* published "The Color of Money," a series of articles that received extensive

---

[85] Different agencies are responsible for overseeing different kinds of financial institutions. The CRA applies to each of these agencies as they oversee their relevant financial institutions. Thus, the OCC oversees national banks, the Federal Reserve oversees state-chartered banks that are members of the Federal Reserve system, and the FDIC oversees state-chartered banks that are not members of the Federal Reserve system. See Richard Marisco, "Democratizing Capital: The History, Law, and Reform of the Community Reinvestment Act," *New York Law School Law Review* 49 (2004): 712–26, 718.

Power-Oriented Policy Design   189

national attention and exposed widespread redlining in that city.[86] In 1992, the Federal Reserve Bank of Boston conducted a rigorous study that concluded that race had a strong influence in lending decisions.[87] The study received broad media coverage, confronting banks with discrimination allegations from a particularly authoritative source.

Similarly, in a number of cities, the CRA's provision allowing community groups to invoke federal regulatory involvement helped catalyze a broader effort among community organizations to organize and expand their engagement with local banks.[88] The background threat of federal regulatory enforcement incentivized banks themselves to engage with these community groups and negotiate for mutually agreeable community lending programs. In Boston in the 1990s, groups like the Community Investment Coalition (CIC) formed out of a combination of labor unions, community development corporations, and the state's affordable housing association.[89] The CIC then developed neighborhood reinvestment plans for the Roxbury area of Boston and prepared CRA challenges. In response, many of the larger banks in the area, including the Bank of Boston and the Bank of New England, agreed to negotiate, culminating in an affordable mortgage lending plan for the region.[90] The Pittsburgh Community Reinvestment Group formed in 1988 as a multiracial advocacy coalition to conduct local research on CRA scorecard data provided by federal agencies. Invoking the CRA, this group was able to organize and empower other community development corporation leaders, and negotiate with local banks to channel more investment to poorer neighborhoods. The group even convinced the City of Pittsburgh and its board of education to put their money in banks that performed better on their CRA obligations.[91]

In the 1990s, the accuracy and scope of CRA data continued to improve: disclosure became more frequent; data quality increased; more financial institutions were required to report; and data were collected and distributed

---

[86] In 1989, Bill Dedman was awarded a Pulitzer Prize for this series, published May 1–4, 1988.

[87] Alicia H. Munnell, Lynn Elaine Browne, James McEneaney, and Geoffrey M. B. Tootell, "Mortgage Lending in Boston: Interpreting HMDA Data," *American Economic Review* 86, no. 1 (1996): 25–53. Originally published as a working paper in 1992.

[88] Gregory Squires, "The Rough Road to Reinvestment," chapter 1 in *Organizing Access to Capital: Advocacy and the Democratization of Financial Institutions*, ed. Gregory D. Squires (Philadelphia: Temple University Press, 2003), 1–26.

[89] Munnell, Browne, McEneaney, and Tootell, "Mortgage Lending in Boston."

[90] William Tisdale and Carla Westheirn, "Giving Back to the Future: Citizen Involvement and Community Stabilization in Milwaukee," chapter 3 in *Organizing Access to Capital*, ed. Squires, (Philadelphia: Temple University Press, 2003), 42–54.

[91] Stanley Lowe and John Metzger, "A Citywide Strategy: The Pittsburgh Community Reinvestment Group," chapter 6 in *Organizing Access to Capital*, ed. Squires, (Philadelphia: Temple University Press, 2003), 85–101.

190   *Civic Power*

electronically.[92] The Clinton administration, meanwhile, issued directives to allow for stronger enforcement of these standards. In particular, regulatory oversight was more effective after revisions in 1995 that specified three tests by which these firms would be evaluated: a lending test, an investment test, and a service test.[93]

Today, the CRA has less of an effect on bank lending and on community participation. CRA oversight is now more generally a process of agency rubber-stamp approval, while courts have been hostile to legal challenges from individuals and groups seeking judicial review of agency decisions under the CRA.[94] These trends have diminished the ability of community groups to monitor bank and agency conduct. Furthermore, the Trump administration has made an overhaul of the CRA part of its legislative agenda.[95] But in its heyday, the CRA offered a glimpse of how a well-designed enforcement and transparency process, combined with active and strategic organizing by grassroots constituencies, can produce genuine shifts in power.

Beyond Good Governance

Indeed, citizen audits represent a distinctive rethinking of conventional approaches to democratic and participatory theory and institutional design, going well beyond the kinds of "good governance" approaches to transparency and participation discussed earlier. Like good governance and civic tech reforms, these participatory monitoring approaches rely to some degree on data transparency and civic engagement. But whereas in good governance and civic tech approaches the public is implicitly characterized as a *passive recipient* of improved services, in cases like copwatching, the SDI pavement census, and the CRA, the dynamic is very different. Here the public is an *active participant* in policy – organized through civil society organizations, generating its own data, and with statutory or regulatory or political levers

---

[92] These improvements were introduced through subsequent amendments of the Federal Reserve Board's Regulation C, which implements HMDA.

[93] Barr, "Credit Where it Counts," 112.

[94] Brescia, "Part of the Disease or Part of the Cure," 652–55. See *Lee v. Board of Governors of the Federal Reserve System*, 118 F.3d 905 (2d Cir 1997) and *Lee v. Federal Deposit Insurance Corporation*, SDNY 1997, discussed in Brescia, 655–61. As he notes, courts have shifted to viewing legal claims brought by community groups on CRA grounds as failing to meet standards of causation and redressability, finding that the statute's stated goals of expanding community access to credit are amorphous and precatory.

[95] Rachel Louise Ensign and Ryan Tracy, "Trump Administration Seeks to Change Rules on Bank Lending to the Poor," *Wall Street Journal*, January 10, 2018, www.wsj.com/articles/trump-administration-seeks-to-change-rules-on-bank-lending-to-the-poor-1515624418.

Power-Oriented Policy Design 191

through which it can exercise direct influence on policymakers as a result. Nor are these cases where participants are awash in so much data that it becomes useless; the focus here is not on dumping data for its own sake, but rather on more "targeted" transparency that focuses on the metrics and goals that matter to the participants themselves.[96]

Indeed, distinguishing citizen audits from conventional transparency regimes reveals an important difference between these approaches in their underlying diagnoses of the sources of governmental failure as well as in their theories of democratizing reform. In both transparency and open data interventions, the primary defect of the political process is understood as a *lack of information* in one or two typical accounts: (1) if only voters knew more of what policymakers were doing, they could hold these officials accountable; or (2) if only policymakers had better information about facts on the ground, they could do their jobs better. Informational gaps and asymmetries are a reality and worth addressing, but citizen audits as described above exhibit a more sophisticated diagnosis of governmental failure, rooted in an analysis of power. For these activists, the problem is not a lack of information on the part of policymakers or even that there is a mass of nebulously uninformed voters. Rather the root problem is a systematic political indifference on the part of policymakers toward the needs, concerns, and voices of the marginalized communities.

In many ways, this is a more realistic vision of political failure than that which underlies the open government framework. Here, policymakers are rightly seen as embedded in fields of influence and social context that shape their behavior. The neglect of minority and marginalized communities is a product of concrete disparities in political power and influence – in the capacity of different communities to hold policymakers accountable – and not just disparities of information. The remedy, then, is to acquire better information about policymaker activities and facts on the ground, while also actively leveraging this information to generate greater political power and influence on those policymakers.

In recent years, some democratic theorists have turned to the idea of citizen monitoring and surveillance of government officials as a distinctive form of democratic action and power. In this view, when citizens watch, as an audience, this is more than an act of passive observation; indeed, they can thereby

---

[96] This is what Archon Fung, Mary Graham, and David Weil call "targeted transparency," distinguishing it from ordinary transparency regimes that simply disclose information, untethered to any particular topical focus or any link to an enforcement or advocacy response. See their *Full Disclosure*, 39–40.

192   *Civic Power*

exercise a powerful form of influence that relies not on the metaphor of citizen voice (through speech, voting, or deliberation), but rather on the metaphor of the citizen's *gaze* – observing, monitoring, and surveilling decision-makers, and in the process placing these decision-makers under additional burdens of persuasion, accountability, and efficacy.[97]

Citizen monitoring, or surveillance of policymakers, represents what theorist Pierre Rosanvallon calls a form of "organiz[ed] distrust," and, as such, it is a *"mode of action ... [that] cannot be dismissed as mere passivity."*[98] What might look like a passivity and apathy on the part of modern voters may in fact be something quite different: a shift or displacement of political activity away from formal and conventional channels of democratic voice toward such alternative modes of building and exercising political power. Such citizen monitoring may not take the form of a public speech or a voting action, and it may emphasize a negative critique of government rather than proposing an alternative solution. But it nevertheless represents a thoroughly *active*, and *public* assertion of civic power.[99] Indeed, the idea of citizen monitoring is more suited for operating in a real, nonideal political world: rather than positing an overly utopian vision of civic virtue, voice, or participation, monitoring taps into a more realistic form of civic engagement suited to the existing opportunities and capacities of most laypersons. It also takes preexisting evils and disparities of power as given, yet seeks to mitigate them by expanding popular modes of accountability, rather than trying to bracket or elide these disparities.[100] Citizen audits are thus not just about information, but rather link information to a specifically adversarial and oppositional stance of monitoring, accountability, and influence.

Citizen audits also represent a mode of democratic participation that is distinct from conventional interest in deliberation and voice. Deliberative democracy often casts the project of participation in the light of virtuous, good faith citizens engaging in articulating reasons in public, while seeking

---

[97]   Jeffrey Edward Green, *The Eyes of the People: Democracy in an Age of Spectatorship* (New York: Oxford University Press, 2009). It is worth noting that this focus on building power and organizing constituents also distinguishes citizen audits from the kind of spectator power that Green valorizes. Green focuses on the power of *unorganized* spectators, "linked together in their shared experience of nondecision, nonpreference, and relative subordination to political elites" (63). While the activists in citizen audits are generally outside of the decision-making or reason-giving spaces, they nevertheless are deliberately organized and mobilized as groups.

[98]   Pierre Rosanvallon, *Counter-Democracy: Politics in an Age of Distrust*, trans. Arthur Goldhammer (New York: Cambridge University Press, 2012), 4, 34.

[99]   See Rosanvallon, *Counter-Democracy*, 185.

[100]   Green, *The Eyes of the People*, 24.

Power-Oriented Policy Design

consensus and mutual understanding. The implicit goal is to minimize – or at least economize – disagreement so as to enable progress on matters of common concern.[101] But many citizens lack opportunities to engage in this kind of deliberative voice. Furthermore, the realities of marginalization and disempowerment mean that even in these deliberative settings, such power disparities can often persist in the background.[102] Unlike deliberation, citizen audits do *not* seek consensus, or citizen voice; rather they aim to mobilize and sharpen *disagreement* through the citizen's gaze.[103] But this is not to say that such citizen audits are meant to be purely inhibitory and conflictual; they do seek to contribute to systematic policy change and reform. The key is that citizen audits take a stance of *productive contestation* – neither seeking consensus, nor collapsing into raw and unchecked conflict.

Indeed, it is this combination of contestation and policy-relevant engagement that generates responsiveness from political elites by building an accumulation of power on the part of formerly powerless groups. It is the adversarial and oppositional stance that creates this necessary friction, which is enhanced by channeling disagreement and contestation toward productive ends. Furthermore, it is the knowledge and capacity of community groups to facilitate effective governance and policy implementation – by monitoring outcomes and providing relevant data to policymakers – that makes this contestation ultimately productive and not solely negative.

Citizen audits thus make two important moves relative to other accounts of civic engagement: (1) they are an adversarial and oppositional form of participation; and (2) they are focused on monitoring and enforcement, not on policymaking in the first instance. What makes citizen audits work effectively is how they place the power over monitoring in the hands of constituencies themselves. By creating this form of civic power, citizen audits provide for an important mode of accountability and contestation that ultimately drives the kind of policy improvements and responsiveness celebrated by other democratic and participatory accounts of governance.[104] But for citizen audits to be productive in generating accountability and responsiveness – and for them to extend beyond particular instances of community organizing – they need to be

[101] For canonical accounts of deliberative democracy, see the work of Amy Gutmann and Dennis Thompson in their *Democracy and Disagreement* and *Why Deliberative Democracy?*
[102] Jennifer M. Morton and Sarah K. Paul, "Grit," *Ethics* (forthcoming), 18, available at https://philarchive.org/archive/PAUG-5v1.
[103] Green, *The Eyes of the People*, 59–61, 179–81.
[104] Rosanvallon suggests that citizen surveillance can be inhibitory and counterproductive by incentivizing inaction (*Counter-Democracy*, 253–59). But if embedded in an institutional structure, such monitoring and accountability can be exactly the kind of adversarial check and spark that drives productive shifts in policy responsiveness.

194   *Civic Power*

embedded in a larger policy design strategy that makes room for this kind of participatory monitoring and accountability.

INSTITUTIONALIZED REPRESENTATION

In our analysis of civic power, we have continually returned to the importance of institutionalized linkages between constituencies and organizing on the one hand, and governance bodies and policymakers on the other. Processes like participatory budgeting or citizen audits provide such linkages by giving constituencies leverage within policymaking or policy implementation. More broadly, democratic reformers have long explored more macro institutional designs that would institutionalize dedicated representation within government bodies, for example through the creation of "regulatory public defenders"[105] or offices for "proxy advocacy."[106] Such offices would create footholds for countervailing interests within the black box of the agency itself. Furthermore, they would be even more forceful in checking agency assumptions and balancing the power and influence of other groups within the agency ecosystem, if they in part possess a more direct connection to "client" constituencies.

A similar approach would establish such links between constituencies and policymakers at the level of an agency office – what Margo Schlanger has dubbed an "office of goodness."[107] Such offices codify and institutionalize a substantive ethos and commitment to a particular mission – for example, civil rights protections or internal dissenting checks and balances within an agency.[108] By providing advice, assistance, or even independent investigation of complaints and checking of agency analyses, these offices can provide an institutionalized form of countervailing power within the agency.[109] Crucially, such offices are for the most part dependent on the

---

[105] See Mariano-Florentino Cuellar, "Rethinking Regulatory Democracy," *Administrative Law Review* 57 (2005): 411–501, 491.

[106] See Daniel Schwarz on examining case studies of how proxy advocacy and tripartism have helped mitigate the risk of capture in state-level insurance regulation, in "Preventing Capture through Consumer Empowerment Programs: Some Evidence from Insurance Regulation," in *Preventing Regulatory Capture: Special Interest Influence and How to Limit It*, ed. Daniel Carpenter and David A. Moss (New York: Cambridge University Press, 2014), 366.

[107] Margo Schlanger, "Offices of Goodness: Influence without Authority in Federal Agencies," *Cardozo Law Review* 36, no. 1 (2014): 55–62.

[108] Ibid.

[109] In this, Schlanger's account relates to other studies of internal checks and balances between offices within the same agency. See Daniel Farber and Anne O'Connell, "Agencies as Adversaries," *California Law Review* 105 (2017): 1375–1469; Neal K. Katyal, "Internal Separation of Powers: Checking Today's Most Dangerous Branch from Within," *Yale Law*

rest of the agency, particularly on its leadership, for their autonomy and independence.[110]

These kinds of quasi-representation are surprisingly common in regulatory bodies at the federal, state, and local levels, and often arise in proposals to remedy institutional capture by dedicating representative or ombudsmen-type officials within regulatory agencies.[111] But as an institutional strategy for shifting power, this approach can be used more widely and in more aggressive ways. Consider two recent experiments in creating whole policymaking bodies that institutionalize countervailing power and representation of marginalized powers at the local level.

Institutionalized Representation at the Local Level: Community Benefits

Consider for example recent efforts by community organizations to democratize urban development processes through the use of community benefits agreements (CBAs). Beginning in the 1990s, CBAs were deployed as a way to hold real estate developers more accountable for investing in local communities rather than simply exploiting these neighborhoods for elite-serving and gentrifying projects.[112] Generally, CBAs refer to contractual agreements between private developers and grassroots community groups (though increasingly local governments have also become direct parties to more modern agreements), committing developers to invest some degree of resources into

---

Journal 115 (2006): 2314–49, describing internal checks within agencies; Jennifer Nou, "Subdelegating Powers," *Columbia Law Review* 117, no. 2 (2017): 473–526, modeling the incentives for agency heads to subdelegate certain functions to other offices within the agency; Jennifer Nou, "Intra-Agency Coordination," *Harvard Law Review* 129 (2015): 421–90; and Daphna Renan, "Pooling Powers," *Columbia Law Review* 115, no. 2 (2015): 211–91.

[110] Schlanger, "Offices of Goodness are internal and dependent on their agency" ("Offices of Goodness," 61); see also Daniel Carpenter, "Internal Governance of Agencies: The Sieve, the Shove, the Show," Harvard Law Review Forum 129 (2016): 189–96, warning that agency subdelegation of this sort can just as often be used to silence internal dissent as to enable it; and Nou, "Subdelegating Powers," noting that subdelegation of power to an internal office is more likely to occur when the incentives and goals of the agency head and the suboffice align.

[111] K. Sabeel Rahman, "Envisioning the Regulatory State: Technocracy, Democracy, and Institutional Experimentation in the 2010 Financial Reform and Oil Spill Statutes," *Harvard Journal on Legislation* 48, no. 2 (2011): 555–90; see also Rahman, "Policymaking as Power-Building," *Southern California Interdisciplinary Law Journal* 27 (2018): 315–77.

[112] See generally Virginia Parks and Dorian Warren, "The Politics and Practice of Economic Justice: Community Benefits Agreements as Tactic of the New Accountable Development Movement," *Journal of Community Practice* 17 (2009): 88–106; and Edward W. De Barbieri, "Do Community Benefits Actually Benefit Communities?" *Cardozo Law Review* 37 (2016): 1773–1825.

local needs – such as parks and infrastructure – while also committing to certain labor requirements, including hiring from local communities and complying with higher wage and worker safety and security standards.[113] CBAs have been praised as a way to hold developers accountable for more inclusive and equitable development.[114] But they also have their critics. In some cases, CBAs have been vehicles for more narrow constituencies to extract concessions that may or may not serve the larger neighborhood.[115] Even if CBAs are successful, there remain challenges of scope, as they are limited to the particular development or project and often lack a larger connection to regional or citywide zoning, housing, and land use decisions.[116]

Key challenges for CBAs include not only assuring representativeness of the community groups negotiating with developers, but also assuring that developers actually follow through on these commitments.[117] Community benefits are often agreed to but ignored, as developers capture or simply run roughshod over local government bodies. As one study suggests, successful CBAs are often marked by the presence of well-organized, effective community groups capable of holding developers accountable to the terms of the agreement.[118] But in recent years, newer experiments with CBAs suggest a further set of requirements – success depends not just on the involvement of well-organized community groups, but rather on the involvement of well-organized community groups that are connected to institutional levers of influence and power.[119]

This is well demonstrated in Oakland, California. In 2013, developers seeking to make use of a former army base there entered into a CBA and a project labor agreement with the City of Oakland and a coalition of community organizations, spearheaded by Revive Oakland, an umbrella group bringing together faith groups, labor organizations, racial and economic justice organizations, and community members.[120] Revive Oakland is a broad campaign that cuts across a range of constituencies; it was led in

---

[113] Parks and Warren, "The Politics and Practice."
[114] Ibid.
[115] See De Barbieri, "Do Community Benefits," 1788–91.
[116] For a recent overview and analysis of CBAs, see De Barbieri, "Do Community Benefits."
[117] Ibid.; and see Parks and Warren, "The Politics and Practice."
[118] See generally, Parks and Warren, "The Politics and Practice."
[119] Ibid.
[120] See Partnership for Working Families (website), "EBASE and Revive Oakland Win Big," June 29, 2012, www.forworkingfamilies.org/article/ebase-and-revive-oakland-win-big; and K. Sabeel Rahman, "The Key to Making Economic Development More Equitable Is Making It More Democratic," Nation, April 26, 2016, www.thenation.com/article/the-key-to-making-economic-development-more-equitable-is-making-it-more-democratic/.

Power-Oriented Policy Design

part by the East Bay Alliance for a Sustainable Economy (EBASE), the San Francisco Bay Area affiliate of the Partnership for Working Families.[121]

The Oakland CBA involves two notable elements. First, in order to implement the local hire requirements, the city formally created the West Oakland Job Resource Center.[122] The CBA requires the developers to work with the job center when hiring for the project.[123] The job center meanwhile proactively recruits qualified candidates, while providing support and referrals for job seekers, helping them leverage their engagement with the army base project into longer-term jobs and careers.[124] As a workforce development and jobs plan, this has proven successful, particularly in transitioning local hires into longer-term trades and careers.[125] For our purposes, it is the creation of the job center itself, and the role of EBASE in taking on responsibility but also a share of power over the hiring for the project, that are notable.

The key role of community groups in the Oakland CBA is even more apparent in the enforcement regime set up for the project. The development and CBA are both monitored by a newly created, city-chartered oversight body comprised of representatives of the developers and the community organizations.[126] This commission is comprised of eleven members appointed by the mayor,[127] removable for cause.[128] There is a requirement that five of the members be appointed from various community organizations and coalition groups specified in the ordinance, with an additional two members appointed from organized labor.[129] The remainder of seats are split between two members from city government and two from the developer.[130] This distribution of seats is telling: not only are local stakeholders included, but they hold the balance of power on the commission. The city and developers combined hold only four of eleven seats; the Revive Oakland coalition and its partners and labor together hold seven seats.[131] The powers of the commission are also significant. It is charged with reviewing the implementation of the CBA, monitoring

---

[121] See "EBASE and Revive Oakland Win Big"; and Rahman, "The Key to Making Economic Development."

[122] Ibid.

[123] Ibid.

[124] Ibid.

[125] See Fran Smith, "Oakland Army Base Is a Model for Equitable Development," Next City (website), February 19, 2016, https://nextcity.org/daily/entry/oakland-army-base-jobs-community-benefits-development.

[126] See Oakland, Cal., Ordinance 13140 (November 13, 2012).

[127] Oakland, Cal., Ordinance 13140. at § 3.

[128] Oakland, Cal., Ordinance 13140. at § 6.

[129] Ibid.

[130] Oakland, Cal., Ordinance 13140. at § 3.

[131] Ibid.

198   *Civic Power*

compliance with the agreement, and negotiating directly with the developers for remedies of possible violations.[132] The city itself is committed to enforcing the agreement as a backstop if such negotiations fall short.[133] Additionally, the commission is charged with issuing reports and findings and is empowered to develop additional procedures for its monitoring functions.[134]

The commission provides a foothold of oversight power for all affected stakeholders. It also provides a forum for airing grievances, empowering community organizations and civil society groups to bring claims for the alleged failures of developers to meet commitments on local hiring or community benefits investments.[135] As a result, the commission both serves as a unique focal point for civic engagement and as a vital point of leverage for community members to influence the project on an ongoing basis. According to Revive Oakland members, the project is not only meeting its local hiring benchmarks, but exceeding them.[136] More importantly, this substantive outcome has been achieved through a structure that has created greater power and influence for the communities themselves. The national Partnership for Working Families is already developing newer iterations of this model for CBAs around the country.[137]

State Wage Boards

Another similar experiment involves state-level regulatory agencies in the context of labor and employment law. Among the biggest policy debates facing workers in today's highly unequal economy involves wages: both the setting of minimum wages in different industries and the problem of "wage theft," where employers fail to provide wages or benefits to which workers are entitled, for example by denying overtime pay or misclassifying full-time employees as "independent contractors."[138] As new worker organizations (of

---

[132] Oakland, Cal., Ordinance 13140. §§ 1, 2a–2c.
[133] Oakland, Cal., Ordinance 13140. § 2d.
[134] Oakland, Cal., Ordinance 13140. § 5.
[135] Rahman, *Democracy against Domination*.
[136] EBASE interview.
[137] See Partnership for Working Families (website), "Policy & Tools: Community Benefits Toolkit," www.forworkingfamilies.org/resources/policy-tools-community-benefits-agreements-and-policies.
[138] Steven Greenhouse, "More Workers Are Claiming 'Wage Theft,'" *New York Times*, August 31, 2014, www.nytimes.com/2014/09/01/business/more-workers-are-claiming-wage-t heft.html; and Linda H. Donahue, James Ryan Lamare, and Fred B. Kotler, *The Cost of Worker Misclassification in New York State* [electronic version] (Ithaca, NY: Cornell

Power-Oriented Policy Design

the sort described in Chapter 4) have gained a foothold of political power in some states, they have sought not just to establish substantive worker-friendly policies, but also to build new *institutions* that could structurally establish more worker power. Like the CBA model in Oakland, a key experiment in this domain has involved the creation of "wage boards" that include dedicated labor representatives and have the authority to set wages and punish companies for wage theft.

Consider New York State's wage board mechanism. Under state Labor Law § 653, the New York State Labor Commissioner can set minimum wages for different sectors through the commissioning of a wage board.[139] These boards consist of at most nine individuals, divided equally among representatives of industry employers, employees, and "general public" members.[140] The board is selected by the state commissioner and chaired by one of the public members.[141] Once established, the board is empowered to conduct public hearings, issue subpoenas, and conduct investigations.[142] The board must also recommend wage levels to the commissioner.[143] This wage board system was harnessed in 2015 to issue a major policy shift, raising the minimum wage for tipped workers (such as restaurant waitstaff), who for many years had been legally exempt from the state's overall minimum wage law.[144] New York is not alone in authorizing and deploying this mechanism; governors of states including

---

University, School of Industrial and Labor Relations, 2007), http://digitalcommons.ilr.cor nell.edu/reports/9/.

[139] National Employment Law Project (website), "New York Department of Labor Wage Board for Fast-Food Workers," Fact sheet, May 2015, www.nelp.org/content/uploads/Fact-Sheet-New-York-Labor-Department-Fast-Food-Wage-Board.pdf. See NY Labor Law (hereinafter "LAB") § 653 (1) (2017), http://codes.findlaw.com/ny/labor-law/lab-sect-653.html: "If, on the basis of information in his possession with or without such an investigation, the commissioner is of the opinion that any substantial number of persons employed in any occupation or occupations are receiving wages insufficient to provide adequate maintenance and to protect their health, he shall appoint a wage board to inquire into and report and recommend adequate minimum wages and regulations for employees ..."

[140] NY LAB § 655 (1) (2017), http://codes.findlaw.com/ny/labor-law/lab-sect-655.html: "A wage board shall be composed of not more than three representatives of employers, an equal number of representatives of employees and an equal number of persons selected from the general public. The commissioner shall appoint the members of the board, the representatives of the employers and employees to be selected so far as practicable from nominations submitted by employers and employees in such occupation or occupations. The commissioner shall designate as the chairman one of the members selected from the general public."

[141] Ibid.

[142] NY LAB § 655 (3).

[143] NY LAB § 655 (4).

[144] Ibid.

200   *Civic Power*

California, Massachusetts, and Wisconsin have a similar authority to set wage levels without legislative action.[145] The New York wage board is a promising governmental tool, but its potential remains relatively limited. On the one hand, it is built on a tripartite structure with members of labor, business, and the government. On the other hand, the scope of the board's authority is limited to wages and does not extend to other workplace issues. Additionally, the ability of the board to facilitate negotiation between workers, employers, and policymakers is contingent and circumstantial.[146]

Nevertheless, this wage board mechanism is indicative of the potential for governmental power shifting through institutional and policy design. As in the Oakland CBA case, a key to the recent revival of interest in wage boards has been the *combination* of bottom-up pressure from worker organizations, a creative focus on institutional design proposals aimed to codify greater worker power, and the presence of policymakers amenable to these demands. Indeed, the rise of "worker centers" around the country – worker-run organizations that provide advocacy and support services for workers outside of the Wagner Act model of collective bargaining – has helped catalyze other similar institutional innovations.[147] The Coalition of Immigrant Worker Advocates (now known as the Coalition of Low-Wage and Immigrant Worker Advocates) in California, for example, worked with the Secretary of Labor as well as the Workforce Development Agency of California to form a low-wage worker advisory board aimed at ensuring industry compliance with state labor regulations.[148] Similarly, on a federal level, Interfaith Worker Justice (IWJ), a nonprofit organization with offices in Chicago, Washington, DC, and Texas,[149] has been a leader in "forming coalitions with state and federal government agencies, including working closely with the Federal Department of Labor Wage and Hour Division."[150]

CONCLUSION: POWER, PARTICIPATION, AND POLICY DESIGN

Shifting power depends not just on strategies of membership building and organizing, as discussed in Chapters 2 and 3. The ability of even well-organized groups to exercise influence over policy depends in part on the

---

[145] "New York Department of Labor Wage Board for Fast-Food Workers."
[146] Andrias, "The New Labor Law," 63–68.
[147] Fine, *Worker Centers*, 2.
[148] Ibid., 436.
[149] Interfaith Worker Justice (website), "About," www.iwj.org/about.
[150] Fine, *Worker Centers*, 451.

larger institutional context. Public policy design involves not just questions of substantive problem-solving; it also implicitly structures the terrain of political action. Thus, we can design public policies with an eye to their *political* and *democratic* effects, not just their substantive outcomes. In this chapter we have seen examples of alternative policy design strategies that take *power* as a central problem to be managed. Creating meaningful interfaces for civic engagement requires: (1) structured participation that follows transparent rules, (2) *contestation* over real levers of influence, (3) participation focused on a distinct set of outcomes, and (4) institutionalization of participation, moving beyond pilots or one-off experiments.

By implementing a participatory process in the initial policy formation stage, traditional policy decisions (like budgeting) can become vehicles for balancing disparities of power and bringing marginalized voices into governance. By creating policy designs that provide the data and levers to enable citizen audits or participatory monitoring, conventional substantive policy issues can become sites of expanding countervailing power. This power orientation to policy design thus represents a major shift in conventional policy discussions. As suggested in Chapter 4, policy design debates will continue to focus on cost–benefit analyses, efficiency, and substantive technical disputes. But in addition to those issues, an orientation toward power and democracy can inflect policy design in important ways.

These examples, however, are not perfect. They still arguably fall short in terms of power and scale. Participatory budgeting in cities or the community monitoring involved in the heyday of CRA are both processes key to very specific policies – neighborhood improvement budgets and the bank merger approval process, respectively. They do not by themselves speak to power disparities in other policy domains. Nor is either currently well entrenched. As we have seen in this chapter, the ability of such policy designs to actually shift power dynamics turns on both the degree to which they are institutionalized (or dismantled) as well as the degree to which government officials devote significant resources and personnel commitment to their success. Thus, a more codified, institutionalized approach to shifting power through policy design also depends on the kinds of internal bureaucratic shifts described in Chapter 5. Furthermore, these power-shifting policy designs require the presence of robust external movement organizing, of the sort described in Chapter 3. Indeed, this should be unsurprising in a sense: given the pervasive disparities of power driving inequality and exclusion in American democracy today, it is fitting that the rebuilding of civic power and democratic inclusion requires a similarly multifaceted approach. The work of creating a real democracy requires transformations in the larger political ecosystem, stretching from organizing to bureaucracies to policy-making. As we will see in the next and final chapter, it is only by operating in all these dimensions that American democracy can be renewed for the twenty-first century.

PART III

CONCLUSION

7

Democracy's Future

In the summer of 2017, a coalition of neo-Nazi and white supremacist groups held a "Unite the Right" rally in Charlottesville, Virginia, leading to counterprotest and clashes.[1] One white supremacist, James Alex Fields Jr., drove a car into a crowd of counterprotesters, killing Heather Heyer and injuring several others.[2] The stark images of an unvarnished, unrepentant, and seemingly unshackled neo-Nazi far right encapsulated the sense of democratic crisis under the specter of exclusionary populist movements for many who diagnose this as the main feature of the Trump era.[3] At the same time, this is not the only "crisis" facing the ideals of American democracy. Concerns about rampant inequality, stagnant wages, the future of work, and the collapse of the safety net have threatened the "American Dream" of economic opportunity for many. Corporate power too seems on the ascent, from the increasing corporate influence on elections after the loosening of campaign finance regulations to corporate pressure on state legislatures and the growing merger wave creating mega-firms that dominate their markets.

DEMOCRATIC RESISTANCE AND RECONSTRUCTION

These myriad social and economic conflicts are beyond the scope of this book, but this book does seek to show that there is a common underlying set of dynamics animating the simultaneous explosion of these many different issues. First, the current "crisis of democracy" is neither just about resolving

---

[1] Jud Esty-Kendall, Mitra Bonshahi, and Emma Bowman, "Loved Ones of Charlottesville Victim Heather Heyer Cope with Their Loss Together," NPR, August 10, 2018, www.npr.org/2018/08/10/636871546/loved-ones-of-charlottesville-victim-heather-heyer-cope-with-their-loss-together.

[2] Ibid.

[3] Hochschild, *Strangers in Their Own Land*, 136.

the unique pressures placed on American institutions and political discourse by Donald Trump, nor should it be seen as the tragic loss of a sense of bipartisanship or civility. Rather, the deeper crisis of American democracy is rooted in underlying structural challenges: (1) the growing crisis of economic inequality that has helped further magnify the gap in power between big business on the one hand and ordinary communities on the other; (2) the systemic crises of exclusion particularly along racial and gender lines preventing many communities from being fully empowered as agents in our democracy; (3) the fusion of rising corporate power as well as media and organizing infrastructures helping sustain the rise of exclusionary populism; and (4) the concurrent thinning out of the organized countervailing power of workers, communities of color, and other marginalized constituencies.

These structural challenges are exacerbated by a further limitation *within* many of the discourses of democracy reform itself. Conventional attempts at democracy reform have often emphasized relatively thin forms of civic engagement that focus only on voter mobilization and voice – or worse, are easily co-opted by corporate and other interests seeking to launder their political influence through the veneer of public engagement. Meanwhile conventional approaches to institutional reform often invoke a "good governance" framework, focusing on making government more rational, technocratic, and efficient. Such approaches to reform, while perhaps attractive and easy to support, do little to redress these deeper inequalities of power and influence.

This is an era where the organized political power of exclusionary populism on the one hand and corporate and wealthy interests on the other have successfully gained control over government at the federal, state, and local levels. These pressures have driven the systematic dismantling of policy regimes that would ensure greater inclusion – like civil rights enforcement and the social safety net – as well as attacks on civil society organizations that empower workers and marginalized communities. In the face of such pressure, conventional democracy reform is not enough. Democracy reformers must embrace a more radical – and radically powerful – concept of democracy, one that is committed to building up the countervailing power of marginalized and traditionally overlooked communities through a combination of durable movement organizing and transformative institutional change.

In this book we have sketched a way of thinking about such long-term, durable power building. Civic power, we have argued, requires the deep investment in grassroots organizing aimed at creating durable coalitions and civil society organizations capable of exercising political influence – and

Democracy's Future

oriented to forge new collective identities and target deep drivers of economic inequality and social exclusion, from the inequities of geography to the precarity of modern work. We have also argued that civic power requires a concurrent shift in the institutional infrastructure of policymaking. Movement organizations by themselves will only have limited influence; what is also needed is the shift among bureaucracies and policymaking institutions and processes to incorporate a commitment to democracy, and to institutionalize approaches that embed greater opportunities for grassroots groups to participate, exert leverage and influence, and thereby exercise power in policymaking.

In some ways, the rise of "Resistance" movements in response to the Trump presidency offer a potentially major opportunity to build this kind of inclusive democracy. Indeed, the Trump era has sparked a remarkable mobilization of grassroots political engagement, starting with the Women's March, the largest single day of collective action in American history on the day after Trump's inauguration,[4] running through the airport protests in reaction to the travel ban,[5] and continuing since then, including such high points as public school teacher strikes in deeply conservative states like Oklahoma,[6] the youth-led March for our Lives focused on gun violence in schools,[7] and mass mobilizations in defense of communities of color and immigrants in response to violent separations of families at the border.[8] Early indicators are that "Resistance" mobilizing has activated a wide swath of Americans, not just Democrats, as emergent groups and local chapters are forming all over the country.[9] We realize that by the time of publication, there will have been several more crises and responses with subsequent lessons for researchers and practitioners. But

[4] Erica Chenoweth and Jeremey Pressman, "This Is What We Learned by Counting the Women's Marches," *Washington Post*, February 7, 2017.

[5] Lauren Gambino, Sabrina Siddiqui, Paul Owen, and Edward Helmore, "Thousands Protest against Trump Travel Ban in Cities and Airports Nationwide," *Guardian*, January 29, 2017, www.theguardian.com/us-news/2017/jan/29/protest-trump-travel-ban-muslims-airports.

[6] Dana Goldstein and Alexander Burns, "Teacher Walkouts Threaten Republican Grip on Conservative States," *New York Times*, April 12, 2018, www.nytimes.com/2018/04/12/us/teacher-walkouts-threaten-republican-grip-on-conservative-states.html.

[7] Peter Jamison, Joe Heim, Lori Aratani, and Marissa J. Lang, "'Never Again!' Students Demand Action against Gun Violence in Nation's Capital," *Washington Post*, March 12, 2018, www .washingtonpost.com/local/march-for-our-lives-huge-crowds-gather-for-rally-against-gun-violence-in-nations-capital/2018/03/24/4121b100-2f7d-11e8-bobo-f706877db618_story.html.

[8] Dara Lind, "'Families Belong Together' Rallies Are Protesting the Separation of Immigrant Children from Parents," *Vox*, June 14, 2018, www.vox.com/2018/6/14/17463732/families-belong-together-rally-protest-separate-children-immigrants.

[9] Charlotte Alter, "How the Anti-Trump Resistance Is Organizing Its Outrage," *Time*, October 18, 2018, http://time.com/longform/democrat-midterm-strategy/.

208 *Civic Power*

there are perennial questions about whether the potential of this moment – like similar ones that have come before it, such as Occupy or even the Movement for Black Lives – will be realized, and doubts remain about its implications for building civic power in the future. A key challenge is that, even with a focus on elections and advocacy, this upsurge of funding and activism may or may not result in long-term political power and change. This challenge manifests on several fronts in key issues that must be addressed.

First, to what extent are these newly activated communities connected to other grassroots social movements, especially among workers and communities of color? And to what extent do the flashpoint mobilizations of "Resistance" feed into the kind of long-term organizing and power building described above? As scholars of social movements have argued, long-term political influence often stems not just from flashpoint moments of mobilized protest, but from the long-term work of grassroots organizing – the painstaking work of building durable mass movements through mass-membership-based civil society organizations. As Marshall Ganz has argued, the enthusiasm and activism of these "resistance groups" needs to be channeled into organizations that thicken relationships, cultivate new leaders, and build the organizational muscle needed to exert durable political influence at the national and local levels.[10] Lara Putnam and Theda Skocpol have documented a generational awakening among suburban, middle-aged, college-educated white women.[11] Meanwhile, the average age of participants in some of these mobilizations ranged from thirty-nine at the March for Racial Justice to forty-four at the People's Climate March.[12] These constituencies could prove an enormous addition to fueling the kinds of bottom-up movements discussed in previous chapters. But they also may not. The very tendencies described in earlier chapters – the trends toward professionalized advocacy over grassroots, federated, and locally rooted organizing, the preference for nonideological "good governance" reforms – cut against this kind of long-term power building.

---

[10] Marshall Ganz, "How to Organize to Win," *The Nation*, March 16, 2018, www.thenation.com /article/how-to-organize-to-win/.

[11] Lara Putnam and Theda Skocpol, "Middle America Reboots Democracy," *Democracy: A Journal of Ideas*, February 20, 2018, https://democracyjournal.org/arguments/middle-america-reboots-democracy/.

[12] Dana R. Fisher, Lorien Jasny, and Dawn M. Dow, "Why Are We Here? Patterns of Intersectional Motivations across the Resistance," *SocArXiv*, last edited July 2, 2018, 14. The authors note, however, that "IRB protocol required that we only collect data from participants over the age of 18" (n. 8). Cf. Sarah Ruiz-Grossman, "Millennials Are the Foot Soldiers of the Resistance," *Huffington Post*, February 23, 2017, www.huffingtonpost.com/entry/trump-protest -poll_us_58addc16e4b0d0a6ef47517e.

Second, there is a question over the degree to which this "Resistance" will drive deep policy and institutional change. Much of this recent enthusiasm has been focused directly on opposition to Trump or on upcoming elections, including congressional midterm elections and a wider range of state and local elections. But it is unclear to what extent existing party systems – particularly the Democratic Party in its opposition to Trump – are capitalizing on these movements to revitalize and transform themselves.[13] Without either the power of a major political party or deep base building and organizing, the degree to which this "Resistance" movement can drive policy change is unclear.[14] The Tea Party was able to begin generating genuine momentum through its distance from the established Republican Party, and then ultimately the party incorporated many of the Tea Party viewpoints and positions. Does the Resistance need to stay independent from the traditional Democratic machinery? What is the right level of support and tension with more established structures?

If part of the concern about the long-term impact of the Resistance stems from its potential separation from the work of deep movement and organization building, there is also a third concern that operates in reverse. That is, are those organizations and movements that *do* in fact engage in the painstaking work of building bottom-up durable movements and organizations actually succeeding in building enough power to overcome institutional inertia and the entrenched power of established interests? Thus many of the case studies noted in this book focus on genuine efforts by organizers, policymakers, and reformers to build civic power. Our story is for the most part an optimistic one, highlighting positive avenues for power building. But the long-term success of these efforts remains to be seen. The existing institutional and organizational powers of the business lobby and of exclusionary populism present formidable barriers to building genuinely countervailing power, particularly when combined with cultural opposition to dislodging current power dynamics as well as sheer inertia. When inclusionary grassroots movements actually do succeed in claiming a share of governmental power, it is critical that they use that moment of control to create durable institutions that can further expand their ability to exercise leverage and influence going forward – including

---

[13] See Skocpol and Putnam in "Middle America Reboots Democracy": "In an era in which political consultants get big-ticket contracts to work with Big Data, as far as we can tell, the party is still not gathering even the most basic *small* data about local membership or the state or local party efforts that could nurture or leverage ongoing participation."

[14] See Jacob S. Hacker, "Afterword: What the Resistance Means for American Democracy," in *The Resistance: The Dawn of the Anti-Trump Opposition Movement*, ed. David S. Meyer and Sidney Tarrow (New York: Oxford University Press, 2018).

through the kinds of institutional reform and bureaucratic reform approaches sketched above.

Indeed, the opportunities created by the Resistance can, however, still be harnessed to drive a deeper, more radical transformation and renewal of American democracy. Democracy, as we have suggested throughout this book, requires building a more equitable balance of power as well as nurturing a commitment to the kinds of civil society organizations and political institutions that can realize and defend this balance of power. This is what we have termed the *civic power* view of democracy reform. Done right, building civic power means creating the kind of *inclusive populism* that is the antidote to both the specter of Charlottesville as well as the concentration of economic power. Investing in bottom-up power of a more diverse and inclusive coalition of communities is part of the toolkit for wresting political power back for the people – for *all* of the people – and embedding that power in long-lasting institutions and policy regimes.

The first pillar of an inclusive populism involves civil society and community organizing. If the crisis of American democracy today is one of exclusion and alienation of marginalized groups from political voice, resulting in government that is unresponsive to significant real needs, then a key to overcoming this challenge is to build independent, grassroots associations that can empower and engage ordinary Americans. Furthermore, done right, these kinds of associations are critical to forging identities that cut across traditional boundaries of race, gender, and geography. The ways in which we go about organizing communities can play a large role in constructing new identities and solidarities – or in reinforcing existing exclusions and divisions.

Too often, organizing is viewed as a thin, short-term project of mobilizing voters for winning elections or rallying behind issue-advocacy campaigns, particularly during legislative pushes. Instead, long-term democratic revival requires a deeper investment in grassroots organizing to build bottom-up participatory capacity and power. Without this kind of durable, independent, civil society muscle, it will be impossible to remedy the disparities of political power and influence skewing our politics. Furthermore, this kind of deep engagement is necessary to build civic power in ways that tighten relationships and thicken networks through shared bonds and identities especially across racial, gender, and geographic lines.

The second pillar for building civic power and driving an inclusionary populism focuses on institutions. Government is not just the target of civil society mobilization, and policy is more than just an outcome of political struggle. Rather, policymaking institutions and policy regimes themselves shape the terrain of political contest itself. Policies can be designed to leave in place existing disparities of power, or they can be designed to build up countervailing power, embedding more hooks and levers through which affected but often underpowered constituencies can exercise more political influence. Bureaucracies, meanwhile, can be radically transformed to be more hospitable to such democratic participation – and to be better counterparts in the larger project of governing in an inclusive way. Truly democratic governance requires different institutional structures for governing agencies as well as different cultures and personnel within the agencies themselves. This means moving from the technocratic, expertise-based model of governance to an inclusive, democratic one.

Combining these two pillars – building bottom-up power through deep organizing and creating radically democratic, participatory institutions and policy designs – produces a major shift from conventional civic engagement or good governance models of reform. Ultimately, such conventional liberal models of governance are at best a mitigation strategy, not a transformational one. Without more far-reaching transformation, the deep disparities of power that subvert democratic ideals cannot be overcome.

Real democracy, then, is a *radical* concept, and as we have argued throughout this book, it requires major shifts in power through deep investments in organizing and institutional transformation. This radicalism must be embraced. But at the same time, we have shown throughout this book that radical democracy is also *achievable*. Concrete on-the-ground examples illustrate ways to build bottom-up power through novel coalitions, from multiracial organizing around infrastructure in urban, suburban, and rural spaces, to new modes of worker organizing. We have also seen how bureaucracies and policy designs can be made more democratic in practice, creating new cultures and cultivating personnel supportive of participation and inclusion, as in bodies like the Mayor's Office of New Urban Mechanics in Boston or the CFPB under Obama. Policies can also help build up countervailing power, as in the cases of the Community Reinvestment Act, Participatory Budgeting, and more. These case studies are indicative, not exhaustive; indeed, these new democratic practices are portable and modular – variants can be implemented at all levels of government and for all types of issues, from the local to the federal, from economic policy to labor.

These ideas therefore have far-reaching implications and potential. At the same time, we are mindful of the limits of even these more radical power-building approaches. There are deep institutional failings that hobble American democracy, from the electoral college to gerrymandering, to the ways in which an asymmetrically polarized party system has enabled a minority of far-right voters to exercise outsize influence on the federal

212   *Civic Power*

government.[15] Systematic voter suppression and the ongoing problem of money in politics remain urgent concerns. Nevertheless, the ideas developed in this book have important implications for the day-to-day work of democracy reform.

RECOMMENDATIONS: BUILDING CIVIC POWER

Our approach in this book has been to view civic power and the task of democratic reconstruction as an ecosystemic matter, requiring shifts in power, major investments of time and resources, and new forms of institution building by a wide range of actors. We have foregrounded the work of organizers and activists on the one hand and policymakers on the other. But the arguments of this book also carry major implications for how two other key constituencies, funders and scholars, can better support and encourage these power-shifting and democracy-enhancing endeavors.

Recommendations for Organizers

As noted in previous chapters, there are a number of common underlying themes that emerge from the focus on building durable, bottom-up, grassroots power. As we have noted above, these lessons are increasingly broadly shared, as a new wave of grassroots leaders and organizations develop powerful and compelling new approaches to grassroots organizing. These new approaches point to a number of key lessons.

First, experiences such as those described in Chapter 3, highlight the importance of activating and organizing communities in part by focusing on concrete problems that affect the lived reality of community members and offering clear solutions, while also linking these experiences to larger collective and structural, rather than individualized, understandings of cause and effect. This means starting from where individuals are experiencing real challenges but working to shift their understandings of those challenges as collective problems, solvable through political action.

Second, it is crucial for organizers to connect the mobilization of communities to very real levers of power. People want to participate, but where mobilization does not yield impact, the resulting frustration can make long-term organizing very difficult. By contrast, where mobilization yields tangible and visible changes, even more widespread and deeper organizing can become possible. At the same time, since so many of the problems that affect

---

[15]   See Hacker, "Afterword."

marginalized communities are deeply structural, organizations must balance the need to show tangible victories (e.g., at the local level) against the rival need to pursue solutions and strategies that operate at more macro, systemic, and structural levels beyond the local or neighborhood context. For example, mobilizing on-the-ground organizing in municipalities to produce even lasting local changes may require addressing the significant structural power of special interests and corporations that pressure state legislatures to pre-empt local ordinances.

Third, organizers need to integrate in-person and online tools. Key case studies show that this is a successful strategy. From the online organizing platform Coworker.org to organizations like the National Domestic Workers Alliance (NDWA), the "alt-labor" movement is particularly effective at leveraging online tools while also investing in people on the ground. High-touch, face-to-face organizing is essential for building solidarities and deep relationships. But it is also true that in the modern era not everyone can meet face-to-face. Online tools can be invaluable in connecting individuals to larger communities – but only if leveraged appropriately to build genuine relationships, rather than substituting "thin" mobilization in place of real organizing. This, in turn, means structuring community engagement in ways that encourage building and strengthening relationships. This requires, among other things, better support for broader participation, via tools like stipends for participation, convenient meeting times and locations, transportation grants, childcare, and food.

Fourth, this kind of real organizing requires a significant investment of resources. Organizers are more effective when they cultivate local leaders, build skills, and construct more inclusive solidarities and narratives over time. Truly bottom-up organizing must offer community members real opportunities to develop themselves and each other as movement leaders and skillful advocates. Even on-the-ground organizing falters when it is seen only as a mobilization tool to be deployed by professionalized managers. Yet this all requires a more sustainable funding pipeline that provides core support for organizing groups rather than issue- or project-based models. It also means that as organizations seek to develop more political and policy impact, they need *political* resources in the form of effective alliances with policymakers, whether elected officials or bureaucrats.

Fifth, these models demonstrate the necessity and power of political organizing around the formation of more inclusive identities. New narratives can break down silos between communities long divided, but this requires finding new common points of entry across identities as well as a commitment to using these common points to shape new common goals and stories. As we have shown, organizations such as Faith in Texas and the Center for Rural Strategies are working on innovative techniques and strategies for new identity formation. Over the long term, building these new narratives includes cultivating local leaders, building skills, and constructing more inclusive solidarities. During an era of exclusionary populism based on "us" vs "them" identities and xenophobia, constructing these narratives requires hard work and difficult conversations. Given the polarized contemporary political climate, people may want to retreat from such engagements and further divide themselves. Trying to generate a shared vocabulary to build trust among people who distrust one another is difficult. Yet the important work of building shared narratives requires breaking down these silos and misconceptions.

Finally, localities and rural areas are good places to test new processes and new collaborations. While it is difficult to generalize about these communities, which are diverse, often they can implement change faster than larger regions. Trust is a critical factor for motivating civic engagement, and local and rural communities retain relatively high levels of trust and social cohesion.[16] The move to innovate government in cities cannot leave behind rural communities. Indeed, as the examples show, powerful organizing partnerships can be built that embrace local issues with approaches that extend beyond municipal borders to include rural and exurban communities, constructing effective urban-rural coalitions that are key in many states where legislatures can greatly restrict municipal powers.

Recommendations for Policymakers

Policymakers too, as we have suggested in this book, will have to approach their work very differently in order to provide the kind of forums and governance institutions needed to house genuinely democratic participation and engagement. Here too recent innovations and experiments suggest some important directions for future policy innovation that builds civic power.

First, policymakers need to make the positive case for government. This is perhaps most familiar to governance reformers. There is already a widespread sense that civil services need to show that government can *work*, that it can be responsive to community needs, and that it can actually get positive things done. Making this case is particularly essential to overcoming community distrust as well as decades of anti-government narratives and critiques.

---

[16] Allen J. Smart and Betsey Russell, "What Rural America Can Teach Us about Civil Society," *Stanford Social Innovation Review*, August 21, 2018, https://ssir.org/articles/entry/what_rural_america_can_teach_us_about_civil_society.

From the standpoint of civic power, however, it is important that the concept of effective governance be expanded beyond merely efficient "good governance"; it must embrace a sense of genuinely "democratic" or "participatory" government. Policymakers and theorists must come to see that governance that routinely, structurally excludes certain community voices cannot be effectively democratic. Participatory monitoring, as outlined in this book, offers one compelling example of how to genuinely empower citizenry. Thus, policymakers must move beyond the glamour and attraction of seemingly easy-fix civic tech and good governance solutions. Open data and consumer- or user-experience reforms aimed at making government more transparent, more technologically advanced, or more streamlined from a service delivery perspective all may be useful. But they do not by themselves produce genuine shifts in power and long-term support for or ability to engage in equitable policymaking. Effective and inclusive civic engagement will require a mix of in-person and online tools. Institutions that genuinely shift power will require support of both policymakers and organizers on the ground. Examples in the book include the formation of the CRA, the CFPB, Boston's MONUM, and New York City's Public Engagement Unit. We have argued in this book that mechanisms like participatory monitoring or participatory policymaking work best when they are: (1) backed by independent social movement organizations, (2) codified in institutions that provide real leverage and influence for constituencies on the ground, and (3) facilitated by government officials who are resourced and oriented to promote this kind of democratic decision-making.

Third, and relatedly, a truly democratic institutional ecosystem requires governmental bodies that do more than simply provide services effectively. They must also create meaningful points of leverage and participation through which communities can exercise a share of decision-making power. Thus, policies and institutions must be designed specifically with an eye toward institutionalizing countervailing power especially for those traditionally disempowered communities. This reorientation around civic engagement requires procedures that go beyond simple town halls or invitations for public comment. Examples in the book have included participatory budgeting, participatory monitoring, and citizen audits. As these examples suggest, meaningful civic engagement requires providing occasions for actual influence over policy outcomes. But it also requires that *visibility, authority, and accountability* must be present together. This can create some tension for government officials, as it places them in positions that are somewhat open-ended, unstable, and open to potential conflict with community participants. But without this tension, it is unlikely that such participation would be meaningful.

Fourth, these shifts in the practice of governance will need dedicated commitment from governmental leaders. Effective civic engagement will necessarily require more experimentation, but such experimentation itself requires "political air cover" with support from above giving space for lower-level governmental officials to try – and potentially fail – with alternative modes of participatory engagement. Furthermore, developing and implementing such participatory procedures requires that officials have the necessary support and resources in order to pursue these often time- and resource-intensive efforts.

Fifth, democratizing bureaucratic institutions requires a radically different view of what governmental expertise and personnel look like. Civic engagement requires its own form of expertise: interfacing with communities requires a wide range of linguistic, interpersonal, and locally rooted expertise. This means that government will have to change its view about how to recruit, train, and deploy staff. A governmental bureaucracy committed to democratic participation and to sustaining and implementing these kinds of power-shifting policies and processes will have to train and invest in existing staff, creating incentives and supports for learning new approaches. Such a governmental body must also develop new creative ways to bring in a more locally rooted and diverse workforce particularly through concerted outreach to marginalized communities. This means modifying the talent pipeline to be more diverse and more inclusive, so that more individuals from nontraditional backgrounds enter public service.

Sixth, building civic power within government requires leadership willing to take risks. Genuinely empowering people in more than public affairs or a perfunctory capacity will require tackling trust gaps: many people inside government are mistrustful of the public, and many marginalized communities distrust governmental authorities. Confronting this problem requires more than one-off, tightly controlled events; there must be enough room for iteration and for developing tools to let people express themselves. Experimentation with the public will require that public leaders develop a higher risk tolerance for public criticism.

Within government, this shift in personnel could be achieved through other mechanisms. For example, rotational teams of lawyers, policy designers, ethnographers, and community organizers might be formed to provide ongoing support to movement campaigns or to civic engagement processes. New public service fellowships could be institutionalized and financed so that colleges, professional schools, and vocational training facilities could

Democracy's Future

frequently partner with philanthropists, organizers, and bureaucrats to offer "residencies" that cultivate talent by exposing future organizers to government work and future bureaucrats to organizing and advocacy work. There is a proven track record for the fellowship model within a sector, including in examples like the long-standing Presidential Management Fellows (PMF) program, which tackles some of the same challenges to attracting early career recruits to public service, and in the Obama administration's Presidential Innovation Fellows (PIF) program.[17]

These civic fellowships, however, should be inter-sectoral, rather than only intra-sectoral. The goal would be to create lifelong civic leaders, not fund limited-scope projects through short, time-bound appointments. Indeed, the importance of early career rotations to developing key staff is increasingly recognized by governmental bodies. For example, in New York City, the relatively new HPD-HDC Housing Fellows Program recruits recent graduates of professional programs in law, urban studies, planning, and management to spend two years rotating between different offices within the Department of Housing Preservation and Development (HPD) and the New York City Housing Development Corporation (HDC).[18] Meanwhile, the Department of State's second Quadrennial Diplomacy and Development Review included a recommendation for how the department could better invest in an "agile, skilled workforce," by allowing workforce mobility, enabling employees to move between department bureaus, rotating between the state department and the United States Agency for International Development (USAID), being detailed to other federal agencies, or even taking sabbaticals from federal service into academia or the private sector.[19] As the state department's Tom Perriello has said, "We're managing people's entire careers, not just managing them to the next tour."[20]

Academia, the private sector, and philanthropy could help support these types of fellowships and further institutionalize them. For example, Harvard Business School's Leadership Fellows program helps place recent graduates in meaningful public sector and social sector offices in local government. Harvard subsidizes part of the salary and provides mentorship opportunities.

---

[17] Presidential Innovation Fellows (website), home page, https://presidentialinnovationfellows .gov/.
[18] NYC (City of New York website), "HPD-HDC Housing Fellows Program," www1.nyc.gov/si te/hpd/about/hpd-hdc-housing-fellows-program.page.
[19] Quadrennial Diplomacy and Development Review, *Enduring Leadership in a Dynamic World* (Washington, DC: U.S. Department of State and USAID, 2015), 67–78.
[20] Eric Katz, "How One Agency Will Use Sabbaticals and Rotations to Retain Employees," *Government Executive*, April 29, 2015, www.govexec.com/pay-benefits/2015/04/how-one-agency-will-use-sabbaticals-and-rotations-retain-employees/111424/.

218   *Civic Power*

Chris Osgood, who went on to cofound Boston's New Urban Mechanics, began his work at city hall as a Harvard Leadership Fellow.[21] The fellowship's goals are to invest in leaders and to demonstrate the value of multisector or "tri-sector" expertise.[22] Unlike other business school fellowships that put a premium on business expertise and translating findings into profits, the goal of these civic fellowships is to create leaders who will remain place based and tied to their communities. This requires gaining expertise outside of one's existing academic and professional communities.

Equity and inclusion must be paramount goals in forming a truly inclusive pipeline of civic leaders. Currently, there are high obstacles to civic work, from crushing student loans to an overreliance on unpaid internships and well-established networks. Through the work of building carefully designed and funded rotational fellowships, equity and inclusion can be placed front and center to ensure a more inclusive civic workforce. Furthermore, fellows should be matched with mentors who ideally will help support them even after the formal fellowship obligations are complete, in order to further overcome structural retention problems and guide lifelong career development. Universities, industry, and philanthropy can all play a strategic role in recruiting new talent by providing funding and training opportunities and by working to develop a diverse pipeline. This should include community colleges and not be limited to four-year degree-granting programs. The government needs to ensure that inclusive talent from across the country can have opportunities to serve in government.

Recommendations for Funders

All of these approaches to power building require financial resources. In an era when civil society groups and governmental bodies alike are struggling to maintain budgets and are working in a risk-averse environment, philanthropy and private funding have become even more important in shaping the dynamics of civic engagement, policymaking, and advocacy. Indeed, the nonprofit sector has long noted the difficulties of funder-dependence, where nonprofits must compete for scarce funding resources, leading them to more

---

[21] Jen Myers, "Leading Boston and Beyond: How HBS Leadership Fellows Have Reinvented How We Think about Governance," Harvard Business School (website), December 1, 2015, www .alumni.hbs.edu/stories/Pages/story-bulletin.aspx?num=5001; and Harvard Business School, "Social Enterprise" www.hbs.edu/socialenterprise/for-organizations/Pages/leadership-fellows.aspx.

[22] Nick Lovegrove and Matthew Thomas, "Why the World Needs Tri-Sector Leaders," *Harvard Business Review*, February 13, 2013, https://hbr.org/2013/02/why-the-world-needs-tri-sector.

Democracy's Future 219

and more convoluted programs and projects in search of funding. Instead, durable power building requires more flexible funding models.

First, funders need to provide more general operating support and no-strings -attached resources. They also should invest more in talent, leadership development, pipeline projects, and organizational infrastructure rather than focusing on specific campaigns or policy outcomes. Through enabling more low-risk catalytic support for experimentation, funders can help organizers and the government itself to be more risk tolerant. Philanthropy can play the role of external champion to provide another layer of support for innovative leaders trying to more effectively encourage civic power.

Second, funders should further explore how to support alternative funding models such as collaborative funding structures across philanthropy. Examples of such structures include the NetGain Partnership, and the Public Interest Technology Program, which includes a collaborative of foundations (including the MacArthur Foundation, the Mozilla Foundation, the Ford Foundation, Open Society Foundations, and the Knight Foundation). The Public Interest Technology Program is focused on how to leverage technology for public good across different fields, including training and investing in future community leaders.[23] The Reimagining the Civic Commons Initiative, a three-year national initiative across Akron, Chicago, Detroit, Memphis, and Philadelphia, is bringing together national foundations and local partners to strengthen and revitalize local communities; and the Smart Chicago Collaborative works with community-based organizations and is now merged into an effort dubbed civic tech.[24] Such models can help structure funding to encourage more cooperation and less competition between organizations. A holistic approach to funding ecosystems could also work to ensure that different funders collaborate to support different aspects of governance reform. For example, currently there are silos between funders investing in government or civic technology and those funding on-the-ground organizing and institutional building. As we argue in this book, building civic power will require investment and collaboration across both of these axes.

Third, make learning and research a key grant prerequisite. Given people's busy schedules, collaboration with external stakeholders, especially researchers, could be integrated more directly into grant proposals. If working with external researchers or learning and evaluation efforts are baked into grant

---

[23] See the Netgain Partnership, https://netgainpartnership.org/; See Public Interest Technology, www.fordfoundation.org/campaigns/public-interest-tech/; See $18 M in Grants to Advance Public Interest Technology, www.macfound.org/press/publications/18m-grants-advance-public-interest-technology/.

[24] Reimagining the Civic Commons (website), "About," http://civiccommons.us/about/.

proposals at their onset, this could help to engender overall support for collaboration and additional time afforded to external researchers and evaluators. This can help, in turn, to generate broader lessons and findings for the field. Key goals of governance reform should include fostering wider dissemination of the results of local efforts to a broader network of civil society, governmental, and external actors and generating institutionalized knowledge. Especially in the context of fast-moving pilots and experimentation, institutional knowledge of past successes and failures can be lacking.[25]

Fourth, while data, human-centered design thinking, and evidence-based policymaking are critical components of governance innovation, they do not replace the need for on-the-ground organizing and place-based knowledge. One aspect of this is building public interest technology within city hall that has the capacity to leverage innovations in data, digital technology, human-centered design, and evidence-based decision-making.[26] One promising model is Bloomberg Philanthropies' Harvard City Leadership Initiative, which provides training to mayors that includes in-person learnings, coaching, research, and fellowships.[27] Currently, there are dispersed efforts and tools but there is not enough government capacity to fully harness digital technologies to improve governance. This is especially true in smaller townships, rural communities, and cities that lack the resources of the major cities and coastal metropolises. Without investing internally to spur government capacity and innovation, there is the risk of capture by the private sector, which will continue to monetize people's data and their attention span in the pursuit of providing goods. Moreover, once technological capacity is reached, accountability mechanisms should be put in place to ensure that data, user-centered design, and evidence-based decision-making include built-in feedback from citizens. Without feedback loops to engage citizens, incorporating new tools and technologies into government runs the risk of making policy invisible. Funders should explore project requirements to staff new pilots in data, technology, and design thinking with community organizers, sociologists, anthropologists, or ethnographers, who can help translate human-centered feedback to the very constituents affected on the ground. The result is combined efforts that blend offline and online approaches.

[25] Micah Sifry, "Learning from the Civic Tech Graveyard," *Civicist*, October 1, 2018, https://ci vichall.org/civicist/civic-tech-graveyard/.

[26] Michael Brennan, "Public Interest Tech: A Growing Field You Should Know," *Equals Change Blog*, Ford Foundation, April 2, 2018, www.fordfoundation.org/ideas/equals-change-blog/posts/public-interest-tech-a-growing-field-you-should-know/.

[27] See Blooomberg Harvard City Leadership Initiative, www.bloomberg.org/program/govern ment-innovation/bloomberg-harvard-city-leadership-initiative/#overview.

Fifth, while the push for local innovations and investments is powerful, it needs to be integrated into a broader strategy that grasps how local innovations can be upended by political and legal structures at the state and national levels. Changes that occur merely at the municipal level are particularly vulnerable to such interference, as for example, when corporations put pressure on state legislatures to pre-empt local initiatives that could benefit communities such as a soda tax or a new paid sick leave law. Therefore, funding for local initiatives needs to be coupled with a longer-term and more geographically dispersed investment strategy.

Recommendations for Scholars

Finally, these arguments about civic power suggest that a very different approach to the study of democracy and democracy reform is needed.

First, the problem of building durable power requires an interdisciplinary research approach, engaging qualitative as well as quantitative measures of success to get a more nuanced understanding of how citizens' views are shifting through new interactions with government. This approach should combine ethnography and sociological research with political science, law, and public policy. Even within disciplines such as political science or legal history, there is often a disconnect between those who study federal policy and urban power politics. However, the study of civic power requires understanding the interplay of local, regional, and national laws, policies, and regulations as well as the constituencies that navigate these frameworks at multiple levels.

Second, academics can play important roles not only in studying power building but also in building civic power, if they embrace research approaches that create more bridges between the academy and the work of practitioners. Furthermore, such roles may indeed be necessary for scholars to be able to gain adequate and detailed understandings of power building. Typically, when academics and practitioners come together it is in time-bound projects with constrained funding. However, power building requires a longer-term investment of multiyear commitments to build communities of practice. These communities, in turn, can further develop trust between academics and practitioners to ensure access and respect surrounding sensitive topics.

Given the current pressures facing tenure-track faculty, these types of deep, ongoing learning engagements will require departmental and administrative support, including from tenured faculty toward graduate students and junior faculty. Universities can also encourage junior faculty to achieve real-world practice and view this as a part of their cocurricular engagements. For example, external funders could support course buy-outs for faculty to help

222   *Civic Power*

encourage less established faculty to participate in such projects. One aspect could include making active research – i.e., being embedded in community organizations or government agencies as active research participants – a requirement for graduate students, including doctoral students, in relevant fields. This could take the form of field coursework where students would receive course credit.

Third, the focus on power we articulate here suggests a host of critical questions for future researchers. Much more should be known about what specific strategies and civic engagement approaches are most effective at encouraging more participation in the future, at building new identities and durable coalitions, and at generating real political power and impact. What are the relationships, for example, between online engagement through social media or other types of online discussion and offline identities and political action? How can one form of participation such as participatory budgeting influence other forms of participation such as voting or protest in the future? How can civic engagement be structured so that it is satisfying and compelling enough to overcome distrust or cynicism? What mechanisms for participation and collaboration are most effective at empowering and activating traditionally underrepresented and marginalized constituencies, particularly communities of color? Addressing these questions will require creative and concerted scholarly effort, from longitudinal studies to in-depth qualitative case studies, and more. It will also require scholarship that is closely connected to, and embedded in, the work of on-the-ground democracy reformers outside of the traditional contexts of party politics and studies of electoral behavior.

***

As this book is going to press, much of the discussion in the United States revolves around a pervasive sense of a crisis of American democracy – and potentially an existential one. As we have suggested above, this crisis is real, but it is not really (or at least, not entirely) the product of the Trump era or the Trump administration. Rather, the deeper crises of American democracy stem from systemic and chronic crises of economic inequality and social exclusion. These crises, in turn, are not just products of nature; rather there is real power and real organizational and institutional structures that enable, drive, and make durable these crises – and make less real the aspirations for a democracy that is truly of, for, and by all of us.

True democracy reform must be transformative and bold enough to meet these challenges. Democracy is not going to be achieved by tinkering around the edges of existing economic, social, and political regimes. Neither optimizing government to make it more efficient, nor generating mass numbers of online petition signers will suffice. Democracy is a radical, transformative aspiration, committed to building the deep and durable power of grassroots communities to author their own destinies through the shared exercise of the powers and responsibilities of governance. Democracy is also radical in its hostility to the kinds of concentrations of unaccountable power that effectively deny these claims of individual and collective agency.

But radical democracy is not utopian; it is rather very real and achievable. That realness is often mundane: radical democracy can be found in the painstaking door-by-door work of organizing new movements, coalitions, and communities; of forging common identities; and of building the relationships and organizational muscles needed to assert political power. Radical democracy can be found in the work of policy design optimized not for efficiency, but for inclusion. Radical democracy can be found in the work of bureaucratic culture shifting, transforming staid government organizations into open and inclusive forums and counterparts, where communities can engage and participate in the business of decision-making. We have offered here glimpses of how this more radical yet achievable democracy can be (and is already being) built. The examples we have provided represent only a small selection of the work that many organizers, reformers, and thinkers are doing to make these aspirations for radical democracy and civic power real.

Indeed, these are broad aspirations; they will require significant organizing and advocacy work on the part of civil society actors as well as radical institutional and policy change on the part of governments. But this is not the first time America has faced a crossroads where the survival of democracy is at stake. Reconstruction after the Civil War, the Populist and Progressive movements culminating in the New Deal response to the upheavals of industrial capitalism, and the civil rights movement (and its successive inclusionary movements) of the 1960s and 1970s all represent major transformative moments when American democracy created new institutions that expanded its responsiveness and staved off the pathologies of corruption, systemic exclusion, and deliberate de-democratization. Whether today's movements, organizations, and institutions will similarly be able to restore and even deepen American democracy in the twenty-first century remains to be seen.

Bibliography

18 F. Home page. Accessed December 5, 2018. https://18f.gsa.gov/.

Abello, Oscar Perry. "Oakland Lets Residents Decide How to Prioritize Federal Grant Money." *Next City*, May 3, 2017. https://nextcity.org/daily/entry/oakland-participatory-budgeting-residents-decide-spend-cdbgs.

Abello, Oscar Perry. "Participatory Budgeting Fans Say State DOT's Embrace Is 'Revolutionary.'" *Next City*, September 20, 2017. https://nextcity.org/daily/entry/california-transportation-participatory-budgeting-process.

Abers, Rebecca, Igor Brandão, Robin King, and Daniely Votto. "Porto Alegre: Participatory Budgeting and the Challenge of Sustaining Transformative Change." World Resources Report Case Study. Washington, DC: World Resources Institute, 2008.

Achen, Christopher H., and Larry M. Bartels. *Democracy for Realists: Why Elections Do Not Produce Responsive Government*. Princeton, NJ: Princeton University Press, 2016.

Ackerman, Bruce, and James S. Fishkin. *Deliberation Day*. New Haven, CT: Yale University Press, 2005.

Agranoff, Robert. "Inside Collaborative Networks: Ten Lessons for Public Managers." *Public Administration Review* 66 (2006): 56–65

Aitken, Rob. "Everyday Debt Relationalities: Situating Peer-to-Peer Lending and the Rolling Jubilee." *Cultural Studies* 29 (2015): 845–68.

Akbar, Amna. "Policing 'Radicalization.'" *UC Irvine Law Review* 3 (2013): 809–83.

Alesina, Alberto, and Edward Glaeser. *Fighting Poverty in the US and Europe: A World of Difference*. Oxford: Oxford University Press, 2004.

Alesina, Alberto, Edward Glaeser, and Bruce Sacerdote. "Why Doesn't the United States Have a European-Style Welfare State?" Brookings Papers on Economic Activity, no. 2 (2001): 187–254.

Alexander, Michelle. *The New Jim Crow: Mass Incarceration in the Age of Colorblindness*. New York: New Press, 2010.

Allen, Hilary J. "Putting the 'Financial Stability' in Financial Stability Oversight Council." *Ohio State Law Journal* 76 (2015): 1087–1152.

Alter, Charlotte. "How the Anti-Trump Resistance Is Organizing Its Outrage." *Time*, October 18, 2018. http://time.com/longform/democrat-midterm-strategy/.

Bibliography

American Bar Association. "Public Interest Law Community." April 26, 2018. www
.americanbar.org/groups/public_services/public_interest_law1/.
Analyst Institute. "Our Mission." Accessed December 5, 2018. https://analystinstitute
.org/our-mission/.
Andersen, Travis. "Boston Hopes Data Can Aid Its Efforts in Fighting Fires." *Boston Globe*, April 4, 2016. www.bostonglobe.com/metro/2016/04/04/city-boston-using-data
-improve-firefighting-and-other-services-report-says/vCspAKEgRYkAB4mMxz7qw
N/story.html#comments.
Anderson, Carol. *White Rage: The Unspoken Truth of Our Racial Divide*. New York: Bloomsbury, 2017.
Anderson, Elizabeth. *Private Government: How Employers Rule Our Lives (and Why We Don't Talk about It)*. Princeton, NJ: Princeton University Press, 2017.
Anderson, Elizabeth, and Richard H. Pildes. "Expressive Theories of Law: A General Restatement." *University of Pennsylvania Law Review* 148 (2000): 1503–75.
Anderson, Lisa. "Demystifying the Arab Spring: Parsing the Differences between Tunisia, Egypt, and Libya." *Foreign Affairs* 90, no. 3 (2011): 2–7.
Anderson, Monica, Skye Toor, Lee Rainie, and Aaron Smith. *Activism in the Social Media Age*. Washington, DC: Pew Research Center, July 2018. www.pewinternet.org
/2018/07/11/activism-in-the-social-media-age/.
Andrias, Kate. "Separations of Wealth: Inequality and the Erosion of Checks and Balances." *Michigan Journal of Constitutional Law* 18 (2016): 419–504.
Andrias, Kate. "The New Labor Law." *Yale Law Journal* 126 (2016): 2–100.
Ansell, Chris, and Alison Gash. "Collaborative Governance in Theory and Practice." *Journal of Public Administration Research and Theory* 18 (2008): 543–71. doi:10.1093/
jopart/mum032.
Ansell, Christopher K. *Pragmatist Democracy: Evolutionary Learning as Public Philosophy*. New York: Oxford University Press, 2011.
Anti-Defamation League. "Murder and Extremism in the United States in 2017." Accessed December 5, 2018. www.adl.org/resources/reports/murder-and-extremism-
in-the-united-states-in-2017#the-incidents.
Arnstein, Sherry R. "A Ladder of Citizen Participation." *Journal of the American Institute of Planners* 35, no. 4 (1969): 216–24. doi:10.1080/01944366908977225.
Aspen Institute. "An Interview with Job Quality Fellow Jess Kutch." February 20, 2018. www.aspeninstitute.org/longform/job-quality-fellows-profile-series/jess-kutch/.
Awrey, Dan. "Complexity, Innovation, and the Regulation of Modern Financial Markets." *Harvard Business Law Review* 2, no. 2 (2012): 235–94.
Baez, Nancy, and Andreas Hernandez. "Participatory Budgeting in the City: Challenging NYC's Development Paradigm from the Grassroots." *Interface* 4, no. 1 (2012): 316–26.
Balkin, Jack M. "Constitutional Hardball and Constitutional Crises." *Quinnipiac Law Review* 26 (2008): 579–98.
Barber, Benjamin, ed. *Strong Democracy: Participatory Politics for a New Age*. Berkeley: University of California Press, 2004.
Barker, Derek W. M., Noëlle McAfee, and David W. McIvor. *Democratizing Deliberation: A Political Theory Anthology*. Dayton, OH: Kettering Foundation, 2012.

Barr, Michael S. "The Financial Crisis and the Path of Reform." *Yale Journal on Regulation* 29, no. 1 (2012): 91–119.

Barr, Michael S. "Comment: Accountability and Independence in Financial Regulation: Checks and Balances, Public Engagement, and Other Innovations." *Law and Contemporary Problems* 78, no. 3 (2015): 119–28.

Bartels, Larry M. "Uninformed Votes: Information Effects in Presidential Elections." *American Journal of Political Science* 40 (1996): 194–230.

Bartels, Larry M. *Unequal Democracy: The Political Economy of the New Digital Age*, 2nd ed. Princeton, NJ: Princeton University Press/Russell Sage Foundation, 2016.

Baumgartner, Frank R., and Beth L. Leech. *Basic Interests: The Importance of Groups in Politics and Political Science*. Princeton, NJ: Princeton University Press, 1998.

Baumgartner, Frank R., and Bryan D. Jones. *The Politics of Information: Problem Definition and the Course of Public Policy in America*. Chicago: University of Chicago Press, 2015.

Bean, Lydia. *The Politics of Evangelical Identity: Local Churches and Partisan Divides in the United States and Canada*. Princeton, NJ: Princeton University Press, 2014.

Bell, Monica. "Police Reform and the Dismantling of Legal Cynicism." *Yale Law Journal* 126 (2017): 2054–2150.

Benkler, Yochai. *The Wealth of Networks: How Social Production Transforms Markets and Freedom*. New Haven, CT: Yale University Press, 2006.

Benkler, Yochai. "A Free Irresponsible Press: Wikileaks and the Battle over the Soul of the Networked Fourth Estate." *Harvard Civil Rights – Civil Liberties Law Review* 46 (2011): 311–97.

Bennett, W. Lance, and Alexandra Segerberg. *The Logic of Connective Action: Digital Media and the Personalization of Contentious Politics*. Cambridge: Cambridge University Press, 2013.

Bergen, Peter, and David Sterman. "What Is the Threat to the United States Today?" In *Jihadist Terrorism 17 Years after 9/11*. Washington, DC: New America, updated September 10, 2018. www.newamerica.org/in-depth/terrorism-in-america/what-threat-united-states-today/.

Berman, Ari. *Give Us the Ballot: The Modern Struggle for Voting Rights in America*. New York: Picador, 2015.

Berry, Jeffry M. *The New Liberalism: The Rising Power of Citizen Groups*. Washington, DC: Brookings Institution, 1999.

Berry, Jeffrey M., and Clyde Wilcox. *The Interest Group Society*, 5th ed. New York: Routledge, 2016.

Berry, Wendell. "Southern Despair." *New York Review of Books*, May 11, 2017. www.nybooks.com/articles/2017/05/11/southern-despair/.

Best, Samuel J., and Brian S. Krueger. "Analyzing the Representativeness of Internet Political Participation." *Political Behavior* 27, no. 2 (2005): 183–216.

Beukes, Anni. "Know Your City: Community Profiling of Informal Settlements." International Institute for Environment and Development (IIED) Briefing (June 2014). http://pubs.iied.org/pdfs/17244IIED.pdf.

Bimber, Bruce, Andrew Flanagin, and Cynthia Stohl. *Collective Action in Organizations: Interaction and Engagement in an Era of Technological Change*. New York: Cambridge University Press, 2012.

Bibliography

Bingham, Lisa Blomgren. Tina Nabatchi, and Rosemary O'Leary. "The New Governance: Practices and Processes for Stakeholder and Citizen Participation in the Work of Government." *Public Administration Review* 65 (2005): 547–58.

Bloomberg Philanthropies. "Where We've Worked." Accessed December 5, 2018. https://whatworkscities.bloomberg.org/cities/.

Boyd, Aaron. "Trump Budget Calls for Slight Increase in IT Spending." *Nextgov*, February 12, 2018. www.nextgov.com/cio-briefing/2018/02/trump-budget-calls-slight-increase-it-spending/145914/.

Boyd, James. "Nixon's Southern Strategy." *New York Times*, May 17, 1970. www.nytimes.com/1970/05/17/archives/nixons-southern-strategy-its-all-in-the-charts.html.

Boyer, Dave. "Trump Plan Cuts CFPB's Budget by One-Third." *Washington Times*, February 13, 2018. www.washingtontimes.com/news/2018/feb/13/trump-plan-cuts-cfpbs-budget-by-one-third/.

Brazil: Toward a More Inclusive and Effective Participatory Budget in Porto Alegre. Washington, DC: World Bank, 2008.

Brennan, Michael. "Public Interest Tech: A Growing Field You Should Know." *Equals Change Blog*, Ford Foundation, April 2, 2018. www.fordfoundation.org/ideas/equals-change-blog/posts/public-interest-tech-a-growing-field-you-should-know/.

Brescia, Raymond H. "Part of the Disease or Part of the Cure: The Financial Crisis and the Community Reinvestment Act." *University of South Carolina Law Review* 60 (2009): 617–77.

Briggs, Xavier de Souza. *Democracy as Problem Solving: Civic Capacity in Communities across the Globe.* Cambridge, MA: MIT Press, 2008.

Brown, Meta S. "City Governments Making Public Data Easier to Get: 90 Municipal Open Data Portals." *Forbes*, April 29, 2018. www.forbes.com/sites/metabrown/2018/04/29/city-governments-making-public-data-easier-to-get-90-municipal-open-data-portals/.

Bryson, John M., Barbara C. Crosby, and Laura Bloomberg. "Public Value Governance: Moving beyond Traditional Public Administration and the New Public Management." *Public Administration Review* 74, no. 4 (2014): 445–56.

Burbank, Stephen, Sean Farhang, and Herbert Kritzer. "Private Enforcement." *Lewis & Clark Law Review* 17, no. 3 (2013): 637–722.

Bureau of Labor Statistics. "Union Members Summary." Economic News Release. January 19, 2018. www.bls.gov/news.release/union2.nr0.htm.

Burgin, Angus. *The Great Persuasion: Reinventing Free Markets since the Depression.* Cambridge, MA: Harvard University Press, 2012.

Cadwalladr, Carole. "Revealed: How US Billionaire Helped to Back Brexit." *Guardian*, February 25, 2017. www.theguardian.com/politics/2017/feb/26/us-billionaire-mercer-helped-back-brexit.

Campbell, Andrea Louise. "Self-Interest, Social Security, and the Distinctive Participation Patterns of Senior Citizens." *American Political Science Review* 96, no. 3 (September 2002): 565–74.

Campbell, Angus, Gerald Gurin, and Warren E. Miller. *The Voter Decides.* Evanston, IL: Row, Peterson, 1954.

Carlson, Edward, and Justin Goss. "The State of the Urban/Rural Digital Divide." National Telecommunications and Information Administration, United States

Department of Commerce. August 10, 2016. www.ntia.doc.gov/blog/2016/state-urbanrural-digital-divide.

Carnes, Nicholas. *White Collar Government: The Hidden Role of Class in Economic Policy Making*. Chicago: University of Chicago Press, 2013.

Carpenter, Daniel. "Internal Governance of Agencies: The Sieve, the Shove, the Show." *Harvard Law Review Forum* 129 (2016): 189–96.

Cashman, Tim. "The Economic Impact of Open Data." *Socrata*, February 27, 2014. https://socrata.com/blog/economic-impact-open-data/.

Castells, Manuel. *Networks of Outrage and Hope: Social Movements in the Internet Age*. Cambridge: Polity, 2012.

Center for Rural Strategies. "Broadband Advocacy." Accessed December 5, 2018. www.ruralstrategies.org/broadband/.

Center for Rural Strategies. "Rural Assembly." Accessed December 5, 2018. www.ruralstrategies.org/national-rural-assembly/.

Center for Rural Strategies. "The Daily Yonder: Keep It Rural." Accessed December 5, 2018. www.ruralstrategies.org/the-daily-yonder/.

Centers for Disease Control and Prevention. "Suicide in Rural America." Last updated May 2, 2018. www.cdc.gov/ruralhealth/Suicide.html.

Centers for Medicare and Medicaid Services. "Office of Equal Opportunity and Civil Rights." Last modified September 5, 2018. www.cms.gov/About-CMS/Agency Information/CMSLeadership/Office_OEOCR.html.

Change.org. Home page. Accessed December 5, 2018. www.change.org/.

Chanley, Virginia A., Thomas J. Rudolph, and Wendy M. Rahn. "The Origins and Consequences of Public Trust in Government: A Time Series Analysis." *Public Opinion Quarterly* 64 (2000): 239–56.

Chapman, Ben, and Lisa L. Colangelo. "NYC Rolling Out New Unit to Connect Residents in Need with Social Services." *New York Daily News*, September 20, 2015. www.nydailynews.com/new-york/exclusive-nyc-creates-unit-connect-needy-nyers-article-1.2366942.

Chenoweth, Erica, and Jeremey Pressman. "This Is What We Learned by Counting the Women's Marches." *Washington Post*, February 7, 2017.

Chetty, Raj, Nathaniel Hendren, and Lawrence Katz. "The Effects of Exposure to Better Neighborhoods on Children: New Evidence from the Moving to Opportunity Project." *American Economic Review* 106 (2016): 855–902.

"Chicago's 'Menu' Program for Aldermen: 50 Ways to Waste Your Money." (editorial) *Chicago Tribune*, April 20, 2017. www.chicagotribune.com/news/opinion/editorials/ct-menu-chicago-aldermen-cdot-infrastructure-city-council-0421-jm-20170420-story.html

Choi, Matthew. "Texas Payday Lenders Face Tougher Standards with New Federal Rules." *Texas Tribune*, October 12, 2017. www.texastribune.org/2017/10/12/texans-hope-for-better-protections-from-payday-loans-following-federal/.

City of Boston. "Mayor's Office of New Urban Mechanics and Code for America Partner to Build Nation's First Backpack Apps." February 15, 2011. www.cityofboston.gov/news/default.aspx?id=4988.

City of Boston. "BOS:311 App." Last updated December 4, 2017. www.boston.gov/departments/new-urban-mechanics/bos311-app.

City of Boston "BOS: 311." Accessed December 5, 2018. https://311.boston.gov/.

Bibliography

City of Boston. "Housing Innovation Lab Now a Permanent Office." July 19, 2017. www
.boston.gov/news/housing-innovation-lab-now-permanent-office.

City of Boston. "Boston Recognized by Bloomberg Philanthropies for Excellence in
Government Services." January 25, 2018. www.boston.gov/news/boston-recognized-
bloomberg-philanthropies-excellence-government-services.

City of Boston. "Housing a Changing City: Boston 2030." Last updated September 27,
2018. www.boston.gov/departments/neighborhood-development/housing-changing-
city-boston-2030.

City of Boston. "Housing Innovation Lab." Last updated June 26, 2018. www.boston.gov
/departments/new-urban-mechanics/housing-innovation-lab.

City of Boston. "Intergenerational Homeshare Pilot." Last updated May 1, 2018. www
.boston.gov/departments/new-urban-mechanics/housing-innovation-lab/intergenera
tional-homeshare-pilot.

City of Boston. "Urban Housing Unit Roadshow." Last updated April 20, 2018. www
.boston.gov/departments/new-urban-mechanics/urban-housing-unit-roadshow.

City of Boston. "Simplifying the Home Buying Process." Last updated October 4, 2017.
www.boston.gov/departments/new-urban-mechanics/simplifying-homebuying-
process.

City of Boston. "Youth Lead the Change." Last updated October 2, 2018. www
.boston.gov/departments/boston-centers-youth-families/youth-lead-change.

City of Boston. "Innovation and Technology." Accessed December 5, 2018. www
.boston.gov/departments/innovation-and-technology.

City of Boston. "New Urban Mechanics." Accessed December 5, 2018. www.boston.gov
/departments/new-urban-mechanics.

City of Chicago. "Capital Improvement Program." Accessed December 5, 2018. www
.cityofchicago.org/city/en/depts/obm/provdrs/cap_improve.html.

City of Philadelphia. "PHL Participatory Design Lab Announces Project Partners and
Fellows." November 9, 2017. www.phila.gov/2017-11-09-phl-participatory-design-lab-
announces-project-partners-and-fellows/.

City of Vallejo California. "Vallejo's PB Program." Accessed December 5, 2018. www
.ci.vallejo.ca.us/cms/One.aspx?pageId=52101.

Clark, Susan, and Woden Teachout. *Slow Democracy: Rediscovering Community,
Bringing Decision Making Back Home*. White River Junction, VT: Chelsea Green
Publishing, 2012.

Clemens, Elisabeth. *The People's Lobby: Organizational Innovation and the Rise of
Interest Group Politics in the United States, 1890–1925*. Chicago: University of
Chicago Press, 1997.

Code for America. Home page. Accessed December 5, 2018. www.codeforamerica.org/.

Coffee, Jr., John C. "Political Economy of Dodd-Frank: Why Financial Reform Tends
to be Frustrated and Systemic Risk Perpetuated." *Cornell Law Review* 97, no. 5 (July
2012): 1019–82.

Cohen, Amy. "Governance Legalism: Hayek and Sabel on Reason and Rules,
Organization and Law." *Wisconsin Law Review* (2010): 357–88.

Cohen, Amy. "Negotiation, Meet New Governance: Interests, Skills, and Selves." *Law
and Social Inquiry* 33 (2008): 503–62.

Cohen, Cathy J., and Joseph Kahne. *Participatory Politics: New Media and Youth
Political Action*. Oakland, CA: Youth and Participatory Politics Research Network,

Bibliography

June 2012. https://ypp.dmlcentral.net/sites/default/files/publications/Participatory_Politics_New_Media_and_Youth_Political_Action.2012.pdf.

Cohen, Cathy J., and Michael C. Dawson. "Neighborhood Poverty and African American Politics." *American Political Science Review* 87 (1993): 286–302.

Cohen, Joshua, and Archon Fung. "Radical Democracy." *Raisons Politiques* 42 (2004): 23–34.

Cohen, Joshua. "Deliberation and Democratic Legitimacy." In *Debates in Contemporary Political Philosophy*, edited by Derek Matravers and Jon Pike, 342–60. New York: Routledge, 2007.

Community Development Project at the Urban Justice Center and the Participatory Budgeting in New York City Research Team. *A People's Budget: A Research and Evaluation Report on Participatory Budgeting in New York City*. New York: Urban Justice Center, 2015.

Community Voices Heard. "Our Mission" and "Our Vision." Accessed December 5, 2018. www.cvhaction.org/what-we-do/.

Confessore, Nicholas. "Koch Brothers' Budget of $889 Million for 2016 Is on Par with Both Parties' Spending." *New York Times*, January 26, 2015. www.nytimes.com/2015/01/27/us/politics/kochs-plan-to-spend-900-million-on-2016-campaign.html.

Consumer Financial Protection Bureau. "Field Hearing on Debt Collection in Sacramento, Calif." Last updated July 28, 2016. www.consumerfinance.gov/about-us/events/archive-past-events/field-hearing-debt-collection-sacramento-calif/.

Consumer Financial Protection Bureau. "Consumer Complaint Database." Accessed December 5, 2018. www.consumerfinance.gov/data-research/consumer-complaints/.

Consumer Financial Protection Bureau. "The Bureau." Accessed December 5, 2018. www.consumerfinance.gov/about-us/the-bureau/.

Cook, Lauren. "City Council Program Lets You Choose What Public Projects to Fund in Your Neighborhood." *amNewYork*, updated April 13, 2018. www.amny.com/news/participatory-budgeting-nyc-1.17864253.

Cooper, Terry L., Thomas A. Bryer, and Jack W. Meek. "Citizen-Centered Collaborative Public Management." *Public Administration Review special issue* 66 (2006): 76.

Cordray, Richard. "The Trump Administration Is Trying to Undermine the CFPB. It Will Fail." *Washington Post*, February 14, 2018. www.washingtonpost.com/opinions/the-trump-administration-is-trying-to-undermine-the-cfpb-it-will-fail/2018/02/14/cab18f18-10d2-11e8-8ea1-c1d91fcec3fe_story.html.

Coren, Michael J. "Silicon Valley Tech Workers Are Talking about Starting Their First Union in 2017 to Resist Trump." *Quartz*, March 24, 2017. https://qz.com/916534/silicon-valley-tech-workers-are-talking-about-starting-their-first-union-in-2017-to-resist-trump/.

Cortes, Amber. "Person of Interest: Candace Faber, Civic Technology Advocate for the City of Seattle." *The Stranger*, February 1, 2017. www.thestranger.com/features/2017/02/01/24853520/person-of-interest-candace-faber.

Council of the City of New York, Office of Communications. "Council to Vote on Landmark Rules Reform Package." May 14, 2014. http://council.nyc.gov/html/pr/051414stated.shtml.

Bibliography

Coworker.org. "Coworker.org Victories." Accessed December 5, 2018. https://home.coworker.org/victories/.

Coworker.org. "Tech Workers Coalition." Accessed September 25, 2018. www.coworker.org/partnerships/tech-workers-coalition.

Coworker.org. "To: Starbucks: Let Us Have Visible Tattoos!!!" Accessed December 5, 2018. www.coworker.org/petitions/let-us-have-visible-tattoos.

Coworker.org. "Starbucks: Give Us a Fair Workweek!" Accessed December 5, 2018. www.coworker.org/petitions/starbucks-employees-need-a-fair-workweek.

Coworker.org. "Tech Workers Stand with Our Security Officers." Accessed September 25, 2018. www.coworker.org/petitions/solidarity-with-tech-security-officers.

Coworkers.org. "Grounds for Change: How Baristas Won Visible Tattoos at Starbucks." *Medium*, February 20, 2018. https://medium.com/@TeamCoworker/grounds-for-change-how-baristas-won-visible-tattoos-at-starbucks-a1b578e3a417.

Craig, Stephen C., Richard G. Niemi, and Glenn E. Silver. "Political Efficacy and Trust: A Report on the NES Pilot Study Items." *Political Behavior* 12 (1990): 289–314.

Cramer, Katherine J. *The Politics of Resentment: Rural Consciousness in Wisconsin and the Rise of Scott Walker*. Chicago: University of Chicago Press, 2016.

Crawford, Susan, and Dana Walters. *Citizen-Centered Governance: The Mayor's Office of New Urban Mechanics and the Evolution of the CRM in Boston*. Cambridge, MA: Berkman Klein Center for Internet and Society, July 30, 2013.

Cuellar, Mariano-Florentino. "Rethinking Regulatory Democracy." *Administrative Law Review* 57 (2005): 411–501.

Cummings, Scott. "Empirical Studies of Law and Social Change: What Is the Field? What Are the Questions?" *Wisconsin Law Review* (2013): 171–204.

Dahl, Robert A. *Polyarchy: Participation and Opposition*. New Haven, CT: Yale University Press, 1971.

Data.gov. "Datasets Published per Month." Last updated July 13, 2018. www.data.gov/metric/federalagency/dataset-published-per-month.

DataSF. "Data Academy." Accessed December 5, 2018. https://datasf.org/academy/.

Davidson, Joe. "Top Civil Servants Leaving Trump Administration at a Quick Clip." *Washington Post*, September 9, 2018.

Davidson, Nestor. "Localist Administrative Law" *Yale Law Journal* 127 (2017): 564–634.

De Barbieri, Edward W. "Do Community Benefits Actually Benefit Communities?" *Cardozo Law Review* 37 (2016): 1773–1825.

Democracy Fund Voter Study Group. "Insights from the 2016 Voter Survey." June 2017. www.voterstudygroup.org/publications/2016-elections/executive-summary.

Denhardt, Janet V., and Robert B. Denhardt. *The New Public Service: Serving, Not Steering*, 3rd ed. New York: Routledge, 2015.

DeSante, Christopher D. "Working Twice as Hard to Get Half as Far: Race, Work Ethic, and America's Deserving Poor." *American Journal of Political Science* 57 (2013): 342–56.

DiIulio, John J. *Deregulating the Public Sector: Can Government Be Improved?* Washington, DC: Brookings Institution, 2011.

Donahue, Linda H., James Ryan Lamare, and Fred B. Kotler. *The Cost of Worker Misclassification in New York State*. Ithaca, NY: Cornell University, School of Industrial and Labor Relations, 2007. http://digitalcommons.ilr.cornell.edu/reports/9/.

Doward, Jamie, and Alice Gibbs. "Did Cambridge Analytica Influence the Brexit Vote and the US Election?" *Observer*, March 4, 2017. www.theguardian.com/politics/2017/mar/04/nigel-oakes-cambridge-analytica-what-role-brexit-trump.

Downs, Anthony. *An Economic Theory of Democracy*. New York: Harper, 1957.

Drutman, Lee, and Steven Teles. "A New Agenda for Political Reform." *Washington Monthly*, March/April/May 2015. https://washingtonmonthly.com/magazine/marapr may-2015/a-new-agenda-for-political-reform/.

Drutman, Lee, and Steven Teles. "Why Congress Relies on Lobbyists Instead of Thinking for Itself." *Atlantic*, March 10, 2015. www.theatlantic.com/politics/archiv e/2015/03/when-congress-cant-think-for-itself-it-turns-to-lobbyists/387295/.

Drutman, Lee. *The Business of America Is Lobbying*. New York: Oxford University Press, 2015.

Drutman, Lee. "Donald Trump's Candidacy Is Going to Realign the Political Parties." *Vox*, March 1, 2016. www.vox.com/polyarchy/2016/3/1/11139054/trump-party-realignment.

Easton, David. *A Framework for Political Analysis*. Englewood Cliffs, NJ: Prentice-Hall, 1965.

Easton, David. *A Systems Analysis of Political Life*. Hoboken, NJ: Wiley, 1975.

Eaves, David. "The End of the Beginning of Digital Service Units." *Medium*, June 11, 2018. https://medium.com/digitalhks/the-end-of-the-beginning-of-digital-service-units-cf1fcce8aa57.

"E-Government Act of 2002." 107th Cong., 2nd sess., Congressional Record. January 23, 2002. www.congress.gov/107/plaws/publ347/PLAW-107publ347.pdf.

Eidelson, Josh. "Alt-Labor." *American Prospect*, January 29, 2013. http://prospect.org/a rticle/alt-labor.

Enduring Leadership in a Dynamic World. Quadrennial Diplomacy and Development Review. Washington, DC: U.S. Department of State and USAID, 2015.

Engines of Change: What Civic Tech Can Learn from Social Movements. Washington, DC: Omidyar Network, 2016. www.omidyar.com/sites/default/files/file_archive/Pdf s/Engines%2520of%2520Change%2520-%2520Final.pdf.

Ensign, Rachel Louise, and Ryan Tracy. "Trump Administration Seeks to Change Rules on Bank Lending to the Poor." *Wall Street Journal*, January 10, 2018. www .wsj.com/articles/trump-administration-seeks-to-change-rules-on-bank-lending-to-the-poor-1515624418.

Esty-Kendall, Jud, Mitra Bonshahi, and Emma Bowman. "Loved Ones of Charlottesville Victim Heather Heyer Cope with Their Loss Together." *NPR*, August 10, 2018. www.npr.org/2018/08/10/636871546/loved-ones-of-charlottesville-victim-heather-heyer-cope-with-their-loss-together.

Executive Office of the President, National Science and Technology Council. *Social and Behavior Sciences Team: 2016 Annual Report*. Washington, DC: Office of Science and Technology Policy, September 2016. https://sbst.gov/download/2016% 20SBST%20Annual%20Report.pdf.

Faith in Texas. Home page. Accessed December 5, 2018. https://faithintx.org/.

Farber, Daniel, and Anne O'Connell. "Agencies as Adversaries." *California Law Review* 105 (2017): 1375–1469.

Bibliography

Farina, Cynthia, Mary J. Newhart, Claire Cardie, and Dan Cosley. "Rulemaking 2.0." *University of Miami Law Review* 65 (2011): 395, 477.

Federal Financial Institutions Examination Council. "Home Mortgage Disclosure Act." Accessed December 5, 2018. www.ffiec.gov/hmda.

"The Federalist, No. 10." In *The Federalist Papers*, edited by Ian Shapiro. New Haven, CT: Yale University Press, 2009.

Feeley, Malcolm. *The Process is the Punishment: Handling Cases in a Lower Criminal Court*. New York: Russell Sage Foundation, 1979.

Feintzeig, Rachel. "US Struggles to Draw Young, Savvy Staff." *Wall Street Journal*, June 10, 2014. www.wsj.com/articles/u-s-government-struggles-to-attract-young-savvy-staff-members-1402445198.

Fine, Janice. *Worker Centers: Organizing Communities at the Edge of the Dream*. Ithaca, NY: ILR Press, 2006.

Fisher, Dana R., Lorien Jasny, and Dawn M. Dow. "Why Are We Here? Patterns of Intersectional Motivations across the Resistance." *SocArXiv*, last edited July 2, 2018). doi/abs/10.17813/1086-671X-23-4-451.

Fishkin, James S. *The Voice of the People: Public Opinion and Democracy*. New Haven, CT: Yale University Press, 1995.

Fishkin, Joseph, and David Pozen. "Asymmetric Constitutional Hardball." *Columbia Law Review* 118 (2018): 915–82.

Fishkin, Joseph, and William E. Forbath. "The Anti-Oligarchy Constitution." *Boston University Law Review* 94 (2014): 669–71.

Fishkin, Joseph, and William E. Forbath. "Wealth, Commonwealth, & the Constitution of Opportunity." University of Texas School of Law Public Law Research Paper No. UTPUB632 (2016). https://papers.ssrn.com/sol3/papers.cfm?abstract_id=2620920.

Flynn, Andrea, Susan R. Holmberg, Dorian T. Warren, and Felicia J. Wong. *The Hidden Rules of Race: Barriers to an Inclusive Economy*. New York: Cambridge University Press, 2017.

Foa, Roberto Stefan, and Yascha Mounk. "The Danger of Deconsolidation." *Journal of Democracy* 27, no. 3 (2015): 5–17.

Fones-Wolf, Elizabeth A. *Selling Free Enterprise: Assault on Labor and Liberalism, 1945–60*. Urbana: University of Illinois Press, 1994.

Ford, Cristie. "New Governance in the Teeth of Human Frailty: Lessons from Financial Regulation." *Wisconsin Law Review* (2010): 441–89.

Foroohar, Rana. *Makers and Takers: The Rise of Finance and the Fall of American Business*. New York: Crown, 2016.

Frederickson, Caroline. *Under the Bus: How Working Women Are Being Run Over*. New York: New Press, 2015.

Freeman, Jody, and Adrian Vermeule. "Massachusetts v. EPA: From Politics to Expertise." *Supreme Court Review* 2 (2007): 51–110.

Friedman, Tami J. "Exploiting the North-South Differential: Corporate Power, Southern Politics, and the Decline of Organized Labor after World War II." *Journal of American History* 95 (2008): 323–48.

Frost, Mary. "NYC's 'Participatory Budgeting' Procedure Doles Out Millions, Though Few Actually Vote." *Brooklyn Daily Eagle*, updated May 16, 2018. brooklyneagle

234 *Bibliography*

.com/articles/2018/05/15/nycs-participatory-budgeting-procedure-doles-out-millions-though-few-actually-vote/.

Frug, Gerald E. "The City as a Legal Concept." *Harvard Law Review* 93, no. 6 (1980): 1057–1154.

Frug, Gerald E. *City Making: Building Communities without Building Walls.* Princeton, NJ: Princeton University Press, 2001.

Frug, Gerald E., and David Barron. *City Bound: How States Stifle Urban Innovation.* Ithaca, NY: Cornell University Press, 2008.

Fukuyama, Francis. *The End of History and the Last Man.* New York: Avon, 1992.

Fung, Archon. "Recipes for Public Spheres: Eight institutional Design Choices and Their Consequences." *Journal of Political Philosophy* 11, no. 3 (2003): 338–67.

Fung, Archon. *Empowered Participation: Reinventing Urban Democracy.* Princeton, NJ: Princeton University Press, 2006.

Fung, Archon. "Varieties of Participation in Complex Governance." *Public Administration Review* 66 (December 2006): 66–75.

Fung, Archon. "Putting the Public Back into Governance: The Challenges of Citizen Participation and Its Future." *Public Administration Review* 75, no. 4 (2015): 513–22.

Fung, Archon. "It's the Gap, Stupid." *Boston Review*, September 1, 2017. http://bostonreview.net/class-inequality/archon-fung-its-gap-stupid.

Fung, Archon. "Understanding Power" (working paper, Gettysburg Project on Civic Engagement, June 2017), on file with authors.

Fung, Archon, Hollie Russon Gilman, and Jennifer Shkabatur. "Six Models for the Internet + Politics." *International Studies Review* 15 (2013): 30–47.

Fung, Archon, Mary Graham, and David Weil. *Full Disclosure: The Perils and Promise of Transparency.* New York: Cambridge University Press, 2007.

Fung, Archon, and Jennifer Shkabatur. "Viral Engagement: Fast, Cheap, and Broad, but Good for Democracy?" European University Institute Max Weber Lecture no. 2013/04 (April 17, 2013). http://cadmus.eui.eu/bitstream/handle/1814/27060/MWP_L S_2013_04.pdf;sequence=1.

Fung, Archon, and Erik Olin Wright. "Deepening Democracy: Innovations in Empowered Participatory Governance." *Politics and Society* 29(1) (2001): 5–42.

Gambino, Lauren, Sabrina Siddiqui, Paul Owen, and Edward Helmore. "Thousands Protest against Trump Travel Ban in Cities and Airports Nationwide." *Guardian*, January 29, 2017. www.theguardian.com/us-news/2017/jan/29/protest-trump-travel-ban-muslims-airports.

Ganz, Marshall. "Resources and Resourcefulness: Strategic Capacity in the Unionization of California Agriculture, 1959–1966." *American Journal of Sociology* 105 (2000): 1003–62.

Ganz, Marshall. *Why David Sometimes Wins: Leadership, Organization, and Strategy in the California Farm Worker Movement.* New York: Oxford University Press, 2009.

Ganz, Marshall. "Leading Change: Leadership, Organization, and Social Movements." In *Handbook of Leadership Theory and Practice*, edited by Nitin Nohria and Rakesh Khurana, 1–42. Cambridge, MA: Harvard Business School Press, 2010.

Ganz, Marshall. "How to Organize to Win." *The Nation*, March 16, 2018. www.thenation.com/article/how-to-organize-to-win/.

Garcia-Bedolla, Lisa, and Melissa R. Michelson. *Mobilizing Inclusion: Transforming the Electorate through Get-Out-the-Vote Campaigns.* New Haven, CT: Yale University Press, 2012.

Gaventa, John. *Power and Powerlessness: Quiescence & Rebellion in an Appalachian Valley.* Urbana: University of Illinois Press, 1982.

Geltzer, Joshua. "America's Problem Isn't Too Little Democracy. It's Too Much." *Politico,* June 26, 2018. www.politico.com/magazine/story/2018/06/26/america-democracy-trump-russia-2016-218894.

Gerber, Alan S., and Donald P. Green. "The Effects of Canvassing, Telephone Calls, and Direct Mail on Voter Turnout: A Field Experiment." *American Political Science Review* 94, no. 3 (2000): 653–63.

Gerken, Heather K. "Dissenting by Deciding." *Stanford Law Review* 57 (2005): 1745–1805.

Gershgorn, David. "The Industry That Predicts Your Vote – and Then Alters It – Is Still Just in Its Infancy." *Quartz,* May 18, 2017. https://qz.com/977429/the-industry-that-predicts-your-vote-and-then-alters-it-is-still-just-in-its-infancy/.

Gibbons, Lauren. "Rural Communities Suffer the Most without Access to the Web." *Government Technology,* June 29, 2018. www.govtech.com/network/Rural-Communities-Suffer-the-Most-Without-Access-to-the-Web.html.

Gilens, Martin. *Why Americans Hate Welfare: Race, Media, and the Politics of Antipoverty Policy.* Chicago: University of Chicago Press, 1999.

Gilens, Martin. *Affluence and Influence: Economic Inequality and Political Power in America.* Princeton, NJ: Princeton University Press, 2014.

Gilens, Martin, and Benjamin I. Page. "Testing Theories of American Politics: Elites, Interest Groups, and Average Citizens." *Perspectives on Politics* 12 (2014): 564–81.

Gilens, Martin, and Benjamin I. Page. *Democracy in America: What Has Gone Wrong and What We Can Do about It.* Chicago: University of Chicago Press, 2017.

Gillette, Michael L. *Launching the War on Poverty: An Oral History,* 2nd ed. New York: Oxford University Press, 2010.

Gilman, Hollie Russon. *Democracy Reinvented: Participatory Budgeting and Civic Innovation in America.* Washington, DC: Brookings Institution, 2016.

Gilman, Hollie Russon. "Government as Government, Not Business." *Stanford Social Innovation Review,* October 5, 2017. https://ssir.org/articles/entry/government_as_government_not_business.

Gilman, Hollie Russon, and Jessica Gover. *The Architecture of Innovation: Institutionalizing Innovation in Federal Policymaking.* Washington, DC: Beeck Center for Social Impact and Innovation at Georgetown University, 2016. http://beeckcenter.georgetown.edu/wp-content/uploads/2016/10/The-Architecture-of-Innovation_BeeckCenter.pdf.

Gilman, Hollie Russon, and K. Sabeel Rahman. *Building Civic Capacity in an Era of Democratic Crisis.* Washington, DC: New America, September 2017.

Gilman, Hollie Russon, and Brian Wampler. "The Difference in Design: Participatory Budgeting in Brazil and the United States." *Journal of Public Deliberation* (forthcoming).

Glenn, Brian J., and Steven M. Teles, eds. *Conservatism and American Political Development.* New York: Oxford University Press, 2009.

Goldfrank, Benjamin. "Lessons from Latin America's Experience in Participatory Budgeting." In *Participatory Budgeting*, edited by Anwar Shah, 91–126. Washington, DC: World Bank, 2007.

Goldfrank, Benjamin. "The World Bank and the Globalization of Participatory Budgeting." *Journal of Public Deliberation* 8, no. 2 (2012): 1–18. http://blogs.worldbank.org/ic4d/mobile-enhanced-participatory-budgeting-in-the-drc.

Goldman, Jason. "What Happens Next for We the People." *Medium*, December 21, 2016. https://medium.com/@Goldman44/what-happens-next-for-we-the-people-b55da1309d2c.

Goldsmith, Jack. "Will Donald Trump Destroy the Presidency?" *Atlantic*, October 2017. www.theatlantic.com/magazine/archive/2017/10/will-donald-trump-destroy-the-presidency/537921/.

Goldsmith, Stephen, and Susan Crawford. *The Responsive City: Engaging Communities through Data-Smart Governance*. San Francisco: Jossey-Bass, 2014.

Goldstein, Dana, and Alexander Burns. "Teacher Walkouts Threaten Republican Grip on Conservative States." *New York Times*, April 12, 2018. www.nytimes.com/2018/04/12/us/teacher-walkouts-threaten-republican-grip-on-conservative-states.html.

Gonçalves, Sónia. "The Effects of Participatory Budgeting on Municipal Expenditures and Infant Mortality in Brazil." *World Development*, 53 (January 2014): 94–110. doi:10.1016/j.worlddev.2013.01.009.

Gopnik, Adam. "'The John Birchers' Tea Party." *New Yorker*, October 11, 2013. www.newyorker.com/news/daily-comment/the-john-birchers-tea-party.

Gordon, Eric, and Stephen Walter. "Meaningful Inefficiencies: Resisting the Logic of Technological Efficiency in the Design of Civic Systems." In *Civic Media: Technology, Design, Practice*, edited by Eric Gordon and Paul Mihailidis. Cambridge, MA: MIT Press, 2016.

Gordon, Eric, Jessica Baldwin-Philippi, and Martina Balestra. *Why We Engage: How Theories of Human Behavior Contribute to Our Understanding of Civic Engagement in a Digital Era*. Cambridge, MA: Berkman Center for Internet & Society, 2013. http://cyber.law.harvard.edu/publications/2013/why_we_engage.

Gordon, Linda. *The Second Coming of the KKK: The Ku Klux Klan of the 1920s and the American Political Tradition*. New York: Liveright, 2017.

Gore, Al. *From Red Tape to Results: Creating a Government That Works Better and Costs Less; Executive Summary, National Performance Review*. Washington, DC: United States Government Printing Office, 1993.

"GovTech 100: 2018." *Government Technology*. Accessed December 5, 2018. www.govtech.com/100/.

Graeff, Erhardt. "Evaluating Civic Technology Design for Citizen Empowerment." PhD diss., Massachusetts Institute of Technology, 2018. https://dam-prod.media.mit.edu/x/2018/05/17/erhardt-phd-18.pdf.

Green, Donald P., and Alan S. Gerber. *Get Out the Vote: A Guide for Candidates and Campaigns*. New Haven, CT: Yale University Press, 2004.

Green, Donald P., and Alan S. Gerber. *Get Out the Vote: How to Increase Voter Turnout* 3rd ed. Washington, DC: Brookings, 2015.

Green, Jeffrey Edward. *The Eyes of the People: Democracy in an Age of Spectatorship*. New York: Oxford University Press, 2009.

Bibliography

Greenhouse, Steven. "Labor's Decline and Wage Inequality," *Economix* (blog), *New York Times*, August 4, 2011. http://economix.blogs.nytimes.com/2011/08/04/labors-decline-and-wage-inequality.

Greenhouse, Steven. "More Workers Are Claiming 'Wage Theft.'" *New York Times*, August 31, 2014. www.nytimes.com/2014/09/01/business/more-workers-are-claiming-wage-theft.html.

Greensboro North Carolina. "About Participatory Budgeting." Accessed December 5, 2018. www.greensboro-nc.gov/departments/budget-evaluation/participatory-budgeting/about.

Greenwald, Rebecca. "New Urban Mechanics: The Start-Up within Boston's City Government." *Metropolis*, April 11, 2016. www.metropolismag.com/cities/new-urban-mechanics-the-start-up-that-works-within-city-government/.

Griffin, Robert, and Ruy Teixeira. "The Story of Trump's Appeal: A Portrait of Trump Voters." *Democracy Fund Voter Study Group*, June 2017. www.voterstudygroup.org/publications/2016-elections/story-of-trumps-appeal.

Gutmann, Amy, and Dennis Thompson. *Democracy and Disagreement.* Cambridge, MA: Belknap Press of Harvard University, 1996.

Gutmann, Amy, and Dennis Thompson. *Why Deliberative Democracy?* Princeton, NJ: Princeton University Press, 2004.

Haberman, Clyde. "Roger Ailes, Who Built Fox News into an Empire, Dies at 77." *New York Times*, May 18, 2017. www.nytimes.com/2017/05/18/business/media/roger-ailes-dead.html.

Hacker, Jacob S. *The Divided Welfare State: The Battle over Public and Private Social Benefits in the United States.* New York: Cambridge University Press, 2002.

Hacker, Jacob S. "Afterword: What the Resistance Means for American Democracy." In *The Resistance: The Dawn of the Anti-Trump Opposition Movement*, edited by David S. Meyer and Sidney Tarrow. New York: Oxford University Press, 2018.

Hacker, Jacob S., and Paul Pierson. "Business Power and Social Policy: Employers and the Formation of the American Welfare State." *Politics and Society* 30 (2002): 277–325.

Hacker, Jacob, and Paul Pierson. "Drift and Democracy: The Neglected Politics of Policy Inaction." American Political Science Association Annual Meeting, September 2010.

Hacker, Jacob S., and Paul Pierson. *Winner-Take-All Politics: How Washington Made the Rich Richer – And Turned Its Back on the Middle Class.* New York: Simon & Schuster, 2010.

Hacker, Jacob S., and Paul Pierson. "After the 'Master Theory': Downs, Schattschneider, and the Rebirth of Policy-Focused Analysis." *Perspectives on Politics* 12 (2014): 643–62, 65.

Hacker, Jacob S., and Paul Pierson. *American Amnesia: How the War on Government Led Us to Forget What Made America Prosper.* New York: Simon & Schuster, 2017.

Hampton, Keith, Lauren F. Sessions, Eun Ja Her, and Lee Rainie. *Social Isolation and New Technology.* Washington, DC: Pew Research Center, November 4, 2009. www.pewinternet.org/2009/11/04/social-isolation-and-new-technology/.

Bibliography

Han, Hahrie. *How Organizations Develop Activists: Civic Associations and Leadership in the 21st Century.* New York: Oxford University Press, 2014.

Han, Hahrie. "Want Gun Control? Learn from the N.R.A." *New York Times,* October 4, 2017. www.nytimes.com/2017/10/04/opinion/gun-control-nra-vegas.html.

Hasen, Richard. *Plutocrats United: Campaign Money, the Supreme Court, and the Distortion of American Elections.* New Haven, CT: Yale University Press, 2016.

Hayashi, Yuka. "Trump Administration Overhauls CFPB's Mission, Proposes Budget Cuts." *Wall Street Journal,* February 12, 2018. www.wsj.com/articles/trump-administration-overhauls-cfpbs-mission-proposes-budget-cuts-1518480377.

Hayashi, Yuka. "Trump Budget Plan Cuts CFPB's Budget, Restricts Its Enforcement Power." *Wall Street Journal,* February 12, 2018. www.wsj.com/livecoverage/trumps-2019-budget-proposal-live-analysis/card/1518471424.

Heinrich, Carolyn. "Outcomes-Based Performance Management in the Public Sector: Implications for Government Accountability and Effectiveness." *Public Administration Review* 62 (2002): 712–25.

Heller, Nathaniel. "The Sharing Economy Is Not Civic Tech." *Global Integrity.* Accessed December 5, 2108. www.globalintegrity.org/2013/12/the-sharing-economy-is-not-civic-tech/.

Hertel-Fernandez, Alexander. "How the Right Trounced Liberals in the States." *Democracy: A Journal of Ideas* 39 (2016). http://democracyjournal.org/magazine/39/how-the-right-trounced-liberals-in-the-states [https://perma.cc/5Q6E-SY9 W].

Hertel-Fernandez, Alexander. *Politics at Work: How Companies Turn Their Workers into Lobbyists.* New York: Oxford University Press, 2018.

Hibbing, J. R., and E. Theiss-Morse. *Stealth Democracy: Americans' Beliefs about How Government Should Work.* Cambridge.: Cambridge University Press, 2002.

Hochschild, Arlie Russell. *Strangers in Their Own Land: Anger and Mourning on the American Right.* New York: New Press, 2016.

Hofferth, Sandra L., and John Iceland. "Social Capital in Rural and Urban Communities." *Rural Sociology* 63, no. 4 (December 1998): 574–98.

Howard, Alexander. "White House Responds to Remaining 'We The People' E- Petitions." *Huffington Post,* July 28, 2015. www.huffingtonpost.com/entry/white-house-clears-the-backlog-of-we-the-people-epetitions_us_55b788dde4b0074ba5a6165a.

Huq, Aziz, and Tom Ginsburg. "How to Lose a Constitutional Democracy." *UCLA Law Review* 65 (2018): 78–169. www.uclalawreview.org/lose-constitutional-democracy/.

ICMA. Home page. Accessed December 5, 2018. https://icma.org/.

Ifill, Sherrilyn. "President Trump's First Year Was an Affront to Civil Rights." *Time,* January 17, 2018. http://time.com/5106648/donald-trump-civil-rights-race/.

Illing, Sean. "'Rural America' Doesn't Mean 'White America' – Here's Why That Matters." *Vox,* April 24, 2017. www.vox.com/conversations/2017/4/24/15286624/race-rural-america-trump-politics-media.

Interfaith Worker Justice. "About." Accessed December 5, 2018. www.iwj.org/about.

Issacharoff, Samuel, and Richard H. Pildes. "Politics as Markets: Partisan Lockups of the Democratic Process." *Stanford Law Review* 50 (1998): 643–717.

Issenberg, Sasha. *The Victory Lab: The Secret Science of Winning Campaigns.* New York: Crown, 2012.

Bibliography

J. M. Kaplan Fund. "Michelle Miller & Jess Kutch: Project Overview." Accessed December 5, 2018. www.jmkfund.org/awardee/michelle-miller-and-jess-kutch/.

Jacobs, Meg. "'How about Some Meat?' The Office of Price Administration, Consumption Politics, and State Building from the Bottom Up, 1941–1946." *Journal of American History* 84, no.3 (1997): 910–41.

Jaffer, Jameel, and Brett M. Kaufman. "A Resurgence of Secret Law." *Yale Law Journal Forum* 126 (2016): 242–51.

Jamieson, Kathleen Hall, and Joseph N. Cappella. *Echo Chamber: Rush Limbaugh and the Conservative Media Establishment*. New York: Oxford University Press 2008.

Jamison, Peter, Joe Heim, Lori Aratani, and Marissa J. Lang. "'Never Again!' Students Demand Action against Gun Violence in Nation's Capital." *Washington Post*, March 12, 2018. www.washingtonpost.com/local/march-for-our-lives-huge-crowds-gather-for-rally-against-gun-violence-in-nations-capital/2018/03/24/4121b100-2f7d-11e8-bobo-f706877db618_story.html.

Jenkins, J. Craig, and Charles Perrow. "Insurgency of the Powerless." *American Sociological Review* 42 (1977): 249–68.

Jenkins, Rob, and Anne Marie Goetz. "Accounts and Accountability: Theoretical Implications of the Right-to-Information Movement in India." *Third World Quarterly* 20, no. 3 (1999): 603–22.

Joffé, George. "The Arab Spring in North Africa: Origins and Prospects." *Journal of North Africa Studies* 16 (2011): 507–32.

Johnson, Carolina, and John Gastil. "Variations of Institutional Design for Empowered Deliberation." *Journal of Public Deliberation* 11, no. 1, article 2 (2015).

Johnson, Steven. "What a Hundred Million Calls to 311 Reveal about New York." *Wired*, November 1, 2010. www.wired.com/2010/11/ff_311_new_york/.

Judd, Nick. "With 'We the People,' White House Promises to Go E-To-The People." *TechPresident*, September 1, 2011. http://techpresident.com/blog-entry/we-people-white-house-promises-go-e-people.

Kagan, Elena. "Presidential Administration." *Harvard Law Review* 114 (2001): 2245–2385.

Kahane, David, Daniel Weinstock, and Dominique Melissa Williams. *Deliberative Democracy in Practice*. Vancouver: University of British Columbia Press, 2010.

Kahn, Yasmeen. "Poverty and Hardship Make Life Shorter in Brownsville." *WNYC News*, March 28, 2017. www.wnyc.org/story/poverty-and-hardships-make-life-shorter-brownsville/.

Kantor, Jodi. "Working Anything but 9 to 5: Scheduling Technology Leaves Low-Income Parents with Hours of Chaos." *New York Times*, August 13, 2014. www.nytimes.com/interactive/2014/08/13/us/starbucks-workers-scheduling-hours.html.

Kantor, Jodi. "Starbucks to Revise Policies to End Irregular Schedules for Its 130,000 Baristas." *New York Times*, August 14, 2014. www.nytimes.com/2014/08/15/us/starbucks-to-revise-work-scheduling-policies.html.

Kantor, Jodi. "Times Article Changes a Starbucks Policy, Fast." *New York Times*, August 22, 2014. www.nytimes.com/times-insider/2014/08/22/times-article-changes-a-policy-fast/.

Karlan, Pamela S. "Disarming the Private Attorney General." *University. of Illinois Law Review*, no. 1 (2003): 183–209.

Bibliography

Karpf, Dave. "How the White House's We the People E-Petition Site Became a Virtual Ghost-Town." *TechPresident*, June 20, 2014. http://techpresident.com/news/25144/how-white-houses-we-people-e-petition-site-became-virtual-ghost-town.

Karpf, David. *The MoveOn Effect: The Unexpected Transformation of American Political Advocacy*. New York: Oxford University Press, 2012.

Karpf, David. *Analytic Activism: Digital Listening and the New Political Strategy*. New York: Oxford University Press, 2016.

Katyal, Neal K. "Internal Separation of Powers: Checking Today's Most Dangerous Branch from Within." *Yale Law Journal* 115 (2006): 2314–49.

Katz, Eric. "How One Agency Will Use Sabbaticals and Rotations to Retain Employees." *Government Executive*, April 29, 2015. www.govexec.com/pay-benefits/2015/04/how-one-agency-will-use-sabbaticals-and-rotations-retain-employees/111424/

Katznelson, Ira. *Fear Itself: The New Deal and the Origins of Our Time*. New York: Liveright, 2013.

Kaufman, Alexander C. "Starbucks Baristas Fight to Show Tattoos." *Huffington Post*, September 13, 2014. www.huffingtonpost.com/2014/09/12/starbucks-tattoos_n_5811888.html.

Kennedy, Leonard J., Patricia A. McCoy, and Ethan Bernstein. "The Consumer Financial Protection Bureau: Financial Regulation for the Twenty-First Century." *Cornell Law Review* 97, no. 5 (July 2012): 1141–75.

Kessler, Sarah. "Pixel & Dimed On (Not) Getting by in the Gig Economy." *Fast Company*, March 18, 2014. www.fastcompany.com/3027355/pixel-and-dimed-on-not-getting-by-in-the-gig-economy.

Kettl, Donald F. *Reinventing Government? Appraising the National Performance Review*. Washington, DC: Brookings Institution, 1994.

Kettl, Donald F. "Managing Boundaries in American Administration: The Collaboration Imperative." In "Symposium on Collaborative Public Management." *Public Administration Review* 66, no. S1 (2007): 10–19.

Kettl, Donald F. "The Job of Government: Interweaving Public Functions and Private Hands." *Public Administration Review* 75, no. 2 (2015): 219–29.

Kharas, Homi, and Jaana Remes. "Can Smart Cities Be Equitable?" *Brookings*, June 11, 2018. www.brookings.edu/opinions/can-smart-cities-be-equitable/.

Killian, Lewis. "Organization, Rationality, and Spontaneity in the Civil Rights Movement." *American Sociological Review* 49 (1984): 770–83.

Kinder, Molly. *Automation Potential for Jobs in Indianapolis*. Washington, DC: New America, May 17, 2018. www.newamerica.org/work-workers-technology/reports/automation-potential-jobs-indianapolis/introduction.

King, Desmond. "Forceful Federalism against American Racial Inequality." *Government and Opposition* 52, Special Issue (2017): 356–82.

Kiviat, Barbara. "The CFPB Is Making Government More Accountable. The GOP Wants to Stop It." *Washington Monthly*, June 8, 2017. http://washingtonmonthly.com/2017/06/08/the-cfpb-is-making-government-more-accountable-the-gop-wants-to-stop-it/.

Kneese, Tamara, Alex Rosenblat, and danah boyd. *Understanding Fair Labor Practices in a Networked Age*. New York: Data & Society Research Institute, October 8, 2014. www.datasociety.net/pubs/fow/FairLabor.pdf.

Bibliography

Knight Foundation. "Philadelphia." Accessed December 5, 2018. https://knightfounda tion.org/communities/philadelphia/.

Kreiss, Daniel. *Taking Our Country Back: The Crafting of Network Politics from Howard Dean to Barack Obama*. New York: Oxford University Press, 2012.

Kumkar, Nils C. *The Tea Party, Occupy Wall Street, and the Great Recession*. New York: Palgrave Macmillan, 2018.

Kwak, James. "Cultural Capture and the Financial Crisis." In *Preventing Regulatory Capture: Special Internet Influence and How to Limit It*, edited by Daniel Carpenter and David A. Moss, 71–98. New York: Cambridge University Press, 2013.

Land, Molly K. "Democratizing Human Rights Fact-Finding." In *The Transformation of Human Rights Fact-Finding*, edited by Philip Alston and Sarah Knuckey. New York: Oxford University Press, 2015.

Landis, James M. *The Administrative Process*. New Haven, CT: Yale University Press, 1938.

Lapowsky, Issie. "What Did Cambridge Analytica Really Do for Trump's Campaign?" *Wired*, October 26, 2017. www.wired.com/story/what-did-cambridge-analytica-really-do-for-trumps-campaign/.

Lassiter, Matthew D. *The Silent Majority: Suburban Politics in the Sunbelt South*. Princeton, NJ: Princeton University Press, 2007.

Lee, Caroline W. *Do-It-Yourself Democracy: The Rise of the Public Engagement Industry*. New York: Oxford University Press, 2015.

Lee, Woojin, and John E. Roemer. "Racism and Redistribution in the United States: A Solution to the Problem of American Exceptionalism." *Journal of Public Economics* 90 (2006): 1027–52.

Lerner, Josh. *Everyone Counts: Could "Participatory Budgeting" Change Democracy?* Ithaca, NY: Cornell University Press, 2014.

Lerner, Josh. "Participatory Budgeting Increased Voters Likelihood 7%." June 28, 2018. Participatory Budgeting Project. www.participatorybudgeting.org/participatory-budgeting-increases-voter-turnout-7/.

Lerner, Josh, and Donata Secondo. "By the People, for the People: Participatory Budgeting from the Bottom Up in North America." *Journal of Public Deliberation* 8, no. 2 (2012): 1–9.

Lessig, Lawrence. "The New Chicago School." *Journal of Legal Studies* 27 (1998): 661–91, 665–72.

Lessig, Lawrence. *Code and Other Laws of Cyberspace*. New York: Basic Books, 1999.

Lessig, Lawrence. *Republic, Lost: How Money Corrupts Congress – And a Plan to Stop It*. New York: Twelve, 2011.

Lessig, Lawrence, and Cass R. Sunstein. "The President and the Administration." *Columbia Law Review* 94 (1994): 1–123.

Levine, C. H. "Citizenship and Service Delivery: The Promise of Coproduction." In *The Age of Direct Citizen Participation*, edited by Nancy C. Roberts, 78–92. Armonk, NY: M. E. Sharpe, 2008.

Levine, Peter. *We Are the Ones We Have Been Waiting For: The Promise of Civic Renewal in America*. New York: Oxford University Press, 2013.

Levinson, Daryl. "Looking for Power in Public Law." *Harvard Law Review* 130 (2016): 31–143.

Levinson, Daryl J., and Richard H. Piles. "Separation of Parties, Not Powers." *Harvard Law Review* 119 (2006): 2311–86.

Bibliography

Levitin, Adam J. "The Consumer Financial Protection Bureau: An Introduction." *Review of Banking and Financial Law* 32 (2013): 321–69.

Levitsky, Steven, and Daniel Ziblatt. *How Democracies Die*. New York: Crown, 2018.

Lichtenstein, Nelson. *State of the Union*. Princeton, NJ: Princeton University Press, 2010.

Lincoln, Abraham. "The Gettysburg Address." Transcribed by the Smithsonian Institution, National Museum of American History, November 19, 1863. http://americanhistory.si.edu/documentsgallery/exhibitions/gettysburg_address_2.html.

Lind, Dara. "'Families Belong Together' Rallies Are Protesting the Separation of Immigrant Children from Parents." *Vox*, June 14, 2018. www.vox.com/2018/6/14/17463732/families-belong-together-rally-protest-separate-children-immigrants.

Lindblom, Charles E. *The Market System: What It Is, How It Works, and What to Make of It*. New Haven, CT: Yale University Press, 2001.

LinkNYC. Home page. Accessed December 5, 2018. www.link.nyc/.

Littrell, Jill, and Fred Brooks. "In Defense of the Community Reinvestment Act." *Journal of Community Practice*, 18, no. 4 (2010): 417–39.

Livermore, Michael, Vladimir Eidelman, and Brian Grom. "Computationally Assisted Regulatory Participation." *Notre Dame Law Review* 93 (2018): 977–1034.

Lopez, Ian Haney. *Dog Whistle Politics: How Coded Racial Appeals Have Reinvented Racism and Wrecked the Middle Class*. New York: Oxford University Press, 2014.

Lovegrove, Nick, and Matthew Thomas. "Why the World Needs Tri-Sector Leaders." *Harvard Business Review* (February 13, 2013). https://hbr.org/2013/02/why-the-world-needs-tri-sector.

Lowe, Stanley, and John Metzger. "A Citywide Strategy: The Pittsburgh Community Reinvestment Group." In *Organizing Access to Capital: Advocacy and the Democratization of Financial Institutions*, edited by Gregory D. Squires, 85–101. Philadelphia: Temple University Press, 2003.

Lukensmeyer, Carolyn. *Bringing Citizen Voices to the Table: A Guide for Public Managers*. New York: John Wiley, 2012.

Lukensmeyer, Carolyn J., and Lars Hasselblad Torres. *Public Deliberation: A Manager' Guide to Citizen Engagement*. Washington, DC: IBM Center for the Business of Government, 2006.

Luttmer, Erzo F. P. "Group Loyalty and the Taste for Redistribution." *Journal of Political Economy* 109 (2001): 500–28.

MacLean, Nancy. *Democracy in Chains: The Deep History of the Radical Right's Stealth Plan for America*. New York: Penguin, 2017.

"Making Open and Machine Readable the New Default for Government Information." Exec. Order No. 13642, 78 Fed. Reg. 28111. May 14, 2013; signed May 9, 2013.

Malakoff, David. "Trump's Pick to Head White House Science Office Gets Good Reviews." *Science*, July 31, 2018. www.sciencemag.org/news/2018/07/trump-s-pick-head-white-house-science-office-gets-good-reviews.

Maloy, J. S. *The Colonial Origins of Modern Democratic Thought*. New York: Cambridge University Press, 2008.

Mansbridge, Jane. *Beyond Adversary Democracy*. New York: Basic Books, 1980.

Mansbridge, Jane. *Deliberative Systems: Deliberative Democracy at the Large Scale*. Cambridge: Cambridge University Press, 2013.

Mansbridge, Jane, James Bohman, Simone Chambers, David Estlund, Andreas Follesdal, Archon Fung, Cristina Lafont, Bernard Manin, and José luis Martí. "The Place of Self-Interest and the Role of Power in Deliberative Democracy." *Journal of Political Philosophy* 18 (2010): 64–100.

Marisco, Richard. "Democratizing Capital: The History, Law, and Reform of the Community Reinvestment Act." *New York Law School Law Review* 49 (2004): 712–26.

Marquetti, Adalmir. "Participação e redistribuição: O orçamento participativo em Porto Alegre." In *A inovação democrática no Brasil: O orçamento participativo*, edited by Leonardo Avritzer, Zander Navarro, and A. Marquetti, 129–56. São Paulo, Brazil: Cortez Editora, 2003.

Matthews, Dylan. "Studies: Democratic Politicians Represent Middle-Class Voters. GOP Politicians Don't." *Vox*, April 2, 2018. www.vox.com/policy-and-politics/2018/4/2/16226202/oligarchy-political-science-politician-congress-respond-citizens-public-opinion.

Mayer, Gerald. *Union Membership Trends in the United States*. Washington, DC: Congressional Research Service, August 31, 2004. https://digitalcommons.ilr.cornell.edu/key_workplace/174/.

Mayer, Jane. "Covert Operations." *New Yorker*, August 30, 2010. www.newyorker.com/magazine/2010/08/30/covert-operations.

Mayer, Jane. "The Reclusive Hedge-Fund Tycoon behind the Trump Presidency." *New Yorker*, March 27, 2017. www.newyorker.com/magazine/2017/03/27/the-reclusive-hedge-fund-tycoon-behind-the-trump-presidency.

Mayor's Office of New Mechanics. "Urban Housing Unit Roadshow." Last updated April 20, 2018. www.boston.gov/departments/new-urban-mechanics/urban-housing-unit-roadshow.

McAdam, Doug. *Political Process and the Development of Black Insurgency*. Chicago: University of Chicago Press, 1982.

McAlevey, Jane. *No Shortcuts: Organizing for Power in the New Gilded Age*. New York: Oxford University Press, 2016.

McCaney, Shawn. "A New Path for Urban Philanthropy." *William Penn Foundation*, November 29, 2017. https://williampennfoundation.org/blog/new-path-urban-philanthropy.

McCartin, Joseph A. *Collison Course: Ronald Reagan, the Air Traffic Controllers, and the Strike That Changed America*. New York: Oxford University Press, 2011.

McCarty, Nolan. "Complexity, Capacity, Capture." In *Preventing Regulatory Capture: Special Interest Influence and How to Limit It*, edited by Daniel Carpenter and David A. Moss, 99–123. New York: Cambridge University Press, 2014.

McClelland, Edward. "Is Walmart Sticking It to The People or Sticking It to The Man?" *Ward Room*, June 4, 2010. www.nbcchicago.com/blogs/ward-room/Is-Walmart-Sticking-It-to-The-People-or-Sticking-it-to-The-Man-95520589.html.

McCormick, John. "Machiavelli against Republicanism: On the Cambridge School's Guicciardinian Moments." *Political Theory* 31 (2003): 615–43.

McCormick, John. "Contain the Wealthy and Patrol the Magistrates: Restoring Elite Accountability to Popular Government." *American Political Science Review* 100, no. 2 (2006): 147–63.

McCormick, John P. *Machiavellian Democracy*. New York: Cambridge University Press, 2011.

Bibliography

McCue, T. J. "57 Million U.S. Workers Are Part of the Gig Economy." *Forbes*, August 31, 2018. www.forbes.com/sites/tjmccue/2018/08/31/57-million-u-s-workers-are-part-of-the-gig-economy/#285ba9ae7118.

McElwee, Sean, and Jason McDaniel. "Economic Anxiety Didn't Make People Vote Trump, Racism Did." *Nation*, May 8, 2017. www.thenation.com/article/economic-anxiety-didnt-make-people-vote-trump-racism-did/.

McKenna, Elizabeth, and Hahrie Han. *Groundbreakers: How Obama's 2.2 Million Volunteers Transformed Campaigns in America*. New York: Oxford University Press, 2014.

McRae, Elizabeth Gillespie. *Mothers of the Massive Resistance*. New York: Oxford University Press, 2018.

Melish, Tara J. "Maximum Feasible Participation of the Poor: New Governance, New Accountability, and a 21st Century War on the Sources of Poverty." *Yale Human Rights and Development Journal* 13, no. 1 (2010): 1–133.

Mellon, Jonathan, Hollie Russon Gilman, Fredrik M. Sjoberg, and Tiago Peixoto. *Gender and Political Mobilization Online: Participation and Policy Success on a Global Petitioning Platform*. Cambridge, MA: Harvard Kennedy School, Ash Center, July 2017. https://ash.harvard.edu/links/gender-and-political-mobilization-online-participation-and-policy-success-global.

Merle, Renae. "Trump Administration Strips Consumer Watchdog Office of Enforcement Powers in Lending Discrimination Cases." *Washington Post*, February 1, 2018. www.washingtonpost.com/news/business/wp/2018/02/01/trump-administration-strips-consumer-watchdog-office-of-enforcement-powers-against-financial-firms-in-lending-discrimination-cases/?utm_term=.dfc7f9619e42.

Merrill, Thomas. "Capture Theory and the Courts: 1967–1983." *Chicago-Kent Law Review* 72 (1997): 1039–1117.

Mettler, Suzanne. *The Submerged State: How Invisible Government Policies Undermine American Democracy*. Chicago: University of Chicago Press, 2011.

Metzger, Gillian. "1930s Redux: The Administrative State under Siege." *Harvard Law Review* 131 (2017): 1–95.

Metzger, Gillian E. "Through the Looking Glass to a Shared Reflection: The Evolving Relationship between Administrative Law and Financial Regulation." *Law and Contemporary Problems* 78 (2015): 129–56.

Meyer, Jane. *Dark Money: The Hidden History of the Billionaires behind the Rise of the Radical Right*. New York: Anchor, 2017.

Meyer, Robinson. "The Secret Startup That Saved the Worst Website in America." *Atlantic*, July 9, 2015. www.theatlantic.com/technology/archive/2015/07/the-secret-startup-saved-healthcare-gov-the-worst-website-in-america/397784/.

Michaels, Jon D. *Constitutional Coup: Privatization's Threat to the American Republic*. Cambridge, MA: Harvard University Press, 2017.

Middendorf II, J. William. *A Glorious Disaster: Barry Goldwater's Presidential Campaign and the Origins of the Conservative Movement*. New York: Basic Books, 2006.

Miller, Arthur H. "Political Issues and Trust in Government: 1964–1970." *American Political Science Review* 68 (1974): 951–72.

Miller, Michelle. "The Union of the Future: Thought Brief." July 2015. Roosevelt Institute. http://rooseveltinstitute.org/wp-content/uploads/2015/10/Miller-The-Union-of-the-Future.pdf.

Bibliography

Miller, Michelle, and Eric Bernstein. *New Frontiers of Worker Power: Challenges and Opportunities in the Modern Economy.* New York: Roosevelt Institute, February 15, 2017.

Milward, H. Brinton et al. "Managing the Hollow State." Lecture, American Political Science Association Annual Meeting, 1991.

Milward, H. Brinton, and Keith G. Provan. "Governing the Hollow State." *Journal of Public Administration Research and Theory* 10 (2000): 359–80.

Minkoff, Debra C. *Organizing for Equality: The Evolution of Women's and Racial-Ethnic Organizations in America, 1955–1985.* Philadelphia: Temple University Press, 1995.

Misra, Tanvi, and Sarah Holder. "'Workers' Rights, Silicon-Valley Style." *City Lab,* August 31, 2018. www.citylab.com/equity/2018/08/workers-rights-silicon-valley-style/568189/.

MobLab. "Coworker.org to Give Deep Support to Mobilize Workers." March 11, 2013. https://mobilisationlab.org/new-organization-to-give-deep-support-to-mobilize-workers/.

Moore, Mark. *Recognizing Public Value.* Cambridge, MA: Harvard University Press, 2013.

Morozov, Evgeny. *The Net Delusion: The Dark Side of Internet Freedom.* New York: Public Affairs, 2011.

Morris, Aldon D. *The Origins of the Civil Rights Movement, Black Communities Organizing for Change.* New York: Free Press, 1984.

Morton, Jennifer M., and Sarah K. Paul. "Grit." In *Ethics.* Forthcoming. https://phil archive.org/archive/PAUG-5v1.

Mounk, Yascha. "Donald Trump Is the End of Global Politics as We Know It." *Foreign Policy,* November 11, 2016. https://foreignpolicy.com/2016/11/11/donald-trump-will-change-global-politics-as-we-know-it/.

The Movement for Black Lives. "A Vision for Black Lives: Policy Demands for Black Power, Freedom & Justice." Last modified December 5, 2018. https://policy.m4bl.org/.

Munnell, Alicia H., Lynn Elaine Browne, James McEneaney, and Geoffrey M. B. Tootell. "Mortgage Lending in Boston: Interpreting HMDA Data." *American Economic Review* 86, no. 1 (1996): 25–53.

Murray, Peter. "The Secret of Scale: How Powerful Civic Organizations Like the NRA and AARP Build Membership, Make Money, and Sway Public Policy." *Stanford Social Innovation Review* (Fall 2013): 32–39.

Myers, Jen. "Leading Boston and Beyond: How HBS Leadership Fellows Have Reinvented How We Think about Governance." Harvard Business School. December 1, 2015. www.alumni.hbs.edu/stories/Pages/story-bulletin.aspx?num=5001.

Nabatchi, Tina. "Addressing the Citizenship and Democratic Deficits: The Potential of Deliberative Democracy for Public Administration." *American Review of Public Administration* 40 (2010): 376–99.

Nabatchi, Tina. "Putting the 'Public' Back in Public Values Research: Designing Public Participation to Identify and Respond to Public Values." *Public Administration Review* 72, no. 5 (2012): 699–708.

Nabatchi, Tina, and Matt Leighninger. *Public Participation for the 21st Century.* Hoboken, NJ: Jossey-Bass, 2015.

National Bail Out. Home page. Accessed December 5, 2018. https://nomoremoneybail .org/.

National Coalition for Dialogue & Deliberation. "Community Blog." Accessed December 5, 2018. http://ncdd.org/27766.

National Employment Law Project. "New York Department of Labor Wage Board for Fast-Food Workers." Fact sheet. May 2015. www.nelp.org/content/uploads/Fact-Sheet-New-York-Labor-Department-Fast-Food-Wage-Board.pdf.

National Rural Assembly. Home page. Accessed December 5, 2018. http://ruralassem bly.org.

National Rural Assembly. "National Rural Assembly 2018: Building Civic Courage, May 21–23, Durham, NC." Accessed December 5, 2018. http://ruralassembly.org/20 18-rural-assembly/.

Netgain Partnership. Home page. Accessed December 5, 2018. https://netgainpartner ship.org/.

Newkirk II, Vann R. "The Fight for Health Care Has Always Been about Civil Rights." *Atlantic*, June 27, 2017. www.theatlantic.com/politics/archive/2017/06/the-fight-for-health-care-is-really-all-about-civil-rights/531855/.

New Urban Mechanics. "What We Learned from the UHU Roadshow." November 9, 2016. https://medium.com/@newurbanmechs/what-we-learned-from-the-uhu-roadshow-7b33caeed721#.jlopwk58g.

New York City Council. "Participatory Budgeting." Accessed December 5, 2018. https://council.nyc.gov/pb/participate/.

New York City Council. "Speaker Corey Johnson and the New York City Council Kickoff Participatory Budgeting Cycle 8." August 20, 2018. https://council.nyc.gov/press/2018/08/20/1633/.

New York City Council. "Speaker Melissa Mark-Viverito and New York City Council Launch 2015–2016 Participatory Budgeting Cycle." September 21, 2015. https://council.nyc.gov/press/2015/09/21/180/.

Nivola, Pietro S., and David W. Brady, eds. *Red and Blue Nation? Volume 2: Consequences and Correction of America's Polarized Politics*. Washington, DC: Brookings Institution, 2008.

Norris, Pippa. *Digital Divide: Civic Engagement, Information Poverty, and the Internet Worldwide*. Cambridge: Cambridge University Press, 2001.

Nou, Jennifer. "Intra-Agency Coordination." *Harvard Law Review* 129 (2015): 421–90.

Nou, Jennifer. "Subdelegating Powers." *Columbia Law Review* 117, no. 2 (2017): 473–526.

Noveck, Beth Simone. "The Electronic Revolution in Rulemaking." *Emory Law Journal* 53, no. 2 (2004): 433–519.

Noveck, Beth Simone. *Smart Citizens, Smarter State: The Technologies of Expertise and the Future of Governing*. Cambridge, MA: Harvard University Press, 2015.

NYC. "Mayor de Blasio Announces 3–K for All." News release. April 24, 2017.www1 .nyc.gov/office-of-the-mayor/news/258-17/mayor-de-blasio-3-k-all/#/0.

NYC. "Mayor de Blasio's GetCoveredNYC Campaign Announces over 150 Upcoming Health Insurance Enrollment Events Citywide." March 27, 2018. www1.nyc.gov/office-of-the-mayor/news/163-18/mayor-de-blasio-s-getcoverednyc-campaign-over-150-upcoming-health-insurance-enrollment.

Bibliography

NYC. "Find a Summer Meals Program." Accessed December 5, 2018. www1.nyc.gov /nyc-resources/service/4061/find-a-summer-meals-program.

NYC. "HPD-HDC Housing Fellows Program." Accessed December 5, 2018. www1 .nyc.gov/site/hpd/about/hpd-hdc-housing-fellows-program.page.

NYC Analytics. "Meet the Team." Accessed December 5, 2018. www1.nyc.gov/site/an alytics/about/meet-team.page.

NYC Analytics. "Open Data." Accessed December 5, 2018. www1.nyc.gov/site/analy tics/initiatives/open-data.page.

NYC Mayor's Office of the Chief Technology Officer. "Making Tech Work for All New Yorkers." Accessed December 5, 2018. https://tech.cityofnewyork.us/.

NYC Mayor's Office of the Chief Technology Officer. "NYCx Co-Labs." Accessed December 5, 2018. https://tech.cityofnewyork.us/projects/nycx-co-labs/.

Obama, Barack. "Barack Obama's Caucus Speech." *New York Times*, January 3, 2008. www.nytimes.com/2008/01/03/us/politics/03obama-transcript.html.

Okin, Susan Moller. "Justice and Gender ." *Philosophy and Public Affairs* 16 (1987): 42–72.

Okin, Susan Moller. "'Forty Acres and a Mule' for Women: Rawls and Feminism." *Politics, Philosophy and Economics* 4, no. 2 (2005): 233–48.

Olguin-Taylor, Jodeen. "From Grievance to Governance: 8 Features of Transformative Campaigns." *Let's Talk: At the Heart of Movement Building*, January 26, 2016. http://letstalkmovementbuilding.org/grievance-governance-8-features-transformative-campaigns/.

Omarova, Saule T. "Bankers, Bureaucrats, and Guardians: Toward Tripartism in Financial Services Regulation." Cornell Law Faculty Publications, paper 1010 (Spring 2012).

"OpenGov Acquires Citizen Engagement Leader Peak Democracy." *Cision PR Newswire*, October 20, 2017. www.prnewswire.com/news-releases/opengov-acquires-citizen-engagement-leader-peak-democracy-300540434.html.

Open Government Partnership. "01.1A Launch 'We the People.'" Accessed December 5, 2018. www.opengovpartnership.org/commitment/011a-launch-we-people.

OPM.gov. "Profile of Federal Civilian Non-Postal Employees." September 30, 2017. www .opm.gov/policy-data-oversight/data-analysis-documentation/federal-employment-reports/reports-publications/profile-of-federal-civilian-non-postal-employees/.

Orleck, Annelise, and Lisa Gayle Hazirjian, eds. *The War on Poverty: A New Grassroots History, 1940–1980*. Athens: University of Georgia Press, 2011.

Orsenfield, Jack. *What Unions No Longer Do*. Cambridge, MA: Harvard University Press, 2014.

Ortiz, Orlando. "Money in Politics: What Funds Do Elected Officials Have at Their Disposal?" November 29, 2016. Project Six. https://thesecretsix.com/2016/11/29/money-in-politics-what-funds-do-elected-officials-have-at-their-disposal/.

Osborne, David, and Ted Gaebler. *Reinventing Government: How the Entrepreneurial Spirit is Transforming the Public Sector*. Reading, MA: Addison-Wesley, 1992.

O'Toole, Garson. "The Future Has Arrived – It's Just Not Evenly Distributed Yet: William Gibson? Anonymous? Apocryphal?" January 24, 2012. *Quote Investigator*. https://quoteinvestigator.com/2012/01/24/future-has-arrived/.

O'Toole, Jr., Laurence J. "The Implications for Democracy in a Networked Bureaucratic World." *Journal of Public Administration Research and Theory* 7 (1997): 443–59.

Painter II, Matthew A., and Pamela Paxton. "Checkbooks in the Heartland: Change over Time in Voluntary Association Membership." *Sociological Forum* 29 (2014): 408–28.

Pape, Madeleine, and Josh Lerner. "Budgeting for Equity: How Can Participatory Budgeting Advance Equity in The United States?" *Journal of Public Deliberation* 12, no. 2 (2016): 1–15. www.publicdeliberation.net/cgi/viewcontent.cgi? article=1435&context=jpd.

Parks, Virginia, and Dorian Warren. "The Politics and Practice of Economic Justice: Community Benefits Agreements as Tactic of the New Accountable Development Movement." *Journal of Community Practice* 17 (2009): 88–106.

Participatory Budgeting Buffalo. Accessed December 5, 2018. www.pbbuffalo.org/.

"Participatory Budgeting Chicago: Rulebook 2017," 2017, www.pbchicago.org/uploads/1/3/5/3/13535542/2017_pbchi_rulebook.pdf .

Partnership for Working Families. "EBASE and Revive Oakland Win Big." June 29, 2012. www.forworkingfamilies.org/article/ebase-and-revive-oakland-win-big.

Partnership for Working Families. "History." Accessed December 5, 2018. www.forworkingfamilies.org/about/history.

Partnership for Working Families. "National Network of Affiliates." Accessed December 5, 2018. www.forworkingfamilies.org/about/affiliates.

Partnership for Working Families. "Policy & Tools: Community Benefits Toolkit." Accessed December 5, 2018. www.forworkingfamilies.org/resources/policy-tools-community-benefits-agreements-and-policies.

Pasquale, Frank. *Black Box Society: The Secret Algorithms that Control Money and Information*. Cambridge, MA: Harvard University Press, 2015.

Patel, Mayur, Jon Sotsky, Sean Gourley, and Daniel Houghton. *The Emergence of Civic Tech: Investments in a Growing Field*. Miami, FL: Knight Foundation, December 2013. www.knightfoundation.org/media/uploads/publication_pdfs/knight-civic-tech.pdf.

Pateman, Carole. *Participation and Democratic Theory*. New York: Cambridge University Press, 1970.

Pateman, Carole. "Participatory Democracy Revisited." *Perspectives on Politics* 10 (2012): 7–19. https://doi.org/10.1017/S1537592711004877.

Patterson, James T. *Congressional Conservatism and the New Deal: The Growth of the Conservative Coalition in Congress, 1933–1939*. Lexington: University of Kentucky Press, 1967.

Pazmino, Gloria. "'Long Overdue': Mark-Viverito Introduces New Rules." *Politico*, April 30, 2014. www.politico.com/states/new-york/city-hall/story/2014/04/long-overdue-mark-viverito-introduces-new-rules-012586.

Perlstein, Rick. *Nixonland: The Rise of a President and the Fracturing of America*. New York: Scribner, 2008.

Personal Democracy Forum 2018. "How We Make Good." New York Law School Meeting, June 7–8, 2018. www.pdf-18.com/.

Phillips-Fein, Kim. *Invisible Hands: The Businessmen's Crusade against the New Deal*. New York: W.W. Norton, 2009.

Bibliography

Phillips-Fein, Kim. "Conservatism: A State of the Field." *Journal of American History* 98 (2011): 723–43.

Pierson, Paul. *Dismantling the Welfare State? Reagan, Thatcher and the Politics of Retrenchment.* New York: Cambridge University Press, 1994.

Piketty, Thomas. *Capital in the Twenty-First Century.* Cambridge, MA: Harvard University Press, 2013.

Pittsburg United. Home page. Accessed December 5, 2018. www.pittsburghunited.org/.

Plitt, Amy. "NYC's Ballot Measures All Receive Decisive Approval." *NYC Curbed,* November 7, 2018. https://ny.curbed.com/2018/11/7/18071574/election-2018-new-york-results-ballot-proposals.

Polimédio, Chayenne, Elena Souris, and Hollie Russon Gilman. *Where Residents, Politics, and Government Meet: Philadelphia's Experiments with Civic Engagement.* Washington, DC: New America, November 2018. www.newamerica.org/political-reform/reports/where-residents-politics-and-government-meet/.

Polletta, Francesca. "How Participatory Democracy Became White: Culture and Organizational Choice." *Mobilization: An International Journal* 10, no. 2 (2013): 271–88.

Polletta, Francesca, and James M. Jasper. "Collective Identity and Social Movements." *Annual Review of Sociology* 27 (2001): 283–305.

Postel, Charles. *The Populist Vision.* New York: Oxford University Press, 2009.

Pozen, David. "Freedom of Information beyond the Freedom of Information Act." *University of Pennsylvania Law Review* 165 (2017): 1097–1158.

Pozen, David. "Transparency's Ideological Drift." *Yale Law Journal* 128 (2018) 100–65.

Presidential Innovation Fellows. Home page. Accessed December 5, 2018. https://presidentialinnovationfellows.gov/.

Presidential Memorandum M-09–12. "President's Memorandum on Transparency and Open Government – Interagency Collaboration." February 24, 2009. https://obamawhitehouse.archives.gov/sites/default/files/omb/assets/memoranda_fy2009/m09-12.pdf.

"Presidential Memorandum on the White House Office of American Innovation." White House. March 27, 2017. www.whitehouse.gov/the-press-office/2017/03/27/presidential-memorandum-white-house-office-american-innovation.

The Promise of a Progressive Populist Movement: Building a Multiracial, Race-Conscious Movement for Bold Change in Rural and Small-Town America. Chicago: People's Action, April 2018. https://peoplesaction.org/wp-content/uploads/2018/04/PA_Report_Final_digital.pdf.

Purdy, Jedediah. "Normcore." *Dissent,* Summer 2018. www.dissentmagazine.org/article/normcore-trump-resistance-books-crisis-of-democracy.

Putnam, Lara, and Theda Skocpol. "Middle America Reboots Democracy." *Democracy: A Journal of Ideas,* February 20, 2018. https://democracyjournal.org/arguments/middle-america-reboots-democracy/.

Putnam, Robert D. *Bowling Alone: The Collapse and Revival of American Community.* New York: Simon & Schuster, 2000.

Puttick, Ruth, Peter Baeck, and Philip Colligan. *I-teams: The Teams and Funds Making Innovation Happen in Governments around the World.* London: Nesta, 2014. http://theiteams.org/system/files_force/i-teams_June%202014.pdf.

Quaintance, Zack. "What's New in Civic Tech: Bloomberg's What Works Cities Honors Best at Using Data to Improve Residents' Lives." *Government Technology*, January 25, 2018. www.govtech.com/civic/Whats-New-in-Civic-Tech-Bloombergs-What-Works-Cities-Honors-Best-at-Using-Data-to-Improve-Residents-Lives.html.

Quicksey, Angel. "What Works Cities Blog Post: Better Procurement, Better Outcomes: Technology and Design Interventions in Boston." December 2, 2016. Bloomberg Philanthropies. https://whatworkscities.bloomberg.org/better-procurement-better-outcomes-technology-design-interventions-boston/.

Quinn, Garrett. "Former Boston Mayor Tom Menino Was City's Urban Mechanic." *MassLive*, October 30, 2014. www.masslive.com/news/boston/index.ssf/2014/10/bos ton-mayor-tom-menino-urban-mechanic.html.

Raban, Jonathan. "The Tea Party and the Art of the Mean Joke." *New York Times*, January 7, 2017. www.nytimes.com/2017/01/07/opinion/sunday/the-tea-party-and-the-art-of-the-mean-joke.html.

Rabin, Robert. "Federal Regulation in Historical Perspective." *Stanford Law Review* 38 (1986): 1189–1326.

Rahman, K. Sabeel. "Envisioning the Regulatory State: Technocracy, Democracy, and Institutional Experimentation in the 2010 Financial Reform and Oil Spill Statutes." *Harvard Journal on Legislation* 48, no. 2 (2011): 555–90.

Rahman, K. Sabeel. "The Key to Making Economic Development More Equitable Is Making It More Democratic." *The Nation*, April 26, 2016. www.thenation.com/ar ticle/the-key-to-making-economic-development-more-equitable-is-making-it-more-democratic/.

Rahman, K. Sabeel. *Democracy against Domination*. New York: Oxford University Press, 2017.

Rahman, K. Sabeel. "From Civic Tech to Civic Capacity: The Case of Citizen Audits." *PS: Political Science & Politics* 50, no. 3 (2017): 751–57.

Rahman, K. Sabeel. "Constructing and Contesting Structural Inequality." *Critical Analysis of Law* 5 (2018): 99–126.

Rahman, K. Sabeel. "Policymaking as Power-Building." *Southern California Interdisciplinary Law Journal* 27 (2018): 315–77.

Rahman, K. Sabeel. "Reconstructing the Administrative State in an Era of Economic and Democratic Crisis." *Harvard Law Review* 131 (2018): 1682–89.

Rahman, Kazi Sabeel Al-Jalal. "Governing the Economy: Markets, Experts, and Citizens." PhD diss., Harvard University, 2013.

Ray, Rashawn, Melissa Brown, Neil Fraistat, and Edward Summers. "Ferguson and the Death of Michael Brown on Twitter: #BlackLivesMatter, #TCOT, and the Evolution of Collective Identities." *Ethnic and Racial Studies* 40 (2017): 1797–1813. www.tandfonline.com/doi/abs/10.1080/01419870.2017.1335422.

Reardon, Marguerite. "Are AT&T and Verizon Fleecing Rural America?" *CNET*, August 3, 2018. www.cnet.com/news/are-at-t-and-verizon-fleecing-rural-america/.

Reimagining the Civic Commons. "About." Accessed December 5, 2018. http://civic commons.us/about/.

Renan, Daphna. "Pooling Powers." *Columbia Law Review* 115, no. 2 (2015): 211–91.

Renan, Daphna. "Presidential Norms and Article II." *Harvard Law Review* 131 (2018): 2187–2282. https://harvardlawreview.org/wp-content/uploads/2018/06/2187-2282_Online.pdf.

"Research and Evaluation of Participatory Budgeting in the U.S. and Canada." Public Agenda. February 20, 2015. www.publicagenda.org/pages/research-and-evaluation-of-participatory-budgeting-in-the-us-and-canada.

Rhodes, R. A. W. "The New Governance: Governing without Government." *Political Studies* 44 (1996): 652–67.

Rich, Frank. "The Billionaires Bankrolling the Tea Party." *New York Times*, August 28, 2010. www.nytimes.com/2010/08/29/opinion/29rich.html.

Robinson, Kevin. "Wal-Mart Using Fake Community Group to Manufacture Support." *Chicagoist*, January 26, 2010. http://chicagoist.com/2010/01/26/wal-mart_using_fake_community_group.php#photo-1.

Rogers, Brishen. "Libertarian Corporatism Is Not an Oxymoron." *Texas Law Review* 94 (2016): 1623–46.

Rogers, Karl. *Participatory Democracy, Science, and Technology: An Exploration in the Philosophy of Science.* New York: Palgrave Macmillan, 2008.

Rogers, Todd, Alan Gerber, and Craig Fox. "Rethinking Why People Vote: Voting as Dynamic Social Expression." In *The Behavioral Foundations of Public Policy*, edited by Eldar Shafir, 91–107. Princeton, NJ: Princeton University Press, 2013.

Rojas, Francisca M. *Recovery Act Transparency: Learning from States' Experience.* Assessing the Recovery Act Series. Washington, DC: IBM Center for the Business of Government, 2012. www.businessofgovernment.org/sites/default/files/Recovery%20Act%20Transparency.pdf.

Rolf, David. *Fight for Fifteen: The Right Wage for a Working America.* New York: New Press, 2015.

Rosanvallon, Pierre. *Counter-Democracy: Politics in an Age of Distrust*, translated by Arthur Goldhammer. New York: Cambridge University Press, 2012.

Rosenberg, Alyssa. "Before Roger Ailes Created Fox News, He Made Richard Nixon the Star of His Own Show." *Washington Post*, May 18, 2017. www.washingtonpost.com/news/act-four/wp/2017/05/18/before-roger-ailes-created-fox-news-he-made-richard-nixon-the-star-of-his-own-show/.

Rosenberg, Eli. "White House Takes Down 'We the People' Petitions Site before Responding to a Single One." *Washington Post*, December 19, 2017. www.washingtonpost.com/news/the-fix/wp/2017/12/19/white-house-takes-down-we-the-people-petitions-site-without-responding-to-a-single-one/?utm_term=.e692a8886aaf.

Rosenberg, Eli. "The White House Has Finally Restored a Petitions Site that Is Critical of President Trump." *Washington Post*, February 1, 2018. www.washingtonpost.com/news/the-fix/wp/2018/01/31/the-white-house-promised-to-restore-a-petitions-site-that-was-critical-of-trump-it-hasnt/?utm_term=.d5a0053edad5.

Rubenstein, William B. "On What a Private Attorney General Is – And Why It Matters." *Vanderbilt Law Review* 57, no. 6 (June 2005): 2129–77.

Rubin, Lillian B. "Maximum Feasible Participation: the Origins, Implications, and Present Status." *Annals of the American Academy of Political and Social Science* 385, no. 1 (September 1969): 14–29.

Ruiz-Grossman, Sarah. "Millennials Are the Foot Soldiers of the Resistance." *Huffington Post*, February 23, 2017. www.huffingtonpost.com/entry/trump-protest-poll_us_58addc16e4b0d0a6ef47517e.

Rumbul, Rebecca. *Who Benefits from Civic Technology?* London: mySociety, 2015. https://research.mysociety.org/publications/who-benefits-from-civic-technology.

Rumbul, Rebecca, and Emily Shaw. *Civic Tech Cities*. London: mySociety, May 16, 2017. www.mysociety.org/files/2017/05/civic-tech-cities.pdf.

Rural Climate Dialogues: State Convening. St. Paul, MN: Jefferson Center, September 2016. www.ruralclimatenetwork.org/sites/default/files/RCD%20State%20Convening%20Report.pdf.

Sabel, Charles, and William Simon. "Minimalism and Experimentalism in the Administrative State." *Georgetown Law Journal* 100 (2011): 53–93.

Sachs, Ben. "The Unbundled Union: Politics without Collective Bargaining." *Yale Law Journal* 123 (2013): 1–265.

Salamon, Lester M. *The Tools of Government: A Guide to the New Governance*. New York: Oxford University Press, 2002.

Scaling Civic Tech: Paths to a Sustainable Future. Miami, FL: Knight Foundation / Rita Allan Foundation, October 31, 2017. https://knightfoundation.org/reports/scaling-civic-tech.

Schattschneider, E. E. *The Semisovereign People: A Realist's View of Democracy in America*. New York: Holt, Rinehart & Winston, 1960.

Scheiber, Noam. "Starbucks Falls Short after Pledging Better Labor Practices." *New York Times*, September 23, 2015. www.nytimes.com/2015/09/24/business/starbucks-falls-short-after-pledging-better-labor-practices.html.

Schickler, Eric. *Racial Realignment: The Transformation of American Liberalism, 1932–1965*. Princeton, NJ: Princeton University Press, 2016.

Schiller, Ben. "Where There Aren't Unions, Can Online Platforms Organize Workers?" *Fast Company*, July 6, 2015. www.fastcompany.com/3047759/where-there-arent-unions-can-online-platforms-organize-workers.

Schiller, Reuel. "Enlarging the Administrative Polity: Administrative Law and the Changing Definition of Pluralism, 1945–1970." *Vanderbilt Law Review* 53 (2000): 1389–1453.

Schiller, Reuel. "The Era of Deference: Courts, Expertise, and the Emergence of New Deal Administrative Law." *Michigan Law Review* (2007): 399–441.

Schlanger, Margo. "Offices of Goodness: Influence without Authority in Federal Agencies." *Cardozo Law Review* 36, no. 2 (2014): 53–118.

Schlozman, Daniel. *When Movements Anchor Parties: Electoral Alignments in American History*. Princeton, NJ: Princeton University Press, 2015.

Schlozman, Kay Lehman, Sidney Verba, and Henry E. Brady. "Weapon of the Strong? Participatory Inequality and the Internet." *Perspectives on Politics* 8 (2010): 487–509.

Schlozman, Kay Lehman, Sidney Verba, and Henry E. Brady. *The Unheavenly Chorus: Unequal Political Voice and the Broken Promise of American Democracy*. Princeton, NJ: Princeton University Press, 2012.

Schneider, Aaron, and Ben Goldfrank. *Budgets and Ballots in Brazil: Participatory Budgeting from the City to the State: IDS Working Paper 149*. Brighton, U.K.: Institute of Development Studies, 2002.

Schragger, Richard. *City Power: Urban Governance in a Global Age*. New York: Oxford University Press, 2016.

Schwarz, Daniel. "Preventing Capture through Consumer Empowerment Programs: Some Evidence from Insurance Regulation." In *Preventing Regulatory Capture: Special Interest Influence and How to Limit It*, edited by Daniel Carpenter and David A. Moss, 366. New York: Cambridge University Press, 2014.

SeeClickFix. "About SeeClickFix." Accessed December 5, 2018. https://seeclickfix .com/pages/about.html.

SeeClickFix. Home page. Accessed December 5, 2018. https://seeclickfix.com/.

"SeeClickFix Year in Review 2017." *Fixer Stories*, January 2, 2018. https://blog .seeclickfix.com/seeclickfix-year-in-review-2017-f95f78619d30.

Seifter, Miriam. "Second-Order Participation." *UCLA Law Review* 63 (2016): 1300, 1308–10.

Shapiro, Ian. *The State of Democratic Theory*. Princeton, NJ: Princeton University Press, 2003.

Sharockman, Aaron. "It's True: WikiLeaks Dumped Podesta Emails Hour after Trump Video Surfaced." *Politifact*, December 18, 2016. www.politifact.com/truth-o-meter/ statements/2016/dec/18/john-podesta/its-true-wikileaks-dumped-podesta-emails-hour -afte/.

Shelby, Cary Martin. "Closing the Hedge Fund Loophole: The SEC as the Primary Regulator of Systemic Risk." *Boston College Law Review* 58, no. 2 (2017): 639–701.

Shier, Steven. *By Invitation Only: The Rise of Exclusive Politics in the United States.* Pittsburgh, PA: University of Pittsburgh Press, 2000.

Shirky, Clay. *Here Comes Everybody: The Power of Organizing without Organizations.* London: Penguin, 2008.

Shoked, Nadav. "The New Local." *Virginia Law Review* 100 (2014): 1323–1403.

Short, Jodi. "The Paranoid Style in Regulatory Reform." *Hastings Law Journal* 63 (2012): 633–94.

Shueh, Jason. "The Case for 18F: Why Federal IT Procurement, Contracting Need to Change." *Government Technology*, July 12, 2016. www.govtech.com/data/The-Case- for-18F-Why-Federal-IT-Procurement-Contracting-Need-to-Change.html.

Sifry, Micah. "President 2.0." *The Guardian*, June 25, 2008. www.theguardian.com/ commentisfree/2008/jun/25/barackobama.internet.

Sifry, Micah L. "Civic Tech and Engagement: In Search of a Common Language." *Tech President*, September 5, 2014. http://techpresident.com/news/25261/civic-tech- and-engagement-search-common-language.

Sifry, Micah L. "Obama's Lost Army." *New Republic*, February 9, 2017. https://new republic.com/article/140245/obamas-lost-army-inside-fall-grassroots-machine.

Sifry, Micah L. "Learning from the Civic Tech Graveyard." *Civicist*, October 1, 2018. https://civichall.org/civicist/civic-tech-graveyard/.

Sifry, Micah L., Matt Stempeck, and Erin Simpson. "Civic Tech Field Guide. " Google sheet, 2016. https://docs.google.com/spreadsheets/d/1FzmvVAKOOFdixCs7 0z88cz9g1fFPHDlgoAHgHCwhf4A/edit#gid=895533063.

Silk, Leonard, and David Vogel. *Ethics and Profits: The Crisis of Confidence in American Business.* New York: Simon & Schuster, 1976.

Simonson, Jocelyn. "Copwatching." *California Law Review* 104, no. 2 (2016): 391–445.

Singer, Peter W. "National Security Pros, It's Time to Talk about Right-Wing Extremism." *Defense One*, February 28, 2018. www.defenseone.com/threats/2018/02 /national-security-pros-its-time-talk-about-right-wing-extremism/146319/.

Sintomer, Yves, Carsten Herzberg, and Anja Röcke. "Transnational Models of Citizen Participation: The Case of Participatory Budgeting." In *Hope for Democracy: 25 Years of Participatory Budgeting Worldwide*, edited by Nelson Dias, 28–44. São Brás de Alportel, Portugal: In Loco Association, 2014.

Sirianni, Carmen. "Can a Federal Regulator Become a Civic Enabler? Watersheds at the U.S. Environmental Protection Agency." *National Civic Review* 95, no. 3 (Autumn (Fall) 2006): 17–34, 39.

Sirianni, Carmen. *Investing in Democracy: Engaging Citizens in Collaborative Governance*. Washington, DC: Brookings Institution, 2009.

Sitaraman, Ganesh. "The Puzzling Absence of Power in Constitutional Theory." *Cornell Law Review* 101 (2016): 1445–1532.

Sitaraman, Ganesh. *The Crisis of the Middle-Class Constitution: Why Economic Inequality Threatens Our Republic*. New York: Alfred A. Knopf, 2017.

Skinner, Christina P. "Regulating Nonbanks: A Plan for SIFI Lite." *Georgetown Law Journal* 105 (2017): 1379–1432.

Skocpol, Theda. *Protecting Soldiers and Mothers*. Cambridge, MA: Belknap Press of Harvard University, 1992.

Skocpol, Theda. "Unravelling from Above." *American Prospect*, March/April 1996.

Skocpol, Theda. "Associations wthout Members." *American Prospect*, July/August, 1999. http://prospect.org/article/associations-without-members.

Skocpol, Theda. *Diminished Democracy: From Membership to Management in American Civic Life*. Norman: University of Oklahoma Press, 2003.

Skocpol, Theda, and Morris P. Fiorina. *Civic Engagement in American Democracy*. Washington, DC: Brookings Institution, 1999.

Skocpol, Theda, and Vanessa Williamson. *The Tea Party and the Remaking of Republican Conservatism*. New York: Oxford University Press, 2012.

Skocpol, Theda, Ariane Liazos, and Marshall Ganz. *What a Mighty Power We Can Be: African American Fraternal Groups and the Struggle for Racial Equality*. Princeton, NJ: Princeton University Press, 2008.

Smart, Allen J., and Betsey Russell. "What Rural America Can Teach Us about Civil Society." *Stanford Social Innovation Review*, August 21, 2018. https://ssir.org/articles/entry/what_rural_america_can_teach_us_about_civil_society.

Smith, David. "Major Trump Donor Robert Mercer to Sell Stake in Far-Right News Site Breitbart." *The Guardian*, November 2, 2017. www.theguardian.com/media/20 17/nov/02/billionaire-trump-donor-robert-mercer-breitbart.

Smith, David Barton. *The Power to Heal: Civil Rights, Medicare, and the Struggle to Transform America's Health Care System*. Nashville, TN: Vanderbilt University Press, 2016.

Smith, Fran. "Oakland Army Base Is a Model for Equitable Development." February 19, 2016. Next City. https://nextcity.org/daily/entry/oakland-army-base-jobs-community-benefits-development.

Smith, Graham. *Democratic Innovations: Designing Institutions for Citizen Participation*. Cambridge: Cambridge University Press, 2009.

Smucker, Jonathan M. *Hegemony How-To: A Roadmap for Radicals*. Chico, CA: AK Press, 2017.

Snow, David A. "Collective Identity and Expressive Forms." In *International Encyclopedia of the Social and Behavioral Sciences*, edited by Neil J. Smelser and Paul B. Baltes, 2212–19. New York: Elsevier, 2001.

Snow, David A., and Robert D. Benford. "Ideology, Frame Resonance, and Participant Mobilization." In *From Structure to Action: Comparing Social Movement Research across Cultures*, edited by Bert Klandermans, Hanspeter Kriesi, and Sidney G. Tarrow, 197–217. Greenwich, CT: JAI Press, 1988.

Soss, Joe, and Sanford S. Schram. "A Public Transformed? Welfare Reform as Policy Feedback." *American Political Science Review* 101 (2007): 111–27. doi:10.1017. S0003055407070049.

Souris, Elena, and Regina Schwartz. "Case Study Highlight: Q&A with NYC's Regina Schwartz." New America, Participatory Democracy Project, October 24, 2017. www.newamerica.org/political-reform/participatory-democracy-project/civic-engagement/case-study-highlight-q-nycs-regina-schwartz/.

Spencer, Hawes, and Caitlin Dickerson. "Heather Heyer, Charlottesville Victim, Cannot Be Silenced, Mother Says." *New York Times*, August 16, 2017. www.nytimes.com/2017/08/16/us/charlottesville-heather-heyer-memorial-mother.html.

Squires, Gregory. "The Rough Road to Reinvestment." In *Organizing Access to Capital: Advocacy and the Democratization of Financial Institutions*, edited by Gregory D. Squires, 1–26. Philadelphia: Temple University Press, 2003.

Steinhauser, Paul. "'Obama for America' to Morph into 'Organizing for Action.'" *Political Ticker, CNN*, January 18, 2013. http://politicalticker.blogs.cnn.com/2013/01/18/obama-for-america-to-morph-into-organizing-for-action/.

Stephens-Davidowitz, Seth. *Everybody Lies: Big Data, New Data, and What the Internet Can Tell Us about Who We Really Are*. New York: HarperCollins, 2017.

Stewart, Nikita. "De Blasio Seeks to Turn Homeless 'Cluster Sites' into Affordable Housing." *New York Times*, December 12, 2017. www.nytimes.com/2017/12/12/nyregion/homeless-shelter-cluster-nyc-de-blasio.html.

Stewart, Nikita, and William Neuman. "De Blasio Calls for 'Blood and Guts' War on Homelessness. Is His Plan Gutsy Enough?" *New York Times*, February 28, 2017. www.nytimes.com/2017/02/28/nyregion/bill-de-blasio-new-york-homelessness-plan.html.

Stewart, Richard B. "The Reformation of American Administrative Law." *Harvard Law Review* 88 (1975): 1667–1813.

Stone, Clarence. "Civic Capacity and Urban Education." *Urban Affairs Review* 36 (2001): 595–619.

Strike Debt. Home page. Accessed December 5, 2018. http://strikedebt.org/.

Stromer-Galley, Jennifer. "New Voices in the Public Sphere: A Comparative Analysis of Interpersonal and Online Political Talk." *Javnost – The Public* 9, no. 2 (2002): 23–42.

Su, Celina. "Whose Budget? Our Budget? Broadening Political Stakeholdership via Participatory Budgeting." *Journal of Public Deliberation* 8, no. 2 (2012): 1–16. www.publicdeliberation.net/cgi/viewcontent.cgi?article=1227&context=jpd.

Suebasaeng, Asawin. "'My God, What Have We Done?': White House Staffers React to Insane Online Petitions." *Mother Jones*, January 18, 2013. www.motherjones.com/politics/2013/01/we-the-people-white-house-petitions-obama-administration/.

Sunstein, Cass R. "Interest Groups in American Public Law." *Stanford Law Review* 38 (1985): 29–87.

Super, David. "Laboratories of Destitution: Democratic Experimentalism and the Failure of Antipoverty Law." *University of Pennsylvania Law Review* 157 (2008): 541–616.

Swenson, Kyle. "Rebekah Mercer, the Billionaire Backer of Bannon and Trump, Chooses Sides." *Washington Post*, January 5, 2018. www.washingtonpost.com/new

256 *Bibliography*

s/morning-mix/wp/2018/01/05/rebekah-mercer-the-billionaire-backer-of-bannon-and
-trump-chooses-sides/?noredirect=on&utm_term=.9bf5d31782b1.

Talbot, David. "How Obama *Really* Did It." *MIT Technology Review*, August 19, 2008. www.technologyreview.com/s/410644/how-obama-really-did-it/.

Tani, Karen M. "Welfare and Rights Before the Movement: Rights as a Language of the State." *Yale Law Journal* 122, no. 2 (November 2012): 314–521.

Tani, Karen M. "States' Rights, Welfare Rights, and the Indian Problem: Negotiating Citizenship and Sovereignty, 1933–1954." *Law and History Review* 331, no. 1 (February 2015): 1–40.

Tannenwal, David, and Hollie Russon Gilman. A *21st Century Town Hall?* Washington, DC: New America, July 27, 2017. www.newamerica.org/oti/policy-papers/21st-century-town-hall/.

Tapscott, Don. "At Davos, Technology CEOs Discuss the Digital Economy." *Huffington Post*, January 24, 2015. www.huffingtonpost.com/don-tapscott/at-davos-technology-ceos-discuss-the-digital-economy_b_6537772.html.

Tarrow, Sidney. *Power in Movement: Social Movements and Contentious Politics*, 3rd ed. New York: Cambridge University Press, 2011.

Tarrow, Sidney, and Charles Tilly. *Contentious Politics and Social Movements*. Boulder, CO: Paradigm, 2006.

Taylor, Kate. "New York City Will Offer Free Preschool for All 3-Year-Olds." *New York Times*, April 24, 2017. www.nytimes.com/2017/04/24/nyregion/de-blasio-pre-k-expan sion.html.

Taylor, Keeanga-Yamahtta. *From #BlackLivesMatter to Black Liberation*. Chicago: Haymarket, 2016.

Teachout, Zephyr. *Corruption in America: From Benjamin Franklin's Snuff Box to Citizens United*. Cambridge, MA: Harvard University Press, 2014.

Teles, Steven M. "Conservative Mobilization against Entrenched Liberalism." In *The Transformation of American Politics: Activist Government and the Rise of Conservativism*, edited by Paul Pierson and Theda Skocpol. Princeton, NJ: Princeton University Press, 2007.

Terranova, Tiziana. *Network Culture: Politics for the Information Age*. London: Pluto Books, 2004.

Tesler, Michael. "The Spillover of Racialization into Health Care: How President Obama Polarized Public Opinion by Racial Attitudes and Race." *American Journal of Political Science* 56 (2012): 690–704.

Tesler, Michael. *Post-Racial or Most Racial? Race and Politics in the Obama Era*. Chicago: University of Chicago Press, 2015.

Thaler, Richard, and Cass Sunstein. *Nudge: Improving Decisions about Health, Wealth, and Happiness*. New Haven, CT: Yale University Press, 2008.

Thompson, Dennis F. "Deliberative Democratic Theory and Empirical Political Science." *Annual Review of Political Science* 11 (2008): 497–520. doi:10.1146/annurev.polisci.11.081306.070555.

Tieken, Mara Casey. *Why Rural Schools Matter*. Chapel Hill: University of North Carolina Press, 2014.

Tilly, Charles. *Contentious Performances*. New York: Cambridge University Press, 2008.

Tisdale, William, and Carla Westheirn. "Giving Back to the Future: Citizen Involvement and Community Stabilization in Milwaukee." In *Organizing*

Access to Capital: Advocacy and the Democratization of Financial Institutions, edited by Gregory D. Squires, 42–54. Philadelphia: Temple University Press, 2003.

Tocqueville, Alexis de. *Democracy in America and Two Essays on America*, edited by Isaac Kramnick, translated by Gerald Bevan. London: Penguin, 2003.

Ton, Zeynep. *The Good Jobs Strategy: How the Smartest Companies Invest in Employees to Lower Costs and Boost Profits*. New York: Houghton Mifflin, 2014.

Touchton, Michael, and Brian Wampler. "Improving Social Well-Being through New Democratic Institutions." *Comparative Political Studies* 47, no. 10 (2014): 1442–69.

Trippi, Joe. *The Revolution Will Be Televised: Democracy, the Internet, and the Overthrow of Everything*. New York: Regan, 2004.

"Trust in Business vs. Government." *Wall Street Journal*, August 15, 2016. www.wsj.com /articles/trust-in-business-vs-government-1471304776.

"Trust in Government: 1958–2015." In *Beyond Distrust: How Americans View Their Government*. Washington, DC: Pew Research Center, 2015. www.people-press.org/ 2015/11/23/1-trust-in-government-1958-2015/.

Tufekci, Zeynep. "The Medium and the Movement: Digital Tools, Social Movement Politics, and the End of the Free Rider Problem." *Policy and Internet* 6, no. 2 (2014): 202–08.

Tufekci, Zeynep. *Twitter and Tear Gas: The Power and Fragility of Networked Protest*. New Haven, CT: Yale University Press., 2017.

Tushnet, Mark. "Administrative Law in the 1930s: The Supreme Court's Accommodation of Progressive Legal Theory." *Duke Law Journal* (2011): 1565–1637.

Tynan, Roxana. "Unmasking the Hidden Power of Cities." *Medium*, June 14, 2018. https://medium.com/@roxanatynan/unmasking-the-hidden-power-of-cities-dbc 9f1f724c8.

Umhoefer, Dave. "For Unions in Wisconsin, a Fast and Hard Fall since Act 10." *Journal Sentinel*, November 27, 2016. https://projects.jsonline.com/news/2016/11/27/ for-unions-in-wisconsin-fast-and-hard-fall-since-act-10.html.

Urbinati, Nadia. "Unpolitical Democracy." *Political Theory* 38, no. 1 (2010): 65–92.

USDA. "Opioid Misuse in Rural America." Accessed December 05, 2018. www .usda.gov/topics/opioids.

USDA. "Rural Poverty & Well-Being." Economic Research Service. Last updated April 18, 2018. www.ers.usda.gov/topics/rural-economy-population/rural-poverty-well-being/.

The U.S. Digital Service. Home page. Accessed December 5, 2018. www.usds.gov/.

U.S. General Services Administration. "Technology Transformation Services." Last reviewed May 22, 2018. www.gsa.gov/about-us/organization/federal-acquisition-service/technology-transformation-services.

Valentino, Nicolas A., and David O. Sears. "Old Times They Are Not Forgotten: Race and Partisan Realignment in the Contemporary South." *American Journal of Political Science* 49 (2005): 672–88.

Vargas, Jose Antonio. "Obama Raised Half a Billion Online." *Washington Post*, November 20, 2008. http://voices.washingtonpost.com/44/2008/11/20/obama_raised_ half_a_billion_on.html.

Veiga, Christina. "Haven't heard of participatory budgeting? Voters approved it on Tuesday – and here's how it can bring millions to New York City schools."

Chalkbeat, November 7, 2018. https://chalkbeat.org/posts/ny/2018/11/07/havent-heard-of-participatory-budgeting-voters-approved-it-on-tuesday-and-heres-how-it-can-bring-millions-to-new-york-city-schools/.

Vinik, Dann. "America's Government is Getting Old." *Politico*, September 29, 2017. www.politico.com/agenda/story/2017/09/27/aging-government-workforce-analysis-000525.

Véron, Pauline. "Why Paris Is Building the World's Biggest Participatory Budget." Accessed December 5, 2018. NewCities. https://newcities.org/why-paris-is-building-the-worlds-biggest-participatory-budget/.

Walker, Edward T. *Grassroots for Hire: Public Affairs Consultants in American Democracy*. Cambridge: Cambridge University Press, 2014.

Walker, Edward T. "Legitimating the Corporation through Public Participation." In *Democratizing Inequalities: Dilemmas of the New Public Participation*, edited by Edward T. Walker, Michael McQuarrie, and Caroline W. Lee, 69. New York: New York University Press, 2015.

Walker, Jack L. *Mobilizing Interest Groups in America: Patrons, Professions, and Social Movements*. Ann Arbor: University of Michigan Press, 1991.

Wampler, Brian. "A Guide to Participatory Budgeting." In *Participatory Budgeting*, edited by Anwar Shah, 21–53. Washington, DC: World Bank, 2007.

Wampler, Brain, and Michael Touchton. "Brazil Let Its Citizens Make Decisions about City Budgets. Here's What Happened." *Washington Post*, January 22, 2014. www.washingtonpost.com/news/monkey-cage/wp/2014/01/22/brazil-let-its-citizens-make-decisions-about-city-budgets-heres-what-happened/.

Wampler, Brian, Michael Touchton, and Stephanie McNulty. *Participatory Budgeting: Spreading across the Globe*. Transparency Initiative. January 2018. www.transparency-initiative.org/uncategorized/2094/participatory-budgeting-spreading-across-globe/

Wang, Jackie. "'Bills Would Undo Cities' Efforts to Rein in Payday Lenders, Advocates Warn." *Texas Tribune*, April 27, 2017. www.texastribune.org/2017/04/27/texas-bills-would-override-local-regulations-on-payday-lending/.

Warren, Mark. "Governance-Driven Democratization." *Critical Policy Studies* 3 (2009): 3–13.

Weeks, Edward C. "The Practice of Deliberative Democracy: Results from Four Large-Scale Trials." *Public Administration Review* 60 (2000): 360–72.

Weil, David. *The Fissured Workplace*. Cambridge, MA: Harvard University Press, 2014.

Weiss, Mitchell. "New Urban Mechanics." Harvard Business School Case 315–075, January 2015 (revised March 2017). www.hbs.edu/faculty/Pages/item.aspx?num=48429.

"We Make This City." Home page. Accessed December 5, 2018. http://wemakethiscity.org/.

White House. "We the People." Accessed September 25, 2018. https://petitions.whitehouse.gov/.

The White House Office of the Press Secretary. "President Obama Launches Office of Public Engagement." May 11, 2009. https://obamawhitehouse.archives.gov/the-press-office/president-obama-launches-office-public-engagement.

"WhiteHouse/petitions." GitHub. Accessed September 26, 2018. https://github.com/WhiteHouse/petitions.

Wiebe, Robert H. *The Search for Order, 1877–1920*. New York: Hill & Wang, 1967.

Bibliography 259

Wilhelm, Anthony G. *Democracy in the Digital Age*. New York: Routledge, 2000.

Williams, Jake. "Colorado Appoints New Chief Data Officer." *StateScoop*, July 16, 2015. https://statescoop.com/colorado-appoints-new-chief-data-officer/.

Williamson, Vanessa, Theda Skocpol, and John Coggin. "The Tea Party and the Remaking of Republican Conservatism." *Perspectives on Politics* 9 (2011): 25–43. doi:10.1017/S153759271000407X.

Winter, Nicholas J. G. "Beyond Welfare: Framing and the Racialization of White Opinion on Social Security." *American Journal of Political Science* 50 (2006): 400–20.

Winter, Nicholas J. G. *Dangerous Frames: How Ideas about Race and Gender Shape Public Opinion*. Chicago: University of Chicago Press, 2008.

Winters, Jeffrey, and Benjamin Page. "Oligarchy in the United States?" *Perspectives on Politics* 7 (2009): 731–51.

Wiseman, Jane. *Lessons from Leading CDOs: A Framework for Better Civic Analytics*. Cambridge, MA: Ash Center for Democratic Governance and Innovation, Harvard Kennedy School, January 2017. https://ash.harvard.edu/files/ash/files/leasons_from_leading_cdos.pdf.

Wolfskill, George. *The Revolt of Conservatives: A History of the American Liberty League, 1934–1940*. Boston: Houghton Mifflin, 1962.

Wong, Kristine. "Participatory Budgeting Is Gaining Momentum in the US. How Does It Work?" *Shareable*, March 20, 2017. www.shareable.net/blog/participatory-budgeting-is-gaining-momentum-in-the-us-how-does-it-work.

Wood, Colin. "What Is Civic Tech?" *Government Technology*, August 16, 2016. www.govtech.com/civic/What-is-Civic-Tech.html.

Yackee, Jason Webb, and Susan Webb Yackee. "A Bias towards Business? Assessing Interest Group Influence on the U.S. Bureaucracy." *Journal of Politics* 68 (2006): 128–39.

Yaffe-Bellany, David. "A Viral Facebook Fundraiser Has Generated More than $20 Million for Immigration Nonprofit RAICES." *Texas Tribune*, June 27, 2018. www.texastribune.org/2018/06/27/viral-facebook-fundraiser-has-generated-more-20-million-immigration-no/.

Yang, Kaifeng. "Public Administrators' Trust in Citizens: A Missing Link in Citizen Involvement Efforts" *Public Administration Review* 65 (2005): 273-85.

Yankelovich, Daniel. *Coming to Public Judgment: Making Democracy Work in a Complex World*. Syracuse, NY: Syracuse University Press, 1991.

Ziblatt, Daniel. "How Did Europe Democratize?" *World Politics* 2 (2006): 311–33.

Zuckerman, Ethan. "New Media, New Civics?" *Policy and Internet* 6, no. 2 (2014): 151–68.

Zuckerman, Ethan. "Beyond 'The Crisis in Civics' – Notes from My 2013 DML Talk." Accessed December 5, 2018. www.ethanzuckerman.com/blog/2013/03/26/beyond-the-crisis-in-civics-notes-from-my-2013-dml-talk/.

LEGAL DOCUMENTS

424 U.S. 1 (1976)

558 U.S. 310 (2010)

Bibliography

5 U.S.C. § 552

29 U.S.C. §§ 151–169

42 U.S.C. §§ 3601–3631, Title VIII of the Civil Rights Act of 1968

5 U.S.C. § 706

Pub. L. No. 96–511, 94 Stat. 2812, codified at 44 U.S.C. §§ 3501–3521

Pub. L. 92–463, 86 Stat. 770

Pub. L. 79–404, 60 Stat. 237, codified at 5 U.S.C. § 500 *et seq.*

Pub. L. 88–352, 78 Stat. 241

Pub. L 94–200, 89 Stat. 1124

Pub. L. 95–128, 91 Stat. 1147, title VIII of the Housing and Community Development Act of 1977, 12 U.S.C. § 2901 et seq.

Pub. L. 88–452

Pub. L. 79–404, 60 Stat. 237

Exec. Order No. 13642

Dodd-Frank Act § 1013(c) (codified at 12 U.S.C. § 5493)

Dodd-Frank Act § 619 (codified at 12 U.S.C. § 1851)

Oakland, Cal., Ordinance 13140 (November 13, 2012)

NY Labor Law § 653 (2017), http://codes.findlaw.com/ny/labor-law/lab-sect-653.html.

NY Labor Law § 655 (2017), http://codes.findlaw.com/ny/labor-law/lab-sect-655.html.

Metlife, Inc. v. Fin. Stability Oversight Council, 177 F. Supp. 3d 219 (D.C. Cir. 2016).

Lee v. Board of Governors of the Federal Reserve System, 118 F.3d 905 (2d Cir 1997)

The Labor Management Relations Act of 1947, 29 U.S.C. §§ 141–197

Index

accountability
authority paired with, 36, 116, 164–5, 215
civic technology, 133
Consumer Financial Protection Bureau, 146
Financial Stability Oversight Council, 144–6
good governance limits, 115–20
Kenya service delivery, 185
participatory monitoring, 183–6, 190–4
power disparities despite, 116–18
privatization effects, 123
real estate developers, 195–8
Shack/Slum Dwellers International, 184
state wage boards, 198–200
transparency as, 116–18
administrative institutions. *See agencies*
Administrative Procedure Act (1946), 116, 119
administrative procedure reform, 115–20
advocacy. *See professionalized advocacy*
agencies. *See also* institutional design,
regulatory bodies
accountability but power disparities, 116–18
accountability with authority, 36, 116,
164–5, 215
CFPB as bureaucratized participation,
143–50
civic technology movement, 14–15, 33
constituencies across identity groups, 114
constitutional status of, 116
culture change for civic power, 151, 160–2,
206, 210–11
day-to-day governance, 41, 114–15
key against inequality and exclusion,
114–15, 164
Mayor's Office of New Urban Mechanics,
33–5, 151–7, 217

Mayor's Public Engagement Unit, 158–62
nineteenth century movements creating,
54
obstruction of, 114
Open Government Initiative, 13
personnel rotations, 216–18
power shifting for reform, 136–8
privatization effects, 123
responsiveness institutionalized, 140,
194–5
visibility, 164, 165, 170, 215, 220
agency. *See civic power, political power*
ages of civil servants, 167
ages of Trump era Resisters, 208
Ailes, Roger, 78
Air Traffic Controllers strike, 61
Alt-Right, 72, 76–9
American Federation of Labor (AFL), 55,
58
American Legislative Exchange Council
(ALEC), 67
American Liberty League, 64, 76
American Recovery and Reinvestment Act
(2009), 131
Americans for Prosperity Foundation, 76
AmericaSpeaks Citizen Summits, 16
Analyst Institute, 158
Arab Spring movement, 83
argument. *See dialogue, political conflict*
Arnstein, Sherry, 35
Atlanta Journal-Constitution, "Color of
Money," 188
authoritarianism, 3–5, 10
authority with accountability, 36, 116,
164–5, 215

262 Index

balance of power. *See also* civic power, power
  shifting
  citizen audits addressing, 191
  democracy as, 37, 210
  democracy as contest of interest groups,
    49–51, *See also* political conflict
  Oakland community benefits agreement,
    197–8
  responsiveness institutionalized, 140, 194–8,
    See also institutional design
bank transparency, 186–90
Bannon, Steve, 77
Bean, Lydia, 104
Berry, Wendell, 91
Bingham, Lisa Blomgren, 181
#BlackLivesMatter, 84
Blair, Tony, 130
Bloomberg Philanthropies, 153, 154
"bodyless heads" of advocacy groups, 62
BOS:311 infrastructure app, 152
Boston
  Community Investment Coalition, 189
  Mayor's Office of New Urban Mechanics,
    33–5, 151–7, 217
  participatory budgeting, 175
  StreetBump infrastructure tool, 129
bowling to socialize, 18
Brazil using participatory budgeting, 172–4, 181
Breitbart News, 77, 78–9, 93
Brexit campaign, 77
Brown, Michael, 23
Bryan, William Jennings, 54
Buckley v. Valeo (1976), 66
budgeting. *See funding, participatory
  budgeting*
bureaucracies. *See agencies*
bureaucratizing participation
  agency culture change for civic power, 151,
    160–2, 206, 210–11
  Boston Mayor's Office of New Urban
    Mechanics, 33–5, 151–7, 217
  Consumer Financial Protection Bureau,
    143–50
  democratizing from within, 163–8, 216
  need for, 142–3
  New York City Mayor's Public Engagement
    Unit, 158–62
  skillsets of personnel, 150, 155–7, 158–9, 160,
    162, 167–8, 216, 217
Bush, George H. W., 78
Bush, George W., 121

business interests
  business lobby power rise, 6–7, 48, 64–8,
    206
  campaign finance influence, 66
  CFPB to be dismantled, 143, 148–9
  comments on proposed regulations, 119
  community benefits agreement
    accountability, 195–8
  corporate citizenship strategies, 17, 68,
    181, 206
  exclusionary populism support, 205
  financial dominating industrial, 65
  Financial Stability Oversight Council
    creation, 145
  "free" online platforms, 86
  Freedom of Information Act favoring, 118
  funding right-wing movements, 76–8
  nineteenth century populists, 54
  policymaking steered by, 5–8, 65–8
  preemption of local policies, 106, 212, 221
  private realms, 9
  privatizing government, 120–4
  racialized employment, 9
  regulators deferring to, 6, 7, 66, 67
  regulatory agency obstruction, 114
  state wage boards, 198–200
  status quo maintenance, 208
  unions as countervailing power, 61, 65
  War on Poverty backlash, 139
  worker insecurity, 98–9
  worker schedules, 28–30, 99–100
  workers told how to vote, 68
Business Roundtable lobbying group, 64, 65

Cambridge Analytica company, 77
campaign finance system, 5, 66, 83
Carnes, Nicholas, 7
Castells, Manuel, 89
Center for Rural Strategies (CRS), 90, 93–6
CFPB. *See Consumer Financial Protection
  Bureau*
Chamber of Commerce of the United States of
  America, 64, 65
Change.org petition site, 130, 132
Charlottesville, Virginia, white supremacist
  rally, 72, 205
Chávez, César, 59
checks and balances
  autocratic power consolidation, 3
  business lobby power rise, 6–7, 48, 64–8, 206
  civic technology lacking, 133

Index 263

Madison democratic institutional design, 25–6, 38
regulators deferring to industry, 6, 7, 66, 67
Trump's lack of, 1–2, 3
wealth concentration asymmetry, 8
Chicago
neighborhood governance, 181
participatory budgeting, 175, 177–81
Smart Chicago collaborative, 219
CIO. *See Congress of Industrial Organizations*
citizen audits, 183–6, 190–4, *See also* participatory monitoring
Citizens United v. Federal Election Commission (2010), 66, 77
civic capacity
building power and inclusion, 90–1, 210
multiracial progressive movement, 90, 104–7
online labor organizing, 29, 90, 98–104, *See also* digital mobilizing, labor organizing
organizations helping build, 52, 59
politics of place, 90, 91–7, 214
civic engagement. *See participation*
Civic Hall, New York City, 127
civic power
building civic power, 27, 206, 212–22
business lobby power rise, 6–7, 48, 64–8, 206
civic associations having power, 5–7, 28, 30, 35–6, 54–5
civic associations losing membership, 6, 60–4, 82
civic associations proliferating, 62–4
communal identities for durable associations, 35, 48, 52, 88, 206, *See also* communal identities
community organization importance, 35, *See also* community organizing
culture change internal to bureaucracies, 151, 160–2, 206, 210–11
for democratic reform, 11–12, 24–7
description, 12, 22, 47
good governance ethos contrasted, 24, 27, 169
government of, by, and for the people, 43–4
inclusive populism, 210–12
Movement for Black Lives, 23, 183
organizing for, 28–30, 40–1, 59, 212–14, *See also* organizing
participatory monitoring, 192–4, *See also* participatory monitoring
public's low motivation, 5, 11

racial exclusion history, 57–9
recommendations for funders, 218–21
recommendations for organizers, 212–14
recommendations for policymakers, 214–18
recommendations for scholars, 221–2
Resistance in Trump era, 210–12
roadmap for, 37, 49, 51–3, 212
civic technology movement. *See also* digital mobilizing
algorithmic code underpinning, 86
autonomy required, 89
"beneficial inefficiencies" of in-person lost, 85
Cambridge Analytica, 77
CFPB online platforms, 147, 148
citizens as policy co-producers, 131
communal identity lacking, 127
as conventional reform, 2, 14, 115–16
copwatching using, 183
curating required, 131–3
description of, 14–15, 124–8
durability strategies paired with, 82, 85, 88–9, 158, 159–60
elite opinion makers using, 21
expenditures for information technology, 126
funding sources, 125
geographic reach expansion, 126
good governance ethos, 19–20, 124
government capacity improvement, 220
government data transparency, 128–9
growth of, 125
innovation offices, 33, 152
Internet of Things and public services, 129
Mayor's Office of New Urban Mechanics, 153–5
Mayor's Public Engagement Unit, 158–9, 160–1
Obama 2008 campaign, 87–9
Obama administration, 13, 33, 88–9, 121, 152
offline relationships supporting digital, 29, 85, 88–9, 95, 100, 158, 159–60, 213, 220
online community organizing, 29
online small-dollar fundraising, 83
online vs. offline organizing, 40, 82–7
participation in democracy, 124, 129–31
passive recipients vs. active participants, 190
petitions online, 13, 130, 131–3
rational public policy via, 18
regulation commenting platform, 119
"slacktivism" over activism, 85

civic technology movement (cont.)
   social media for political engagement, 84–7,
     See also social media
   Technology Transformation Services, 121
   town halls electronically, 130
   as transparency, 14, 124, 128–9
   Trump election concerns, viii
   vulnerability of technology, 221
Civil Rights Act (1964), 75
Civil Rights movement
   backlash, 75, 114
   Community Reinvestment Act, 186–90
   Democratic party support, 58
   exclusionary populism backlash, 68
   Medicare and racial disparities, 137
   organizing for political power, 57–9
   remaking of democratic institutions, 43
civil servant ages, 167
civil servant fellowships, 216–18
civil society organizations. *See organizing*
civility as democracy reform, 18, *See also*
   political conflict
class divisions. *See business interests, economic*
   inequality, inequality, wealth
   concentration
Clinton, Bill, 121, 189
Coalition of Immokalee Workers, 98
Coalition of Low-Wage and Immigrant
   Worker Advocates, 200
Code for America philanthropic initiative,
   157, 167
Cohen, Cathy J., 16
collaborative governance, 26, 134–6, 181, 182
"color blind" equality, 71
"The Color of Money" (*Atlanta Journal-*
   Constitution), 188
Colored Farmers Alliance (CFA), 57
Colored Farmers' National Alliance and Co-
   Operative Union, 57
Colvin, Claudette, 58
communal identities
   candidacy of Scott Walker, 101
   civic technology lacking, 127
   coalitions across identity groups, 82, 88–9,
     97, 105, 114, 196, 210, 213
   Coworker.org building, 102
   durable associations requiring, 35, 48, 52, 88,
     206, 213
   exclusionary populism, 68–76, 81
   issue-specific appeals motivating, 96–7, 212
   National Rifle Association, 75

offline relationships supporting digital, 29,
   85, 88–9, 95, 100, 158, 159–60, 213,
   220
organizational capacity via, 59
participatory budgeting, 182
participatory monitoring, 185
politics of place, 90, 91–7, 214
rural initiatives, 92–6
strategic capacity building, 51–3
United Farm Workers movement, 59
urban initiatives, 96–7
communications infrastructure
   importance of, 95
   New York City initiatives, 161
   rural initiatives, 93–6
community benefits agreements (CBAs), 195–8
community development corporations, 187
community development financial
   institutions, 187
Community Investment Coalition (CIC), 189
community organizing. *See also* organizing
   Boston Mayor's Office of New Urban
     Mechanics, 33–5, 151–7, 217
   Chicago initiatives, 175, 177–81, 219
   civic power requiring, 35
   common identities among members, 59, 63,
     See also communal identities
   community benefits agreements, 195–8
   Community Reinvestment Act, 188–9
   exclusionary populism, 68–76
   Farmers' Alliance into Populist
     movement, 54
   issue-specific appeals motivating, 96–7, 212
   Montgomery bus boycott, 58
   movements linked with governance, 30–3
   New York City Mayor's Public Engagement
     Unit, 158–62
   Obama 2008 campaign, 87–9
   Office of Economic Opportunity, 139
   online platform Coworker.org, 29, 90,
     99–104
   online platforms for, 29, 40, 90
   organizations building political power, 51–3
   participatory monitoring, 183–6
   Philadelphia New Urban Mechanics
     Office, 156
   reform of day-to-day policies, 38
   reinventing for civic power, 40
   rural communities, 91–6, 214
   Starbucks baristas, 28–30, 99–100
   suburban communities, 90, 104–7

Index

urban communities, 105–6, 195–8, *See also* urban community organizing

War on Poverty power shifts, 138–40

Community Reinvestment Act (CRA; 1977), 186–90

Concerned Veterans for America, 76

conflict. *See political conflict*

Congress of Industrial Organizations (CIO), 55, 56, 58

Congress of Racial Equality (CORE), 58

Congressional Research Service, 67

Consumer Financial Protection Bureau (CFPB)
  accountability, 146
  as bureaucratized participation, 143–50
  as democratic governance, 34
  formation of, 143–5, 146
  grassroots engagement, 146–50
  obstruction by business lobby, 114
  responsiveness to the people, 146–8
  skillsets of personnel, 150
  Trump leadership curtailing, 143

contestation. *See political conflict*

conventional reform of democracy
  campaign finance reform, 5, 66, 83
  citizen audits contrasted, 190–1
  civic technology reforms, 2, 13, 14–15, 115–16, 124–34
  deliberative democracy, 15–17, 18
  deregulation, 115–16
  electoral system corruption, 13
  failure of, 13, 18–22, 206
  good governance reforms, 2, 19–20, 115–20, 142, 206
  "innovating government," 120–4
  participatory budgeting contrasted, 182
  privatization, 115–16, 120–4
  radical reform contrasted, 140, 142
  radical reform instead, 22–7, 222–3
  regulatory agency reform, 115–20
  special interests hijacking democracy, 19
  transparency, 13–14, 18

Conway, Kellyanne, 77

"copwatching" as participatory monitoring, 183

corporate citizenship strategies, 17, 68, 181, 206, *See also* business interests

cost-benefit analysis vs. external accountability, 116, 119

countervailing power
  civic power as, 24
  Consumer Financial Protection Bureau, 148

democratic reform via, 27, 42
institutions facilitating, 25, 37, 38, 210–11, 215
Madison harnessing rivals', 25–6, 38
participatory monitoring as, 185, 192
responsiveness institutionalized, 140, 194–8
thinning of organizations, 205
unions vs. corporate interests, 61, 65
War on Poverty backlash, 140
workers' undermined, 6–8

Coworker.org online platform, 29, 90, 99–104

CRA. *See Community Reinvestment Act*

Cramer, Katherine J., 70, 72, 101

criminal justice system racial inequality, 9

crises of democracy
  authoritarianism already here, 10
  chronic view, 2–5
  civil rights erosion deliberate effort, 48, *See also* racial exclusion
  economic inequality, 5–8, *See also* economic inequality
  organizational power imbalances, 48, *See also* balance of power
  political efficacy waning, 11, *See also* political power
  reinventing democratic institutions, 12, 210–11, *See also* institutional design
  systemic exclusion, 9–10, *See also* exclusion
  true sources of, 222
  Trump election fears, 1–3, 222–3

Daily Yonder digital news platform, 93, 95

Data.gov site, 128

Dawson, Michael C., 16

day-to-day governance. *See agencies, bureaucratizing participation*

de Blasio, Bill
  participatory budgeting, 176
  Public Engagement Unit, 158, 159, 160, 162

deliberative democracy reforms
  citizen audits contrasted, 192
  as conventional reform, 15–17
  "empowered deliberative democracy" initiatives, 181
  participatory budgeting as, 181–2

democracy
  academic vs. on-the-ground, vii
  antidemocracy attitudes, 22, 79
  as balancing of political powers, 37, 48, 210, 222, *See also* balance of power

Index

democracy (cont.)
  as contest of interest groups, 49–51, *See also* political conflict
  crises of, 1–3, 222–3, *See also* crises of democracy
  "democratic backsliding," 3–5, 10
  empowerment for self-governance, 12, 24
  future of, 10, 205
  Madison institutional design, 25, 38, *See also* institutional design
  organized interests vs. mass public, 5, *See also* organizing
  private interest as sentinel over public rights, 50
  public distrusted by government, 134, 143, 216
  public trust in, 11, 44, 47, 143
  public trusted to govern, 22, 79
  roadmap for reconstructing, 37, 49, *See also* roadmap
  threats to, 1–2, 3–5, 205
  unevenly distributed, 10
Democratic National Committee (DNC), 88–9
Democratic Party. *See also* Obama, Barack
  civil rights support, 58
  Clinton enforcing financial standards, 189
  organized interest power magnified, 50
  organized labor aligning with, 50, 58
  privatization support, 121
  Resistance movement relationship, 208
  urban–suburban partisan divide initiative, 90, 104–7
deregulation. *See regulatory bodies*
dialogue. *See also* political conflict
  Boston Mayor's Office of New Urban Mechanics, 34, 153–5
  CFPB and grassroots constituencies, 146–8
  citizen audits, 192
  civility as democracy reform, 18
  deliberative democracy reforms, 15–17, 181, 192
  Farmers' Alliance into Populist movement, 54
  movements engaging with institutions, 136–8
  New York City Mayor's Public Engagement Unit, 158, 159–61
  online labor organizing, 29, 100–4
  online platforms for, 83–7

participatory budgeting, 177, 181–2, *See also* participatory budgeting
  in policy design, vii–viii
  professional advocacy lacking, 63
  public discourse of business interests, 64
  rural narratives to urban audiences, 95
  social media for political engagement, 84
  town halls electronically, 130
  Trump campaign and social taboos on race, 72
  voices of ordinary people gone, 69
  "We the People" online petition site, 133
digital divide, 85, 94
digital mobilizing. *See also* civic technology
  algorithmic code underpinning, 86
  autonomy required, 89
  community organizing sites, 29, 40
  debate over online vs. offline, 40, 82–7
  Obama 2008 campaign, 87–9
  offline relationships supporting digital, 29, 85, 88–9, 95, 100, 158, 159–60, 213, 220
  online labor organizing, 29, 90, 99–104
  rural communities, 93–6
  "thin" digital organizing, 87–9, 91, 213
disintermediated democracy, 39
dissemination of reform experimentation, 219
Dodd-Frank Wall Street Reform and Consumer Protection Act (2010), 144
Domestic Workers' Alliance, 29
Dominican Republic using participatory budgeting, 174
Downing Street E-petitions, 130
Downs, Anthony, 49
Drutman, Lee, 67–8
dues by members. *See membership dues*
DuPont company creating American Liberty League, 76

East Bay Alliance for a Sustainable Economy (EBASE), 196–8
economic inequality. *See also* labor organizing, wealth concentration
  CFPB power shifting, 143
  CIO racial and economic inclusion, 58
  civic leadership development, 218
  class-based institutions empowering powerless, 25
  Community Reinvestment Act, 186–90
  Coworker.org members, 103

Index

267

deliberative democracy pitfall, 16
"deserving" poor, 70
digital divide, 85, 94
Faith in Texas progressive movement, 90,
104–7
history of organizing, 53–6
Home Mortgage Disclosure Act, 188
Housing Innovation Lab, 34, 154–5
Machiavelli restraining elites, 38
New York City Mayor's Public Engagement
Unit, 158–60
organizational power building, 51–3
participatory budgeting, 173, 180
political conflict necessary, 20
political leaders wealthy, 7, 66
political power and, 5–8
rise paralleling union losses, 61, 65
rural communities, 91–6
Starbucks baristas organizing, 28–30, 99–100
as threat to democracy, 205
War on Poverty power shifts, 138–40
worker insecurity, 98–9
Economic Opportunity Act (EOA; 1964), 138
18 F office, 13, 33, 121, 152
electoral system, 13, 25, 54
engagement. *See participation*
Environmental Protection Agency
obstruction, 114
exclusion from the system. *See also* gender
exclusion, racial exclusion
Boston Mayor's Office of New Urban
Mechanics, 33–5
business lobbyist numbers vs. poor
people, 66
civic leadership development, 218
civic power addressing, 12, 22, 24, 35,
210
civic technology not addressing, 133–4
democracy as contest of interest groups,
49–51
democracy as empowerment, 12, 24
digital divide, 85, 94
diverse government workforce, 167, 216
financial regulatory insularity, 144
governance agencies against, 114–15, 164
history of organizing, 53–4, 56–9
New York City Mayor's Public Engagement
Unit, 158–60
organizational power building, 51–3
rural communities, 91–6
as threat to democracy, 205

exclusionary populism
antidemocracy attitudes, 22
Charlottesville white supremacist rally,
72, 205
death toll, 72
description of, 68–9
funding, 76–9
media support, 77–9
media–corporate power, 205
organizing for, 68–76, 81
political potency of, 74–6, 206
product of deliberate power shifts, 48, 69, 79
public trust in government, 11
Tea Party movement, 68, 71–5
Trump version, 1–2, 47, 68, 72, 205
trust building among distrusting people, 213
expertise. *See also* skillsets of personnel
emphasis in policy design, 18, 19–20, 38, 116,
119, 121

Faber, Candace, 125
Facebook, 77, 83, 85
Fair Housing Act (1968), 186
Faith in Texas (FIT) multiracial movement,
90, 104–7
Farage, Nigel, 77
Farmers' Alliance, 54, 57
farmworkers
New Deal exclusions, 56, 59, 98
United Farm Workers of America, 59
Federal Advisory Committee Act (FACA;
1972), 14
federal agencies. *See agencies*
Federal Reserve Bank, 187, 188
Federation of Organized Traders and Labor
Unions, 55
fellowships for public service, 216–18
Fields, James Alex, Jr., 205
financial lender transparency, 186–90
financial lending opacity, 190
Financial Stability Oversight Council
(FSOC), 144–6, 148–50
financing. *See funding*
First Amendment organization protections, 50
FOIA. *See Freedom of Information Act*
Fox News, 78, 93
Freedom of Information Act (FOIA; 1967), 14,
116, 118
Freedom Partners super PAC, 76
funding
alternative funding structures, 219

268   *Index*

funding (cont.)
  Boston Mayor's Office of New Urban
    Mechanics, 154, 156, 157
  building democratic capacity, 42, 218–21
  business lobbying associations, 64–6
  campaign finance system, 5, 66, 83
  CFPB budget reductions, 149
  civic leadership development, 218
  of civic technology, 125
  Code for America, 157, 167
  conservative media, 77–9
  crowdsourcing public works projects, 14
  fellowships for public service, 216–18
  information technology expenditures, 126
  lack as participation obstacle, 143, 166
  membership dues, 53, 59, 61, 63
  New York City Mayor's Public Engagement
    Unit, 158
  nineteenth century movements, 54
  Obama 2008 digital campaign, 87
  online small-dollar fundraising, 83
  organizing requiring, 213
  participatory budgeting, 172, *See also*
    participatory budgeting
  Philadelphia New Urban Mechanics
    Office, 156
  preemption of local initiatives, 221
  professionalized advocacy groups, 62
  public service fellowships, 216–18
  recommendations for funders, 218–21
  research support, 219, 221
  right-wing movements, 76–9
  training personnel, 167
  War on Poverty, 138, 139–40
  What Works Cities initiative, 153
Fung, Archon, 181
future of democracy, 10, 205
future of labor organizing, 98–104

Gaebler, Ted, 121
Ganz, Marshall
  African-American political power, 57
  "bodyless heads" of advocacy groups, 62
  Resistance in Trump era, 208
  storytelling in Obama campaign, 87
  strategic capacity of organizations, 51–3
  United Farm Workers of America, 59
gender exclusion
  chronic systemic exclusion, 9–10
  civic power for inclusion, 35
  democracy as empowerment, 12, 24

  exclusionary populism, 68–76
  governance agencies against, 114–15
  reinventing civil associations, 48
  as threat to democracy, 205
General Services Administration (GSA)
  18 F office, 13, 33, 121, 152
  Technology Transformation Services, 121
gentrification and community benefits
  agreements, 195–8
Gettysburg Address, vii, 43–4
Gettysburg Project, vii, viii
Gibson, William, 10
Goldwater, Barry, 68, 74
good governance ethos
  accountability reform, 115–20
  citizen audits contrasted, 190–1
  civic power contrasted, 24, 169
  civic technology as, 124
  countervailing power alternative, 24–7
  democracy as political engagement, 37
  description of, 19–20
  good governance reforms, 2, 18, 115–20, 206
  innovation offices, 33
  intermediary organizations removed, 39
  participatory budgeting contrasted, 182
  radical reform contrasted, 140, 142, 163
  Resistance durability and, 208
governance
  authority and accountability, 36, 116,
    164–5, 215
  civic technology digital governance, 14
  collaborative or new governance, 26, 134–6,
    181, 182
  culture change for civic power, 151, 160–2,
    206, 210–11
  day-to-day against exclusion and inequality,
    38, 114–15
  democracy as empowerment for self-
    governance, 12, 24
  democratizing from within, 163–8, 216
  deregulation as reform, 115
  expertise in, 20, *See also* skillsets of
    personnel
  "good governance" reforms, 2, 18, *See also*
    good governance
  government of, by, and for the people, 43–4
  "innovating government," 120–4
  local level opportunities, 96, 114
  movements linked with, 30–3
  privatization as reform, 115, 120–4
  public service fellowships, 216–18

Index

public trust in government, 11, *See also* trust
recommendations for policymakers, 214–18
reform overview, 113–16, *See also* reform
responsiveness examples, 136–40, 146–8
responsiveness institutionalized, 140, 194–8
responsiveness to the people, 7, 13
supporting participatory, 150–1, 163, 176–7
Government Accountability Office (GAO), 67
government information technology
expenditures, 126
Grassroots Innovation award, 68
grassroots movements. *See movements,
organizing, participation*

Hacker, Jacob, 50, 65
Han, Hahrie, 52
Harvard Business School's Leadership Fellows
program, 217
Haymarket Square riot, 55
Hertel-Fernandez, Alexander, 67, 68
Heyer, Heather, 205
Hidalgo, Anne, 174
hijacking democracy, 19
history of organizing, 43, 53–9, 60–4
organizational structure as key, 59–60
Hochschild, Arlie Russell, 72
Home Mortgage Disclosure Act (HMDA;
1975), 186–8
housing
community benefits agreements, 195–8
Community Reinvestment Act, 186–90
Fair Housing Act, 186
Home Mortgage Disclosure Act, 186–8
Housing Innovation Lab, 34, 154–5
New York City Housing Fellows
Program, 217
Shack/Slum Dwellers International, 184
human rights via participatory monitoring, 185

identity. *See communal identities*
inclusive democracy
building power and inclusive
coalitions, 90–1
CIO racial and economic inclusion, 58
civic leadership development, 218
civic power for, 12, 22, 24, 35, 210, *See also*
civic power
dismantling of, 206
diverse government workforce, 167, 216
inclusive populism, 210–12
multiracial progressive movement, 90, 104–7

online labor organizing, 29, 90
organizations building trust through, 213
participatory budgeting as, 178–80, 182
politics of place, 90, 91–7, 214
Trump election as opportunity, 207–12
Trump election versus, viii
worker organizing, 90, 98–104, *See also*
organizing
income inequality. *See economic inequality*
India
panchayat reforms, 181
right to information movement, 185
Indonesia using participatory budgeting, 174
industrialization and organizing, 54–9
inequality. *See also* economic inequality
civic power addressing, 12, 22, 24
civic technology because of, 125
deliberative democracy pitfall, 16
democracy as contest of interest groups,
49–51
democracy as empowerment, 12, 16, 24
governance agencies against, 114–15
government data crunching, 131
history of organizing, 53–9
organizational power building, 51–3
as organizational power problem, 60–4
participatory budgeting, 180
political conflict necessary, 20
political leaders wealthy, 7, 66
product of deliberate power shifts, 48
rise paralleling union losses, 61, 65
as threat to democracy, 205
urban local governance, 96
infrastructure. *See also* participatory
budgeting
BOS:311 app, 152
Boston Community Investment
Coalition, 189
Boston Mayor's Office of New Urban
Mechanics, 33–5, 151–7, 217
Boston StreetBump tool, 129
civic technology tools, 129–30
community benefits agreements, 195–8
Community Reinvestment Act, 186–90
New York City housing program, 217
New York City Mayor's Public Engagement
Unit, 158–62
SeeClickFix issue reporting platform,
129–30
Shack/Slum Dwellers International, 184
What Works Cities initiative, 153

Index

innovation offices of government
Boston Mayor's Office of New Urban
Mechanics, 33–5, 151–7, 217
description of, 33, 152
efficiency vs. engagement, 163–4
Philadelphia New Urban Mechanics
Office, 156
institutional design. *See also* policy design
authority with accountability, 36, 116,
164–5, 215
Boston Mayor's Office of New Urban
Mechanics, 33–5, 151–7, 217
CFPB grassroots engagement, 144, 146–50
citizen audits, 183–6, 190–4, *See also* participatory monitoring
class-based institutions empowering
powerless, 25
Community Reinvestment Act, 188–90
countervailing power within, 25, 37, 38,
210–11, 215
for democratic balance of power, 37
democratizing from within, 163–8, 216
governance reform overview, 113–16
history of, 43
hooks and levers for engagement, 41, 113, 115,
136–8, 146–8
institutionalized representation, 194–5
key against inequality and exclusion,
114–15, 164
Madison institutional design, 25, 38
movements influencing federal policy,
136–8
New York City Mayor's Public Engagement
Unit, 158–62
organizational structure as key, 59–60
participation catalyzed by, 30–1, 33–5, 165
power balancing of, 25, 33, 170–1
power shifting made durable, 208
recommendations for policymakers, 214–18
as reform linchpin, 37–40
reinventing democratic institutions, 12,
210–11
skillsets of personnel, 150–1, 155–7, 158–9,
160, 162, 167–8, 216, 217
social movement interaction, 33
visibility, 164, 165, 170, 215, 220
wage boards, 198–200
War on Poverty power shifts, 138–40
institutionalized representation, 194–5
interest group politics. *See business interests,
labor organizing, lobbyists*

Interfaith Worker Justice, 200
intermediary organizations, 39
Internet. *See also* digital mobilizing
digital divide, 85, 94
Internet of Things and public services, 129

Jacob, Nigel, 152
John Birch Society, 75, 76, 77
Johnson, Lyndon, 139

Karpf, David, 85, 132
Kenya
participatory budgeting, 174
service delivery accountability, 185
Knight Foundation, 125, 156
Koch Industries, 76
Koch, Charles G., 76–7
Koch, David H., 76–7
Koch, Fred C., 77
Ku Klux Klan, 75
Kushner, Jared, 122
Kutch, Jess, 100–2

labor organizing
Air Traffic Controllers strike, 61
black strikers abandoned by whites, 57
business interests undermining, 6, 48, 65
civic capacity via, 90
Democratic Party alignment, 50
future of, 98–104
history of, 53–6
innovation needed, 35, 48
lobbyist numbers vs. business, 66
Oklahoma school teacher strikes, 207
online platforms for, 29, 90, 99–104
Pullman strike, 55
racial exclusion, 56–8
right to work laws, 32, 61, 98
Starbucks baristas, 28–30, 99–100
structural allocations of power, 31–3
"unbundled unions" for worker power, 99
union membership numbers, 56, 60
unions losing membership, 60–4, 65, 69
wage boards, 198–200
Wisconsin union busting, 101
worker insecurity, 98–9
"A Ladder of Citizen Participation"
(Arnstein), 35
Landis, James M., 20
law enforcement accountability, 183
leadership

Index

autonomy, flexibility, and decentralization, 89
Colored Farmers Alliance producing, 57
Coworker.org building, 102–3
Faith in Texas training, 105
fellowships for public service, 216–18
funding development, 219
"good governance" reforms, 2, 18
inability to develop, 62–4
Leadership Fellows program, 217
organizations building political power, 52, 59, 212–14
participatory budgeting delegates, 177
responsiveness institutionalized, 140, 194–8
responsiveness to the people, 7, 13
risk-taking willingness, 216, 219
support of power shifting necessary, 166, 176–7, 216
supporting participatory governance, 150–1, 163
Tea Party, 73
wealth class representation, 7, 66
Lee, Caroline W., 181
Lee, Robert E., 72
lending disparities, 186–90
Lessig, Lawrence, 86
Levine, Peter, 87
Liazos, Ariane, 57
Libertarian Party candidate, 77
Lincoln, Abraham, vii, 43–4
lobbyists
  business interest "public participation," 17, 68, 181, 206
  business lobby power rise, 6–7, 48, 64–8, 206
  business numbers vs. labor, 66
  campaign donation growth, 66
  civic association political efficacy, 5
  Financial Stability Oversight Council pressure, 148
  Koch network, 76
  Obama versus, 1
  preemption of local policies, 106, 212, 221
  professionalized advocacy groups, 62–4
  public sector shrinking against, 67–8
  regulatory agency obstruction, 114
  subverting political system, 19
local governance. *See also* agencies
  Boston Mayor's Office of New Urban Mechanics, 33–5, 151–7, 217
  civic technology expansion, 126
  dissemination of reforms, 219

financial lender transparency, 186–90
India panchayat reforms, 181
innovative government test sites, 214
New York City Mayor's Public Engagement Unit, 158–62
opportunities in, 96, 114
participatory budgeting, 172–81
participatory budgeting lessons, 181–3
participatory monitoring, 183–90
power shifting of institutions, 138–40
preemption by state legislatures, 106–7, 212, 221
privatization, 123
responsiveness institutionalized, 140, 195–8
responsiveness to the people, 7, 13
SeeClickFix issue reporting platform, 129–30
state wage boards, 198–200
technology as vulnerability, 221
town hall electronic platform, 130
urban–suburban coalition, 106–7
War on Poverty backlash, 139–40

Machiavelli, 38
Madison, James, 25–6
March for Our Lives, 207
March for Racial Justice, 208
March on Washington for Jobs and Freedom, 58
Martin, Trayvon, 23, 84
Mayor's Office of New Urban Mechanics (MONUM)
  bureaucratizing participation, 151–7
  designed for participation, 33–5, 151, 155–7
  Harvard Leadership Fellowship, 217
  Housing Innovation Lab, 34, 154–5
Mayor's Public Engagement Unit (PEU)
  culture shift internally, 160–2
  reaching out for participation, 158–60
media. *See also* social media
  Breitbart News, 77, 78–9
  conservative media megaphone, 78–9
  Coworker.org connecting with, 103
  Daily Yonder digital news platform, 93, 95
  exclusionary populism support, 77–9, 205
  Facebook countering state-controlled, 83
  Fox News, 78
  radio conservatives vs. liberals, 78
  rural community organizing, 93–6
median-voter theorem, 49
Medicare and racial disparities, 137

272   *Index*

Melish, Tara, 184
membership dues of organizations
  history of organizing, 53
  organizations leveraging resources, 59
  professional advocacy groups, 63
  right to work laws and union dues, 61
Menino, Thomas, 151, 152
Mercer Family Foundation, 77
Mercer, Rebekah, 77–8
Mercer, Robert, 77–8
#MeToo, 84
Miller, Michelle, 101–2
minimum wage, 198–200
minipublics, 15–17
mobilizing
  business interest "public participation," 17,
    68, 181, 206
  Community Reinvestment Act, 188
  digital mobilizing, 29, 40, *See also* digital
    mobilizing
  hooks and levers to catalyze, 41, 113, 115,
    136–8, 146–8, 212, *See also* participation
  impact importance, 212
  Montgomery bus boycott, 58
  organizations building power, 51–3, *See also*
    organizing
  Trump sparking, 207–8
monitoring. *See participatory monitoring*
Montgomery bus boycott, 58
MONUM. *See Mayor's Office of New Urban
  Mechanics*
Moore, Joe, 175
Morozov, Evgeny, 85
Movement for Black Lives (M4BL), 23
  participatory monitoring, 183
movements. *See also* Civil Rights movement,
  organizing
  Arab Spring, 83
  backlashes, 64, 68–71, 74–5, 114, 116,
    139–40
  Center for Rural Strategies, 90, 91–6
  civic power description, 22–7
  civic technology movement, 124, 129–31,
    See also civic technology
  coalitions across identity groups, 82, 88–9,
    97, 105, 114, 196, 210
  common identities among members, 59, 63,
    See also communal identities
  connections among, 208
  consumer rights and CFPB, 146
  funding right-wing, 76–9, *See also* funding

  governance linked with, 30–3, 136–8
  history of, 43, 54–9
  labor organizing, 98–104, *See also* labor
    organizing
  March for Our Lives, 207
  March for Racial Justice, 208
  March on Washington for Jobs and
    Freedom, 58
  Movement for Black Lives, 23, 183
  MoveOn.org, 40, 88
  Occupy, 47, 83
  Office of Price Administration, 136
  organizational structure, 59–60
  organizing for civic power, 28–30, 40–1, 59,
    See also organizing
  People's Climate March, 208
  political opportunity structures, 28, 30,
    41, 170
  politics of place, 90, 91–7, 214
  recent mobilizations, 47
  reinventing for civic power, 40
  Resistance in Trump era, 207–12
  Tea Party movement, 68, 71–5, 76, 208
  Women's March, 207
MoveOn.org, 40, 88
Mulvaney, Mick, 149
Murdoch, Rupert, 78
mySociety civic technology organization, 124

Nabatchi, Tina, 135, 181
National Domestic Workers Alliance
  (NDWA), 29, 90, 98
National Guestworker Alliance, 98
National Labor Relations Act (1935), 56
National Ocean and Atmospheric
  Administration (NOAA), 128
National Performance Review, 121
National Rifle Association (NRA), 50, 75
National Rural Assembly, 93, 94
Navarro, Jannette, 28–9, 99–100
NetGain Partnership, 219
New America think tank, vii, viii–ix
New Deal
  American Liberty League hostility to, 64, 76
  domestic worker exclusions, 98
  farmworker exclusions, 56, 59, 98
  Landis as an architect of, 20
  modern conservatism from, 74
  organizing leading to, 48, 55, 56, 58
new governance, 26, 134–6, 181, 182
new public management (NPM), 120–4

Index

New Urban Mechanics. *See Mayor's Office of New Urban Mechanics*

New York City
  Civic Hall, 127
  HPD-HDC Housing Fellows Program, 217
  Mayor's Public Engagement Unit, 158–62
  participatory budgeting, 176–81

New York state wage board, 199–200

Nixon, Richard, 68, 78

norms of political behavior, 4, 72

Noveck, Beth Simone, 20

O'Leary, Rosemary, 181

Oakland, California
  community benefits agreements, 196–8
  participatory budgeting, 175

Obama for America (OFA), 13, 88–9

Obama, Barack
  birth certificate, 72
  campaign of 2008 digital revolution, 87–9
  e-petitions platform, 13, 130, 131–3
  government data machine readable, 128
  innovation offices, 33, 152
  Office of Public Engagement, 163
  racism of conservative opposition, 70, 72
  revival of democracy, 1, 13–15
  technologists for expertise, 121

Occupy movement, 47, 83

Office of American Innovation, 122

Office of Economic Opportunity, 139

Office of Equal Health Opportunity, 137

Office of Fair Lending and Equal Opportunity, 149

Office of Price Administration, 136

Office of Public Engagement, 163

Office of Science and Technology Policy, 122

Office of Social Innovation and Civic Participation, 13

Oklahoma school teacher strikes, 207

Omarova, Saule, 145

Omidyar Network foundation, 125

on-demand scheduling of workers, 28–30, 99–100

online organizing. *See digital mobilizing*

Open Government Initiative, 13

Open Society Foundations, vii

openness. *See transparency*

organizing
  backlashes propelling, 64, 68–71, 74–5, 114

Boston Mayor's Office of New Urban Mechanics, 33–5, 151–7, 217

business lobby power rise, 6–7, 48, 64–8, 206

civic associations having power, 5–7, 28, 30, 35–6, 54–5

civic associations losing membership, 6, 60–4, 82

civic associations proliferating, 62–4

civic capacities via, 52, 59

for civic power, 28–30, 40–1, 59, 212–14
  See also civic power

coalitions across identity groups, 82, 88–9, 97, 105, 114, 196, 210

common identities among members, 59, 63, *See also* communal identities

community organizing required, 35, *See also* community organizing

democracy as contest of interest groups, 49–51, *See also* political conflict

democratizing force of, 53–9

description of, 28–30

exclusionary populism, 68–76, 81

First Amendment protections, 50

funding of right-wing movements, 76–9, *See also* funding

governance authority and accountability, 36, 116, 164–5, 215

history of, 43, 53–9, 60–4

inequality diminishing power, 60–4

institutional context importance, 41, *See also* institutional design

labor organizing for the future, 98–104, *See also* labor organizing

membership dues, 53, 59, 61, 63

movements linked with governance, 30–3, *See also* movements

offline relationships supporting digital, 29, 85, 88–9, 95, 100, 158, 159–60, 213, 220

online platforms for, 29

organizational structure as key, 59–60

"organized distrust" in action, 192–4, *See also* participatory monitoring

political parties magnifying power, 50

political power building, 51–3, *See also* political power

professionalized advocacy, 62–4, 82–7, 91, 208

recommendations for organizers, 212–14

reinventing organizing strategies, 35, 40–1, 48, 212–14, *See also* roadmap

Index

organizing (cont.)
  Resistance in Trump era, 207–12
  resources required, 213, *See also* resources
  rural communities, 91–6, 214
  strategic capacity of organizations, 51–3
  suburban communities, 90, 104–7
  support of participation, 213, *See also*
    participation
  "thin" digital organizing, 87–9, 91, 213
  "thin" organizing, 63, 82–7, 91, 133–4,
    169, 210
  thinning of countervailing power, 205
  urban communities, 105–6, 195–8, *See also*
    urban community organizing
Osborne, David, 121
Osgood, Chris, 152, 157, 217

Parks, Rosa, 58
participation in democracy. *See also* dialogue
  active participant vs. passive recipient, 190
  bureaucratizing participation, 142–3,
    See also bureaucratizing participation
  business interest "public participation," 17,
    68, 181, 206
  citizen input in rulemaking, 119
  civic power reclaiming, 22–7, 35, *See also*
    civic power
  civic technology movement, 124, 129–31,
    See also civic technology
  community organizing online platforms, 29,
    40, 90, *See also* community organizing
  contestation as requirement, 171, *See also*
    political conflict
  deliberative democracy reforms, 15–17, 181–2
  early in policymaking process, 171, *See also*
    policy design
  financial grassroots engagement, 145–6
  funding lack as obstacle, 143, *See also*
    funding
  hooks and levers to catalyze, 41, 113, 115,
    136–8, 146–8, 212
  institutional design catalyzing, 30–1, 33–5,
    38, 165, *See also* institutional design
  intermediary organization involvement, 39
  issue-specific appeals motivating, 96–7, 212
  local level opportunities, 96, 114
  Obama 2008 digital campaign, 87–9
  Obama administration, 13–14, 88–9
  offline relationships supporting digital, 29,
    85, 88–9, 95, 100, 158, 159–60, 213,
    220

online community organizing platforms, 29,
  40, 90
online discussion platforms, 83
online petitions, 13, 130, 131–3
organizations building political power, 51,
  See also organizing
participatory budgeting, 172, *See also*
  participatory budgeting
public trust in government, 11, 214, 216,
  See also trust
responsiveness examples, 136–40, 146–8
responsiveness institutionalized, 140, 194–8
responsiveness to the people, 7, 13
scaling up as problem, 17, 21
social media for political engagement, 84–7,
  See also social media
structured participation required, 171
support of participation, 213
supporting participatory governance, 150–1,
  163, 176–7
system-level disparities of power, 9–10, 21
thick participatory monitoring, 185
thick vs. thin, 171, 208
trust as critical factor for, 214, *See also* trust
urban local governance, 96
War on Poverty backlash, 139–40
participatory budgeting (PB)
  benefits of, 181–3
  Brazil, 172–4, 180
  description of, 172
  "empowered deliberative democracy," 181
  institutionalization of, 180
  international use, 174, 175
  process of, 177–81
  US cities, 175–81
participatory monitoring
  citizen audits, 183–6, 190–4
  community benefits agreements, 195–8
  Consumer Financial Protection Bureau, 149
  financial lending opacity, 190
  financial lending transparency, 186–90
  models of, 183–6
  "organized distrust" in action, 192–4
  power of, 148, 190–2
  state wage boards, 198–200
partisan politics. *See political conflict*
Partnership for Working Families (PFWF)
  civic capacity, 90, 91, 96–7
  Oakland community benefits agreement,
    196–8
Pateman, Carole, 27

Index

payday lending, 105–6, 149
Peak Democracy open town hall platform, 130
People's Action Network, 29, 92
People's Climate March, 208
Perriello, Tom, 217
Personal Democracy Forum, 127
Peru using participatory budgeting, 174
petitions online, 13, 130, 131–3
Philadelphia New Urban Mechanics
    Office, 156
Philippines using participatory budgeting, 174
Phillips-Fein, Kim, 74
Pierson, Paul, 50, 65
Pittsburgh Community Reinvestment
    Group, 189
Pittsburgh United, 96
police officer accountability, 183
policy design. *See also* institutional design
    behavioral insights for, 121
    Boston Mayor's Office of New Urban
        Mechanics, 33–5, 151–7, 217
    business power rise from, 64
    business steering, 5–8, 65–8
    citizen input, 34, 119, 136–8, 147–8, 153–5, 180
    citizens as policy co-producers, 131, 134
    Community Reinvestment Act, 188–90
    conflict reduction as democracy reform,
        18–22
    deliberative democracy reforms, 15–17
    dialogue toward, vii–viii, *See also* dialogue
    expertise emphasis, 18, 19–20, 38, 116, 119, 121
    feedback loops against rollback, 170
    "good governance" reforms. 2, 18, *See also*
        good governance
    hooks and levers for engagement, 41, 113, 115,
        136–8, 146–8
    "innovating government," 120–4
    institutional design catalyzing participation,
        30–1, *See also* institutional design
    nineteenth century movements and, 54
    nonpartisan analysis reductions, 67
    organizing to influence, 49–52, 57–9,
        See also organizing
    participatory budgeting, 172, *See also*
        participatory budgeting
    participatory monitoring, 183–6, *See also*
        participatory monitoring
    participatory policy making, 181–3
    political opportunity structures, 28, 30,
        41, 170
    privatizing government, 115, 120–4

public opinion influence on, 113, *See also*
    public opinion
recommendations for policymakers, 214–18
visibility and durability, 170
voting influence on, 113
wage boards, 198–200
War on Poverty power shifts, 138–40
wealthy steering, 5–8, 206
policymakers, recommendations for, 214–18
political agency. *See political power*
political conflict. *See also* dialogue
    citizen audits, 192–4
    civic power managing, 24–7, 215
    democracy as political engagement, 37
    good governance contrasted, 19–22
    institutional design facilitating, 25, 37, 38, 171
    organized interest group contests, 49–51
    participatory budgeting, 182
    participatory monitoring, 183–6
    reducing as democracy reform, 18–22
    rural narratives to urban audiences, 95
    scorched-earth as democratic backsliding, 3
political leadership. *See leadership*
political opportunity structures, 28, 30, 41, 170
political organization. *See organizing*
political parties. *See also* Democratic Party,
        Republican Party
    Libertarian candidate David Koch, 77
    organized interest power magnified, 50
    privatization supported by all, 121
    Resistance movements, 208
    Tea Party, 68, 71–5, 76, 208
    urban–suburban partisan divide initiative,
        90, 104–7
political power. *See also* civic power, power
        shifting
    autocratic power consolidation, 3
    business interest "public participation," 17,
        68, 181, 206
    business lobby power rise, 6–7, 48, 64–8, 206
    campaign finance system, 5, 66, 83
    civic technology not empowering, 131, 132–4
    Colored Farmers Alliance, 57
    deliberative democracy pitfall, 16
    democracy as balancing, 37, *See also*
        balance of power
    democracy as empowerment, 12, 24
    economic inequality and, 5–8, *See also* eco-
        nomic inequality
    of exclusionary populism, 68–76
    good governance pitfall, 20–1

Index

political power (cont.)
  of movements, 28, *See also* movements
  organizational structure as key, 59–60
  organizations building power, 51–3, *See also* organizing
  organizations needing alliances with, 213
  organized interest power magnified, 50
  organizing for African-American, 57–9
  Partnership for Working Families' focus, 96
  political efficacy waning, 11
  politics of place, 90, 91–7, 214
  public opinion chasing, 49
  recommendations for policymakers, 214–18
  status quo maintenance, 208
  structural allocations of, 31–3
  systemic exclusion, 9–10, *See also* exclusion
  War on Poverty backlash, 139–40
political science
  business advocacy influence, 6–7
  concentration of wealth vs. democracy, 8
  deliberative democracy, 15–17
  democracy as contest of interest groups, 49–51
  history of organizing, 53–9
  median-voter theorem, 49
  new governance, 26, 181, 182
  recommendations for scholars, 221–2
  research, 219, 221–2
politics of place, 90, 91–7, 214
Polletta, Francesca, 181
populism. *See also* exclusionary populism
  Farmers' Alliance into Populist movement, 54
  inclusive populism, 210–12
  Populist racial exclusion, 56, 57
  us populism vs. them populism, 81
Portugal using participatory budgeting, 174
poverty. *See economic inequality*
power. *See political power*
power shifting
  business lobby power rise, 6–7, 48, 64–8, 206
  CIO shifting Democratic Party, 58
  civic power shifting participation, 24, 35, 206, 215
  collaborative or new governance, 26, 134–6, 181, 182
  Consumer Financial Protection Bureau, 146–50
  copwatching participatory monitoring, 183
  durable institutions from, 208
  exclusionary populism rise, 48, 69, 79

federal bureaucracies, 136–8
financial lender transparency, 186–90
Financial Stability Oversight Council creation, 145
institutional design with power in mind, 25, 33, 170–1, *See also* institutional design
leadership support for durability, 166, 176–7, 216
local governance, 138–40
participatory budgeting, 183, *See also* participatory budgeting
power balancing of institutional design, 25, 33, 170–1, *See also* balance of power
responsiveness examples, 136–40, 146–8
responsiveness institutionalized, 140, 194–8
responsiveness to the people, 7, 13
  as risky, 216, 219
state wage boards, 198–200
War on Poverty, 138–40
preemption of local policies, 106–7, 212, 221
Presidential Innovation Fellow program, 121, 216
Presidential Management Fellows program, 216
private realms, 9
privatization, 115–16, 120–4
Professional Air Traffic Controllers Organization strike, 61
professionalized advocacy
  limits of, 62–4
  Resistance durability and, 208
  "thin" organizing, 63, 82–7, 91
Progressives, 43, 54–5, 56, 57
Public Affairs Council Grassroots Innovation award, 68
public engagement. *See participation*
Public Engagement Unit (PEU), 158–62
Public Engagement, Office of, 13
public opinion
  mythical "center," 49
  organizing to influence, 49–51, 57–9, *See also* organizing
  policymaker influence, 113
  racial resentments, 71
  Trump supporter racial attitudes, 72
  trust in democracy, 11, 44, 47, 143, *See also* trust
public participation. *See participation*
public sector shrinking, 67–8, 167
public service fellowships, 216–18

Index

Pullman strike, 55
Putnam, Lara, 208
Putnam, Robert D., 18, 63

racial exclusion. *See also* exclusionary
  populism
  chronic systemic exclusion, 9–10
  CIO racial and economic inclusion, 58
  civic power for inclusion, 35, *See also* civic
    power
  civil associations reinvented, 48
  "color blind" equality, 71
  Colored Farmers Alliance political
    advocacy, 57
  Community Reinvestment Act, 186–90
  Coworker.org members, 103
  deliberative democracy pitfall, 16
  democracy as empowerment, 12, 24
  diverse government workforce, 167, 216
  exclusionary populism, 68–76, *See also*
    exclusionary populism
  Faith in Texas progressive movement, 90,
    104–7
  governance agencies against, 114–15, 164
  history of organizing, 53–4, 56–9
  Medicare shift to civil rights, 137
  Movement for Black Lives, 23, 183
  New Deal farmworker exclusions, 56
  organizational power building, 51–3,
    See also organizing
  Reconstruction, 43
  rural initiatives, 92, 93
  as threat to democracy, 205
  urban–suburban partisan divide initiative,
    90, 104–7
  War on Poverty power shifts, 138–40
radical reform of democracy. *See also* roadmap
  achievable, 222–3
  bureaucratizing participation, 142–3,
    See also bureaucratizing participation
  civic power, 12, 22, 169, 206, *See also* civic
    power
  collaborative or new governance, 26, 134–6,
    181, 182
  dissemination of results, 219
  "empowered deliberative democracy," 181
  good governance contrasted, 140, 142, 163
  organizing strategies reinvented, 40–1,
    212–14, *See also* organizing
  participation support, 213, *See also*
    participation

participatory budgeting, 172, *See also*
  participatory budgeting
participatory monitoring as, 183–90, *See also*
  participatory monitoring
power shifting, 136–40, *See also* power
  shifting
Resistance in Trump era, 207–12
radio conservatives vs. liberals, 78
Reagan, Ronald, 61
recommendations for building civic power
  about, 212
  for funders, 218–21
  for organizers, 212–14
  for policymakers, 214–18
  for scholars, 221–2
Reconstruction, 43, 56
Recovery.gov accountability site, 131
redistributive policies, 66, 172–4
reform of democracy. *See also* conventional
  reform, radical reform, roadmap
  dissemination of results, 219
  funder and advocate support, 42
  history of organizing, 53–9
  institutional design as linchpin, 37–40,
    See also institutional design
  intermediary organizations' role, 39
  reinventing democratic institutions, 12
  to pre-Trump norms, 2
Regulations.gov commenting platform, 119
regulatory bodies
  anti-regulatory organizing, 64, 114
  bank mergers, 187, 188
  CFPB as bureaucratized participation,
    143–50
  citizen auditing of, 184–5
  civil servants leaving, 167
  collaborative or new governance, 26
  day-to-day governance, 41, 114–15
  deregulation as backlash, 116
  deregulation as reform, 115–16
  expertise-based, 20, 117, 119
  financial lender transparency, 186–90
  financial regulatory fragmentation, 145–6
  Financial Stability Oversight Council, 144–6
  good governance reforms, 115–20
  "interest representation" emerging, 116
  key against inequality and exclusion,
    114–15, 164
  nineteenth century movements creating, 54
  privatization effects, 123
  public comments on regulations, 119

Index

regulatory bodies (cont.)
  regulators deferring to industry, 6, 7, 66, 67
  regulators manipulated by industry, 119
  regulatory public defenders, 194–5
  responsiveness institutionalized, 140, 194–5
  state wage boards, 198–200
Reimagining the Civic Commons
    Initiative, 219
Reinventing Government (Osborne &
    Gaebler), 121
relationships. *See communal identities*
Republican Party. *See also* Trump, Donald
  activity by Mercers, 77
  business alignment with, 6, 65
  CFPB to be dismantled, 143
  exclusionary populism, 68–76
  Fox News and Roger Ailes, 78
  National Rifle Association alignment
    with, 50
  organized interest power magnified, 50
  privatization support, 121
  Reagan and Air Traffic Controllers strike, 61
  Tea Party incorporated into, 208
  urban–suburban partisan divide initiative,
    90, 104–7
research
  dissemination of, 219
  recommendations to scholars, 221–2
Resistance in Trump era, 207–12
resources. *See also* funding
  citizen resource investment for power, 172
  for implementing participation, 216
  organizing requiring, 213
  as participation support, 213
  participatory budgeting, 180
  personnel skillsets, 150–1, 155–7, 158–9, 160,
    162, 167–8, 216, 217
  personnel training, 167–8
  recommendations for funders, 218–21
  for scholarship of power building, 221
Restaurant Opportunities Centers United
    (ROC), 98
revenue. *See funding*
right to work laws, 32, 61, 98
risk taking of power shifting, 216,
    219
roadmap for reconstructing democracy.
    See also reform
  book layout, 37
  contest between interest groups, 49, *See also*
    political conflict

organizational power building, 51–3,
    212,
  See also civic power, organizing
recommendations for funders, 218–21,
  See also funding
recommendations for organizers, 212–14,
  See also organizing
recommendations for policymakers, 214–18,
  See also institutional design, policy design
recommendations for scholars, 221–2,
  See also political science
Roosevelt, Franklin Delano, 56, 58, *See also*
    New Deal
Roosevelt, Theodore, 54
rural community organizing, 91–6, 214
RuralAmerica.org advocacy platform, 94, 95

Schattschneider, E. E., 64
scheduling workers, 28–30, 99–100
scholars
  recommendations for, 221–2
  research dissemination, 219
Schwartz, Regina, 158, 159
Seattle Civic Technology Advocate, 125
SeeClickFix issue reporting platform, 129–30
The Semisovereign People
    (Schattschneider), 64
separation of families at the border, 207
Service Employees International Union
    (SEIU), 101
Shack/Slum Dwellers International (SDI), 184
shootings of African Americans, 23, 183
Sifry, Micah L., 88, 124, 127
Simonson, Jocelyn, 183
Simpson, Erin, 124
skillsets of personnel
  democratizing government from within,
    167–8, 216
  Harvard Leadership Fellowship, 217
  Mayor's Office of New Urban Mechanics,
    155–7
  for participatory policymaking, 150–1
  Public Engagement Unit, 158–9, 160,
    162
Skocpol, Theda
  African-American political power, 57
  civic association emergence, 53
  professional advocacy groups, 63
  Resistance in Trump era, 208
  Tea Party, 73
Smucker, Jonathan M., 52

Index

social media
autonomy required, 89
#BlackLivesMatter, 84
civic technology movement, 14
Coworker.org campaign, 103
#MeToo, 84
Movement for Black Lives, 23, 183
on-the-ground organizing, 83, 85
political engagement via, 84–7
rationality in good governance, 18
rural resources, 95
social movements. *See movements*
Social Security entrenched, 170
South Korea using participatory budgeting, 174
special interests. *See business interests, labor organizing, lobbyists*
Starbucks
barista on-demand scheduling, 28–30, 99–100
barista visible tattoos, 103
Coworker.org campaigns, 103
state agencies. *See agencies*
state legislatures
American Legislative Exchange Council influence, 67
preemption of local policies, 106–7, 212, 221
privatization, 123
technology as vulnerability, 221
urban–suburban coalition pressuring, 106
War on Poverty backlash, 139–40
state wage boards, 198–200
Stempeck, Matt, 124
storytelling in Obama campaign, 87
strategic capacity of organizations, 51–3
strikes by labor
Air Traffic Controllers strike, 61
black strikers abandoned by whites, 57
Oklahoma school teacher strikes, 207
Pullman strike, 55
Student Nonviolent Coordinating Committee (SNCC), 58
suburban community organizing, 90, 104–7
Sunstein, Cass R., 20
Sustainable Development Goals (UN), vii

Taft-Hartley Act (1947), 60–2
Tani, Karen, 137
Tarrow, Sidney, 28
tattoos on Starbucks baristas, 103
Tea Party movement
exclusionary populism, 68, 71–5

funding, 76
organizational capacity, 73–5
Republican party independence, 208
technology. *See civic technology movement*
Technology Transformation Services, 121
technology workers' coalitions, 103–4
Teles, Steven, 67–8
Texas progressive movement, 90, 104–7
"thin" organizing, 63, 82–7, 91, 169
"thin" digital organizing, 87–9, 91
Tilly, Charles, 28
Ton, Zeynep, 100
town halls electronically, 130
training of personnel, 167–8, 216
academics, 221
transparency
as accountability, 116–18
agency authority plus, 116
citizen audits, 183–6, 190–1
civic technology movement, 14, 124, 128–9
Consumer Financial Protection Bureau, 146–8
as democracy reform, 13–14, 18
elite opinion makers using, 21
financial lenders, 186–90
good governance, 19, 116–18
Obama administration, 13–14
participatory budgeting, 172, 175, 179
participatory monitoring, 185
as radical reform in CFPB, 143–50
Trump's lack of, 1
travel ban protests, 207
Trump, Donald
Cambridge Analytica payment, 77
CFPB to be dismantled, 143, 148, 149
Community Reinvestment Act hostility, 190
"democratic backsliding," 3–5
deregulation, 167
election as implausible, viii, 1
election as opportunity, 207
exclusionary populism, 1–2, 47, 68, 72, 205
information technology expenditures, 126
Mercer introducing to advisers, 77
norms violated, 4, 72
Office of American Innovation, 122
Resistance movement, 207–12
supporter demographics, 72
threats to democracy, 1–2, 3–5, 205
"We the People" petition site, 13, 130, 131–3
white supremacist encouragement, 1, 47, 205

Index

trust
  between academics and practitioners, 221
  CFPB core mission, 147, 149
  critical factor for civic engagement, 214
  FOIA building distrust of government, 118
  "organized distrust" of participatory
    monitoring, 192
  public distrusted by government, 134,
    143, 216
  Public Engagement Unit building, 159
  public trust in democracy, 11, 44, 47, 143
  public trust in government, 11, 214, 216
  rural community social cohesion, 214
  shared vocabulary to build, 213
  trust in "the people" to govern, 22, 79
Tufekci, Zeynep, 85

unions. *See also* labor organizing
  membership numbers, 56, 60
  "unbundled unions" for worker power, 99
  Wisconsin union busting, 101
United Farm Workers of America, 59
United Kingdom
  Brexit campaign, 77
  Downing Street E-petitions, 130
  Financial Services Authority, 145
United Nations (UN) Sustainable
  Development Goals, vii
United States Digital Service, 13, 33, 121, 152
urban community organizing
  community benefits agreements, 195–8
  disparities of power, 96
  Partnership for Working Families, 90,
    91, 96–7
  payday lending campaign, 105–6
  rural narratives to urban audiences, 95
  urban–suburban partisan divide initiative,
    90, 104–7

visibility of an institution
  civic engagement effectiveness, 215
  protection against rollback, 170
  requirement for, 164, 165
  technology risk of invisibility, 220
votes and voting
  Cambridge Analytica on Facebook, 77
  corporate pressure on employees, 68
  electoral system, 13, 25, 54
  issue-specific appeals motivating, 96–7, 212
  lack of information vs. power imbalance, 191
  median-voter theorem, 49

participatory budgeting, 174, 176, 178–9
Pittsburgh United voter engagement, 96
policymaker influence, 113
Trump supporter demographics, 72
urban–suburban partisan divide, 90, 104–7

wages and state wage boards, 198–200
Wagner Act (1935), 56
Walker, Edward T., 181
Walker, Scott, 101–2
Walmart "Community Action Network," 68
Walter, Stephen, 153
War on Poverty power shifts, 138–40
"We the People" online petition site, 13, 130,
  131–3
wealth concentration
  checks and balances asymmetry, 8
  electoral system corruption, 13
  funding right-wing movements, 76–9
  policymaking steered by, 5–8, 206
  political conflict necessary, 20
  political leaders wealthy, 7, 66
  as threat to democracy, 205
welfare
  federal bureaucracy power shifting, 137–8
  local power shifting, 138–40
Weyrich, Paul, 67
What Works Cities initiative, 153
white supremacists. *See also* exclusionary
    populism
  in "golden era" of mass organizing, 56
  rally in Charlottesville, 72, 205
  Trump encouraging, 1, 47, 205
William Penn Foundation, 156
Williams, Kristie, 103
Wisconsin
  union battles, 101–2
  worker employment transitions, 181
Women's March, 207
worker centers for support services, 98, 197, 200
worker insecurity, 98–9, *See also* labor
    organizing
  employment transitions, 181
  voting pressure, 68
  work schedules, 28–30, 99–100
World Bank on participatory budgeting,
  172, 174
Wright, Erik Olin, 181
WRTP/BIG STEP (Wisconsin), 181

Zimmerman, George, 84